D1554495

HIGHEST AND HARDEST

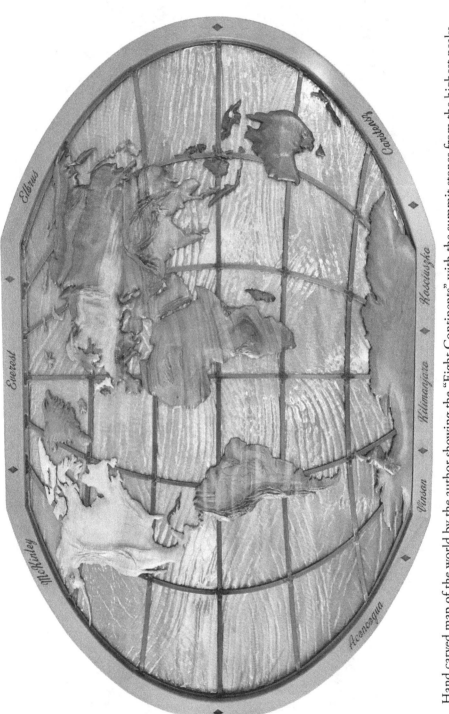

Hand carved map of the world by the author showing the "Eight Continents" with the summit stones from the highest peaks.

HIGHEST AND HARDEST
A MOUNTAIN CLIMBER'S LIFETIME ODYSSEY TO THE TOP OF THE WORLD

CHRIS KOPCZYNSKI

FALCON®

Guilford, Connecticut

FALCON®

An imprint of Globe Pequot, the trade division of
The Rowman & Littlefield Publishing Group, Inc.
4501 Forbes Blvd., Ste. 200
Lanham, MD 20706
www.rowman.com
Falcon and FalconGuides are registered trademarks and Make Adventure Your
Story is a trademark of The Rowman & Littlefield Publishing Group, Inc.

Distributed by NATIONAL BOOK NETWORK

British Library Cataloguing in Publication Information available

Library of Congress Cataloging-in-Publication Data available

ISBN 978-1-4930-6647-6 (hardcover)
ISBN 978-1-4930-6648-3 (e-book)

DEDICATION

I thank my parents, Bernard and Maxine, my former wife Sharon, my wife Michelle, and my children Jae, Jon, Kelly and Quinn for their undaunted support.

I thank all the teammates mentioned in this book who have allowed me to age "Into Thin Hair."

And I thank the Spokane Mountaineers.

Contents

Foreword

Chris Kopczynski and I have been friends and climbing partners for over 55 years. We met as teenagers while enrolled in the Spokane Mountaineers basic mountaineering course in 1965. Like the great French alpinists, Lionel Terray and Louis Lachenal, whom we admired and sought to emulate, Chris and I quickly discovered our individual strengths were stronger working together than competing against one another.

We prided ourselves in becoming all-around mountaineers—bouldering on the granite and gneiss outcrops around Spokane, scampering up the Cascade volcanoes, and climbing for days on the vertical and technical big walls throughout the Pacific Northwest. Nine years after learning to tie an old nylon climbing rope around our waists with a bowline-on-a-coil, Chris and I were on the Eiger North Face challenging one of the world's most sought-after alpine walls. Our early climbs together over the years proved to be the key that unlocked the Eiger's defenses. The summit, like so many others, was ours.

Descending off the summit and down the West Face of the Eiger, fatigue from three days of strenuous climbing in bad weather penetrated our weakened muscles. As Chris details in his chapter, *Eiger North Face*, he made a common climbing error, leaned into the ice while crossing the gully, and fell. We weren't roped together, so there was nothing I could do but watch my friend die as he slid to his death. After bobsledding on his seat face forward for several hundred feet and flying off two small vertical cliffs, he spread-eagled, like a wall spider, scratching and clawing on a narrow band of steeply sloping ice and scree and came to a stop just short of a 1000-foot drop, one that a base jumper would relish. He had badly sprained his ankle. We roped together again and, with Chris limping along and in pain, the two of us picked our way down the West flank. The last rays of the sun sneaking a peak under the dark clouds ignited our descent. Within an hour, we stopped and bivouacked for a third night 2,000 feet above and a mile and a half from Kleine Scheidegg.

With cowbells echoing off the surrounding walls and stars shining brightly in the rarified air, we ate what little we had left and settled in for a cold night. Hungry, exhausted, and sore, our situation wasn't grim any longer. In fact, I think a climbing buddy should twist an ankle every few years. Chris and I, after years of the kind of underlying tension only brothers and really good friends can create, got to know each other again during that unplanned bivouac. Our friendship, weakened over the years by competition and pride, returned with an understanding of each other's needs. Once our pride had "fallen" away on the flanks of the Eiger, we each found a lost friend.

Highest and Hardest awakened me to the fact that, despite knowing Chris for so many years, my knowledge of his life was superficial, essentially a short story I had created for myself from our many climbing and personal experiences. Chris is not someone who indulges in idle chatter. His friends, like me, feel special to get a word out of him; a sentence is something we do not treat lightly; and a full-on conversation demands an explanation to the question, "Are you feeling okay, Chris?" Chris's autobiography, then, is especially intriguing, as it is an open window into the complexities of his life that he seldom, if ever, spoke about.

Chris, like so many outstanding athletes, has dedicated his life to fulfilling almost impossible dreams. If I were asked who I thought was the most under-rated American mountaineer, I would not hesitate to say Chris Kopczynski. His summits and attempts that fill this book speak for themselves. But there is so much more to this man's personality I never knew. After years of hearing him say he was going to write a book, it's here. It's fascinating, in-depth, and a well-written personal account of his life focused on achieving personal goals at great cost to him and his family. There's a downside, of course, to writing a book—Chris is going to have to do a lot more talking.

—John Roskelley

Introduction

Driven to 'The Death Zone'

LIFE AS WE KNOW IT on earth is not sustainable above 17,000 feet. Nevertheless, Himalayan peaks rise miles above that elevation, catching the human eye with glistening beauty and luring climbers into The Death Zone above 23,000 feet. Metamorphic, sedimentary, and igneous rock jut out from under the snow and ice at these extreme altitudes in an alien atmosphere. In many respects, The Death Zone is another planet. The moon rises as bright and crisp as an ocean salmon through the uncluttered air and appears larger than it would at sea level. Even in the daytime, the sky ranges from dark blue on the horizon to purple and almost to the blackness of outer space as you gaze straight up. The sun's ultraviolet rays burn exposed skin like a blowtorch. Without the protection of special sunglasses, your retinas will fry and leave you snow blind if not permanently sightless. Ice at these extreme elevations may have been frozen for centuries.

No lichens, plants, moss or bugs cling to existence there. No trees, weeds, grass of any kind take root; no animals visit. Humans show up, but the clock is ticking toward their demise without supplemental oxygen.

I once saw a wayward raven soaring up to this altitude, but other than the occasional bird, life forms without wings to quickly descend cannot live, not for long. According to physiologists, a human being can go to this altitude temporarily, but the body immediately begins to eat its own tissue. Fat cells provide nutrients until they are depleted to little more than a few atoms. As muscle cells atrophy, the body dissolves them one by one to provide nourishment, causing immediate loss of strength and weight. The brain numbs and the thought process slows when subjected to thin air with a third less oxygen than we breathe at sea level. The heart rate accelerates. The bone marrow tries desperately to produce new red cells, which must flatten out in the lungs to collect the scant oxygen molecules in the atmosphere. The eyes begin to look like a Los Angeles road map as the hemorrhaging starts at the retinas.

You become lethargic, slow to react. Moving a mere 250 feet in elevation can take an hour, requiring five or six breaths for each step. Every movement is slowed to a crawl. The air temperature is below zero and sometimes the wind can knock you off your feet. Climbers must be wary of HAPE (high altitude pulmonary edema), which can be lethal in more subtle ways than a James Bond girlfriend. HAPE shackles your appetite. You must aim each spoonful of food to your mouth and hope you don't immediately hurl all the precious nutrition you've consumed. Red blood cells are one body element that prospers in this environment, eventually thickening the blood to the consistency of tomato paste. High altitude sickness can strike with a blood clot in your leg, your arm, or anywhere in a thousand miles of veins and capillaries. If the clot thickens and won't pass, it can cause an embolism in your leg, or worse, higher up. If a clot forms in your brain at this altitude you will likely die from cerebral edema. Death from pulmonary edema is even more ghoulish. The membrane in your lungs can break, allowing blood and water to flow between cell tissues, flooding the bronchial trees. Without evacuating quickly to lower elevations, a victim will drown in a raw, gurgling, internally prepared stew.

On October 20, 1981, as I climbed the last few feet to a wind-shredded nylon tent at 26,300 feet on Mount Everest, I briefly questioned my sanity in the course of assuring myself I wasn't nuts. The temperature was 20 degrees below zero and the wind was around 50 miles per hour. I was almost two vertical miles higher than I'd been on the summit of the first completed mountaineering goal of my life, the North Face of the Eiger. Two ultimate challenges I'd set at the age of 15 were to be the first American to climb the Eiger North Face, "the hardest," and to scale Mount Everest, "the highest." No American had accomplished that deuce. Years later, I was less than 3,000 vertical feet from reaching my top of the world. Odds makers with any research on mountaineering would have given me no better than a 3 percent chance of succeeding. On the Eiger North Face in the early 1970s, for every climber who reached the top, one had died. On Everest, 108 climbers had reached the summit, but 53 climbers had lost their lives. The chances of a rescue in The Death Zone of Everest were close to zero if I got sick or in trouble. Despite the odds, I was confident, as I'm reminded in reviewing the detailed diary I kept of my climbs.

No one else really cared if I succeeded. The public didn't understand the challenge I'd taken. The two questions commonly asked when I returned from the climb were, "How cold was it?" and "How do you go to the bathroom?" No trophy, MVP award, or million-dollar contract was waiting if I returned alive from the summit; no Olympic gold medal or even a Sports Illustrated mention as athlete of the week. Only my immediate family and a handful of friends even knew I was on Everest. Only a couple of my teammates knew Sherpa Sungdare and I were hunkering into a frozen nest at Camp Four. None of that mattered because if I were merely seeking recognition I'd have chosen the surer, safer route of running naked across the field during a Seattle Seahawks game. We were deep into The Death Zone, yet I've never felt more alive. At this daunting height on Everest, the only signs of life outside our tent were tiny fossils in sedimentary rock laid down in a seabed more than 550 million years ago. This was an unlikely place to find happiness, yet I knew it was the last pit stop on the way to what I wanted. I remembered my father's words, "The man who doesn't know what he wants is already there." My parents had given me the genes to be able to climb Everest, but it's the brain that tells the body to move. It was up to me to decide whether I would complete the journey to the top of the world and return to tell the story.

HIGHEST AND HARDEST

ONE

LIFE WITH MEANING

I OFTEN THINK ABOUT the vastness of space and wonder about all the amazing things we have yet to discover, from Jupiter and other planets to galaxies beyond. And then I think about everything we haven't discovered right here on earth, including things undiscovered in my hometown.

Anthropologists claim Homo sapiens evolved from Africa and then wandered northward to Europe, Asia, and finally crossed the Siberian land bridge to walk into the relatively hospitable desert of what we call Eastern Washington. Native Americans had populated and thrived along the Spokane River for thousands of years before my ancestors arrived. I was born in Spokane, a moment of incredible endurance, faith, and bravery for my mother, I'm sure. But our predecessors had a much more arduous journey. How did people manage to travel all that way on foot, covering all that distance? These questions were the food for my imagination.

Spokane is a great big little town, a generally peaceful, quiet home for a quarter million or so people, bisected by an interstate highway with farm fields or forests an easy bicycle ride from any quadrant. The area enjoys four distinct seasons with a comforting serenity in the absence of natural disasters like hurricanes, typhoons, earthquakes, or avalanches to worry about. Geologically speaking, this is the calm after the storm. Between 12,000 and 15,000 years ago, the largest flooding in the history of our planet carved the landscape for Spokane and much of Eastern Washington. Waters of the Rocky Mountains to the west filled a huge basin called Glacial Lake Missoula. As the Cordilleran ice sheet advanced to block the Clark Fork River draining the basin near what is now Sandpoint, Idaho, about 80 miles north of Spokane, this "reservoir" expanded. The ice dam was huge, about 2,100 feet high. When the waters crested and breached the dam, geologists have calculated that 500 cubic miles of water were released in a torrent comparable to the combined flows of all the rivers in the world. Somewhere around 40 of these unfathomable floods occurred over thousands of years. Glacial Lake Missoula would empty and the Cordilleran ice sheet would advance again to block the river. The water backed up until the dam would be breached again. Dozens of humongous floods, perhaps the grandest in the solar system, flowed over Spokane, Washington, to the Pacific Ocean leaving scores of deep blue lakes and potholes scoured out of basalt bedrock. Any evidence of early human settlements was erased. The slate was clean. Only Mars has the same flooding scars to prove water existed and raged in torrents that could have rivaled the flooding of North Idaho, Eastern Washington, and Oregon.

My Caucasian ancestors were far away from these catastrophic floods, on another continent finding their way to the rolling grasslands in Europe. After surviving in Poland and Germany for centuries as farmers and builders, my great-great grandfather August left Poland in 1846 for the United States seeking new opportunities and the possibility of a better life. His search took him to Chicago, Kansas, British Columbia, and finally to Idaho where my dad was born. As far as our family tree can be traced, my ancestors were reared in the discipline of the Catholic Church.

My father was born in Cottonwood, Idaho. My mother was born in an even smaller community called Kueterville about 15 miles west of Cottonwood. When my mom and dad married, they eventually made their home in Spokane where they raised five children. Both sides of my parental lineage were farmers, builders, or blacksmiths.

I was born at 8 a.m. on February 24, 1948. My first vivid memories date back to 1950 as a two-year-old, living in a small wooden house on the US Air Force Base called Garden Springs. Our home was surrounded by dozens of almost identical homes built for military families.

My mother told me about a family trip to Northwest Seed and Pet Store, where my sister and I took a liking to the reptiles. A small turtle from that showcase became our first family pet. One day, the turtle escaped, or more likely, I simply took it out of the bowl and put it on the floor for some exercise and lost track of it. The missing turtle didn't show up until years later when we began moving to our newly built house on Montavilla Drive. I was 2 or 3 years old and I remember Dad pulling out the refrigerator and revealing my pet on the dusty floor, shriveled and lifeless as a hockey puck. The experience shook me. I poked the turtle with my fingers to make him move—to no avail. The mummified creature was my first introduction to the finality of death. The turtle never crawled or ate a cricket again. Never again did I think of life as forever.

My adventures started close to home as a three-year-old, highlighted by the one-block walks to the grocery store, guided in a stroller or wagon by my mother and older sister, Dawne. I soon learned that the dirt road to the "polka dot store" was also our local sledding hill during the winter. The Pokka Dot store, as my sister and I called it, was grocery magnate Mert Rosauer's first supermarket in Spokane. The building was white with big red, blue and yellow painted balls on the exterior, and I suppose the artist intended for them to look like balloons, but to Dawne and me they were big polka dots.

Record snowfall buried Spokane in the winter of 1950-1951. Snow piled halfway up the windows of the house. I would stare in amazement at the frost that formed on the windows and wonder how these pretty patterns of ice molecules made their own natural paintings. My best friend in Garden Springs was Mary Beth Phelps, who lived across the street. Some of my fondest childhood memories are the birthday parties and playing on the swing set with Mary Beth. When Dad bought a lot on Montavilla Drive, the Phelps family bought the house across the street from us, so we remained close pals.

In 1951, we moved into our new house, of which I had a hand in building, although it was a very small hand, which was usually in the way. Dad was a hard worker, a gifted musician, and a talented carpenter. Dad liked to boast that when he built his new home, he did all of the trade work including the concrete foundation, framing, electrical, plumbing, landscape work, masonry, concrete work, sidewalk and patio, and painting. He loved to tell his kids that the only trade he did not perform with his own hands on this house was the plasterwork. The contractor he hired had only one eye, and dad would scrunch up his face, close one eye, and mimic the plaster man to show us how the end product was pretty good considering the man's handicap.

At the age of six, I also helped with an addition to the house. The most memorable contribution was the day Dad trusted my budding skills to install the 1-by-10 shiplap over the roof joists. I eagerly jumped at this chance to prove my worth to earn praise and extra candy bar credit. He gave me a hammer and a nail pouch and laid out the shiplap before giving me instructions for cutting the boards with a handsaw and how to nail them in place. Dad left for work and I immediately applied myself to the job. I toiled all day, installing board after board, and was pretty impressed with my progress. When Dad returned after work, he came up on the roof for inspection. His jaw dropped. This was my first time I saw his temper flare. "Oh no! You've put on all the shiplap upside down!" I remember helping him rip off and reinstall all the boards that had taken me hours to attach. After this humbling episode, I remember going to the huge woodpile we had stacked up from the cutting of all the pine trees in the back yard. Here was something I could do and not screw up. I could chop wood! I remember splitting the wood with maul and wedge all day and making fire size pieces out of all those logs. At the end of the day I practically had the entire pile split. I was very proud of my effort and so was my dad.

Forty years after the shiplap incident, Dad told me he worried that yelling at me about my installation mistake may have scarred me for life. I admit that it was something I never forgot, and it made me think twice before proceeding on any construction project. But the incident was another building block in my upbringing.

LIFE LESSON: Do a job right the first time. It takes more time and energy to correct a mistake. Always think first, and then do a job one time.

Dad's first cabinet shop was started in the Spokane Valley with help from a friend who loaned him $500. He started out making window sashes, new doors and frames, and eventually built cabinets. His second shop building was located on Third Avenue and Maple Street. Large grocery stores eventually took over the site and the building was renovated by a car dealership. Occasionally, I was allowed to tag along with him to work, and I would hang out playing in the sawdust and watching him build cabinets. One day, we went to meet a customer who owned a grocery store on North Division Street. I gazed at the wonderful items on the shelves as though it was a museum. Dad distinctly told me to refrain from touching anything, as these items belonged to the store owner. My discipline was put to the test when I spotted a big candy bar. I told Dad I wanted that candy bar, and he refused. I begged, and he still refused. I sulked and pouted, and when my dad was busy talking to his client, I just reached up, grabbed the candy bar, and put it in my pocket. Then we left the store.

We drove down Division Street for a couple miles toward town, and I thought to myself that plenty of time had passed so my dad wouldn't notice me eating my "forbidden fruit." I pulled it out of my pocket, peeled off the wrapper, and took a big bite of chocolate. Dad looked around at me in the back seat munching away and immediately realized he was driving with a little thief.

"Where did you get that candy bar?" he demanded.

I immediately confessed, and he turned the car around and headed straight back to the store. I sweated in dead silent fear. They chop kids' hands off in some cultures for this behavior. I didn't know that, but I couldn't have been more scared if I did. I knew my dad was furious. Back to the store, he grabbed my hand, walked me into the building, and asked to see the owner. As I stood before a giant of a man with a white butcher apron, Dad said, "My boy has something to tell you."

I stuttered to get the words out, admitting that I had taken this candy bar without paying for it. The man was congenial. Dad said a few words, reached into his pocket and gave the man some money.

No pain was inflicted, but Dad lectured me on the way home, giving me my first formal moral building block:

LIFE LESSONS: Do not steal. Always be honest in your actions with people. Do not take things that do not belong to you, unless you pay for these items with money you have earned. You build a "track record" in life, Dad explained, and "only the Indian was able to cover his tracks."

Dad and I often went fishing on weekends. We drove to Lake Pend Oreille in Idaho and rented a barebones 12-foot boat at Bayview. I would help him carry it to the lake and clamp on our outboard motor. Like most little boys,

I thought my dad could do no wrong, and that green Evinrude motor was handsome, the best looking outboard on any boat around. It powered us out across the lake for great adventures. We would buy some juicy worms, launch out over the expanse of water to fish for kokanee—"bluebacks" as the locals called them. These land-locked sockeye salmon were prolific in the lake during the 1950s. The catch limit was 50 fish a day per person! Changes in the lake made the waters less hospitable for kokanee. In the 1990s the fishery crashed so dramatically that fishing for kokanee was prohibited for a few years, making the lake less welcoming for anglers, and their kids, too.

My dad never stopped exploring for new places to fish. His first salmon trip in the San Juan Islands hooked him for life. We started taking family vacation trips to Comox, British Columbia, where Dad's father lived and worked for a short period in his life before moving to Cottonwood, Idaho. I always wondered why my grandfather would move away from a place as beautiful as Comox, but it allegedly had to do with citizenship. If the family was going to stay in Canada, they would have to become Canadian citizens, so they returned to the United States.

LIFE LESSON: Give a boy a fish, and you give him a meal. Teach a boy to fish and you feed him for life.

Me with a king salmon at Leonard Piket's resort on the Little River, near Comox, BC, 1955.

Two

Whittier School

Whittier School

Going to school was a roller coaster experience. I recall hanging from a branch of a pine tree in our front yard when Mrs. Nissen, a Whittier School teacher, drove by. "Next year I'm going to first grade," I shouted to her at the top of my five-year-old lungs. I was fully ready to ascend from the dirtbag life of preschool to the higher calling of education—until the first day of school.

"Chris, stop crying, you will be fine," Dad said, holding my hand and trying to comfort me as we walked toward the huge square building. "You already know lots of kids at this school." Not to be pacified, I cried with all my might, complete with hysterical convulsions. I was openly terrified of what was going to happen inside the brick walls. I bawled as we walked through the double-door entrance; tears streamed down my cheeks as we proceeded through the cavernous hallway, and my anxiety spilled over until Dad opened the big white door to the first grade classroom and held my hand while I soaked

7

it in. About 20 little kids like me were sitting quietly in steel chairs with desks attached. One of them was my friend, Mary Beth. All was well in the world.

Meeting new friends came easy for me in first grade at Whittier School, but getting in trouble was even easier. Mischief—and trying to get away with it—was part of the learning curve. The boys restroom seemed like a particularly safe place for boys to be boys. A porcelain urinal stretched across the plaster of Paris north wall. It was about 3 feet high and molded into a trough with constant running water. Perhaps it started with an innocent off-target delivery, but that little squirt led to a game to see who could pee the highest on the wall. Once the competition started, I wanted to win! It was my first incentive to get high marks in school.

Day after day, a few boys including Gwain Oka and I would strut in like little hot shots during our breaks and let it fly. When someone eventually snitched on our competition, justice was swift. The principal, Mrs. O'Donnell, marched us into the boys restroom where the vice principal presented the evidence: urine marks distinguished with pencil lines. Her face went from stern to a horrified, wrinkled, and a colorless expression of disbelief. Apparently this group of first-grade boys had presented the veteran school administrator a new learning experience. We would have been proud of that if we hadn't been so scared. The group punishment was effective. We never peed on the walls of Whittier School again.

Whittier School was built in 1913 at the cost of $55,370 taxpayer dollars. The new school building replaced the first two-room Whittier School that had operated 1891–1892 at Ninth Avenue and A Street. The new Whittier School, named after the poet John Greenleaf Whittier, was touted as "one of the most beautiful buildings in the city." It was built on a bluff with a spectacular view overlooking Spokane to the east and north. The building was constructed with light golden pressed brick and huge Corinthian pillars at the front steps. However, the front steps were never used as the proposed street across the front area was never built, probably because of the steep, sandy bank that plunged into thick pinewoods that lay between the school and the Burlington Northern Railroad track below. Every day, steam engines would chug their way in and out of town along these tracks. To the east was Government Way, the road to Fort Wright, which was occupied by military commissioned officers.

Whittier was the school their children attended. No school bus operated in 1913 so parents arranged for their children's transportation. No sweat for the Kopczynskis, since our new home built in 1950 on 720 Montavilla Drive was only two blocks from the school.

Fighting was natural to me, but I honed the techniques through my years at Whittier where I became good at dishing out fighting words and then proving that I could get physical. If testosterone is the chemical that triggers aggression in boys, I had it in abundance. The last big fight in grade school was with Ray McElfish, whom I had sparred with over the years until the ridiculous issues came to a showdown in eighth grade. We agreed to fight just like professional boxers do, and we agreed the bout would be at the newly constructed park next to the school. Ray was much taller than I, but that didn't scare me away. With half the school watching, we squared off with fists cocked and ready. I had been previously successful wrestling other kids to submission, so I planned to stick with what I knew.

"Ok, let's do this!" Ray snapped at me. We jumped at each other like two fighting cocks, and somehow in the tornado of fists, I wrestled Ray to the ground. Being on the top for an instant, I managed to get Ray into a "rear naked choke," and then it was just a matter of waiting for him to either give up or pass out. Squeezing with all my might I yelled into his ear, "Give up!" He wouldn't. I continued to squeeze with everything I had for another very, very long minute before Ray finally said, "I give!"

We got up off the ground, and from that day forward we were fast friends.

My other major grade school challenge came from the architects who built Whittier School with a concrete band they poured as a separation barrier between the school foundation and the main two-story building above. This concrete band was exposed forming an 8-inch ledge—just wide enough for kids to get their feet on. With our backs firmly pressed against the brick wall, it was possible to shuffle sideway completely around the building on this ledge. No sweat, depending on how far a kid dared to go.

Whittier was built on a slope, so as the ledge remained level, the exposure gradually increased on the north and east side of the building into a 25-foot drop to the dirt below. The rate of difficulty increased at the very highest corner on the northeast side as the ledge narrowed to about 4 inches, probably to allow for an air duct behind the brick. Getting around the narrowest part of the ledge system required turning your body around to face the wall, and then stretching as far as possible to reach around the corner and grasp a half-inch joint in the brick with your fingertips. If you had arms long enough to make this tricky move, holding on with all your might, you could creep along inch by inch, nose planted into the bricks, tippy toes sliding on the 4-inch ledge, finger tips smeared in masonry joints.

No prize waited for us around the building. It was purely the challenge that dared us to make this move at the risk of broken bones or much worse if we fell. We walked the ledge for the thrill and the satisfaction of personal victory. And we never fell. This was my introduction to mountaineering.

THREE

THE SCIENCE PROJECT

THE FORMATION OF OUR NEIGHBOR GANG began like most other hoodlum groups. We were young boys looking for adventure. Gwain Oka, Ward Walker and I felt like giants the day we put our creative heads together and dubbed our gang, officially, The Three Musketeers. This was huge. Gwain was a natural born athlete, composed, subdued, and always thoughtful and graceful in his actions. Ward was the brains of the gang, already the neighborhood piano savant, and a chess champion as well. I was still trying to find out what I was good at. Piano wasn't my calling and neither was chess, so raising hell while trying to discover my purpose in life became my mission.

One warm, summer day, the Musketeers were palling around together near the school when the sky darkened with storm clouds that swelled with moisture until they unleashed a downburst rivaling a waterfall. Clothed in T-shirts, jeans, and tennis shoes, we danced around splashing in the mud. As the rain began to puddle into a large pond in front of the school, Ward saw the potential to mimic Mother Nature. "Hey! Let's channel the dirt to make a river!" he yelled. We had been studying erosion in our fourth-grade science lessons. The rainstorm had turned our school yard into a laboratory for understanding the power of water.

With the big pond growing larger in front of us, Ward, Gwain, and I tooled up like cavemen, using tree limbs and our bare hands to dig a trench that channeled the water flow down the east alleyway in front of the school's main entrance. As the rain poured down even harder, the street flooded and the pond grew into a lake that began to overflow its banks into our diverted streambed.

We watched in astonishment as the little stream swelled into a river and then into a drainage of Amazon proportions. The entire watershed surrounding the school seemed to be funneling into our manmade gorge. Cutting a channel down the east sand bank, the torrent gathered power, gouging deeper and deeper into the sand bank and hauling topsoil like a runaway train toward the railroad tracks below. Our force of nature raged past a huge pine tree, quickly stripping away the soil and exposing its tangled roots. Like any scientist witnessing such immediate and overpowering success from his experiment, we were amazed, then proud, then petrified with fear.

"Geez you guys!" Gwain said urgently. "How do we stop this? What's going to happen next?"

Ward and I were speechless. Was the entire school going to fall down the bank? Cubic yard upon cubic yard of sand and mud was being fanned into a huge delta on the railway's service road. Within minutes the road was blocked by a newly formed mountain at the end of the newly formed 4-foot wide, 4-foot deep canyon.

The Three Musketeers stood in awe before doing the right thing—running away. The city had to deploy a huge earthmover at taxpayer expense to repair the damage we'd unleashed with our hands and a few sticks.

LIFE LESSON: Controlling nature can lead to unforeseen problems.

Four

Teacher from Hell

THE WHITTIER SCHOOL sixth grade teacher was Art Manor, a towering man, more than 6 feet tall, with a big chin and a long, bulbous nose under his thick glasses and butch haircut. He drove to school in a white Thunderbird convertible with spoke wheels and white sidewall tires. He proudly kept this car spotless. Coats of wax made it shine. Every day at school we would ogle at this car and then cower under the tutelage of its driver.

Mr. Manor had developed a mantra of discipline that made military schools patsy in comparison. On his desktop, he kept a paddle about two feet long and an inch thick. He'd drilled perfect holes through the wood and coated it with varnish as though it were a prized piece of furniture custom made for making an impression on mischievous boys. Mr. Manor quickly sensed that my calling at this juncture in life was to cause and instigate trouble from any angle. He began to hone in on me, as well as Russ Shover and Ray McElfish, as the bad boys. The pee contest in first grade was five years in the past, but as my dad had told me, "Only the Indian could cover his tracks." Manor had probably been waiting for his chance to straighten us out.

One afternoon, Russ, Danny Simmons, and I wandered across the playground not minding the time, and we casually walked to the annex where the sixth-grade classroom was separated from the main school building. Manor was waiting stern-faced as we entered the door. We were late for class.

"You boys come up to the front of the classroom," he boomed in the voice of a drill sergeant about to set an example. "Now who is going to be first?"

Terrorized and red with embarrassment, I blurted, "I will Mr. Manor."

"Bend over and grab your ankles tight!" Manor commanded. I obediently bowed to the ground, reached for my ankles, and began to sweat with my heart beating in my throat. Manor calmly grabbed the big paddle off his desktop, walked behind me and wound up like Babe Ruth initiating a home run swing. I mustered all my inner strength, closed my eyes and "POW!" Two more "POWS" and my dose of educational discipline had been administered. I walked away with my ass throbbing—so sore that I couldn't sit down. Then Russell took his punishment. "POW" came the first hack. "POW" again. Manor reached even deeper into his morbidity for the third whack and, instead of a "pow" when the board connected, we heard a loud "CRACK." He'd broken the paddle on Russell's butt. "Well," said Manor, "I guess Danny will have to pay the consequences."

Manor opened his lower desk drawer and pulled out a shiny new correctional tool. He held the paddle up for all to see and to our horror one side of the board had nails sticking out!

"Grab your ankles Danny," Manor said, turning his instrument of pain over to make sure that Danny saw the nail points protruding like daggers from the back side of the paddle. "POW" came the slap. Danny snapped erect, swung his hands firmly to his butt, and then quickly lifted his hands in front of his face to see if there was any blood. Manor, with his sadistic personality, had switched the board over at the last second from the nail side to the flat side, but poor Danny was barely able to stand up after getting two more whacks.

Manor had a way of maiming student attitudes even without his paddle. Playing flag football in the park across the street against our rival, Irving School, I missed pulling a flag on one of the runners who scampered by to score the winning touchdown. Manor stopped the game, and in front of my teammates and the Irving team, said, "Son, I'm going to paint a yellow stripe down your back for missing that flag." I never played football again.

Fortunately, there was only one Art Manor in my life. But I give him credit for giving me my first taste of revenge. During the year, Manor began leaving his white convertible at home and commuting to school in a small, compact car similar in size to a Volkswagen Beetle. Staring at this little car one day gave me an idea.

"Hey, Gwain and Russ come over here and give me a hand." With our hands gripped under the undercarriage of the car, we lifted with all our might and we were stoked to see one wheel come off the ground!

Over the next several days, I convinced the strongest boys in school to join us after classes on the day of teacher conferences. Manor's car was perfectly parked out of sight from the school. With 15 of us surrounding the car, we made a combined "Heave-ho!" and were able to lift the vehicle entirely off the ground. We carried the car about 100 feet and up a small embankment. We angled it sideway with the front and rear bumpers tightly against the foundation walls of two houses. It couldn't be driven out! Then we scattered like birds.

The car was gone the next morning. Maybe Manor had to hire a crane to remove it, since none of us could imagine a man of that ilk could have any friends. But it was gone, and we never heard a word from anyone. My dad would later tell me another Chinese proverb: "Chris, if you seek revenge, first dig two graves." My first taste of it was sweet. Not until years later would I understand what Dad meant.

LIFE LESSON: A bad teacher can leave a scar for life.

Five

Trestle Trauma

"I'll go down this afternoon, fill this gallon jar with gas, and then I'll see you guys at 11 tonight at the base of the train bridge." The Three Musketeers had expanded to a Gang of Four and this would be another crazy stunt in our repertoire of raising hell.

Starting at the age of 10, I delivered newspapers, a job that rousted me out of bed by 4:30 a.m. every day. I developed the life-long habit of reading the paper during the hour and a half it took me to walk the route. One morning I read about the civil war in the Soviet Union and my attention was captured by a photo of what appeared to be teenage kids throwing home-made bombs at armored tanks. This was my introduction to the Molotov cocktail, a weapon the young rebels could make with nothing more than a rag, a bottle, and gasoline. If a beer bottle was a bomb that could terrorize an army, I tried to imagine what a kid could do with a full gallon of gas!

The plan fell into place like a Lincoln Logs cabin. In the 1950s, milk came in gallon glass containers delivered to your doorstep by the milkman, who'd leave fresh milk regularly and pick up the empties. Since we lived a few blocks from the railroad tracks, we knew the train schedules and routes pretty much by heart. Spokane was known throughout the United States as "the city of bridges." Dozens of major spans for vehicles or trains were built in the town core to flow traffic and commerce over the geologic escarpments of Latah Creek, the Spokane River, and the undulating basalt terrain. One of the longest railroad trestles in the world was just half a mile from our house. This magnificent steel trestle was more than a mile long and a couple hundred feet high above the Spokane River. A wooden walkway ran along one side for inspectors and train men to use, but it was clearly posted as dangerous and off-limits to the public. Marc Mercury, Gwain Oka, and especially Russell

Shover agreed that throwing a Gang-of-Four-sized Molotov cocktail off this trestle was an outstanding idea.

We'd graduated to the Gang of Four when Marc joined up with us for a few years, making us at least 25 percent more trouble. I took a milk container off our back porch, walked to the local gas station, and filled it to the brim. That evening I pretended to go to bed, then snuck out of the house after dark. I mounted my Columbia bicycle while holding in one hand the gallon of gas with a rag sticking out the top as I pedaled down the road to Russell's house in the cloak of night. The gang assembled at the prearranged meeting spot at the south end of the trestle. The sense of excitement was explosive. We had to venture out on the wooden walkway for two thirds of a mile before reaching the point where the Spokane River was directly below the towering trestle. I set the giant "cocktail" on top of the white wooden railing. Russ struck a match and lit the rag. The flame was as sudden and intense as our panic! The torch wrenched us from the stealth of darkness and into a spotlight for everyone to see. I tried desperately to extinguish the blaze by clasping the flames with my bare hands. Gwain and Russ stood frozen while Marc took off running back along the gangway.

I looked at Russ and said, "We got to put this out!" Before the last word left my mouth, Russ raised his foot and kicked the "cocktail" off the bridge. Three heads swung to the railing and peered over. The bomb streaked down with a tail of flame, hit a pillar and exploded into a huge fireball that blazed all the way to the river. Our jaws dropped even farther when we saw the water ablaze. Dogs began barking and we could hear people yelling from below in the trailer park, which was almost directly under the south end of the bridge. I looked up and to my horror, I was standing alone, as Russ and Gwain also had started fleeing. And run we did! Those two thirds of a mile on that rickety old boardwalk seemed endless. As we sprinted we heard sirens over the din of barking dogs and people hollering.

We made it to the end of the bridge, hopped on our bikes, and rode home as fast as we could. I snuck inside and took a hot bath trying to wash away the pungent smell of gas. I nearly rubbed my skin off trying to get rid of the odor. Still sweating I crawled into bed. The morning paper reported an "explosion" had occurred in Peaceful Valley. Mom commented about the small article to my father at breakfast. I said nothing. No one beyond the Gang of Four knew what happened that night.

LIFE LESSON: Do not play with matches around gasoline.

At Latah Creek, only the foundations remain of what was once the longest train trestle in the Northern Hemisphere.

Six

Birdman

"Oh my God, what is in this package, Cary?"

The postman had just delivered a large wooden crate to our doorstep, and when my mother read the label she sounded agitated.

"Don't worry Mom; it's just a big bag of bees," Cary calmly replied. "The queen is in the middle of a big bee ball inside."

My younger brother Cary was a deep thinker with a savant-type personality. As a boy, he engaged in hobbies like building ant farms and raising bees for honey. Cary had previously ordered the hives and built the bases necessary to begin his honey farm. Once the bees were released into their new home, they went to work.

The first honey harvest was great—about a pound for every hundred bee stings Cary suffered tending the hives. Getting stung was part of the job, and as meticulous as he was about covering himself from head to toe with a coat, hat, and bee netting, he was stung quite often. One day Cary ran into the house to tell Mom he had been stung again, and then he went in the bedroom to lie down. Minutes later, Mom helped Cary to the car and rushed him to the hospital. His throat was swelling and he could barely breathe. She got him to the emergency room just in time.

In a progression that no one could have predicted, my brother's brush with death led to the birth of my interest in conquering vertical challenges. Bee farming was no longer safe for Cary, so he decided to raise pigeons. He became fascinated with homing pigeons, especially an odd type called Pensom Rollers. When let out of the cage, these pigeons would fly straight up in the air several hundred feet and roll backward over and over until nearly reaching the ground, where they would flap back up high and repeat this crazy flight pattern. Before he could order these pigeons through the mail, he needed a cage. I helped him level the ground and construct a bird house out of plywood and chicken wire. It was big enough to hold a couple dozen birds. I offered my services to trap additional pigeons for him because I knew just where to start.

Spokane, "The City of Bridges," had a magnificent concrete span on Sunset Boulevard—1,070 feet long over Latah Creek with seven Roman arches that were 128 to 150 feet across. This haven for pigeons was only a half mile from our home. The birds nested about 150 feet off the ground on top of the arches that held the roadway above, but we could not figure out how to reach them. The bridge builders seemed to have done a great job of eliminating any access 12-year-old boys might exploit, that is until we discovered a possibility on the southwest corner. The transition between the arch on the west end and the first concrete pillar was only 20 feet off the ground. Bill Tresko was my one and only climbing friend at this time. Bill was huge for his age, big and strong, perfect for the job at hand.

We searched the adjacent forest and found a dead tree to use as a temporary ladder. Together, we dragged the tree from the forest and leaned it against the lower part of the arch. I climbed up the tree first, clutching dead limbs and bear hugging the trunk until I gained the concrete crotch of the arch. Climbing into the arch, to my amazement I saw a two-inch-wide hemp rope hanging from the pilaster above. Bill didn't seem so excited, but I was, and immediately began to pull myself hand over hand up the rope. This was no ordinary rope; it was thick woven manila and hemp rope with plenty of braids for excellent handgrip. The builders must have left these ropes hanging from the pilasters at the top of the curving arches for rappelling down as they stripped the wooden forms. I didn't know much about construction. To me, it was just a big rope to climb. As I pulled myself up hand over hand I was putting a hundred feet between me and the ground, so the situation was dangerous. Upon reaching the pillar where the rope was tied, I had to carefully skirt my body around the small concrete pilaster with great caution to gain the top of the arch.

I lay down, stuck my head over the lip of the arch and yelled, "Hey Bill! I'm up here at the top of the arch!"

"Holy Cow! How did you get way up there! Wait for me! I'm coming up too!"

With trepid care, Bill followed my route to join me at the top. Silence and fear of the height gripped us into a new emotional state. "Man, this is pretty hairy up here," I said trying to stay somewhat composed and hide my anxiety.

The dangerous part of the mission started at the top of the arch. The pigeons all lived on the highest section of the bridge four arches to the east and over Latah Creek. The immediate problem was to reach the arches on the north side of the bridge, where we knew from previous scouting that a repairmen's walkway hung in place directly underneath the highway.

From the top of the arch, we inched our way around the second pilaster with even greater vertical drop to gain access to another construction rope, which was lying right where the construction men left it in 1912 when the bridge was completed. In 48 years it had been touched only by whatever the wind and weather delivered until I grabbed it. Carefully, I climbed down hand over hand on the rope, my feet guiding me along the arch, until I landed in the Y where it joined into the supporting vertical pillar. I was standing on a wooden plank, probably 12 inches wide by 4 inches deep the contractors had left for access to the far side (north side) arches. We had to walk this plank about 40 feet to the Y of the north arch at the same elevation. The plank was 90 feet off the ground, high enough to create the illusion that a foot-wide board was more like a tight rope. I carefully walked the plank using one arm for balance touching a hand to the concrete pillar. Bill followed my lead until we were staring at another old construction rope that went up the north pillar, exactly like the ones we had just used. We climbed this last arch to gain a walkway—complete with a handrail! This repair walkway transgressed the length of the bridge next to the water line and gas lines offering access to the eastern arches where the pigeons lived. Huck Finn and Tom Sawyer had nothing on Bill and me.

Having worked out the route to reach the birds, we retreated to figure out how to trap them. Using blueprints in one of Cary's books, we built several wooden traps from apple crates. Then we cut wire from coat hangers to make the one-way entrance. Constructing the traps was easy. Getting them into place was not. In my mountaineering career that followed, I never went 10 feet off the ground without a protection belay. Here on this bridge, Bill and I were climbing on old ropes, over old wooden planks, and precariously tiptoeing around narrow concrete ledges with a vertical drop of a hundred feet to get two traps in place and baited with bird seed.

Returning the next day, we found to our delight that the bait had worked and we had a pigeon in each trap. Bill wasn't interested in the birds at all, so the job was over as far as he was concerned. Getting the birds back home to Cary's cages would be a challenge for one person who didn't have ropes. I decided to put the birds down my T-shirt next to my body. This way, my arms were free to do the climbing necessary to get down. I was pleased with my solution, and the pigeons seemed to like the idea, too. They didn't move. Later I refined this method and added an extra sweater over the T-shirt next to my body. The pigeons seemed comfortable there, and I could easily see how magicians keep these birds calmly hidden from the public while performing magic shows. I trapped a dozen or more pigeons this way until one trapping incident nearly ended my life.

The huge concrete arches had a hollow section in the middle. Where Bill and I climbed from the Y joint, the arch continues down another 75 feet or so to the ground level in this hollow section. One day while checking our traps, I told Bill, "Hey, I'm going to rappel down inside this pillar. I'll place a trap down where the nests are." We could see several pigeon nests on what appeared to be solid concrete or dirt. Once we gathered enough old construction rope and tied it off at the uppermost pillar, I let myself down hand over hand toward the bottom.

"Kop! Are you sure you can climb back outta there?" Bill yelled. Good question, I thought, but not until I was near the bottom of the arch where the angle was very nearly vertical and more than a hundred feet straight down. Still, I was confident. When I got near the vertical bottom of the arch, all my body weight was transferred to my hands and arms, and it became much harder to hold onto the rope. As I neared the floor, and what looked like concrete or dirt, I let go of the rope to step onto solid ground and rest from the down climbing.

To my horror, I broke through a false floor and went up to my armpits in slime. The water surface was under a 12-inch head of moldy bird shit laid down over the past 48 years! I found myself in a desperate situation. "Bill! Bill!

Help!" I yelled with all the volume I could crank out of my voice, but there was nothing Bill could do for me. On the verge of panic, I assessed the situation and realized my hands were still dry and holding on to the rope. I tried in desperation to stem with my feet and hands to move myself upward, but the goo on my shoes acted like grease. "Bill, try to pull me up!" I could hear Bill grunting and gasping as I clung to the rope, but I barely moved an inch.

With my heart in my throat, I could see only one way out. I started pulling myself hand over hand up the rope, inches at a time. My feet and body were saturated with crap and worse than useless. Slowly I gained a few feet. My arms ached and I nearly blacked out from the exertion. Somehow, about the moment that I felt I could hold on no longer, I managed to semi-wrap the rope around my slimed foot. By pressing the side of my foot hard to the concrete with the rope wrapped around it, I could take a tiny bit of weight off my hands. It allowed the blood to flow back to my wasted forearms. With this stop-and-go method, I found the strength to continue and pull myself hand over hand more than a hundred feet up and out of a death trap to Bill's position at the top of the arch. I collapsed totally spent and laid on my back shivering in my slimed and smelly clothes.

"Kop, we got some trouble coming," Bill whispered. "Look over the edge here." Our yelling back and forth had attracted attention, probably from pedestrians directly above us on the sidewalk. I peered over the lip of the arch and below on the dirt road I saw a police car easing to a stop right below our position. "Oh shit!"

The policemen got out of the car, and one of them was holding a bullhorn. "You boys get off that bridge right now and come down!"

I had to think of something quick. I didn't want to go to jail. Bill and I discussed bolting on the catwalk but running away would certainly mean the cops would see how we go up there. I decided to try negotiating from our loftier position. I yelled down with as much command as I could. "We were just looking for pigeons, we will never come up here again, and if you leave, we will come down."

The police officers didn't move for what seemed like an eternity. They just sat there, and again the bullhorn sounded. "You boys come down here right now!"

"If you leave we will come down, I promise!" I replied firmly. We were holding the upper ground, and I wasn't going to budge. I guessed that the cops couldn't climb to us, so I felt confident in the faceoff.

Both policemen eventually climbed into the squad car and slowly drove under the bridge and out of sight to the south. Bill and I climbed onto the catwalk and ran to the other side, climbed the arches and got down off the bridge. I kept my promise and never returned for another pigeon, nor did I ever climb the bridge again.

LIFE LESSON: Quicksand looks like solid ground.

Latah Creek Bridge has seven huge Roman arches.

SEVEN

PENANCE & PENOLOGY

EARLY LESSONS FROM LIFE came from outside as well as inside the walls of Whittier grade school. One day after classes my friend Bob Rooney and I climbed to the top of the hills behind my house and discovered a contractor's construction shack next to a new home on the cliff. This was the first new home to be built on the hill above us. I learned later this was to be the home of Dr. Larry Pence and his family. The house was constructed over solid basalt and the contractor had to use dynamite to break the rock for the foundations. I was 10 years old at the time and didn't have a clue what I was looking at, but my friend Bob was 13 and I was tagging along with a real man.

"Hey Chris, take a look; these are blasting caps!" Bob held up a couple of wires that had a lollypop-like device at one end. We looked at the construction shack and put two and two together.

We tried our best to break the lock and get our hands on some real big firecrackers. Thankfully, we failed in our attempt, but this brush with destructive adventure whetted Bob's appetite for mischief. We started walking home down a dirt road, later named West Drive, and saw an old coupe parked alongside the road. I've never been enthralled by the average American's love affair with type, make, or name of cars, and this didn't look like anything special to me. The vehicle was locked, but Bob said, "Let's break inside." We scrounged around in the dirt and found an old pipe that Bob used to smash in the windows. Then he handed the pipe over so I could have some fun. Before long, we had broken every window. Next we unlocked the hood, pounded on the motor, pulled out wires, unhooked the tubes and pipes, smashed the fenders and scratched the paint all around the car. I have no explanation of what was going through my numbskull, hormone-surging brain. We walked home feeling pretty high from the thrill of smashing something to bits.

When he came home from work, I told Dad I needed to tell him something in private, so he followed me into the back den of our house. I dug deep and managed to spit out the understatement of my life: "I think I did something bad today."

"Well, what did you do?"

I recounted exactly what happened, telling him about trying to break into the contractor's shack, then finding the "abandoned" car, and destroying it. I went through all the excruciating details. When I finished spewing my guts, I felt somewhat better, and awaited my fate.

Dad stood in silence for a few moments, then put his huge hand on my shoulder. A slight smile creased his mouth. "Chris, I'm glad you told me the truth," he said, uttering words I'll never forget. "You did something very bad and wrong, but you told me the truth, and that's the most important thing. There are going to be consequences for your action."

I didn't have any idea what the word "consequence" meant, but it didn't sound like candy.

The vehicle belonged to the mother of our neighbor, Judge Willard Roe. I can only imagine Judge Roe's face when my dad called and told him what Bob and I had done. Dad also called Bob's father, Ed Rooney, who was a Spokane police detective. He responded to the news by giving his son the whipping of his life. My friendship with Bob was over.

Dad and Judge Roe set a date for my sentencing, and that was to be when the estimate for the auto repairs was received. About a week later, Dad and I walked up to the judge's house and he handed me my half of the estimate for the damage, as the other half was to be paid by Bob. My portion was $849. In 1958, that was a good sum of money. We had done serious damage to that car, and maybe they had to total it for all I know.

At the time I was already doing small construction jobs and chores like lawn mowing for my parents, but I realized, being pretty accomplished at math, that I would be many years paying off this debt at the 25 cents an hour I was getting paid. Dad and Judge Roe found out that the local paper route delivery boy was quitting, and The Spokesman-Review was looking for a new paperboy for our neighborhood. The Review was a morning paper, and there was an afternoon paper called The Chronicle. The difference was the Review was delivered seven days a week, including a large Sunday edition with expanded advertising section that was quite heavy. The Review also paid much better, between $10 and $12 profit each week depending on the number of customers. I wrote a letter with much help from Dad and applied in person at The Review office for this position as I was underage to work as a paperboy. Dad and particularly Judge Roe had some influence with the newspaper managers, and I was hired. Now I was a 10-year-old with a real paying job, and the responsibility to go with it.

Mom bought a clock for my bedside, and at 4 a.m., rain or shine, seven days a week, the alarm sounded and off I went into the darkness to pick up my papers two blocks away on F Street. This sentence and my penitence turned out to be one of the most rewarding experiences in my life. Every morning for the next seven and a half years, until I turned over the paper route to my brother Cary before my senior year in high school, I delivered the newspapers. Getting up before sunrise became fun. I evolved into a student of natural history. I tried to calculate the exact time of the sunrise through summer, fall, winter, and spring. I marveled at the change of the season with the distinct difference in weather that Spokane has. I was especially delighted by the songs of birds—robins, wrens, and sparrows chirping in the morning quiet. I looked forward to the job. I developed a connection with nature and made money at something I liked to do.

It took a couple years to pay off my debt for the car damage, but my dad and Judge Roe were kind enough to let me keep an extra couple bucks a week after paying my weekly payment. Not only was I learning about justice and how it can be dealt, I also was learning about human nature. Some of my customers did everything they could to avoid paying me. Thankfully, there were only a couple of bad apples among my 70-some subscribers.

After every cent of my debt was paid, I saved my earnings and bought my first snow skis. I paid $165, all in $1 bills, all laid out on the counter at Simchuck Sporting Goods. I was 15 years old, and this was the proudest moment of my life.

LIFE LESSONS: Bad decisions are costly and consequential. Good decisions pay off.

EIGHT

BUDDING MOUNTAINEER

Me climbing the East Ridge of Edith Cavell, British Columbia.
Photo by Joe Collins.

My climbing career began in the summer of 1963. I was 15, already had a record with the law from vandalizing a car and breaking the neighbors picture window. Doubtless I was heading for more trouble when my dad convinced me to go on a family vacation to British Columbia. I will never forget the first views of a real mountain as we were driving along the southern flank of Mount Verendrye near Vermillion Crossing in Banff National Park. I scanned the rocky cliffs thousands of feet above for mountain goats. I was smitten with the view from our Banff hotel room window of Mount Cascade bathed in early morning sunlight. Love at first sight. I desperately wanted to climb up there to see how far I could see, what the rock was composed of and how it felt. "What animals live up there?" I wondered. I wanted to touch the indigo blue sky.

I carried on about my desire to climb these big mountains and was a bit surprised when Dad, to whom I owe everything, said, "Chris, if you really want to do this sort of thing, you should get hold of a business associate of mine, Bill Boulton. Bill is president of the Spokane Mountaineers Club, and you should go through the school they have to properly learn how to climb mountains."

Back in Spokane, I called Boulton, got the information needed, and joined the club, which has been around in one form or another since 1915. The introductory meeting was held at a downtown bank. Joe Collins was the featured storyteller, and his slide show hooked me. At the meeting I noticed a puny, smart-aleck skinny kid who didn't, in my estimation, have any business being in an "athletic" club. His name was John Roskelley, who eventually taught me the folly of making too much of first impressions.

I soon abandoned my love for baseball the way a dog races from a chew toy to a big meaty bone, and started reading every mountaineering book I could find. The first was "Annapurna," the detailed account of the 1952 French expedition that made the first ascent of a peak higher than 8,000 meters. Eventually I read "The White Spider," by Austrian climber Heinrich Harrer, who, along with three companions, made the first ascent of the most famous mountain wall in the world, the North Face of the Eiger in Switzerland.

I soon realized that mountaineering was the right fit for my personality. I was on the high school baseball and wrestling teams, but these activities never inspired me physically or mentally. Wrestling was tough for six or eight minutes, but then you rested. Baseball was challenging, but it wasn't like climbing, a discipline in which one must be tough mentally and physically hour after hour for extended periods. A climber thinks about succeeding while depending on judgment to stay alive. I realized mountaineering not only fit my personality, it could tap my potential.

I went through weeks of Mountain School sessions and especially reveled in the weekend of on-snow practice near Lookout Pass. We trained in ice-axe arrest, roping up in teams for glacier travel, and camping in the snow, and then applied what we'd learned up the St. Regis Basin in Montana. Later that summer, the school's "graduation" climb would take me to the top of Mount Hood in Oregon.

By the time I bought my first ice axe I already had lofty ambitions. I used my wood burner to sear goals into the ash shank:

EIGER
V
E
R
E
S
T

I aspired to climb Mount Everest because it was the highest mountain in the world, and the Eiger North Face because it was recognized by the fraternity of world mountaineers as "the ultimate test of how good you are." At the time I spelled out my goals, Everest and the Eiger North Face had been climbed, but no mountaineer had climbed both of these mountains. With my goals carved into my axe, I could see them every time I went into the mountains, but years, luck, hundreds of climbs and almost as many failures would be needed. My dad, always a man of few words, was a man of no words when I told him how much I loved climbing, and that my goal was to climb Everest. A famous French mountaineer named Lionel Terray wrote, "A man's nature determines his fate." It certainly proved true for my life.

Higher Education

After graduation from high school, I was eager to make a living as a carpenter and continue to train and prepare for my mountaineering goals. Dad countered by lecturing that going to college and completing higher education was the single most important thing I could do in my life. Dad loved statistics, and he continually reminded me that people who do not start college directly after high school rarely achieve a college degree. He preached the long-term economic value of college. He was convincing. I chose Washington State University for its Construction Management studies as well as the wrestling program in the competitive Pacific Eight National Collegiate Athletic Conference.

From the first day I arrived on the WSU campus, I loved it. Many students get all the adventure they want from textbooks and that's the main mission of college, but in my case, hunting the wheat fields near Pullman and venturing out to the mountains on weekends were the fulfilling experiences I sought. I wanted to make myself stronger. My wanderlust habits from high school continued as I left town whenever possible.

I studied physics, economics, architecture, genetics, surveying, building materials, and construction management. During my freshman year, I took an elective class in geology, which proved to be fascinating, and the most beneficial science class of my life. I followed up with a mineralogy class. For our class "graduation" field trip, a few students were selected for a 10-day rafting float down the Green River and Yampa River in Colorado and Utah through Dinosaur National Monument. The trip, which was before the route was on the radar of tourists, was one of the best field learning experiences I have ever had. Combined with mineralogy, basic geology studies gave me an understanding of what mountains were made of, how old they were, and the stories they could tell. With this education, going into the mountains was like reading the pages of a book. I developed a deep love for all the sciences, but I just could not figure out how to make my living at geology or genetics, so I stayed the course in construction management.

College athletics competed with my studies. I worked out from 2 p.m. to 6 p.m. daily to measure up to my NCAA wrestling opponents. During my last year at WSU, I set my sights on a medal at the Pacific Eight finals. For four years on varsity, I always had a winning record, only to be edged out of the medals platform at the conference tournament. I was determined to change that story in my final year.

Workouts started with a 7-mile run from Bohler Gym to the end of the golf course and back. Then I ran up and down the stadium stairs a dozen times. The cardiovascular training was followed by 30 to 45 minutes of weightlifting before heading to the wrestling mats in Smith Gym for the final two hours of competitive wrestling and technical training with the team. Making the varsity team was not easy. Each year there would be one or two high school state champions from my weight class who would challenge me. As a freshman, I won a varsity position at the 158-pound class and never lost it in four years of challenges. I should have wrestled at the 167-pound division, as that was my natural weight, but our team was stronger if I dropped the pounds to the lighter weight. You could say I took one for the team on that count. Dropping weight for wrestling is detrimental and I wouldn't do it again.

I was proud of my NCAA career. I worked hard to win, and eventually placed third in the PAC Eight Conference in 1970, which earned me a trip to the Nationals in Evanston, Illinois, where I lost by decision in the first round to the Big Ten Champion. The overriding lesson I gained from my high school and college varsity sports years was how competitive humans are and what lengths people will go to win.

I thought I worked hard to succeed until I saw the world's greatest wrestling champion, Dan Gable, at Evanston. I was working out three to four hours a day while the NCAA champions were training all day long. It became their life to be Number One. I realized what I already knew deep down, that to reach my goals of climbing Everest and The Eiger North Face, I would have to up my training program a couple notches to succeed.

Athletics also revealed that people have a genetic predisposition for success in sports and other activities. I realized that if I had trained 24 hours a day, seven days a week, my success may or may not have been slightly better as a wrestler. However, I knew that if I were to lead every NCAA wrestling champion on a race to the summit of Mount Rainier, I could win that contest, as I was born with a high Ventilatory Maximal Oxygen uptake, (VO2 Max), and a super high Hypoxic Ventilatory Response (HVR). These technical terms I would not understand until much later in my life, but simply put, I was born with the right genes to excel and excel at high altitude mountaineering.

My parents knew my dedication and passion for wrestling and mountain climbing would never make me any money, so they continued to push me to get my college degree. I frustrated Dad in the summer of 1970 by going to Yosemite Valley to climb for three weeks. Instead of coming right back and getting to work on my construction career, I bought a racing bicycle in Oakland and pedaled it all the way back to Spokane. This lifestyle was completely irresponsible in the eyes of my parents.

My senior year at WSU came to an end in the spring of 1971, as I had to take an extra semester the fall of 1970 to pass a mandatory accounting class. I moved back to Spokane and applied for work at Boulton Insulation Company, moved out of my parents' house to a cabin on the Little Spokane River, and went to work. A career in construction paled to my ambition for being one of the world's best mountaineers, but I had to support myself. Being a climbing bum, like so many of the Yosemite rock jocks, wouldn't advance me toward my goals. Getting invited to join an Everest expedition required more than just being good.

LIFE LESSONS: Competition is fierce for every goal you set, and there is a price to pay for your passion.

Nine

Matterhorn & Eiger

The Matterhorn as seen from Zermatt, Switerland.

My heroes as a budding teenager included the odd combination of world-class mountaineers and explorers including Edward Whymper, Sir Edmund Hillary, and Lionel Terray, as well as the greatest Greek thinkers—Aristotle, Socrates, and Plato. In some ways, I was not a mainstream kid.

The youth of the tumultuous 1960s made headlines for the sexual revolution, the "me" generation, their rebellion of the Vietnam War, and for being the greatest optimists of all times. The hippies of the '60s were mostly young people my age who dropped out of mainstream society to live a life of drugs and sex and escape from things their parents would recognize as civilized. They had a vision of Utopia and they pursued it with abandon. I was one of these tumultuous teenagers, but I used to poke fun at the revolutionaries, and particularly the hippies and draft dodgers. In my view, they were people with no goals for improvement. To me they came across as no nothing people. But I was no authority on the culture. While many youths were experimenting with drugs, the focus of my teenage years was trying to climb one rock after another, and then one bigger mountain after another. I never ran into marijuana because I never ran around with people I considered to be "losers." I didn't even know the sexual revolution was underway. "The Pill" didn't give me freedom from my fear of commitment to women. I did have girlfriends at the time, but if the relationship got too serious I became terrified of what I thought my girlfriends wanted to happen. From my observation, next to eating, reproduction of the species was the highest priority of the billions of people before me. I was determined to accomplish more in my life than having children and then spending the rest of my life trying to educate, house, and feed them. Women are intuitive, and they figured me out quickly. My passion was not about being a sperm donor or good father, so I didn't break any hearts as I headed for the mountains every weekend where the romance never let me down.

I yearned for a life of adventure and achievement. Success in my mind was becoming an Air Force pilot, scaling unclimbed mountains, going to the moon—certainly there was no time for sitting on my butt and complaining about the past, or the present. I was determined to make a name for myself as an adventurer and athlete. Wilderness was to be my road to "success," so I founded my own club: "Youth for Mountain Climbing and Getting Rich."

My years at Washington State University were dominated by weekend climbing adventures when I wasn't consumed by wrestling for the varsity team. I will always be grateful to my father for insisting I get a college degree. Dad couldn't complete college because he didn't have the money. I was reluctant to go to college because I didn't have a purpose. When I graduated from high school, I felt ready, eager, and capable to make a living on my own. I was strong and knew I could excel in the construction market. I couldn't see over the horizon because there were mountains in the way. I needed only enough money to get that far and conquer them. Dad pitched the long-term value of a college education every time we were alone: "Even if you never use the degree you earn, the fact that you finished college will be a badge that will pay off tenfold in your life." Dad also blessed me with good jobs. Every summer of my teenage years, my brother and I would work on one of his construction projects. The pay was about $2.50 an hour for a laborer, and about $3.50 an hour for a carpenter, which was top dollar for any job at that time. We had to join the laborers union, and then eventually the carpenters union to work on his projects. These jobs were tough physical work, but we were able to live at home and save nearly every dime we earned. After working all day shoveling concrete and gravel, we had little energy left over for nightlife.

Dad helped keep me on the right course at WSU, but my mind still wandered from my studies. I spent a lot of my free time perusing the American Alpine Journals in the library and finding the newest mountain books on the market. Adventures of world travelers hooked me. I longed to give myself a big test. The Matterhorn in Europe eventually stood out because of its formidable reputation for aesthetic and romantic adventure. I set my mind on climbing it.

John Roskelley, my main climbing partner at the time, desperately wanted to go to Europe but he could not afford the trip. I tried a couple other climbing mates with no success, so I made up my mind to go solo. The roundtrip airfare from Vancouver, British Columbia, to Amsterdam was $235. The decision to go solo climbing in Europe was very tough on my parents, particularly my mother. I don't think she slept much the entire time I was in Europe.

In the summer of 1969, my dad had won a construction contract to build the Lamplighter Lodge at Sullivan Road and Interstate 90. Just like the previous four or five summers, I could make good money working as a laborer and carpenter, live at home, climb on the weekends, and save my earnings. This transition between my junior and senior years at WSU seemed like a perfect time to buy a vehicle. Dad passionately tried to discourage me from buying a car, any car. He knew the costs went far beyond the purchase price. My great brainstorm was to buy a car in Amsterdam, tax-free. The total price for a brand new MGB in Holland was only $2,100, and I had saved the money. I also had banked enough for my college tuition for the next year. Then, to my discouragement, I learned about the costs of barge shipping the car home, in addition to the US import duty that nullified any tax savings. The barge went across the Atlantic from Amsterdam to New York, then through the Panama Canal to Seattle. Nevertheless, as in many emotional decisions, I tricked myself into believing this was my only reasonable alternative. I needed some form of transportation while touring Europe, so this MGB classic convertible seemed to fit my style. (I might as well jump forward to point out that upon returning from Europe to the USA, I would take a train from Spokane to Portland to pick up my little sports car. Just 50 miles out of Portland, I would pass a stopped school bus, prompting a $150 ticket from the State Patrol. The prestige of owning a car would eventually wipe out my savings, but not before I had an excellent adventure.)

On August 20, I finished packing my clothing, climbing hardware and ropes, kerosene stove, boots, pack, helmet, gloves, and other gear for the journey to the airport in Vancouver, British Columbia. When I bought my airline ticket, I realized that among the passengers was Yvon Chouinard, one of the most famous mountaineers in the world, I requested to be seated next to him on the plane. The excitement of my expedition had me stir-crazy, and my heart rate never returned to normal for the next 30 days. Looking back out the window as the plane door shut, I remember seeing my parents standing at the terminal concourse to watch the plane take off. It was a polar flight, and a spectacular clear day, so I could view all the mountains that I had climbed in the Canadian Rockies thousands of feet below. I am embarrassed to say that I virtually talked Chouinard's ear off, asking question after question until he finally just fell asleep. However, he did warn me of how big a climb the Matterhorn was, as he had to turn around on his attempt. "It's well over 6,000 feet of climbing," he said. "Don't take it lightly."

Except for dozens of travels to Canada, I had never been to a foreign country. The first issues of money exchange and the foreign accents were pretty easy to deal with, but the fact that I was completely on my own started to sink in. I couldn't afford to make any mistakes.

My MGB was supposed to be at the Amsterdam airport, but to my dismay, I found out the car hadn't even been shipped from London, leaving me to deal with a three-day delay in my plans. I took a bus into Amsterdam and managed to find a decent room, for double the amount of my budget. This would be the only room I remember staying in for the entire month. When planning my adventure, I had bought the book "Europe on 5 Dollars a Day" and was determined to stick to that allowance. The three-days delay in the city put a substantial hole in my pocket. My original plan was to sleep and camp in my car the entire month. At the end of my travels, I averaged about $7.50 a day.

I rented a bicycle in Amsterdam, saw Anne Frank's house, walked all over the downtown district and spent one day going on a tour of the Heineken brewery. I got drunk on free beer at the end of the tour. Art museums were an eye-opening diversion. I was amazed at the huge size of some paintings like "The Night Watchman." The last night, I inadvertently wandered into the red-light district. The women were just opening up their shops where they would advertise their wares and services by sitting bikini-clad on a stool behind a street-side display window as though they were a cross of butcher shop meat and department store mannequins. The values of my upbringing and the sexual lassitude in Europe were worlds apart. Women sell their bodies in Amsterdam the way Macy's sells skirts and high heels, and locals don't blink an eye. One couple bought their two kids ice cream and walked right by one of the windows as a nearly naked hooker calmly sat in wait for her next customer. One woman must have been particularly outstanding, as there was a line of five men outside her apartment. I was too naïve about sex to even consider exploring this wilderness of cultural differences. Besides, I didn't come to Europe to stand in lines, and sex wasn't in my budget.

When my car finally arrived, I traveled on the autobahn toward Frankfurt. I remember the German countryside of rounded rolling hills were green and picturesque. How could there ever have been such a terrible war here? I thought. When I needed a break, I would pull off at a rest area, and either sleep in the car or pull my sleeping bag out and sleep right next to it. I used a small camp stove to boil water for a freeze-dried meal with a cup of tea or hot cider. It was very Spartan living, but I didn't starve. I had gained 5 pounds by the time I returned to the United States, mostly from consuming Swiss chocolate and German beer as though they were meat and potatoes. That doesn't mean I was always fat and happy in pursuit of my mountaineering goal. My anxiety peaked the night before reaching the Alps as I camped in a field off the autobahn in Germany. Loneliness and doubt began setting their hooks. I questioned my judgment. I tossed and turned wondering if the Matterhorn was more than I could handle. Was I strong enough? Could I do it alone? Why the hell was I attempting something like this? Dawn finally appealed my sentence to a sleepless night. I stuffed my sleeping bag, got in the car, my only companion, and headed south toward Switzerland. As I drove toward the mountains, I felt myself entering my comfort zone. Self-doubt gradually submitted to confidence.

Changes were striking as I made a beeline through Zurich and Luzerne. Small villages were built on steep mountain slopes surrounded by cattle grazing in lush green pastures. High-quality construction was the norm, from the stone and wood homes to the deftly engineered mountain roads. The precise Swiss train system, the seemingly impossible tunnels for railroads and highways, the high-altitude dams for hydropower all blend in with the eye-grabbing landscape to keep this little country ticking like a Rolex. No wonder James Bond movies were filmed here.

The winding road over a pass toward Zermatt was perfect for my little green MGB. I descended thousands of feet into a huge, U-shaped glacial valley that dissected the Northern and Southern Alps. In 1969, there was no auto road to Zermatt, so I parked my car at a railway station and rode a train on August 29 for the final 30 miles up the valley to the small village. The train wound its way up the valley, and, like the last chapter in a story book, it rounded a corner to reveal one of the grandest mountain scenes in the world. The first sight of the Matterhorn is awe-inspiring. High, grand, and seemingly chiseled like a huge sculpture, it stands proud and majestic, isolated from the surrounding peaks, and towering above Zermatt. The famous Swiss artist Ferdinand Hodler said he would not paint the Matterhorn because it was "too awesome a subject to capture on canvas."

On the train I met Maurice Alliure, a French Canadian, roughly my age, from Montreal, Canada. He was dressed in casual hiking and trekking clothes, so I struck up a conversation about my plans to climb the Matterhorn. He was impressed and mentioned he had come to hike to the base of the mountain and perhaps find a guide if not too expensive to attempt the climb. I assured him I was quite capable, and why not team up with me for a shot at the summit? Maurice looked very fit and athletic. I needed a climbing companion to belay me on the steep sections of the route, and I figured in a couple days I could teach him the ropes. Although Maurice was inexperienced, he had an abundance of desire to climb one of the world's great mountains.

We went directly to a mountain shop to rent climbing boots, ice axe, and crampons for Maurice. My huge pack already contained all the pitons, rope, stove, tent, and all the other climbing hardware needed. Zermatt was still a tiny village surrounded by small farming terraces. To find a place to camp, we merely walked out of town uphill for a short distance toward the Matterhorn and put down our sleeping bags in a farm pasture nestled in the Alps. On that clear, starry night I finally got a good night's sleep.

The next morning, August 31, we trekked back into town and purchased fuel and enough food to feed us generously for a week. Switzerland's cheese, bread, nuts, and soups were outstanding, but very expensive. Maurice was a light eater and was reluctant to carry so much food. I assured him I would eat it all! We hiked a long day bearing heavy packs and gaining 4,000 vertical feet on the winding trail to reach the two-story shelter at the base of the mountain where the real climbing begins. Maurice seemed strong and never uttered a complaint—a good sign.

Our eyes rarely strayed from the Matterhorn, which was plastered white from top to bottom from a recent snowstorm that had deposited 14 inches of fresh snow and ice. Reaching the Hornli Hut at about 10,000 feet at the base of the ridge by the same name, we found little temperature difference inside or out. After a brief debate on whether to sleep outside among the rocks, we found cots inside. After paying the innkeeper I struck up a long conversation with the middle-aged woman as she questioned why a young man would come all the way from the United States to Zermatt. When she learned of my intentions to try and climb the Matterhorn, she became quite upset and agitated and did everything in her body language and broken English to discourage me from my foolishness. I learned that several climbers had died already that summer. (Indeed, in that summer alone, a total of 11 climbers would die, which is about the average yearly number of fatalities for the Matterhorn.) The old graveyard in Zermatt is a testament to the perils of climbing. The innkeeper had already been set on edge by a man with his son, about 10 years old. I remember the man telling me that his son was going to be the "youngest climber ever" to scale the Matterhorn. All night long I listened to the poor kid whimper and cry. He was scared out of his mind. I would learn weeks later that the father and son had disappeared on the Matterhorn. They had fallen off either the great north face or east face and died.

The Matterhorn and Hornli Ridge are much different up close than they appear from Zermatt. The rock is metamorphic schist, highly compressed granite that is shattered into layers of minerals almost to the point of being rotten. Glaciers easily carved the mountain into its classic shape. More than 5,000 feet of intense climbing commitment rose above us. My first-day goal was to ascend about 3,000 feet of the knife edged ridge to the Solvay Hut, a small emergency shelter built to accommodate about six climbers in cramped quarters. I had given Maurice belay lessons and some common bouldering tests. Since the Matterhorn is not too technically difficult by rock climbing standards, I figured Maurice would be capable. I would do all the leading, and I could top-rope Maurice on the harder pitches. This was my game plan as we set out in semi-darkness at 6 a.m. on August 31.

Climbing conditions were worse than I anticipated. Crampons had to be used from the very beginning of the ascent, and the wind was fierce. I led and belayed Maurice up rock and ice for hours to about the 12,000-foot level, but a new snowstorm and fog forced us to retreat. We spent another miserable night in the ice-cold Hornli Hut as the storm raged and caked another 4 inches of snow on the peak. Conditions were getting worse and my spirits plunged.

Maurice and I awoke to see three climbers making their way up through the new powder snow to the hut. They were from Munich. Although I had taken German in high school, I could speak only in broken phrases, and they were equally challenged with English. The Germans communicated that they were prepared for four nights of bivouac if necessary. Maurice and I still had five days supplies on our backs, so we essentially joined forces. In less than an hour, we were roped up and on the rock, climbing the Hornli Ridge with Josef Seemeier, Heinz Gundel, and Helmut Butlner. We had to stay directly on the ridge crest, as avalanches were pouring off the east face to our left. Crampons and constant belaying were necessary for the entire ascent to the Solvay Hut at 13,200 feet, which we finally reached about 6 p.m. The long, hard day of climbing was rewarded with a view rivaling a perch on the wingtip of an airplane.

From the Solvay Hut, the climb becomes harder as you ascend near-vertical slabs and cracks for about 800 feet to the height of the "shoulder" of the mountain. Conditions were terrible. The cold was piercing, and a new storm of wind and snow hammered our spirits all morning. At about 14,000 feet we realized that continuing was hopeless, so we reluctantly turned around. The 800-foot descent back to the Solvay Hut required seven hours of careful down climbing and belaying.

Two and a half days of arduous climbing had taken a toll on Maurice, who was ill and exhausted and felt he could not continue the climb. We had all planned to descend the next morning, but the sky began to clear about 1 a.m. Despite my poor grasp of their language, my German friends had little trouble understanding my body language as I convinced them to let me join their group for a summit attempt.

At 5 a.m., the Germans and I set out in temperatures near zero Fahrenheit for the last 1,600 feet of climbing to the summit. Maurice chose to remain in the shelter to rest and wait our return. I roped up with my German comrade, Helmut, and eagerly took the lead. We reached our previous high point by 6:30 a.m. and we were onto the "head" of the Matterhorn. Plotting the route above with my eyes, I remembered the words the great guide Peter Tangwalder who told Edward Whymper on the first ascent of the Matterhorn, "Now for something altogether different." The route from this point is near vertical. The fixed ropes installed by Swiss guides for their clients were encrusted beneath inches of verglas and useless, but we were able to use the fixed steel pitons. After five hours of continuous belaying and the most difficult ice climbing I had ever experienced, we crawled above the head to reach the ice slopes that angle 45-

50 degrees to the summit. I spotted the 5-foot high iron cross gleaming in the sunlight on the ridge between the Swiss and Italian summits. Language was no barrier to expressing our happiness for the moment. Around 11 a.m. we were taking turns belaying each other to stand on the pointed and corniced summit of the Matterhorn.

My two German teammates and I on the summit of the Matterhorn.

All the time, effort, expense, and planning had paid off. Threatening storm clouds couldn't dampen the fulfillment of standing at 14,780 feet, on a giant granite needle overlooking a heart-stopping view of the Alps, with Zermatt a speck nearly 2 vertical miles below. The photo of me on the Italian summit was badly overexposed. My only record is the photo from the Swiss summit mailed to me in the United States by my German climbing mate, Helmet.

Most of the many fatal accidents on the Matterhorn have involved climbers getting down the summit slopes. On the first ascent of the Matterhorn by Edward Whymper, four of his companions fell to their deaths just a couple hundred feet from the top. I reassured Helmet that I would be belaying him every step of the tedious descent. He was much heavier than I, and it took all my strength to keep him on a solid belay. When we'd descended to the top of the Matterhorn's head, we had to drive pitons for rappelling the vertical sections to the shoulder of the mountain. Maurice was waiting patiently at the Solvay Hut when we arrived. We gathered our equipment and continued our descent through dangerous snow conditions in a 13-hour ordeal that required highly concentrated effort by all. We narrowly escaped disaster at 12,000 feet when Maurice slipped and sent stones crashing down on Josef and Helmet, shattering Josef's left hand and bruising Helmut's shoulder. This slowed our descent considerably, but we all safely reached the base of the east face under a clear, starlit night.

We made the hike back down to Zermatt with our climbing ambition temporarily satiated. Everything in life seems expanded after an intense activity that puts your life at stake. The air seems fresher, the food tastes better, people seem friendlier, and your self-confidence makes you feel as though the world is at your service.

I was still in a dream state while walking down the trail about a mile from Zermatt when I had the small-world experience of meeting my next-door neighbor. Warren and Katy Heylman and their two children had traveled on the same plane with me from Amsterdam. They arrived in Zermatt the day I came down from the mountain. Katy was happy to see me, and she promptly called my mother to let her know I was OK. It's embarrassing to look back and realize that I did not call anyone during my great adventure. I was still too immature to understand the concern parents have for their kids.

Climbing the Matterhorn in itself is worthy of a trip to Europe, but my adventure was far from over as I set my sights on the long road trip through Italy, Yugoslavia, and on to Greece. Maurice was enthusiastic to join me on this journey, but he had no money to share the expenses for gas and food. He assured me that he had a stable job and upon his return to Canada would pay any expenses owed me for the trip. (Indeed, Maurice was a man of his word.

He mailed the money about a month after my return to WSU.) Having a companion for the next leg of the journey would prove to be invaluable. I probably would not be writing this story if I had done the trip alone.

ON TO THE EIGER

We drove to Brig, Switzerland, and over a mountain pass into Italy, through Venice, and into Yugoslavia. The Tito government was in power and the dictator controlled dozens of ethnic tribes and cultures. Unsaddled by any understanding of the precarious political situation, Maurice and I naïvely breezed through the countryside in my MGB. We drove down the coastline, through the cities of Split and Dubrovnik. The Yugoslavia coastline was a destination for elite European families attracted by picturesque villages built on rugged limestone cliffs within walking distance of the Adriatic Sea. The walled city of Dubrovnik was particularly photogenic with its buildings of red roofs and terra cotta tiles, white and beige stucco against the azure water.

The Yugoslavian coastline runs a couple hundred miles from the Italy border to the Albania border where we planned to head east over the mountains to what is now Serbia. What was once the country of Yugoslavia has been piecemealed into other smaller countries such as Bosnia and Herzegovina, Croatia, Montenegro, Slovenia, and Macedonia. These "cultural" or tribal areas as I call them, have always been under internal civil war and fighting between warlords. These countries are the original home of the traveling gypsies. We were about to drive right through the heart of it all. Of course, neither Maurice nor I had read any of the history of the strife and knew little about this area of the world, so we had no clue about the potential for adventure ahead.

The last night on the coast of Yugoslavia was spent camped in a small Adriatic inlet where we enjoyed music from a live band that played from a floating barge. This was one of the most memorable nights of music in my life. The musicians were talented, the starlit night was calm, and listening to the band on a floating barge on the sea between the limestone cliffs of the inlet was surreal. The music echoed off the cliffs, and lingered in my eardrums.

The next morning we headed south and east along the shoreline of a large lake, then directly east. The map I had purchased showed a red line for the most traveled route, but no topography was shown. It was a pretty good map, but this part of Europe was just not well documented and seldom traveled. We had no warning that the road was going to deteriorate into a poorly kept rock-and-dirt route over a 9,200-foot mountain pass. The high-class friendly tourist scene vanished just a few miles up from the coastline. Driving down this highway in a convertible sports car, we stuck out like a sore thumb among the poor who hung out along the road. For the next three days we would be driving up and over a rugged truck route, past clans of gypsies, through war-torn territories. English was not spoken here. The dialect seemed to change in every new valley. We had the unsettling feeling of not being safe.

My MGB in Yugoslavia.

Driving through the last small village shown on our map before heading up to the mountain pass, I filled the car with gas until it overflowed. We just didn't know what was on the other side. The road became one lane in places and rough as an alpine trail, sometimes requiring us to get out and move rocks or tree limbs. On several occasions we would round the corner to see a band of gypsies pushing an oxcart. The destitute vagabonds would run up like a pack of wolves, surround us and try and grab anything loose inside the car. I would stomp on the accelerator, trying my best not to run over any children. The gypsy men were fierce looking, sporting long black mustaches and unkempt black hair and wearing woolen clothes that appeared as though they'd never been washed.

This was my first experience with cultural shock. Of course, not all the people lived like wild animals, but on this route Maurice and I realized we had better not stop our car and fall asleep. We placed our ice axes next to the steering wheel. We were fully prepared to use them if necessary. The road from the Mediterranean side of the mountains, down into what is now Serbia was about 200 miles, and we passed perhaps a half dozen merchant trucks going the other way. It was a positive sign. These trucks came from somewhere that had a gas station. We crested the pass and slowly drove through the night and at dawn, much to our relief, we were able to refuel at a village. We were really some dumb North American tourists who had stumbled into the backyard of primitive humanity. We continued out of the mountains to some fine rolling hills and pastures as the sun rose. Seeing some farmers who looked friendly, we asked if we were on the correct road to Skopje. As this day turned into night, we had been wired and awake for 36 hours and desperately needed sleep. We pulled off the road onto a green field and threw out our sleeping bags, with our ice axes underneath our mats.

I awoke groggy and sleep-deprived to the sound of men's voices. The dawn was just breaking so there was enough light as I bent up off the ground to see four men walking toward our little camp. I could see they had rifles slung over their shoulders. I yelled at Maurice to wake up and tucked my axe under my right arm. Obviously, an ice axe would be pretty useless against four rifles, but if there was going to be a fight, I was determined to at least make a stand. In my mountain adventures there have been situations of high anxiety, exposure, and fatigue, where life and death hung by a thread. But at least I had control of my fate. Here in the wilds of Serbia, I was trembling with fear. There is just no predicting what people of extreme political motives will do.

Fate was on our side that morning. These men were in high spirits as they chatted and laughed, and when they saw us lying on the ground with a camp stove between us next to a green sports car, they all burst into a roar of laughter. Fortunately for Maurice and me, these guys had either won an all night card game, had good wives, or a good dinner the night before, or all of the above. Maurice started babbling something in French, and I tried to say something in English, but our riflemen just laughed all the more. The two older men's faces were deeply age-etched; the other two were younger men. Perhaps they were two fathers with their sons. They seemed crazed with happiness from some recent event, but Maurice and I were of no interest to them. They continued their march, laughing all the way up the road.

We reached Skopje, the birthplace of Mother Teresa, late in the afternoon. It was a beautiful little town, built next to a hillside in a forested area surrounded by farms and healthy fields. Here the people were much wealthier in dress and character, and we felt safe getting out of the car and walking a short distance up the main street to take pictures. We were quite relieved to have the stress behind us. We drove several more hours and reached the northern border of Greece. Maurice got down on the ground and kissed the dirt.

Entering the heartland of legendary Greek stories, the mountains were beautiful white limestone covered with trees, with small farms etched into the valleys that gave way to seaside villas built along the coastline. Athens treated us to the Parthenon overlooking the glimmering sea. I felt enlightened at the steps of the ancient Agora where Plato, Aristotle, and Socrates meditated. After a couple days of visiting the ancient ruins, fattening up on greasy tacos, and staying in a cheap rooftop flat, we drove to Patrasa on the west Aegean seacoast, where I ramped my car onto a ferry that sailed to Brindisi, Italy. The ocean ride provided some of the most relaxing hours of my time in Europe.

We drove to Pompeii and stayed beneath Mount Vesuvius. Seeing people mummified into plaster forms of death from hot ashes is disturbing and unforgettable. I needed an escape. Maurice and I climbed Vesuvius to the huge summit crater still belching a plume of sulfur gas. In geologic time, a couple thousand years is nothing, and this mountain was still hot, barren of trees, and hinted that it could explode again and do more damage.

Driving northward we spent four days visiting Rome and Florence, seeing all the engineering marvels and structures like the famous Roman roads and aqueducts, the Coliseum, Catacombs, The Vatican with no pope visible, and numerous ancient building sites. Moving on to Florence and Pisa, we saw the famous Leaning Tower and the Statue of David. After 40 years of traveling and visiting many great cities and their museums full of artwork, nothing surpasses my amazement upon seeing the ancient Greek and Italian wonders for the first time. Continuing north, I was able to drive through the highly touted and newly completed roadway/tunnel that connected Italy and France through Mont Blanc, the highest peak in Western Europe!

On the French side of the tunnel we entered the world-renowned destination resort of Chamonix, where we stopped for a brief break before continuing the drive over another pass heading back toward Zermatt. Here I said farewell to my traveling companion, as Maurice was taking a train to Zurich, and then flying home to Montreal. We said bon voyage after our two-week adventure and headed our separate ways.

I drove north to visit the village of Grindewald and Kleine Scheidegg at the base of the highest mountain wall in the Alps, the North Face of the Eiger. I arrived late in the afternoon, found a campsite and pitched my tent. These campsites are always full of mountain transients such as myself, and I struck up a conversation with a New York climber named Eric Stern, who had come to climb the northwest flank of the Eiger. He asked if I would be interested in doing the climb with him. Since I had another week to get back to Amsterdam, I eagerly agreed.

We took the train to the small village of Kleine Scheidegg on the morning of September 21 and began the climb that morning. The northwest ridge is not technical, however, one must be very careful not to slip, as the exposure is great. We had planned a two-day climb, bringing bivouac gear, a stove, and extra food, but no tent. We climbed fast and mostly un-roped to a series of small ledges about 500 feet from the summit. Here we hacked out a platform and spent a cold night, rising at first light to continue the ascent to the summit of the Eiger.

Having all day to descend, we carefully explored down the west ridge to peer over at the most famous mountain wall in the Alps, the Eiger North Face. I took several good photographs, and thought to myself that the route looked insane and impossible. Five years later I would climb the Eiger North Face with John Roskelley.

My driving route back to Amsterdam went through Interlaken, Bern, and Neuchatel, where I spent the last of my cash on a Swiss watch. Owning a Swiss timepiece was something I always felt would be a "status symbol," but forking over $50 for this watch was a big expenditure for me. And it was a waste of money. In the next couple years, the watch proved to be a dud. It wouldn't keep perfect time, and broke easily. I would have been better off with a cheap Timex.

I spent a couple days driving north through Germany, and on my final night as I approached the border with the Netherlands, I pulled off the autobahn on a side road in farm country to find a pasture to spread out my sleeping bag. It was a beautiful night with a full moon rising, no clouds, and very still, perfect for my last night after a month of memorable adventures. This side road was quiet and far enough away that I couldn't hear vehicle traffic. I collected my down sleeping bag and mattress, a water bottle, and my staple of candy bars for the night. Both sides of the road had nice pastures, but they were fenced with a 5-foot high barbed wire. No fence had ever stopped me before, so I carefully climbed over and walked out into the field. For some reason, I wanted be far out into the field, so I walked several hundred feet from the car. I stripped off my clothes and crawled into my bag and began to reminisce about my adventures, which surpassed the goals I had set. I was exhausted from driving and drifted into sleep as I dreamed of the beautiful places I had seen.

The snort that woke me with a start was sharp and powerful. It certainly wasn't a small dog. I sat up and looked around the moonlit field. The unmistakable silhouettes of three bulls were a couple hundred yards away. One of the bulls, roughly the size of a Mack truck, pawed the ground a few times before launching into a dead run—straight for me.

I grabbed my stuff and ran for my life. Sprinting in nothing by my underpants, I could feel the hot blasts of breath out of the bull's nostrils and onto my back as I reached the barbed-wire fence. I leaped in the air as high as my strength would take me, putting my left hand on the top strand and doing a high jump type roll-over as the bull came pounding and snorting to a stop just inches from my face on the other side of the fence.

Feathers were drifting down from the sky. As I'd cleared the fence, the sleeping bag snagged and ripped nearly in half, exploding like a goose suicide bomber. Blood dripped on my thigh from a deep, three-inch-long gash in the palm of my hand. I collected my thoughts, too pumped up to feel pain, bandaged my hand with my T-shirt, and lay down next to the car and stared at the bull, which just stood and stared at me for the longest time. So, I learned another of life's lessons. Barbed wire fences are in place for a purpose.

The next morning I rose at dawn and finished the drive into Amsterdam and arranged for my car to be shipped back to Portland, Oregon, via the Panama Canal. I used all my remaining money to pay the import duty fees and shipping costs. I would break even financially with this car. At the end of my senior year in college, I sold it for what I had originally paid. Although I sometimes cursed myself for the financial drain, the car was a good learning experience. It gave me a joyride through Europe and was an instrumental vehicle to another discovery: completing one goal is the starting point to another.

Ten

Breakthrough on Chephren

John Roskelley mid-way up the mile-high Chephren East Face.

ATHLETES DREAM OF SUCCESS on an international stage. Wrestling had taken me to the national stage where I got my education in real competition, but I wanted to be competitive on a world scale. I always felt that I had the right stuff to find success in alpinism, but there was a nagging question in my mind: Was I mentally tough enough to tackle the world's greatest climbs?

Since climbing the Eiger West Ridge in 1969, my desire to try the North Face waned as I let myself believe it was beyond my abilities. It made my fear barometer spin. But the goal carved into my ice axe shaft with a wood burner was staring at me every time I went climbing. I was maturing into a good mountaineer, but in order to prepare for the Eiger I needed to push the limits of my mental and physical abilities. I was confident in leading rock and ice climbs of 5.9 and 5.10 (the upper limit on the scale of route technical difficulty achieved at the time). My body strength was there, and I was in top form, but could I do sustained fifth class, technical climbing with 45 pounds on my back at 12,000 feet in a blizzard after three days of no sleep? The unknowns in climbing create the competition. I had a hunch that Everest could be climbed without supplemental oxygen even though no one had done it at that time. There were opportunities. No American climbing team had climbed the Eiger North Face. Did I have the right stuff? A lot of people before me had died competing for the answer to the question.

Mountaineers advance in baby steps before taking the leap to a big climb. John Roskelley and I traveled through the Canadian Rockies bagging routes for many years before we could look with anything beyond slack-jawed awe at the 5,000-foot wall on the east face of Mount Chephren. Located south of the Columbia Icefield off Highway 1 between Banff and Jasper highway, Chephren, at 10,850 feet stands guard over the valleys below with its black, pyramid-shaped tower of limestone and ice. It looks like the North Face Eiger in many respects, but the big Canadian wall was oriented to the east. The face was bathed in warmth and sunshine during much of the daytime. The summit of Chephren is nearly 3,000 feet lower than the Eiger, and predicting the high pressure and stable weather patterns for the Canadian Rockies is relatively reliable. Still, the mountain is 5,000 feet of total commitment. In 1971, only one team had succeeded in climbing the wall after three full days of epic adventure.

Staying in the black was a struggle for me that year as I ventured out for the first time onto the bumpy road of financial independence. I wanted experience working for someone other than my father's company, so took a big pay cut and found steady work with Boulton Insulation Company. The pay was one penny per lineal foot of insulation installed. To earn the basic survival wage of $230 a week after taxes, I had to install about 30,000 lineal feet of insulation. This would pay my rent, make the payment on my vehicle, buy gas, food, and leave me broke until the next paycheck. It was a hard way to make a living. My training workouts after work were over as I simply had no energy to go practice climbing on the east side of Spokane at the Minnehaha Rocks.

My finances took another hit, but my goal of a career in the building industry advanced when I landed a job with Warren Heylman, a prominent Spokane architect. It was an 8-to-5, shirt-and-tie job starting as an architectural draftsman on building projects. The pay was $1.75 an hour, which entrenched me on poverty row. I moved from the small cabin on the Little Spokane River into a tiny apartment in Browne's Addition, and began walking to work to save gas money. During the winter, I made a few extra dollars as a ski instructor on Mount Spokane. Several hours of teaching the little kids on the weekends earned enough to buy a whole tank of gas! The financial sacrifice of an entry-level job with a downtown architect was worthwhile in the sense that I had the energy to continue working out in the evenings at the Minnehaha Rocks—and my weekends were free for the mountains.

My climbing partners varied, but I could always count on Roskelley. During our college years, Roskelley and I climbed the East Face of Liberty Bell in the North Cascades and many hard routes in Yosemite Valley, the Grand Tetons, the Valhalla Range of British Columbia, and several big peaks in the Rockies. Upon leaving college, John dedicated himself to a course that would make mountaineering his career and eventually win him kudos as one of the premier mountaineers of the time. He anchored his status among the best in 1973 after he was invited on an expedition and successfully reached the summit of Dhaulagiri, the world's seventh highest mountain. After that expedition, Roskelley earned endorsements and corporate support that enabled him to devote nearly full-time to climbing. The world's universally recognized greatest mountaineer, Reinhold Messner of Italy, remarked, "The American, John Roskelley, was stronger than I."

ASCENT OF MOUNT CHEPHREN

On August 13, 1971, the sun set with nothing but stars and Canadian Rockies peaks above us. It was a short night and mostly sleepless at that, as most nights are for climbers. Roskelley and I were up at 2 a.m. and started hiking to the base of Chephren. At last. In the dark above was more than a vertical mile of limestone and ice, culminating at the 10,850-foot summit.

The plan was much as it had been on dozens of climbs on the way to this challenge. I would lead on any ice pitches, and since John was the better rock climber, he would lead on the rock. I was more comfortable carrying a heavier pack and camera to record our journey. In many respects, climbing second is harder because of all the pitons that must be pounded out and organizing the rack for the next lead. This climb would favor John, who felt more confident and in control when he was in the front.

We began the ascent on the black ice of the small glacier at the mountain base, clawing our way up the steep ice on our crampons and using ice axes. A slip on this section would be deadly. We were cautious, climbing simultaneous without the rope to move as quickly as possible. Speed translated to safety. After a few hundred feet we reached the solid polished limestone above the bergschrund and continued free soloing for the first thousand feet of moderate rock before roping up and belaying. The sun was beginning to warm the rock as the exposure on the knife-edge buttress intensified. We weren't carrying enough pitons to rappel the 2,000 feet we had climbed. We were committed to go up.

On every serious climb there is a "crux", the place where the climb demands the most technical knowledge and strength. On Chephren East Face, we were following the central prominent buttress that falls directly below the summit all the way to the valley floor. The buttress is interrupted two-thirds of the way up by a 300-foot band of smooth limestone. The first ascent party had taken a full day to climb this vertical and overhanging section. It was dead vertical with no cracks above us, so we traversed left to view the cracks and chimney system the first ascent party had climbed, and found water running down from the ice above. It looked out of the question.

We decided to traverse back to the prow and then go right to a chimney and crack system that led straight up. It appeared to extend above the overhanging section. Beyond that was a question mark. In order to lead the rock crux, which proved to be 5.10 climbing, I would have to carry Roskelley's pack as well as mine, as there is no way he could lead this section encumbered with 40 pounds on his back. To save weight, we hadn't brought a haul line. I took a huge breath. If Roskelley could make it up, I would have to follow, climbing with jumars while shouldering 95 pounds. We had to do it.

Up the vertical crack system, John gained altitude rapidly. That was his style. But he began grunting and gasping as he approached the overhang. I heard some frenzied wheezes and the occasional curse, which were signals the climbing was at his limit. Since I knew he was capable of more than 5.10, I began fretting over my turn. I huddled close to the rock in my belay stance and tried to contain myself with slow controlled breathing to maximize my strength and not turn to butter. No way I could free climb this section with two full packs. If John could negotiate the overhang, I would have to jumar 180 feet of vertical and overhang packing all that weight.

John disappeared above the overhang with a masterful display of gymnastics and finesse. I was alone in what seemed like an eternity of tension before he gave the rope two pulls, meaning he was tied off. We were out of sight and beyond shouting distance. I gingerly started to inch my way up with John's pack tied onto mine. The pack was an awkward handicap and I was in a world of hurt. After 50 feet, I hooked on the jumars so I could free my hands from the rock. This proved no easier. It merely shifted the world of hurt to pulling back my shoulders and arching my back like a bow. I progressed sweating like a fully loaded mule hoofing out of a desert canyon.

When I removed the last piton before the overhang, I put all faith in my partner, clasping both hands onto my lifeline, which may or may not have been manufactured under the watch of a disgruntled laborer. I closed my eyes and swung into space, spinning slowly in circles. The rope held, answering my initial doubt. Now, with all my strength focused to my aching arms, the next 30 feet to get over the overhang was pure adrenalin with 3,000 feet of nothing between me and the rocks below. With each spin I would look at the Banff-Jasper Highway far below and question my sanity. I inched, scratched, clawed, and cursed my way over the lip of the rock overhang and saw John about 30 feet above me in a sketchy down-sloped bench. The rope I was banking my life on was tied off in two upside-down knife blade Chouinard pitons he'd pounded into a small horizontal crack.

"Chris, don't make any unusual pulls on the rope," John said in a voice that was calm but filled with tension. "These two pins are all I could get in and they are marginal."

I slowly climbed, pulling on the rope as little as possible, up the slanted gulley to his precarious perch. John was able to take his pack now, as the terrain was an easier angle of about 70 degrees. We were clinging like two tiny mites on a giant's back, and I hoped the giant didn't notice and try to shake us off. One more pitch led to a broad horizontal ledge where we both lay down and counted our blessings.

With only a few hours of daylight left, the terrain above us was relatively easy fourth and low fifth class rock climbing. Relief flooded our veins and empowered our exhausted bodies.

At 10 p.m., after 18 hours on the wall, we stood together on the peak of Chephren and coiled the rope. We had beaten the first-ascent team's time by two full days. The glass ceiling I'd been bumping my head against was a thousand feet below me. We pulled out our sleeping bags and watched a glorious sunset transform to heavy clouds and snow. It snowed six to eight inches that night.

Well aware that going down is where 90 percent of climbers get in trouble, we were able to let our bodies rest for a few cold hours before beginning a predawn climb down in a raging snowstorm in the gully between Mt. Chephron and White Pyramid. The snow turned to a continuous rain that required full concentration. At the bergschrund where the glacier connects with the mountain, I jumped onto a huge block of ice that collapsed, sending me flying through the air and onto the glacier, one of the scariest moments of the climb. We finally found relief at the Waterfowl Lakes parking lot along with my brother, Cary, and Joe Collins, who had climbed Mount Athabasca after dropping John and me off at the start of our climb. Our celebration was brief but well attended by just the four of us. And then we headed home, one day ahead of our plan.

Words from the Wild

- If you wouldn't trust your life with that guy, don't climb with him.
- In the mountains, speed is safety.
- Successful people have strength, knowledge, and an abundance of will.

After 18 hours of total focus, we coiled the rope on
the summit of Mount Chephren.

Eleven

Robson

Mount Robson.

Mount Robson is the highest mountain in the Canadian Rockies, and in my opinion, one of the 10 greatest mountains in the world. Although there's no positive record for the origin of its name, the local Native American tribes called it "mountain of the spiral road" because of the horizontal layering of the limestone bands that overlay the granite base rock. Geologically, the limestone and dolomite layers were laid down between 500 and 300 million years ago in shallow inland seas and then uplifted gradually and very recently—only 60 million years ago—to weather-pounded heights.

Robson, at 12,972 feet above sea level, stands alone, proud, and supreme among hundreds of surrounding lofty mountains. The summit is permanently capped with thick glacial ice. At the 10,000-foot level, these glaciers plunge over the harder sedimentary limestone bedrock and form a ruffled skirt of vertical blue cliffs around the mountain. Below this ice band are beautiful rock arêtes that rise straight and true to the ice-capped summit block. The combination of hanging glaciers and rock is a formidable shield to thwart climbers who might still be full of confidence after scaling the initial wave of Robson's vertical rock cliffs. Many mountaineers have lost their lives trying to scale its heights. There is simply no safe or easy way to the top.

The Rev. GB Kinney and a trapper named Curly Phillips came very close to making the first ascent of Robson. Kinney had become obsessed with summiting the peak, with attempts in 1907 and 1908 before taking his final shot in 1909, when he came very, very close. After trekking and bushwhacking more than 200 miles and crossing dangerous rivers all the way from Edmonton, Kinney and Phillips' ascent of the southwest face to a point only 60 feet from the summit ranks as one of the most magnificent failures in mountaineering lore.

The first ascent of Robson's true summit was by the great guide Conrad Kain in 1913. "Mount Robson is one of the most beautiful mountains in the Rockies, and certainly the most difficult one," he wrote. "On all my mountaineering in various countries, I have climbed only a few mountains that were hemmed in with more difficulties. Mount Robson is one of the most dangerous expeditions I have ever made."

After reading several books and wild tales about Robson, I set my goal to stand on its summit, too. I endured several failures over five years but persevered.

My first attempts were made with Roskelley in late 1966 and 1967. We never even reached the Ralph Forester Hut perched at 9,600 feet on the southwest arête! We had sadly underestimated the scope and length of the route, as the southwest arête route above Kinney Lake is nearly 10,000 feet of continuous climbing.

These two failed attempts whet our desire. In 1970, Roskelley and Bob Christianson were the first from our Spokane Mountaineers club to succeed on Robson. I cannot recall exactly why I could not make that expedition, but the round trip from Spokane to the summit of Robson realistically is a five-day expedition. Although I tried to climb something every weekend, the responsibilities of my summer construction jobs sometimes prevented me from leaving town. When I heard that Roskelley and Christianson had made the summit, I salivated with jealousy. It was my idea to climb Robson, and Roskelley had succeeded first. Now there was no stopping me.

Finding partners for a serious expedition was always difficult, and rounding up a capable partner to climb Mount Robson was even harder. Roskelley was moving onward to Dhaulagiri in the Himalayas, and he had no interest in going back up Robson. In early 1972, I contacted a high school classmate, Craig Kopet, who had been on the wrestling team with me. Kopet was about 10 pounds heavier than I, and had tremendous upper body strength. Once he grabbed an opponent with his granite arms it was all over. Kopet was also a strong mountaineer as I had learned in 1971 when he joined my brother Cary and me to climb the East Face of Mount Stanley on the July 4 holiday weekend. Craig was attending summer school at the Mayo Clinic in the Midwest, so we exchanged letters and he agreed to try Robson with me in the following summer. I would be going on our annual family salmon fishing trip to Campbell River in the latter half of July, and then planned to board the bus with my backpack and travel from Campbell River to Nanaimo, then ferry to Vancouver, then bus to Radium Hot Springs where I would meet Kopet with his family car.

We had two weeks to prepare and climb. The first week Craig and I climbed Storm Mountain above Vermillion Crossing via the north ridge. Craig was nervous at first, but he was very strong and athletically capable for all the technical rock challenges. After three days of moderate rock climbing, I felt strong and ready to do battle, and Craig was strong and naïve.

Our two-man attack on Robson began the morning of August 4. We sweated and cursed under the burden of full packs during the 5,000 feet of continuous steep climbing to the Ralph Forester Hut. The next morning, we made an attempt on the summit, but stopped at about 12,000-feet at the Swartz ledges as they were plastered with snow and ice. The stormy conditions forced us to stay at the hut another day before the weather began to clear. Our second attempt to the summit began on the south-southwest arête at 2 a.m. the morning of August 7. During the stormy weather, I had been able to scope out the Extinguisher Glacier Hourglass route, which appeared to be in much safer condition than our original planned route. I decided to try the Hourglass and then reach the southwest ridge for the final ascent to the summit.

The weather was brilliantly clear and cold, perfect for the task! We made good progress crossing the rock cliffs to the glacier, and then up the steep mixed rock and ice climbing to the top of the Hourglass. We broke trail through fresh, steep snow to the southwest arête, and then followed this most beautiful, undulating, corniced and knife-edged ridge to the final summit plateau. The climbing was spiced with dramatic exposure. Views off our right shoulders looked directly down into the beautiful Berg Lake more than six thousand feet below our feet. After much step cutting and belaying up several steep pitches, we reached the summit about 1 p.m. The day was clear, but we were experiencing an inversion and the air temperatures at the middle mountain elevations were warming rapidly. As we had climbed, I noticed that avalanches were cascading off the mountain beneath us. This was a bad sign and very unnerving, as we had climbed through snow slopes that could avalanche with the warmer air. I was careful not to disclose my "situation awareness" fears to Kopet about the snow conditions, as Craig was already stressed enough with the technical climbing and exposure of this route.

After a short summit ceremony of water and candy, we descended about 1,000 feet on the southwest ridge, where I decided to dig a snow cave and wait for the air to cool. On both sides of the mountain from our precarious stance, the slopes below us were avalanching. My internalized feelings finally surfaced to my lips.

"Craig, I have to put a halt to our descent right now. The conditions are so dangerous with this warm air inversion that if we continue to descend it could be suicide."

"Suicide! Suicide! What do you mean suicide?"

"Well, the snow conditions are very treacherous; you will just have to take my word for it. We have to wait for nightfall for freezing air, or bivouac for the night, or wait for freezing temperatures in the early morning."

"Good God man! What did you get me into?"

Craig Kopet on top of Little Robson.

The snow cave idea sounded good, but when we tried to dig into the cornice, we found solid ice just six inches or so under the snow crust. We dug for an hour, and maybe got another two feet hollowed out, just enough to recline our bodies inside. Our position on this ridge was so exposed to the wind that it became obvious to me that we would freeze to death if we had to spend all night here without thermal pads for insulation. Our climbing gear of leather boots, woolen knickers, and down parkas was soaked from sweat and spindrift. As the wind froze us to the core, we had only one choice: wait until sundown and try and descend in the night before we became immobilized by cold.

When the sun was about half an hour from setting, we began descending the snow slopes. The air was still above freezing but we had to go or freeze to death on the exposed ridge. We had about 1,000 feet of down climbing across treacherous, avalanche-prone slopes to reach the top of the Hourglass. I told Craig, "Walk in my steps like you were on top of eggshells." Each step I sank practically to my knees. On one step the entire slope settled by several inches with a loud WHOOMPH. The conditions were frightening, but if the snow did break loose and avalanche, I was hopeful it would crack and slide off below the steps I was cutting. Craig began to pray out loud. Years later, his mother told me that Craig started the "religious period" of his life at this moment on Mount Robson. Meanwhile, I continued to concentrate on what the military calls "situation awareness."

Slowly, and cautiously, I proceeded down these loaded slopes as gingerly as a ballerina, until at last we reached the top of the Hourglass. Where there had been nice, firm footing on our ascent in the early morning, the snow had avalanched off down to the bare ice! I had brought a half dozen ice screws just for this situation, and we began rappelling into the night skies. We had one good headlamp to light our way, and I used all the ice screws we had to make five rappels down the ice slopes and the head of the Extinguisher Glacier.

Our position was still precarious. The head of the glacier is surrounded by immense cliffs that held unstable snow.

"Craig, listen up!" I said in the most commanding voice I could muster. "We are going to run with the rope between us to the arête." I didn't mention that the safe rock on the southwest arête was still about a mile away over a crevasse-laced glacier.

We ran for our lives in pitch-black darkness over the ice, jumping over crevasses that looked more horrific with only a weak headlamp beam defining its edges. Every few minutes we could hear more snow thundering down from the slopes above us, but we at last reached the safety of the sharp, rocky southwest arête. In all my mountain experiences, I have never had such a scary avalanche predicament. We were much relieved to stumble into the hut at 1 a.m., a full 23 hours round trip from the time we left the hut. I crawled into my sleeping bag, and slept so soundly that upon awaking, I had forgotten who and where I was. I walked out of the hut into a brilliant sunlit sky surrounded by stupendous mountains, with the sun nearly straight above me. This was one of two times in my entire life that I slept so soundly that all feelings of the mortal shell of life were erased. I'd awakened as if I had just been born a new baby. When my memory came flooding back, I looked up to see the horrible slopes that we had crossed the night before with all of our tracks erased from avalanche scars.

Craig and I spent the afternoon drying our clothing and relaxing in the alpine sunshine. The next morning we began the long descent to Kinney Lake and the wooded trail to our car.

Craig Kopet would never climb again. Several months later his mother asked me, "Chris, just what happened up there on that mountain?" Her son had suddenly found God.

"There were a lot of avalanches, and we were lucky," I said.

TWELVE

JOE COLLINS & ROBSON

Joe Collins on the summit of Mount Farnham, highest peak in the Purcells.

A JOE COLLINS SLIDE SHOW was the Spokane Mountaineers' version of a War-ren Miller movie. When I joined the club in 1964, Collins was the featured speaker at the annual Meet the Mountaineers spring program, held that year in the Lincoln Building auditorium. Joe was a diehard climber, one of the most colorful characters in the club, and an amateur photographer who could make professional cameramen drool over his images. That combination made for en-tertaining programs. Anytime Joe staged a slide show, the audience was riveted in their seats in anticipation for the next slide and the corresponding comment. I admired him immediately.

Joe grew up in Winnipeg, Manitoba, to a poor farming family. He never finished high school, as he had to begin working for money in his sophomore year to help his mother and family make ends meet. He met the love of his life, Stella, at a local dance party, and they eventually married. When his new wife convinced him to go to a trade school to earn a living, Joe studied to become a jewelry technician. With jobs scarce in his native country, he and Stella took the train west from Winnipeg to Spokane through the Canadian Rockies where he got his first glimpse of real mountains.

Climbing isn't the first sport that appeals to most people, and it wasn't even in Joe's universe until he and Stella took a weekend car trip to Portland, Oregon. He loathed exercise for exercise sake, but his passion for photography could summon exertion for the sake of a picture. They gazed up at Mount St. Helens as they drove and Joe remarked, "I'd like to go up there and take pictures on that mountain." When Stella doubted his ability to climb the volcano, Joe's manhood suddenly was at stake. A mountaineer was born.

Joe was 26 at the time of his first climb, and in his late 30s when I met him at the Spokane Mountaineers program. He was like the color commentator for the radio sports play by play. His hilarious stories and colorful insight about human nature made long drives to climbing destinations fly by. He became a climbing mentor even though Joe was not athletic. He was about 5-foot 9 inches tall, maybe 140 pounds with a slight build and a full head of black wavy hair and a mustache. He had a nervous habit of almost constantly smoking a cigarette or a pipe—but he never inhaled. Except for his climbing activity, Joe has never exercised. He eats like a fussy hen. As I write this, Joe is 90 years old, and in his lifetime he has never eaten a slice of pizza, or a hamburger. Indeed, he's never dined at a fast food restaurant—ever! His diet consists of selected fruits, grains, and cereals with nuts and raisins, oatmeal and, preferably, buckwheat. He could never travel to a foreign country because, in his own words, "I would die the first week of starvation." Yet at 90 and counting, Joe has never had a family doctor, never once been to a doctor's office, never taken medicine of any kind, never had a flu shot, never swallowed vitamin pills or aspirin. He never once has had a headache, but in his words, "I have caused a lot of headaches." He never called in sick during his 42-year tenure at Teneff Jewelry, nor did he ever miss a day of work. In his old age, he's still healthy as a mule and sometimes just as stubborn.

Like so many of the climbers I know, Joe would be broke if he wasn't so frugal. He made a permanent impression on me during a conversation about money when he pulled out a paycheck stub he had saved. The income box said $24,500—the maximum amount of money he had earned in one year during his career. "Chris, it is not how much money you make, it is all how you manage it," he said, in one of many life lessons he taught me. "I know doctors who make 10 times my wages per year, who are always broke." At those wages, Joe had purchased his own house, paid off the mortgage, owned his two cars, and raised two daughters. He always had money to, as he put it, "eat steak just like anyone else." Even as a teenager, this registered in my still-developing brain.

In 1965, Collins was one of the experienced climbers leading a Spokane Mountaineers trip to climb 9,131-foot Mount Shuksan in the North Cascades. John Roskelley and I were fresh 16-year-old Mountain School graduates, and they took us under their wings. Discipline is one of the first lessons Collins started teaching me on that climb, as he recounted for a story in The Spokesman-Review:

"Chris ate all three-days worth of food the first day," Joe told Outdoors editor Rich Landers. "He came to me and said, 'Joe! Joe! My food's all gone!' as I had all of my food neatly organized in front of me. 'What should I do, Joe?' Chris pleaded as he looked longingly at my food, each meal for each day wrapped and labeled (by Stella). I put each package in my stuff sack, pulled the drawstring tight, put it in my pack and said, 'Chris, next time you will remember. Let's go climbing.'"

Even after THAT, I was eager to join him on more climbs and learn more valuable lessons.

Climbing was no different than anything else for Joe. He did it within his means. He had an impressive climbing resume—more than 400 peaks in 22 years—focused mostly on summits in the West and the Canadian Rockies that he could reach in a tortuous weekend of climbing and all-night driving. Joe never missed a day of work and didn't waste time dreaming beyond his budget. He was never going to the Himalaya. Joe's Everest was Mount Robson. The weekend mountaineer had mentioned to me on many occasions that he would like to make an attempt on the highest peak in the Canadian Rockies, and I agreed to go with him. But I had one reservation. I knew he was mentally tough and disciplined, and it wasn't our 25-year age difference that gave me pause. It was his obsession with photography. Making outstanding photographs takes time you don't necessarily have while trying to climb a peak notorious for being a weather crapshoot. I insisted on one thing: if we were going up Robson, I would be the only one with a camera—a tiny, lightweight camera. Attempting a serious, dangerous, and technical climb requires full physical and mental effort for more than 24 hours. Time-consuming distractions can be deadly.

On the first attempt with Joe in 1972, the weather and mountain conditions were perfect when we arrived at the trailhead after a 12-hour drive, but Joe had worked himself into such a fit of intimidation he couldn't get out of the parking lot. We took a serious reality check and made a vow to come back in one year on Labor Day. Joe vowed to be prepared. He went out every weekend the next summer, as usual, to climb mountains from Wyoming to Canada, but this time it was all in preparation for Robson. I am embarrassed to say, with my construction job schedule, I was not as prepared as Joe. Luckily, I had youth and strength on my side.

On September 1, 1973, Joe and I left Spokane packed for the assault on Robson. We made the 600-mile road trip in the manner to which Spokane Mountaineers were accustomed—alternating the driving to catch a few cat naps and arriving at the trailhead at 5 a.m. ready to climb.

The ascent to the Ralph Forester Hut gains 5,000 feet of elevation with some rock climbing involved. This part of the route I knew well from my successful ascent with Craig Kopet, so we moved steadily. We arrived at the hut in the middle of the afternoon, ate dinner, and immediately crawled into our sleeping bags for a few hours sleep. At midnight, we rose, cooked oatmeal and tea, and headed off at 2 a.m. in the light of our headlamps. A short horizontal distance and elevation gain from the hut, the route traverses under a dangerous ice cliff with rock and icefall exposure from above. Once across this dangerous barrier, we gained the rock on the south-southwest arête and climbed steadily for a thousand feet before reaching the pinnacle called "Little Robson," where the view of the route ahead is very dramatic. The entire route and upper cliffs of the mountain can be seen from this viewpoint, and it's enough to make any capable mountaineer rethink his position on religion.

Looking down the SW Ridge of Mount Robson.

The first challenge is a traverse along a knife-edged ice ridge for several hundred feet to where this ridge butts into a 200-foot sheer cliff. Directly above that is "The Extinguisher," an aptly named hanging glacier that's constantly creeping and threatening to send another block of ice crashing down. The only way to gain the steep upper slopes for the final climb to the summit is to traverse 500 feet along a system of two-foot-wide icy ledges before reaching an ice field that's less susceptible to falling ice. The Swartz Ledges, named for Hans Swartz, the guide who first had the guts to venture through them, are a mandatory risk for reaching the summit. The exposure and danger here are off the scale, with The Extinguisher threatening to crush you with icefall, or several thousand feet of plummeting to your death on the scree slopes above Kinney Lake should you slip. Many climbers had already lost their lives at this dangerous crossing, so I re-emphasized to Joe that we must be sure and swift.

Roped together, I led out on the widest ledge placing ice screws and rock pitons wherever I could find good placement. The crossing went quite well (I didn't look down) and we were able to get under the glacier's hanging ice in less than an hour. I was relieved but not relaxed. Glaciers do most of their moving in the afternoon during warmer temperatures. If we made the summit, returning by this route under The Extinguisher would be like playing with fire.

The upper 2,000 feet of climbing requires setting ice screws and belaying for about 500 feet with tremendous exposure almost straight down into Kinney Lake. Climbing became easier and safer as the ice slope gradually turned into compact snow to the fluted, heavily corniced southeast ridge. I knew we had virtually won the summit as I belayed Joe up the exposed ridge and began appreciating the fruits of our effort. Looking down from my anchored perch, Berg Lake stood out like an azure gem 6,000 feet almost straight below. Off my left shoulder, Kinney Lake was now 9,000 feet beneath us.

Although Joe had become very quiet after crossing the horrific Swartz Ledges, I thought the climb was progressing nicely until he ascended to my stance and riveted his blue eyes onto mine in a look of terror. "I don't think I can climb down!" he said—a few words that hit me with the impact of a fist to the gut.

"Joe, pull yourself together right now!" I shouted with all the force inside me. "Get yourself together; we will make it down; we will go down another way and we will make it down. OK?" I wasn't sure exactly how I would keep that promise, but the words worked, and Joe composed himself.

The ridge eventually broadens and the angle eases. We could see the pointed summit clearly about a hundred yards before crossing beautiful slopes, and climbed onto our goal at 12,972 feet. I stepped up to the responsibility of having the only camera and took a couple photos of Joe on the top of Robson.

As I put away the camera, my mind was racing to figure out the safest way off the pig without having to cross the Swartz Ledges. The Hourglass ice chute from the top of The Extinguisher crossed my mind, but the slopes were always dangerous for avalanches. I had a second rope, and remembered the ice cliff at the top of the south-southwest arête and figured it might be possible to rappel down the vertical ice to the ridge below, that is, if the rope was long enough! This alternative seemed the safest choice, and I set my mind to give it a try.

I felt relief in taking the calculated gamble to descend the hanging glacier to the top of the ice cliffs and rappel off to rock on the arête below, but I was inept at verbalizing any sort of confidence. Joe was worried. Although we had no ice flukes for anchoring into the snow, I tried to assure Joe that the gamble of rappelling was much safer than trying to down climb the dangerous slopes and ledges we had ascended. I said I would make a snow bollard for anchoring. He looked at me in disbelief. I knew, from scoping out alternate routes during the ascent, that with two ropes we could rappel off The Extinguisher Glacier at a narrow cleft in the glacier lip, right over the arête.

After about two hours of down climbing through light snow and intermittent fog, we reached the top of The Extinguisher ice cliffs where they cascade over the top of the SSW arête. The weather began to improve, but our daylight was waning. As I approached the glacier lip, the view looking down into the abyss below was a dizzy sight. Joe stood silently, watching and wondering just what I would do next. I never told Joe that I had never tried rappelling off a snow bollard before this, but I was confident it would work. A snow bollard is essentially a shallow horseshoe shaped trench cut into ice or hard snow. The rope is draped around the bollard in the trench. The bollard is basically a "last resort" anchor. I cut the bollard trench as close to the lip of the glacier as I dare. With a doubled rope, we would have nearly 200 feet, which I'd calculated as being just enough to reach the rock on the ridge below.

Joe looked at the trench, sized up the ice and snow that we were about to hang our lives on, and yelled, "What the hell are you doing! We aren't rappelling on that are we?" Again I assured him the bollard would hold as long as we did not put any upward force on the rope before going over the edge.

The sun had set and darkness was near. I carefully and lightly as my body would allow, put my full downward pressure on the rope and the bollard. It held. Now I was confident to ease myself over the lip of the ice cliff, but it was slightly overhanging, so I could not see if the rope reached the bottom. It wasn't until I had rappelled about halfway down that I could plainly see the end of the rope dangling a good 50 feet above the rock arête! My heart sank to my frozen feet. I would have to implement Emergency Plan B.

I continued the vertical rappel to near the end of the ropes and tied a figure eight knot in the end so I wouldn't rappel off my lifeline. Free-hanging but with both hands free, I cranked my two remaining ice screws into the solid glacier ice. I pulled out of my pack about 30 feet of one-eighth inch thick avalanche cord and another 12 feet of new boot lace and tied them together to make one long string. Securely tying the end of the avalanche cord to the ice screws, I threw the looped cord down. Damn. Five feet short, but it was all I had.

I untied, and carefully put my full weight on these thin cords. To my pleasant surprise, they held my weight. All the time I spent hooking up these lines, I could hear Joe's shouts from above me asking if I was OK. I shouted to answer, but the sound wasn't getting beyond the overhanging ice. Joe couldn't hear me. I slid down as delicately as I could to the end of my bootlaces, and then I was able to chop a couple hand holds in the ice and front point down the last 10 feet of vertical ice to reach the rock below.

I jumped on top of the rock arête and did a spontaneous little dance of euphoria and elation over my success and innovation to get down. Then I climbed down the rock about a hundred feet or so to where I could see Joe at the top of the ice cliff above me. Without trying to explain the circumstances, I yelled at the top of my lungs for him to begin rappelling. Descending with his headlamp on, he survived the initial shock of realizing the rope didn't reach the bottom and I coached him to untie, pull the ropes down, and continue his rappel on the cord and bootlaces. In the darkness of night, we celebrated and breathed a huge sigh of relief on the safety of the rock crest.

We arrived back at the hut around midnight after 23 hours of intense climbing.

We slept for several hours before rising to a beautiful sunny day perfect for the 5,000-foot descent to Kinney Lake and the 5-mile trail hike to the parking lot. Both of us had jobs awaiting; rest was not an option. Riding the euphoria of our success, we drove through the evening and into the middle of the night to reach Spokane. We stunned many people in the know by driving a 1,280-mile roundtrip, climbing to the summit of the highest peak in the Canadian Rockies, and safely returning all on the three-day Labor Day weekend. Luckily, we didn't die on the drive home.

Robson remains as one of my most intense and gratifying climbs, and Joe considers the adventure as his greatest climbing achievement. But he's always regretted that he didn't have along his heavy Hasselblad camera.

Words from the Wild
- Attitude is everything: 49 is not too old to climb big mountains.

Ten Rules of Effective Living according to Joe Collins

1. Only two things you can't live without—oxygen and blood.
2. We are all creatures of habit. Start with good habits, it's harder to change bad habits later.
3. Friends you can choose, relatives you're stuck with.
4. Never burn your bridges. If necessary, take a few detours.
5. Be on time.
6. Never co-sign for anybody.
7. Keep your promise.
8. My check is good; my word is better.
9. Today is the most important day of your life.
10. We are all equal, but some are more equal than others.

Thirteen

Chimney Rock

In 1965, after graduating from the Spokane Mountaineers "Mountain School," I signed up for an outing with Will Murray and Pete VanGelder to climb Chimney Rock at Priest Lake, Idaho. We made the climb via the regular west face route. I returned with John Roskelley to do an early "winter condition" ascent on May 1, 1966. In the next four summers, I completed many more ascents of Chimney Rock with various partners, and we managed to complete first-ascent lines on the east, north, and west faces and the south nose of this dramatic spire of granite.

During the summer of 1968, my dad was building the Indian Creek Marina at Priest Lake and he hired a man named Herb Wagner to run the store and marina. Wagner was a "motor head" and he had every conceivable engine-driven toy, including a new Arctic Cat snowmobile. I was convinced after talking to him that this snowmobile would be my ticket for success in climbing Chimney Rock in the middle of winter. Wagner agreed to loan me the machine, so the following winter, I talked Roskelley into making a real winter attempt.

We returned to Priest Lake in what I believe was the middle of March, as I never recorded the dates of this attempt in my diary. I had picked up the monster snowmobile, and we trailered it to the East Shore Road loaded with a couple hundred pounds of climbing gear and food for a five-day expedition. We strapped one pack on the front of the Arctic Cat, and I carried the other on my back.

The first stretch on the snowmobile was on relatively flat road. Once we hit the Horton Creek Road, the going got steep and it was impossible to ride tandem on the snowmobile. We both brought skis, so after a brief argument as to which one of us would stay on the snowmobile, Roskelley won the coin toss to drive. I would carry my 100-pound pack on my back holding onto a rope tied to the snowmobile as though I were a water skier. I stretched out the entire 150 feet of our climbing rope and tied it to the back of the Arctic Cat. I was going to make a loop for a handle, but then I had the brilliant idea to just tie the rope around my waist using the mountaineer's bowline knot. That way I could balance myself with my arms and ski poles as I was towed. That was my first mistake. My second error was not knowing Roskelley well enough and his callous nature with machines.

The Arctic Cat was a formidable-looking machine, mostly engine sitting over a ribbed tread that spun around a forward and rear axle. I warned John to take it really easy as this machine was powerful: "And go slow." I thought we were on the same page as he roared off and up the road with the line paying out. The jolt when the rope came taut nearly broke me in half. John kept his thumb clamped on the throttle as I wobbled and wavered on my skis with the huge pack on my back. All went well for the first minutes as there were only slight curves in the road at this point. I thought this towing system was going to work.

As I concentrated on keeping upright, I looked over and saw the road much higher to my right. It was immediately across the deep V creek valley, which meant we had a major hairpin corner coming ahead. Surely Roskelley would realize when he made the sharp turn that the 150 feet of rope would lose tension and pile up momentarily across the valley with me still attached. Surely he would realize this!

John continued giving the machine throttle as he brilliantly rounded the hairpin corner. I was shouting at the top of my lungs for him to stop, but my panicked voice couldn't compete with the roar of the Arctic Cat. He continued to accelerate with the focus and concentration of a man in charge. John finished the turn and started roaring up the road right across the creek bed from me. I shouted and then like a madman I tried to untie the bowline knot cinched around my waist. I looked up and John was hunched over the windshield gunning the motor of the snow machine like a bull homing in on a receptive heifer. With the rope temporarily slack, I was standing still and frantically trying to untie myself. But time ran out. The rope drew taut and ripped me off my feet, pulling me headfirst off the road and down into the creek bottom.

With my skis still on my feet, I was being pulled by rope and gravity headfirst into the icy water of Horton Creek. Only when the tension of the stretching rope felt like it was going to cut me in half did the Arctic Cat swerve enough for John to stop its motor. It was either the machine or me, and this time the machine met its match.

I was on my belly, arms outstretched into the water to my shoulders as I kept my face barely out of the rushing stream. The weight of the pack pinned me to the ground. If I rolled one way or the other, I would be engulfed by the icy water. This was another learning experience for both of us. Another lesson in survival as well. One more rough corner of our personalities exposed. Roskelley realized the situation when the snowmobile tipped over, and he slogged back in the snow to see whether his climb would be a solo attempt. When he reached me, he quickly figured out that I had an uncontrollable temper. He deduced that if he pulled me out too quickly his life would be in jeopardy, although he shouldn't take too much credit for that insight since I was promising him with full religious fervor that I would kill him on the spot. John waited several minutes for me to blow off some of my emotion and strength. As I sputtered and gasped, he made me promise not to kill him. Then he finally helped me out of the predicament.

I barely got my act together before committing mistake number two. I tied a loop onto the rope and used it as a handle as John took off up the road. This system went well for a couple miles until a huge swale in the road caused me to let go of the rope. Roskelley was oblivious to the loss of my weight on the machine and continued up the road for what had to be miles before figuring out he was dragging nothing but rope. The snowmobile had no rear-view mirror and Roskelley wasn't prone to looking back for anyone. I waited for more than an hour before I heard the engine coming back down the hill to get me.

I'd had enough. My temper exploded again. The expedition ended right there.

As the 60s came to a close, the clock was ticking on a first winter ascent of Chimney Rock. People were talking about it. The goal was going to be achieved. I thought the only serious competition was John Roskelley, but in 1970 I'd heard that Jim Spearman was keen on snatching the prize of the first winter ascent by himself. Both Spearman and I had climbed the rock some 25 times each. I would be damned to hell to let Spearman beat me for the first winter title. I just had to figure out how to do it.

Meanwhile, the Canadian Rockies were a constant distraction as Roskelley and I were hatching a big, bold plan to make the first winter ascent of the great North Face of Mount Edith Cavell. Why not start on the highest face in the Rockies and work our way down? Roskelley and I were enrolled at Washington State University and every semester break after Christmas we would attempt something "big" in Canada. I had been thinking about a winter ascent of Edith Cavell for a couple of years. In December 1970 we managed to get a snowmobile dealership in Spokane to sponsor our trip. They loaned us a trailer and two new Scorpion Stingers. In return, the company wanted photographs of the snow machines in front of the Canadian peak.

A party of three climbers is safer than two. Roskelley had been communicating with Johnny Waterman, a Western Washington College student who'd already built an impressive climbing resume in Yosemite. He'd climbed Denali at age 16. Waterman came to Spokane, stayed a night at my parents' place, and then the three of us set out on the 500-mile drive to Jasper crammed into my pickup pulling the trailer with two snowmobiles.

Temperatures were bitter cold, dipping to 35 degrees below zero Fahrenheit, yet we saved money by sleeping outside, as usual, on picnic tables in a public park about five miles south of Jasper. Roskelley couldn't get warm. He tossed, tumbled, and whined all night, and we figured out why the next morning. He'd frostbitten his feet —in his sleeping bag! We drove into Jasper, thawed out over coffee and pancakes and watched Roskelley assess the damage to his sore toes. After a few hours, having climbed little more than a few stairs, we abandoned the climb and turned tail back toward Spokane.

A peculiar incident happened on the return trip that offered the first insight into Waterman's complicated personality. We were all disappointed about the aborted climb, but halfway between Eisenhower Junction (later renamed Castle Junction) and Radium, below Mount Verendrye, whatever was going on inside Waterman suddenly boiled over. "LET ME OUT OF THE CAR! RIGHT NOW!" he screamed. "STOP THE CAR!" While I applied the brakes, Waterman yelled, "You guys have girlfriends, I don't! You guys have release and I don't! I only have climbing and I need to get out and climb!"

I pulled off the highway and Waterman bolted out of the truck. He climbed up a nearly vertical cliff, brushing snow off the ledges with his bare hands and muscling his way up technical rock like a madman, kicking into snow and splattering ice while wearing just his boots with no crampons. He plowed through deep powder snow and ascended steep rock bands laced with ice for an hour while Roskelley and I sat and watched from the truck in dazed astonishment. Waterman came down after this long sortie, climbed into the pickup and was calm as a monk.

After going through US Customs, I tried to convince Roskelley to make an attempt into Chimney Rock with me, since we already had the snowmobiles. He'd had enough of the cold for a while, but Waterman was game.

At 5-feet-3-inches tall and slight of build, Waterman had no visible musculature. His hair was "ridiculously long," as he described it. He had large eyes covered by thick glasses that he would nervously push up on the bridge of his tiny nose every few seconds. When trying to carry on a face-to-face conversation with Waterman you needed a pogo stick to jump around with him. Most of the time, he was hyped up like a racehorse dancing behind the starting bar ready for the big race. But once out of the gates, he was a heck of a climber.

All of our gear and supplies were packed, so after just one night in Spokane, Waterman and I drove up to Priest Lake towing the snowmobiles, and camped out again. We started the next morning on the snow machines at Coolin, as the East Shore Road was not plowed in those days. Heavily loaded with gear, we rode for hours up the Horton Ridge road, getting stuck and bucking the machines around. We managed to get to the final hairpin turn below the fire lookout, which was still standing at the time, before bogging down in bottomless fine powder snow. We camped there, and the next morning we broke trail to the lookout, where we spent another night. The next day, we tried in vain to get up to Mount Roothaan in the deepest, lightest snow I have ever seen. "This is shit," I finally concluded. "I've had enough; we are turning around."

Getting to Chimney Rock with the equipment we had was hopeless, but Waterman didn't give up easily. As though he never heard me, he plowed through waist-deep powder huffing, puffing, groaning and trying to make "just one more foot" of progress. After an hour or so, I realized he wasn't coming back. I was freezing, so I packed and started up the mountain only to see Waterman coming back down through the trench he'd plowed into the powder. When we joined up, he had that calmness again. "Well, I had to give it my all, I had to make every step in me to the verge of collapsing before turning around. It feels like a success now, because I gave it all I could. I tell you what Chris, you'll find out when you go to climb Denali just how bad you want it and what it means to you."

Exasperated, we headed for home. After getting down to East Shore Road, Waterman raced his snowmobile ahead of me at top speed, maybe 70 mph. His DNA didn't seem to have any governor for common sense. A few years later, John Mallon Waterman went on to make climbing history. Among other notable ascents, he made the first ascent of the South Face of Mount Hunter in 1973. He got to be known as the "crazy genius" of Alaska climbing, but never meshed with the climbing community. That wasn't necessary to make his mark. As he lost several climbing friends to accidents in the mountains, he increasingly went alone. In 1979, he made the first ascent of the South Spur of Mount Hunter in an epic solo traverse that took 145 days. And then mental illness took control.

A good book was written about Waterman, his brother, and his father and their unusual circumstances and personality issues that culminated in a family tragedy. All three were brilliant scientists but extremely eccentric. All three committed suicide, or at least that's what climbing rangers concluded about Johnny's demise. In April 1981, he disappeared while attempting a solo climb of the east buttress of Denali, which was then called Mount McKinley. Waterman's tracks were spotted going into a dangerous crevasse field and avalanche area with no tracks coming out.

Long before I would learn about Waterman's fate, I continued to be obsessed with that granite spire in the Idaho Selkirks. In February 1973, I would make another fruitless winter attempt at Chimney Rock, this time with Skip Wood. But the fourth time would be the charm.

FIRST WINTER ASCENT

Chimney Rock in winter.

By the end of 1972, I had climbed Chimney Rock 26 times, ascending nearly every crack on all four sides and completing six new routes, including two new routes on the east face. John Roskelley and I made the first free ascent of the east face. Climbing had always been competitive to me, but I was naive to think that no one else would consider climbing such a prominent regional spire against the odds of winter. When I heard Jim Spearman of Spokane was also making plans to be the first, I realized I couldn't wait for all the stars to align into a convenient opportunity. I had to make it happen. In the winter of 1972-73, I was working five days a week as an architectural draftsman for well-known Spokane architect Warren Heylman, and ski instructing on the weekends. The ski school director at Mount Spokane was Skip Wood, a local champion freestyle skier and an accomplished ski mountaineer. When I mentioned I was going to attempt a winter ascent of Chimney Rock, Skip was immediately interested. I knew he would be an able partner, so we began planning.

Chimney Rock East Face in summer.

Reaching the base of Chimney Rock in winter was a significant obstacle to overcome in the 1970s, as logging roads weren't plowed in that direction at the time and snowmobiles were not yet technically advanced enough to handle the terrain and deep snow. Two major failures trying to use snowmobiles had steered me back to my purest roots. The climb took on expedition status as I prepped my cross-country skis, started stuffing my largest backpack, and braced myself for a lot of sweaty grunt work.

On February 14, 1973, Wood and I set off from the East Shore Road along Priest Lake and started skinny skiing up Horton Ridge Road with a one-week food supply, a huge assortment of iron pitons, pots, stove, and a two-man tent, two 60-meter ropes, and all our winter weather clothing complete with double boots. Additionally, we each carried a pair of snowshoes as backup. Our packs weighed just more than 110 pounds each—yes, we weighed them. We would eventually need every piece of gear and food.

The uphill grind of the Horton Creek Road ended at the abandoned Horton Ridge fire lookout, where we crashed the first night. This classic lookout was constructed on top of eight tall poles set on concrete pedestals offering a 360-degree view of the Idaho Selkirks including Priest Lake. The lookout was not heated, but it was luxuriously roomy for two people and offered protection from the bitter cold, wind, and snow. Wood and I needed most of the next day to break trail through deep snow to reach the saddle, elevation 7,000 feet, between the two peaks of Mount Roothaan, where we set up the tent for our base camp. With the short daylight and long winter nights, we were working the late afternoon and the morning hours with headlamps as we cooked and melted water. On February 16, we rose to sub-zero cold, but clear weather, so we skied down the beautiful north face of Mount Roothaan in powder snow and made the trudge up to the base of Chimney with all our heavy "ironmongery" and ropes. Getting to the base of the rock, I found every crack wind-plastered with ice and snow. The west face of Chimney Rock looked like a giant ice cream bar covered with white chocolate.

I chose the west face as the route and looked for an area that had the most rock exposed. The climbing was labor-intensive. I had to chop ice with my axe to clear every hand hold, and then move up a foot at a time, pound in a piton for protection where I could find a crack, then chop and clear the ice above me. I worked all morning and into the afternoon just to do the first lead of about 100 feet. Meanwhile, Wood was freezing to the bone while belaying me for such long periods. It became obvious: we were not going to conquer Rome in one day.

I called off our ascent around 2 p.m. and rappelled down to Wood. Our plan was to sleep in our tent on Mount Roothaan, so I left the extra rope, carabiners and pitons tied off at my high point on the west face, about halfway to the top. We had jumars, so we could return in the morning and ascend the ropes to begin the climb where I'd left off. This seemed like a good plan, but in the high mountains weather can be fickle to the extremes. By the time we arrived back at our campsite, a winter storm had engulfed us in a gale-force blizzard. The next morning, with the wind and snow still raging, Wood felt that he must return to work for fear of losing his new job. We skied the 10 miles past the lookout and down to Priest Lake in one long day. I was disappointed, but not defeated.

Back in Spokane, I immediately began to search for a new climbing mate. The fraternity of climbers in Spokane was quite small, and my search led to Will Parks, who had the time, experience, and equipment to make the return expedition with me. Just two days after Wood and I had returned, Parks and I were packed, headed back to Priest Lake on February 20 under a clear sky. We were much lighter, as my ropes and hardware were already hanging on the West Face of Chimney. We skied the 10 miles from the car all the way to the saddle at Mount Roothaan and pitched our tent. We arose at midnight February 22, and were under way on our skis at 2 a.m., gliding down the basin and up to the base of Chimney Rock. This time, even with numb fingers, I could feel success close at hand. It was very cold, probably around zero degrees, but clear. I ascended the ropes with my jumars back to my previous high point, and then had Will ascend to the same ledge to belay.

From the belay stance, we were about halfway up the west face, but the remaining vertical rock was freshly plastered with snow and ice on top of the already thick winter crust. Although my progress was slow, we had nearly eight hours of daylight remaining to make the last 100 feet of climbing and then descend. I felt confident and giddy as a 6-year-old kid—for a short while.

Climbing hoary ice over the rock snapped me back to reality. The snowy coating was like sugar, too soft to get a grip with my boot tips. I got into a rhythm of chopping away all the ice back to the rock, finding a crack and nailing in a piton, then clipping in a carabineer fixed to my stirrups. I'd wriggle my big boot into the stirrup, stand up in the webbing and repeat the process. I labored all morning and into the afternoon at the glacial pace of only 15 feet per hour. This method of "direct aid" was the only way to safely ascend.

Hours later, I was stoked at the sight of stone cairns about 30 feet above my perch. I surged into a fever pitch and worked like a madman to gain the final feet to the top of Chimney. Sweat was rolling off me as I stood on top with a subzero breeze that froze on my skin. It was only 3 p.m., but the sun was low on the horizon and only about an hour away from setting. It had taken me years, and on this final day, nearly seven hours of hard labor to chop my way up the last hundred feet or so, but here I was standing on top of my hard-won victory. As is the case in many climbs, I spent years planning and calculating how to reach the top of a peak, only to quickly turn around and get off the summit as quickly as possible!

I knew once the sun set the plummeting temperature would be a survival issue. I quickly wrapped a huge sling around one of the ice-plastered cairns, tied off the rope, then laid myself in a prostrate position to get my head over the edge far enough for a visual on Will below. I yelled at my partner to start ascending and make sure to remove all the hardware as he came. Will seemed to get right to the task at hand, but as he strapped on the mechanical jumars and started to ascend, he started yelling like a wounded animal.

"Help, help, help me! HELP ME!"

These are not the words I wanted to hear while standing on top of Chimney Rock in a freezing sweat, the sun nearly setting, and the temperature below zero. Will had been stoic all day patiently belaying me, but the wind and bitter cold had sapped his strength, physically, and mentally. He couldn't get his body to move. I was slowly freezing to death on a pinnacle of rock while roped to a man who could not, or would not, move. I laid on my belly again to get a view of Will below and tried to talk him up.

"Will, what's the matter!" I yelled at the top of my lungs through a blast of arctic wind in my face.

"What do I do? What do I do? I can't get my jumars on the rope; it's frozen! I can't move anything!"

"Will, get hold of yourself," I commanded. "Put your right hand on the jumar. Clamp it on the rope. Make sure your sling is attached. Get your boot into the sling, then do the same for your left hand and left boot."

"OK, OK, I'll try my best."

Oftentimes in stressful situations I have seen people panic, fall apart, and act like babies, or get on their knees and pray. Will took panic to new levels with unnerving dialogue. He seemed to have deteriorated to a state of mush. The adrenalin and emotional overload rendered his wherewithal to the state of a child. In our desperate situation, this was understandable, but unacceptable. I yelled and commanded him like a drill sergeant to make one simple move after another.

Meanwhile, the sun had dropped below the horizon and the cold was cutting deeply into my inactive body. I had to get Will up to my stance as quickly as possible, or rappel down to his stance, cut the ropes and rappel off. My mind was racing to figure out a safe escape plan as I continued to yell directions to him.

Will slowly made upward progress, whining all the way. I talked to myself silently, wondering how I couldn't foresee this circumstance. I had been on many expeditions where people panicked and melted down, but nothing as severe as this circumstance where lives were in jeopardy.

It took two hours for Will to reach the top. By that time, we were standing on a frozen pillar of granite in the dark. I unroped Will, retied the two ropes together, and hooked up the rappel around the stone cairn with a sling and carabineer. Numb with cold, I continued to bark commands, trying to convince myself we could survive this ordeal. I told Will I had to go down first to unwind the ropes to make sure there would be no knots and chop in a platform for a second rappel. Mercifully, the rappels went without a hitch and Will and I reached the bottom of the west face. We were out of the exposure to the bitter wind, but awash in the inky blackness of a winter night with no moon.

As we strapped on our skis at the base, Will was spent. It was obvious that he could not carry any load, not even a light pack, so I put all the gear in my rucksack. The ski back out to the top of Mount Roothaan goes downhill about 400 hundred feet to a basin before climbing up the north slope of the mountain. I carried all the ropes, pitons, carabineers, and slings down to this basin, unloaded the heavy climbing equipment into a bag, and stuffed it under a huge boulder. I would return in the late spring to retrieve all my precious equipment.

To my relief, the remainder of our ski out was uneventful, as we had our ski tracks to follow downhill to the lake. The first winter ascent of Chimney Rock was a hard-won victory for me, and another learning experience.

Words from the Wild

- "Shared joys make a friend, not shared sufferings." —Friedrich Nietzsche, German philosopher

Fourteen

Pamirs & USSR

The American contingent in the 1974 International Pamir Expedition included, front row, kneeling, L-R: Dr. Frank Sarnquist, Bruce Carson; standing, L-R: Fred Stanley, Chris Kopczynski, Marty Hoey, Gary Ullin (hidden behind Marty), Jed Williamson, Jock Glidden, John Roskelley, Pete Schoening (cutting cake) Bob Craig (behind Pete), Pete Lev, Jeff Lowe, John Evans, Allen Steck.

Fifteen climbers died on the 1974 International Pamir Expedition to the USSR, marking one of the worst tragedies in the history of mountaineering. Team member Bob Craig detailed the events in the complete and well-written book "Storm and Sorrow in the High Pamirs." A Hollywood movie based on the book, "Storm and Sorrow," offered good character portrayals and reasonably accurate depiction of events. The ruthlessness of the mountains deeply impacted every expedition member, including me.

In 1973, I learned from American Alpine Club newsletters and the buzz in the climbing community that Pete Schoening, one of the heroes of the American 1953 K2 Expedition, was soliciting resumes to choose 12 of "the best US climbers" for an international expedition to the Union of Soviet Socialist Republics. The nation had reopened relations with the West after decades of secrecy that closed borders to travelers and sporting activities.

The politics of international climbing have always required a legitimate sponsor for exploratory clubs or climbing teams to enter most foreign countries. The American Alpine Club is the premier organization recognized by most countries around the world. Membership in this club allowed expedition leaders to solicit donations on a tax-exempt status. The business and politics of international mountaineering ran through the AAC, and I was not a member.

Competition to be on the first expedition into the USSR since the beginning of the 20th century was fierce. More than 200 serious American alpinists applied. Rumors of more than 400 applicants were never confirmed, as Schoening died before completing his planned book about the expedition. I did not know Schoening at the time, but I telephoned him at his Seattle home expressing my desire to be on the team and followed up with a letter of interest. I listed what I considered sterling qualifications, expeditions, all the difficult routes climbed, plus my recent degree from Washington State University, four years of varsity wrestling and success in team sports. I also emphasized my resume as a construction supervisor and my chosen career in construction.

The pitch hit a chord with Pete, who was a chemical engineer and a contractor. When I called again, he had already chosen his 12 climbers, but he had listed Jeff Lowe and me as alternates and would take me if he could raise the additional funds. I was euphoric. He reminded me that I was not a member of the AAC, and he had many other members to consider. I was still ecstatic. Among the hundreds of serious American mountaineers who'd applied, I was taken seriously as a world-class mountaineer.

A month or so passed without hearing back from Pete. My friend John Roskelley already had been chosen for the team, so I felt that fate had passed me by. Roskelley had been named to the 1973 American Expedition to Dhaulagiri, the world's seventh highest mountain, and he was one of the three members who summited.

I was newly married, and my wife Sharon was charismatic. If an issue festered, she would get aggressive and use her flowery personality to get answers, or her way. I was moping around our apartment when she suddenly picked up the phone determined to apply her power of persuasion to Pete Schoening. I'll never forget her words: "Pete, this is Sharon Kopczynski, Chris's wife. I have known Chris and John Roskelley for a couple years, and Chris is the better man of the two, and you had better take him on your expedition. You won't be sorry, I guarantee it."

She said it with such conviction and zeal, but I grabbed the phone, tried to semi-apologize by saying, "Look, Pete, I may be better at some things but John is a great mountaineer by any definition."

Said Pete, "Well, I can't deny you now; your wife is a good sales agent for you. You will have to join the American Alpine Club, however."

I told Pete I would pay my Alpine Club dues immediately and that he would not regret his decision to take me.

The next step of the strategic plan involved a total commitment on my part for the summer of 1974. I was a husband with a new wife and an adopted daughter. We had little money saved. We were living in a small two-bedroom apartment on 8th Avenue in Spokane. I was working full time during the spring of the year for my father's construction firm as a superintendent on the Iran and Chinese pavilions for Expo '74. Sharon was a salesperson for RE Owes Company, a home interior decorating firm owned by Bob Owes. Even though Sharon and I both had career jobs, we were living paycheck to paycheck, the reason I'd hesitated to pay membership dues to the AAC. The upside of going on an organized, sanctioned expedition was that all the travel costs including food, lodging, clothing, and even camera equipment were underwritten by various private companies willing to sponsor this type of activity in return for the advertising or promotion of their products. I was responsible only for the time loss from my work and some of my climbing equipment. It wasn't my dream trip of being the first man to walk on the moon, but damn close.

Schoening planned to get the entire group together at his home in Seattle, and then climb nearby Mount Rainier and camp in the summit crater for a week. Not much scientific research had been done on humans at extreme altitude in 1974, and the Pamir Mountains were higher than 23,000 feet above sea level. Schoening thought we should acclimate at 14,000 feet for a week before boarding the plane. We climbed to the summit of Rainier on July 2, and then spent a week climbing around the summit crater exploring the thermal ice caves under the peak's ice cap. One day, I climbed with Jeff Lowe down the west side of the mountain to about the 10,000-foot level and climbed back up on the technical ice routes to the Sunset Amphitheater. In the course of the outing I received a good lesson in ice climbing from one of the greatest alpine mountaineers of the times.

St. Peters Square, Moscow.

MOSCOW

The team flew from Sea-Tac Airport directly to Moscow, where the Soviet Union greeted us with culture shock. A KGB agent stripped us of any freedom of movement by taking our wallets, identification, passports, and any other ID that we were carrying. We would be watched and followed 24 hours a day for our entire stay. Two KGB agents accompanied us at the mountain camp. They never let us out of their sight.

Visiting Moscow was interesting for the human cultural experience, but the city in 1974 was drab and depressing. Except for St. Peter's Square, there was no freedom of expression in the architecture or construction. I managed to climb on top of our hotel, called Sputnik, and as far I could see across Moscow the buildings and skyline were all the same, and all devoid of color. Every building was a government-built, mid-rise of unpainted pre-cast concrete. Most of the structures were housing units. None that I saw would get a passing grade from a Western building inspector. The workmanship was poor, the concrete looked like it was just slopped out of the wheelbarrow and much of it was poorly finished. On the inside trim and woodwork, I saw doors that did not even hit the jamb, locks that would not hit the strike plates. As for the plumbing—I would rather have gone in the forest with a wad of toilet paper, if there had been any available. Some buildings had minimal painting decorations, but I never saw a paint job that would pass inspection in a Western country. The lack of competition promoted a lack of quality construction. Craftsmanship was severely lacking, and apparently so was pride.

As I toured Moscow, I never saw one individual with a smile on his or her face. Everyone was deadpan and serious, and most of the Russians smoked cigarettes. Their other favorite pastime was drinking Vodka that tasted to me like some sort of raw kerosene. It was horrible. Soviet society prized gifted musicians, athletes, and mathematicians, who were immediately snatched up by the government and protected. The government seemed to have no boundaries in its mission to be tops on the world stage from the Olympics to the nuclear arms race. Soviet athletes were paid full time to excel. Their mountain climbers competed for the grand prize of "Master of Sports," which had the benefit of a lifetime income.

The Russian people were promised much from a government and system that eventually failed. Despite the "evils" of capitalism, the problems of a free enterprise system pale in comparison with communism. It became obvious to me why my family fled Poland for the individual freedom they craved in the United States. I will always be grateful for the bravery of my ancestors.

When we left Moscow for the airport, we were reminded again that there is no hurry to get anywhere, anytime, in the USSR. We left in the early morning of July 13 and were told that we would board the plane for Osh that same morning, but we waited and waited and finally boarded at 1:30 a.m. on July 14. We were suffering from anxiousness in a muddled culture, and I sure as heck wasn't going to seek treatment for anything in a Soviet hospital.

GETTING STARTED

Arriving in Osh and observing how the local people lived was more interesting to me than trying to find a souvenir. Osh is an ancient trade route along Marco Polo's trail of discovery and adventure. All the territories under the USSR control were interlaced with different ethnic groups and many different languages. The ever-present Soviet Military made sure the native people did not step out of line. As we traveled by truck from Osh to the base camp of the Pamirs, military camps and outposts were frequent. Control by the government meant everything to the communists, and I would say this atmosphere was even worse than the first time I visited China in 1983. I didn't like this feeling of having someone looking over my shoulder day and night, but there was absolutely nothing any of us could do about it.

The Pamir Camp was set up like a Boy Scout jamboree. Every climber was assigned to a little pup tent. While some of the climbers paired up, I chose to be alone. That tent was my base for the next month.

Base Camp with Mount Lenin.

Our mission was to climb and explore the Pamir Mountains and potentially to climb new routes and even make first ascents. My group included Pete Schoening and Frank Sarquist and two top female climbers, Molly Higgins and Marty Hoey. I was pleased to be teamed up with the famous mountaineer. Schoening was the consummate gentleman, with a lifelong passion for mountaineering and exploration, and an icon in American mountaineering. The Soviets had invited 160 of the world's "best" (if "best" can be defined) climbers from around the world, so the main eating tent was always full of interesting conversations. The Russians knew very little English, and none of the climbers I met knew any Russian, so almost all the communication was translated through the Russian-assigned KGB agents. Once all the climbing teams were formed, we packed our gear and headed up the mountain. The most interesting food item the Russians had supplied was fish—whole fish. A 3-foot long dried fish including the head and tail was stuffed into each team's food supply! The first night out, I ate too much of this salted fish, and spent the rest of the night vomiting like a sick dog outside the tent. That was the last I had of the piscatorial delicacy.

PEAK LENIN

My climbing team of Schoening, Hoey, Higgins, Sarquist, and myself had the unique mission to climb over the 20,000-foot pass on the shoulder of Peak Lenin, and then traverse a long high ridge to try scaling two unclimbed mountains. This was a bold and ambitious plan, and unlike all the other climbing teams, ours was the only one trying to discover new peaks to climb. We had no photographs of consequence that showed what was over this pass to the glacier named Dzerzhinsky. We climbed with high anticipation.

For about two weeks, we shuttled loads up and down Peak Lenin to the high camp just under 20,000 feet. I was pleasantly stunned at how strong Marty Hoey was carrying 100 pounds on her back, plus a rather large and heavy hairbrush for grooming her near waist length hair. Marty was proving to me what I already knew, that she was just as strong as she was beautiful.

On July 23, during one of our load carries to establish our Camp Three, I had just crested the shoulder of the mountain and was about to take my pack off when the earth beneath my feet shifted suddenly and I was thrown to the ground on my ass. It was an earthquake! As I sat there, the ground moved about 20 or 30 feet sideways, then moved back and forth and in circles, but not much up and down motion. Standing up was impossible during the violent motion that lasted maybe 10 to 15 seconds. I just sat on my butt and rode it out. I could hear the snow cracking and avalanches falling all around. Later we discovered that the earthquake was about 6.0 on the Richter scale. I can't imagine being in an earthquake of magnitude 9.0.

We quickly summed up this situation as a possible disaster for our climbing mates on their selected routes and made haste to descend the mountain all the way to base camp. We discovered from our walkie-talkie communication system that a miracle of sorts happened with the teams on the north side of Peak Lenin. Some climbers were buried up to their necks from the earthquake-released avalanches, and some were thrown into crevasses, but no one died.

On our side of the mountain, no one was in the wrong place at the wrong time. However, on the east face of Peak Lenin, the five best mountaineers from

Estonia were swept down the face by the avalanches. Three died immediately. Two had survived, but they died shortly after a Soviet rescue team arrived days later. The Soviets managed to hide this fact from all of us, being ultra-sensitive about criticism and how the rest of the world would judge their leadership.

That same night, our relief for the survival of the American team was short-lived as storm clouds formed followed by heavy snowfall. During the middle of the night, an avalanche broke loose on the north face of Peak 19 and covered the tent where Roskelley, John Marts, Bob Craig, and Gary Ullin were sleeping. All we heard on the radio the next morning was that "an American climber had died on the north face of Peak 19." Our team didn't know who the victim was as we continued our descent to base camp, and I worried the whole time about the fate of my best friend, Roskelley. When we reached camp and learned Gary Ullin had died, a pall of grief spread over the American team. Bringing the body down the face of the mountain was impossible, so Marts, Roskelley, and Craig buried him where he died high up on the north face of the mountain in a huge crevasse.

Upon returning to base camp, Marts needed medical attention to cover his swollen and frostbitten hands. He was suffering terribly from the traumatic experience of losing his good friend.

The weather pattern for summer in the high Pamirs was normally calm with safe snow conditions, which is why the Soviets had chosen this area of their country to show off the outstanding climbing potential to the world. However, in the summer of 1974, the weather pattern for the Karakoram and Pamirs was backwards. Summer became winter. We were being hit by back-to-back snowstorms, including below-zero temperatures. None of the senior, seasoned Soviet alpinists had ever witnessed snowstorms in the middle of summer like we experienced that year in the Pamirs.

I believe humans have a hard-wired genetic code of hope. In the case of the weather, we didn't believe that this storm pattern would get worse, and we certainly didn't believe more climbers would be killed. We had a wake for Gary in the adjoining field, restructured our plans, and set out with new goals. My team, led by Schoening, decided to cancel our ambitious trek of discovery, and set our goal to climb Peak Lenin by the Razdelny Pass and the Northwest

Ridge. Peak Lenin is 23,405 feet in elevation, and this was to be my first real test of performance at altitude. Hoey decided not to climb because of her affair with Lev. Our team was now Higgins, Sarnquist, Schoening and me.

All four of us were well acclimated and we made the journey to the high Camp Three at 19,685 feet in just two days. Considering the weather patterns, I did not want to linger up there. On August 3, we rose at 2 a.m., cooked a breakfast of oatmeal and tea, and took off for the summit nearly 4,000 vertical feet above with a long, exposed ridge of ascent. The sky was mostly clear with telltale high cirrus wisps everywhere—a sure sign of instability. I felt like I was at sea level and stormed up the slopes, only to find that my teammates could not match my pace. The climbing was easy, and I elected not to tie into the rope, as in some ways it makes an ascent more dangerous. Philosophies differ among climbers, but to me, speed is safety. When it comes to summit day, I prefer to push to the summit as fast as possible, touch it, and get the hell down. Lingering around above 20,000 feet anywhere on this planet is dangerous. I was soon far above my team.

As the hours passed and the dawn began to break, the strong winds slowly subsided. The route ahead was obvious, a long rock and ice ridge that slowly turned eastward in a long skyward arc toward a broad ridge that ended at the summit. I continued climbing at my own pace, probably a half-mile ahead of my teammates, but I always kept them in sight. After about four hours of climbing, I crested the final ridge and could plainly see the summit. I sat down and waited for the threesome to catch up while enjoying the incredible view of the Pamir Range, which was spanned out below my perch at 23,000 feet. When my three mates reached me sitting on the ridge, we shared a cold drink of water and then climbed the remainaing 400 feet to the summit together.

When we reached the summit of Peak Lenin, I was stunned to see an aluminum bust of Vladimir Lenin placed among the summit rocks. It wasn't a solid head bust like you see on a statue, but a large flat plate with Lenin's bust molded into the cast, and very heavy. Next to the likeness of the leader of Russia's Bolshevik revolution was a small pyramid of metal featuring an ice axe. Only the most dedicated communists would carry those loads to 23,405 feet! We didn't linger on the summit, as more threatening clouds were on the horizon. I was quite proud of my performance at this altitude. Now I knew for certain that climbing another 5,000 feet to the summit of Everest was within my physical and mental limits.

On top. Molly Higgins, Pete Schoening, and me on the summit of Peak Lenin, 23,405 feet. Photo by Frank Sarnquist.

The trip down to the base of the mountain took two long days, and to my surprise was surprisingly uneventful. However, the weather pattern was changing for the worse.

Upon reaching the mountain base, we still had one long day to reach base camp. We learned by radio that the entire Soviet women's team had reached the summit of Lenin, but the next big storm was upon them. The women were attempting to traverse the mountain by climbing up one route and descending by a different route. They had reached the summit with full backpacks late in the afternoon and elected to camp right on the top! Hindsight is crystal clear, but few experienced mountaineers would dare pitch a tent on the summit of a major mountain, especially in unstable weather. I did that in 1966 on top of Mount Hood and nearly died of exposure on the descent. I'd learned my lesson: never hang out on the top of a needle exposed to the full power of nature.

In "Storm and Sorrow," the Soviet women leader Elvira Shataeyeva stated upon reaching the summit of Lenin late in the afternoon with a "storm of major proportions" forecast: "We are strong. We are Soviet women. It is late and we are tired. We will camp here and go down to Razdelny Pass tomorrow."

We all knew they were strong, but the Soviet clothing and particularly their tents were terribly inferior to gear made by modern Western manufacturers. What I saw at the base camp were tents that had late nineteenth century technology. They looked like second-hand Boy Scout pup tents, which might be used at a lakeside campground but never would be suitable for an exposed mountain. Craig gives a painfully detailed description of these military tents in his book. The tents had no zipper closures, but rather a double flap system of folds, which was secured along the seams by wooden toggles, passed through string eyelets attached to the flaps. This closure system hardly kept out the less-potent weather in the same kind of tents provided for us at base camp. A number of us were dumbfounded when we learned that this equipment was what the Soviet women were depending on. Even more depressing was the knowledge that the four poles providing the A-frame suspension at either end of the two-man tents were made of wood. Even a few inches of snow load would buckle these tents.

The gear obviously had been given to this team by the state without proper field-testing. I believe all the KGB officials and the Soviet climbing team were painfully aware of the inferior clothing and technology, but they were terrified to criticize the quality of their country's products for fear of being sent on the next train to Siberia. This was the grim situation in the USSR. The common person was promised the moon by a communist system that could not deliver.

We held up at the base of Peak Lenin in a true blizzard from August 4 to 7, the worst of the several storms we had already experienced, and reportedly one of the worst in recorded Pamirs history, according to the old-timers. The wind was estimated at 50 to 80 miles per hour. More than an inch of snow fell per hour. The temperatures were below zero at base camp, so the temperatures on the summit of Lenin were surmised to be minus 40 to 50 degrees! We could hear the steady roar of winds on the summit of Lenin 10,000 feet above.

My team continued the trek to the base camp the next day, and there we heard via the walkie-talkie that the Soviet women were still trapped on the summit, unable to move. When you climb above 23,000 feet, the oxygen concentration is one-third that of sea level. The effort to survive is magnified even on a good day. Your brain function is numbed, your body movements slowed, and your breathing is rapid as your body tries to adjust by producing millions of red cells from the bone marrow to gather the scant oxygen molecules. A variety of high-altitude sicknesses can be lethal, including pulmonary edema (HAPE), cerebral edema, severe headaches, and blood clots. The only sure cure for any of these ills is descent to lower altitudes. I have seen people with HAPE that have descended just a few hundred feet and recovered. In addition to the threat of HAPE, the Soviet women were trapped and exposed to high winds, a whiteout, and dangerously bitter cold that would not abate.

From the central staging expedition tent at base camp, climbers gathered to listen to the Soviet walkie-talkie conversations with their women's climbing team. The Soviets could not hide anything from us now, because we all knew the women were trapped on the summit of Lenin. We also learned that the Swiss team had tried to make the summit of Lenin the day after our summit climb and were too slow in returning to their high camp. They were forced to bivouac on the exposed ridge in winds they reported to be 80 miles per hour.

A rescue team was formed by our American teammates high on the mountain that included Jed Williamson and Pete Lev with a couple of French climbers that bravely tried to forge through the storm to reach the Russian team. They were unable to go far in the intense storm and had to retreat.

We learned from the 3 P.M. walkie talkie transmission that one of the Swiss women froze to death that morning.

On the morning of August 6, Elvira, the Soviet women team leader, reported by radio that one of the youngest teammates was too sick to move. The climbing leader of Pamir Camp was Abalakov, who insisted that the women leave the sick girl if she could not move and get off the summit to dig snow caves. I knew from being on the summit that there was no place within 3,000 feet to dig a snow cave, as it was solid windblown ice. Mounting a rescue was impossible in the conditions, which raged at a full blizzard even low on the mountain.

TRAGEDY

Over the centuries, poets, priests, and philosophers have written countless words about death. People of faith who believe in heaven talk about how glorious the afterlife will be, like they know exactly what will happen to them when they die. Afterlife is something you believe in, or you do not.

We all view life differently and certainly some of us live life differently, and we all hear words and interpret the meaning of life differently. I was standing by for every radio transmission from Elvira to Abalakov on August 7. When she said her last words, she'd reported that her arms were frozen from the elbow to the fingers. She was pushing the transmitter button with the tip of her frozen elbow. Six of her teammates had died. Only Elvira and one other woman were still alive. What I heard this brave leader say over a period of two days on the radio can be summed up to: "Life is short, life is sacred, and life is fragile. Life is the mountains, and mountain climbing is so beautiful. Life is everywhere, and to be loved to the end, and we love you."

They did not pray, but they helped each other try to survive to their last breaths. They asked forgiveness, as they felt they had failed in their mission, and they wept for their children. They cried, and those of us listening to their last words, cried for them.

I don't know where we go after we die, but the Pamirs experience gave me a lot to think about. Bruce Carson and Marty Hoey died in subsequent climbs. Carson fell off a cornice on Trisul in the Garhwal region of India in 1975. Hoey slid off the North Face of Mount Everest in 1982. In a lapse likely prompted by thin air, she leaned back to rest from a fixed line with her safety harness unbuckled only to come out of the harness and plummet 8,000 feet. Death is something my mind has had to deal with. It's not a mystery I think about, nor pray about, as I believe I have but one life, and my heaven is right here on earth. I believe my children carry my spirit, and hopefully, they inherit some of my love of life. I can say for certain, that the eight Russian women fought the most valiant fight to stay alive in the worst imaginable conditions.

Bodies of Russian women. The frozen bodies of the entire Russian women's team lay where they died. The body of Elvira, the leader, is at the bottom of the snow saddle. Photo by Allen Steck.

What I heard and witnessed in the Pamirs that summer stirs my innermost feelings of sadness, and decades later my emotions override my heart with grief.

On fame's eternal camping ground,
Their silent tents are spread.
And Glory guards with solemn round
The Bivouac of the dead.
—Theodore O'Hara

Words from the Wild
- Common sense is not common.
- Your head is above your heart for a reason.

Fifteen

Eiger North Face

Eiger North Face from West Ridge.

"HOWEVER GOOD HE MAY BE, and however favorable the conditions of his ascent, anyone who returns from the Eigerwand cannot but realize that he has done something more than a virtuoso climb; he has lived through a human experience to which he had committed not only all his skill, intelligence and strength, but his very existence."

These are the words of the French mountaineering hero, Lionel Terray, who, along with his partner Louis Lachenal made the second ascent of Switzerland's Eiger North Face in July of 1947. Three years later, Terray and Lachenal would be members of the historic expedition to Nepal for the first ascent of an 8,000-meter peak. The book "Annapurna" is still regarded as one of the top mountaineering adventure books of all time.

By 1964, the year I took up climbing seriously, 43 successful ascents had been recorded on the Eiger North Face, and 24 men had died trying to climb the wall. These were not favorable odds and the reputation of the Eiger as the "Murderwand" grew internationally. The first two expeditions to attempt the Eiger ended in tragedy, killing six outstanding climbers/guides. They fell or died of exhaustion and exposure. Books were written and movies made of the tragedies, but the climbers kept coming. Some would succeed, and some would perish.

The word "Eiger" in German means "Ogre," as the mountain stands like a frozen, triangular, black, evil, faceless brute casting its north-facing shadow over the Bernese Oberland. To view the Eiger from any angle is hideously intimidating to the mountaineer. The impression leaves it easy to imagine why Europeans felt demons and monsters inhabited the Alps. Until the late 1700s with the ascent of Mount Blanc, the mention of "Eiger" was enough to deter people from climbing mountains.

The North Face of the Eiger is a full 6,000 feet of vertically tilted compact, blackish, polished limestone where the African and European tectonic plates collide. The strata is horizontal bands for the lower third of the face, which is the European plate, then tilted vertically for the upper two thirds of the face, which makes up the African Plate. The upper two thirds of the wall have ice fields that cling to polished ledges and hang like lattice. Icicles cling to the few fractures and cracks. The base of the wall starts at just over 7,000 feet and rises in one vertical pillar to the summit at 13,042 feet. To the untrained eye, the wall appears insurmountable and stands like a giant bastion to the Swiss

Alps behind. To mountaineers, most of its deadly reputation was related to the ease of access to the base of the wall, making it attractive to attempt even the impossible. Rolling pastures for grazing cattle transition right up the base of this spectacular cliff.

Terray's book "Borders of the Impossible" stood out from Eiger literature and inspired me to continue mountaineering and write down my goals to succeed. The Nordwand was not a permanent fixture among them. In 1969 on my solo expedition to Europe and after climbing the Eiger's West Buttress and looking down on the terrible North Face, I erased this goal off my list of dreams. The Eiger North Face looked positively terrifying from my intimate perspective. I couldn't figure out how ANYONE could climb this wall. But fate would hold other plans for me, as time and circumstance can heal all wounds and fears. Between the summer of 1969 and my invitation to climb in the USSR and Pamirs with an "All-American" climbing team, I got married and had a family. I had an anchor.

By the time 1974 arrived, there was still only one American, John Harlin, who had successfully climbed the face. He made the ascent with a European team in August of 1962 but would later die on the Eiger North Face attempting to make the first direct or "Direttissima" route. Every year that passed added more climbing fatalities on the Eiger, and no American team had ever attempted the climb when John Roskelley and I got off the train in Kleine Scheidegg in August of 1974. When Roskelley had learned of his invitation on the Pamir expedition, he dismissed all my horror stories and first-hand impressions of the Eiger North Face. Roskelley immediately changed his airline ticket to add an eight-day extension on the return trip. He saw the opportunity to stop in Switzerland en route to New York for an attempt on the North Face. Roskelley asked if I was interested in joining him, and my response was an emphatic "No way!" From what I had seen in person looking down the face from the West Buttress, the North Face, with its sheer mile-high wall booby trapped with rock fall and ice avalanches looked too dangerous and intimidating for me.

My animated words of caution didn't discourage Roskelley, who began lobbying another Pamir teammate, John Marts of Seattle. Marts had climbed several classic Alpine faces in France and had an international reputation as one of the finest American mountaineers. I felt relieved that Roskelley had a solid partner and wouldn't bug me anymore. But my first written goal, which I had wood-burned into the shaft of my ice axe—EIGER—and confirmed in my diary carried powerful, subliminal messages to my brain.

The expedition in the Pamirs was so traumatizing with the deaths of 15 climbers, that the thought of climbing the Eiger North Face at that time was as distant from my mind as the Planet Pluto. The Pamirs expedition had embossed into my psyche that mountains are dangerous. The word "Eiger" conjured up the vision of the "Death Bivouac." It was hard to shake the thought of the first two men who tried to climb the Eiger, Max Sedlmayer and Karl Mehringer, hanging frozen to death mid-way up the wall. Indeed, the first six men who tried to climb the wall died in their attempts.

But while lying in my sleeping bag at 14,000 feet in the Pamir Camp on a cold, windy night fate came knocking on my tent flap. I was still mourning like all the other climbers over the recent deaths of the Russian women's climbing team when Bob Craig's voice boomed outside my tent flap and asked, "Chris, may I come in your tent?"

"Come inside and get out of the weather, Bob," I replied, a bit stunned from the request. Craig had faced death with Roskelley just a week before on Peak 19 when Gary Ullin had died in an avalanche. John Marts was the fourth teammate of that climbing foursome. Marts was understandably affected by Ullin's death—traumatized into a state of Post Traumatic Syndrome that would stay with him for years. Roskelley, although he, too, was with Gary Ullin when he died, was still determined to go to Switzerland and the Eiger.

"Chris, you know your buddy Roskelley has his mind set on going to climb the Eiger North Face."

"Yes, I know John better than most men, and I know John will be going," I replied in a matter of fact fashion.

"Well, John Marts is in no condition to climb the Eiger. You and I know that, and it would be suicide to even think that he should go. You and John have climbed together for 10 years and would make a strong team. Would you consider going with Roskelley in lieu of Marts?"

Craig's words stunned me. He had guts to come into my tent and lay that trip on me. Why had he asked me to fill in? There are 10 other teammates out there!

I gazed out my tent flap over the Altai Valley, the same valley that Marco Polo traveled on his historic crossing of Europe to China. The sun was setting. Thunder and lightning rattled the skies. Avoiding eye contact with Craig, I watched the violent storm, rolled over in my sleeping bag and continued my gaze through the tent flap into the gray-black sky. A cold wind shook the tent.

"Ok, Bob, I get the picture. I will think about what you said."

The next morning, Roskelley made his presence in the sprawling camp known to me, and the wheels were starting to turn in my brain. Did Roskelley ask Bob Craig to be the go between? Or did Craig just ask me on his own? I was reasonably certain Craig had acted on his own, but didn't know. Roskelley broke the ice and blurted what was on his mind. "Kop, let's meet tonight after dinner and talk about the Eiger."

Somehow, one climb that I was so very adamant to NOT attempt, had surfaced in my mind as a possibility. It was crazy, and confusing to me how I could be so steadfast, yet a twist of circumstances was slowly changing my mind. Psychologically, I was being torn in half. I knew the Eiger's grim reputation. Of a hundred men who had climbed it by 1974, nearly 50 had died trying. My dad's words of wisdom came to mind: "Chris, figures don't lie, and liars don't figure." The odds of living through the experience were worse at that time than chances of surviving an Everest attempt. Yet, on the other side of the coin, climbing the Eiger was still considered the Holy Grail of mountaineering—if you survived.

Couldn't I just say "No!" and stick with it? I had a family to take care of, a young wife I missed terribly, and a young daughter. Plans for a new house were on my mind; my building career looked so promising. I had a solid future to look forward to. But my first goal, my written goal, my purpose for living, to climb the Eiger was still embossed in my ice axe and staring me in the face. It haunted me. Was I good enough? I was strong enough physically, but was I mentally strong enough? What about all those strong men who had died trying to climb it? They lost their wives, kids, futures. What was wrong with them to risk everything for a mountain summit? Was I crazy too?

That evening in the Russian mess tent, Roskelley, as usual, didn't mince words. He was true to character, direct and all business. "Kop, let's go to

Switzerland and try the Eiger. You know I'm looking for a partner, and I'd like you to go. You're up for it Kop; I know you are."

"Look John, there's a bit of a problem. I don't have a ticket, and I'm expected home in a week."

"Think it over and let me know in a couple days. You can switch tickets with John Marts. You know you can find a way if you want to."

"I will think it over." Those were the only words I could muster. I crawled out into the icy air and plunged into my own tent and sleeping bag. Later, I woke in a sweat, dreaming that I was on the Second Icefield of the Eigerwand.

Roskelley approached me again on the morning of our departure from Pamir Camp. My decision had taken me through a ping pong game of emotion, but now I was ready. "Yeah, John, count me in; I'm going."

I was committed. I reasoned the decision in four ways. First, I was in the prime of my climbing career physically. Second, John and I were both extremely competitive. If there was an American team that could climb the Eiger, we were it, especially after climbing for more than a month in the Pamirs, all above 15,000 feet. Both of us were extremely acclimated and fit. Third, I knew that climbing the Eiger required total confidence in your rope mate. We had made great climbs together for the past nine years. We were a proven team. Both of us were very confident, not overconfident or arrogant, but positive that we could succeed. The fourth reason was subconscious, yet it may have carried the most power.

When I'd carved my goal into my axe nine years previously, I started memorizing the route up the Eiger, reading everything written about the geology, the men who died, and the men who succeeded, and why they succeeded. When I climbed a mountain, at one point or another, I envisioned the effort as training for the real Eiger. Every mountain I climbed was mentally preparing me for the hardest climb on earth. I knew the route by heart, as did Roskelley, and now we were both prepared mentally to face the reality. Being prepared mentally was 90 percent of the game. We were not two idiots going off to die, as many of our friends envisioned. We were going off to really live at the outer fringes of life, which was within our grasp.

JUST THE TWO OF US

Saying farewell to the ill-fated Pamir Camp was easy. As we traveled down the Altai Valley heading for Osh in army trucks, life appeared so primitive and simple on the barren slopes, much like Marco Polo must have seen, and the hunger for life back home never felt stronger. On arrival in Moscow 24 hours later, I got a phone connection to Seattle. My wife of one year was on the other end of the line when I shouted "Sharon! I'm going to Switzerland for an additional eight days—I'll be home later than planned!"

"What? Who is this?"

The connection was barely audible, so I yelled through the phone for the fear of her not hearing me. There was dead silence for 30 seconds and the thought of the eight dollar a minute toll charge raced through my mind. "I'm going to Switzerland!"

"What? Chris, is that you?"

With the poor connection we had, this was all I could communicate, but I felt her crying over the phone. She knew from talking to John's wife, Joyce, that we would be attempting the Eiger. Somehow, the loved ones at home always must be braver.

Our Pamir teammates gave us a "Last Supper" feast at a local Moscow restaurant, complete with some poetic songs of fate about the Eiger. Everyone had had enough of war games and death at this juncture, and we shook hands for the last time and bade farewell.

Roskelley and I arrived in Zurich and optimistically purchased round-trip train tickets to the Bernese Oberland. We awoke early the next morning in Grindelwald, a resort town a few miles from the Eiger. Planning for three nights out, we packed carefully and lightly, taking no stove and only lunch-type foods. Since my camera was smaller and lighter, I talked John into leaving his behind; a decision Roskelley would chide me for the rest of my life. We made our way to the train station manager and purchased our tickets to Kleine Scheidegg, the last station, only 1 mile from the Eiger base. We had extra gear, so we purchased a storage locker and placed our bags inside, while the station master read our note: "In the event we do not return, please send these belongings to our wives in Spokane, Washington, United States of America. "We left the home address, carefully printed on each bag with felt pen. The old station master had a reserve key for this locker, and we made sure he understood what our English message said. As he looked at our climbing gear and our youthful faces, his expression went from stern faced to a look of anger and disgust. He knew where we were headed. He had seen this exercise before by other young climbers who never came back. Feeling a bit embarrassed, I knew this would be the look on my father's face too, but I couldn't dwell any longer on my decision to climb. Once on board the train, Roskelley relaxed and puffed a cigar. Suddenly, it was right outside the train window in all its terribleness, the black vertical wall of the Eiger. I didn't dare stare at it too long.

At Kleine Scheidegg, we climbed off the train with all our belongings on our backs and began the 1-mile traverse to the most infamous mountain wall on earth. I was pumped, 100 percent committed, as was John. We'd see if we were the climbers we thought we were. At noon, John and I started upward over fourth-class rock at the base of the wall. I couldn't help noticing all the water pouring down the rock, a taste of things to come. For 500 feet we ascended the edge of the European tectonic plate. The rock had horizontal limestone strata for good hand holds, but I soon demanded the rope. John grumbled but agreed. We climbed 500 feet higher to the base of the first serious obstacle: the Difficult Crack where the horizontal bands end. This is the beginning of technical, vertical climbing. Since water was flowing heavily down the crack, John was forced into gymnastic feats to avoid a drenching. At the end of his lead, he fixed the rope with a piton and climbed up. I decided to stay dry by jumaring on the rope up the blank wall to the right. This system worked fine for 40 feet, until I was forced into the ice water.

I was semi-drenched as we made three more leads up on mixed terrain to a series of narrow, horizontal ledges beneath the Rote Fluh, a huge, slightly overhanging blank wall of compact limestone. This was the start of the infamous Hinterstoisser Traverse, so named for the first man who found the way across to seemly easier rock on the far side. The first six men who made this traverse were unable to come back across it, so it was essentially, a "no-reverse traverse." To me, it looked worse in person than any of the photographs I had seen of this section, and it remains in my mind as the single, hardest section of the Eiger.

Roskelley fixed our rope to a couple of ancient ring pegs and pounded in a good one of our own for a solid anchor as he began the traverse out onto the black, polished rock. Water poured down on him and his rucksack. The scene from my perch on a ledge was incredible as I watched John traverse slightly down and out of sight for a 160-foot rope length on what appeared to have absolutely nothing for holds. After 20 minutes I heard a faint "Belay On!" through the constant roar of the water pouring from above. I had double duty, climbing second on the rope while carrying most of the food and extra gear in my rucksack. Water streamed over the black rock and the rounded holds were just small wrinkles which only got smaller as I gained a foot at a time. Ice water was now finding its way down my back through my "waterproof" anorak. Stories of the Eiger pioneers raced through my mind as it became apparent why the wall had claimed so many lives. I gripped with all the strength I could and focused my mind into the tips of my fingers and toes. It was like trying to cling to a vertical, polished marble tabletop. Inch by inch, and foot by foot I gained ground with an abyss of 2,000 feet below my boots.

"Hurry up Redneck!" Roskelley screamed, providing a flicker of warmth in the frightful surroundings. When I reached the ledge John was clinging to, I grasped onto a big hold in the rock and knew we were now committed to climb the remainder of the wall. There could be no retreat across this traverse.

From a small ledge at the base of a chimney, John led straight up for a full rope length and soon shouted down that he had reached the Swallow's Nest, a favorite and historical bivouac site. My elation was short lived, for when I reached the nest I found water dripping heavily on the only decent sleeping place. John was crouched off to the left, on a small, down-sloping patch of ice only a few feet from the First Icefield. "Welcome to the Swallow's Nest annex," Roskelley said.

The weather, which had been unstable throughout the day, turned to a gray drizzle over our first bivouac site. As the daylight gradually dissipated to blackness, the rain grew heavier; the run-off from the First Icefield increased to a torrent. Flurries of falling stones began to buzz overhead. Nothing was said. We both kept our thoughts to ourselves. This was a terrifying place, and we still had 4,000 feet of sheer wall above us to climb. The rain stopped after a few hours and we settled in for a somewhat restful night in our semi-crouched position on down-sloped ice.

By daybreak we were numb and more than ready to move, but with much apprehension. We strapped on crampons for the ascent of the First Icefield. The first lead ended at a treacherous spot on 55-degree ice with stones buzzing down around us. Up went John again on front points, using his axe and hammer. Lifting my eyes from under my helmet, I watched as he reached the base of the Ice Hose, which had melted away to become more like a water hose! I made my way to the belay and the security of its overhanging rock just as another barrage of rocks crashed down from above.

"Where to from here?" I called out. The Ice Hose was definitely out of condition, and I was surprised to see that it was nearly vertical. From descriptions, I had supposed it to be only 60 degrees. John led up carefully, so as not to dislodge any more stones than were already falling. Some were the size of pumpkins. After 40 feet, climbing up and over a difficult overhang, he was out of sight. Then I heard a buzz coming from high above and a loud CRAACK!

"Roskelley! What's going on?"

He answered in a frenzy: "A rock just hit my helmet!" John hinted later on that at this point he was ready to rappel and retreat. But retreat was impossible. We simply did not have enough rappel anchors to descend.

The three long rope leads that followed were straight up over intensely difficult terrain with shingle-type, down-sloping layered rock. Water ran everywhere. At the base of the famous Second Icefield we continued with three more leads straight up the black ice to the bergschrund and safety from falling rock. Except for the distant whir of stones, the face once again appeared peaceful. We relaxed for a few minutes and could hear the cowbells ringing far below. The scene was surreal. We were fighting for our lives while thousands of feet below children were herding cows.

The next stretch of ascent became somewhat enjoyable as we traversed four full leads across the top of the Second Icefield to the cliff below the Flatiron. Three leads of moderate climbing led to the notorious Death Bivouac where the first two men who tried to climb the Eiger froze to death. We paused here for a much-needed rest and ate a late lunch. Off to the left lay the Third Icefield, the steep passage to the Ramp. As we climbed out onto the ice, a barrage of stones shot past.

"We gotta move fast, Kop."

"I'm going as fast as I can!"

With the aid of picks and front points, we reached the safety of the Ramp where the worst of the stonefall ended. The Ramp is a chimney system completely protected from the falling stones and water, and it felt solid and safe underfoot as we quickly moved up 450 feet. The chimney narrows eventually to a crack splitting the face above. We figured that would be the crux of the climb.

At the top of the Ramp we sat on a two-foot wide ledge beneath the crack, which had water pouring down it. The only route was straight up the waterfall.

"John! The waterfall is too dangerous and icy to climb tonight. Let's bivi here and climb this in the morning! We'll be drenched and frozen to the bone if we continue."

Before I could finish that thought, Roskelley was already climbing the waterfall crack.

"No way, Chris!" he yelled down to me. "We got to climb this pitch tonight!"

After just a few minutes he was soaked to the skin. I watched as the ice water poured down his legs and gushed into his boots. His toes had been severely frostbitten only a year previously while climbing Dhaulagiri in Nepal, but he didn't say a word as he slowly progressed. I knew the pain was excruciating, but finally he mantled onto the ledge at the lip of the waterfall and I heard a low, agonized "I'm up Kop, get ready."

I stripped off my semi-dry clothing and stuffed it into my rucksack. Glancing downward far below, the clouds were gathering and the sun setting, coloring the horizon with brilliant pinks and oranges. I heard the clang of a cowbell and the bark of a dog drifting up from an invisible pasture, and I was flooded with peace. Turning my gaze upward to the overhanging waterfall, however, brought me back to reality. Moving off the exposed stance, I shivered in the freezing air and ascended as fast as the jumars would bite into the rope. Removing the pitons plunged me into frustration as I became drenched in ice water.

John was sitting on a ledge 3 feet by 6 feet with his boots off when I arrived. "How are your feet, man?" he asked.

"They're wet but okay. My hands are still numb."

We sat watching the sparkling lights of Grindelwald a mile below us, and the lights of several other small villages in the Bernese Oberland. We felt fortunate to have stable weather for the evening. Nevertheless, we endured a miserable night clinging to the cliffside and shivering to keep warm. Every piece of clothing we had was soaked.

At the break of dawn we prepared our wet gear and tried to warm our hands for what we hoped would be our final hours on the North Face. John led out to the left, and then went straight up verglas-covered rock. He had to continually blow on his hands, and I realized that the pace was agonizingly slow. Fifteen feet above me he came to a short, overhanging section. With infinite delicacy and poise he crawled upward and over. On a small stance just above this, he strapped on his crampons. When 50 feet of rope was out, it stopped, played out a few more feet, and then dribbled back into my lap.

"Chris! I have to take off my pack! I'll tie my pack to the wall, and you will have to carry both sacks up when you reach here." That wasn't good news, as my strength was eroding from being two nights out without sleep. Twenty minutes passed before I finally heard, "Belay off." John had made it past the frozen waterfall known as the Ice Bulge through the most difficult ice climbing on the Eigerwand. Mustering all my remaining strength, I thrutched and wriggled my way up the ice pitch carrying both packs. Just below John I shamelessly went hand over hand up the rope to the stance.

"Let's move man; time's a wasting!" he said.

"What do you think I've been trying to do?" I shot back.

Steep ice, alternating with belts of bad rock finally brought us to the beginning of the fabled Traverse of the Gods. Although scary with 5,000 feet of air below our boots, our minds had adjusted to the vertical environment and the traverse seemed technically easier than the climbing we had completed. After three lengths of rope, we reached the White Spider, the icefield that catches all the frequent avalanches from above that sweep the upper mountain face. Luckily, the weather was holding so we had no problem ascending this icefield in two rope lengths.

Above the spider, we traversed up and left into the first Exit Cracks. Roskelley moved cautiously up these cracks and overhangs, with much deliberation and delicate climbing for both of us. It was like a tap dance up vertical rock, but now we could smell the summit and what was left of our adrenalin began to surge. We reached a small, finger-like projection called the Pedestal. Securing our own rope, and hooking into an old rope, we rappelled to the base of a wide chimney. We followed this vertical chimney for 400 feet, and then the angle eased off from vertical to about 60-degree ice. We ascended three more rope lengths on ice-covered, down-sloping rock to the summit icefield.

The North Face of the Eiger was all below our feet now, and we climbed the last hundred feet and stood victoriously on the summit of our long-sought goal. John and I shook hands and unleashed huge smiles of relief. I felt the summit ice was melting under our boots from the glow of our pride and accomplishment. The first American team to climb the mountaineers' Holy Grail was comprised of two dreamers from a town in Eastern Washington who didn't have a mountain of consequence on the horizon.

REGRETTABLE DECISIONS

However, the Eiger was not giving up its soul that easily. In the game of mountaineering, only the round trip counts, and we still had to climb down. The sun was very low on the horizon when we started our descent. The West Ridge, the standard route of ascent, is a difficult climb in itself as route finding can be difficult through steep gullies, steep rock ledges and short ice fields. In 1969 I had climbed this route with a vagabond climber I befriended in the climbers' camp near Kleine Scheidegg, and found the route very demanding the entire way. Now, with the waning light of day, exhaustion was taking its toll on both of us. We had been climbing steadily for two and a half days with two miserable, freezing bivouacs. We descended for a couple hundred feet, and then the rocky route ended in a steep ice gulley that fell off the face to the south. Here I made a colossal mistake. In an imperious decision I yelled, "John, take off the rope! I climbed this route five years ago and know the entire way down from here!"

"Chris, are you crazy! We should keep it on for safety! We're both tired, man!"

"No! Goddammit John! Take off the rope! We can climb down twice as fast un-belayed and be in Kleine Scheidegg in four or five hours drinking beer!"

I was adamant and untied my figure of eight knot, unhooked the steel carabiner attached to my swami belt and threw the rope down. I knew that 90 percent of mountaineering accidents occur on the descent of the mountain, not the ascent, but my mind was made up. After all, I had just climbed the Eiger North Face! My arrogance surged and I felt that I was one of the greatest mountaineers alive. I was invincible.

Roskelley, still bewildered at my actions slowly began to untie the rope from his swami belt. After the rope was coiled, John graciously placed the five-pound rope on his rucksack and we continued our climb down the ice and rock spine of the West Ridge. All went well for the next couple hundred feet until we came to another ice gulley that split the ridge from the south face. We had to down climb the steep ice for a hundred feet or so, then begin our traverse over some shattered ledges to gain the ridge crest again. With Roskelley below me, I barked orders like a commando chief when I felt he was off the route of descent as I knew it.

"John, go to your right now; you're going down too far!"

I stood on the ice slope with my face planted into the mountain and the front points of my crampons firmly sticking into the hard black ice. My right hand clutched the bamboo shaft of my prized 70 centimeter custom Chouinard ice axe. I had a one-inch safety loop of nylon attached around my wrist that was also tied to the shaft of the adze of my axe. All was well, we were descending as I'd envisioned when I looked down again and saw Roskelley still descending.

"John, you're going too low!"

As I twisted my tired legs slightly to my left to look straight down at him, my left leg collapsed under me. There didn't seem to be any communication from my brain to my leg. I failed to comprehend that the electrolytes in my bloodstream, and my adrenalin were expended. My brain commands weren't transmitting to my muscles. I wheeled around violently to grab my ice axe firmly with my left hand, and to my horror, gravity had pulled me down so quickly that I couldn't grab the shaft, and the full weight of my body and pack went on my right arm and wrist. I commanded my hand to grip but, like my collapsed leg, the grip was so weakened from the climb that my hand slipped down the ice axe shaft in a split second and I began to fall down the ice slope looking at my ice axe still firmly embedded into the ice above!

This was it! God, what a fool. What a complete fool. Here I was falling down the West Buttress of the Eiger with no ice axe, no rope, not a prayer of hope. In a matter of a second, I flew by Roskelley who was helpless to save me, and in a couple more seconds I was skidding at what seemed like 60 miles per hour. The slope I was sliding down was probably 40 degrees of compact ice that terminated hundreds of feet below me at a 1,000-foot sheer cliff that dropped onto the glacier. The cliff below was coming up fast.

I cursed my terminal decision. "You stupid ass; you stupid arrogant ass," I thought as I dug my fingers, toes, legs, and arms in a spread eagle to get as much body friction as possible onto the mountain. Luck turned a cold shoulder as I bounced over a 30-foot cliff and went airborne over the ice slope below. I wasn't finding much friction while flying, and another 30-foot cliff zooming at my feet. Whoosh! I was airborne again.

Somehow, during both flights, I managed to not tumble. If I had started cartwheeling I would certainly be another Eiger death statistic. Maybe there would be asterisks behind my name as I had actually climbed the North Face, only to die descending. My mind snapped into crystal clearness, and with all my determination I spread my body like a flattened roadkill against the ice. I had slid hundreds of feet and could see the cliff rapidly approaching below my feet, maybe only a hundred feet away. Another small cliff propelled me airborne and again and I landed butt first. One smaller cliff remained between me and oblivion. Whoosh! I was flying again, but somehow I managed to keep looking down, not tumbling and came crashing straight down on my ass with my pack between my butt and the rocks. I had stopped! I was sitting still. Motionless, I sat frozen in place not moving an eyelash, staring in shock at the cliff below me and certain death. I sat in disbelief for a few surreal seconds frozen in place. I was still alive. I looked down at my right leg and my crampon strap was wrapped around my knee. My right ankle began to flood with pain. My hands were bloodied with the flesh ripped into serrated semicircular tears on both palms from the struggle against the unplanned descent.

"Chris!"

I heard Roskelley yelling, from far above me now. I tried to stand up, but the pain in my ankle was so severe that I couldn't put any pressure on the leg.

The swelling in my ankle forced me to open the laces entirely to keep the boot on my foot.

The sun had dropped below the horizon as I started crawling upward, then eventually hopping on one leg, placing my right knee into the ice for whatever grip I could manage. Slowly, more determined than ever, I crawled my way hundreds of feet back up. Meanwhile, Roskelley had grabbed my ice axe and descended to meet me halfway, where he stared at me in disbelief. All the way I cursed myself unmercifully a million times for my foolish, arrogant mistake, and vowed a million times over never to make the same mistake again, if I survived this one. My ankle and leg were useless. We would spend another cold night out on the Eiger. No beer tonight!

The next morning, before dawn, we began our descent with the rope tied around me. I hopped and climbed down the entire way on one leg, using my right knee for support. The final 2,000 foot descent wasn't easy, but we made it to the pastures below and passed by a few incredibly clean jersey cows. There were only a few people up when we made it to the station where a milkman in a horse-drawn wagon greeted us. We took the first train to Grindelwald, and from there we boarded the trains to Zurich and slept in the airport to await our flight home in the morning.

Roskelley and I went home to our wives and families. We came, we saw, and we conquered, virtually unnoticed. The Eiger had spared my life, barely. I went to the hospital to have my ankle examined. Soon the doctor came in and said, "OK Chris, which one is it that's bothering you?" as he held up the x-ray showing nine fractures. It was one more image to add to the 40 photos I snapped during the climb. Roskelley was unhappy with me for years because I'd insisted that we take only my camera on the Eiger to save weight. Maybe he imagined that he was fast enough to capture an action shot of me flying past him.

I needed a couple years to gain back full strength in my right ankle, and to recover mentally from the expeditions of 1974, but as I slowly regained form after achieving my goal, my second major goal, Everest, began to enter my mind.

John Roskelley on top of the Eiger.

Sixteen

DENALI: THE GREAT ONE

Rich Landers on the West Buttress of Denali, Mount Foraker in the distance.

AFTER CLIMBING THE NORTH FACE of the Eiger in 1974, my first major mountaineering goal was under my belt and I made a conscious decision to take a fork in the trail out of expedition climbing for a few years. Marriage and family life agreed with me, and I gratefully went back to work in my father's construction company. Life was good, as long as I could bring home a steady paycheck. However, I never stopped thinking about the mountains. K2 and Everest were familiar images in my dreams.

Climbing workouts were limited to sessions at Minnehaha Rocks along the Spokane River one or two nights a week, and weekend summer climbs in Canada. John Roskelley, my main climbing partner, had become a full-time professional mountaineer. His financial situation seemed much better than mine, as his wife was a full-time schoolteacher. I was jealous of his freedom to train and go climbing whenever he wished, but the grass always looks greener across the street. The thought of making a profession in climbing crossed my mind. On the other hand, a USA climber accomplishing a newsworthy pioneer ascent could count on sponsorship for clothing, technical gear, and perhaps an airline ticket, but that's about it. Unless you climbed Everest, no one had a clue who you were. The public didn't know much about any other mountain.

Another alternative for making money in the mountains was to become a guide on Mount Rainier and yo-yo the route over and over with novices. Guides could earn a decent living as long as they stayed physically and mentally healthy. I had no patience with myself, let alone tolerance to be a guide responsible for others.

Finding new climbing partners was a challenge, but over time I managed to connect with a boyhood friend, Gwain Oka, a high school friend, David Coombs, and later with Gary Silver, Kim Momb, and Jim States, a medical intern working at Deaconess Hospital. And I could always depend upon my longtime friend, Joe Collins, when attempting a less technical route. Joe was the best. All of these men were excellent companions and experienced mountaineers, so we became "weekend warriors," attacking all the mountain ranges within 500 miles.

K2 REJECTION

In 1976, word spread in the American alpine community that Jim Whittaker, the first American to summit Everest, was forming a team to climb K2. I desperately wanted to go, maybe too much. I tried calling Whittaker, writing a letter and calling again, all to no avail. I met Whittaker in 1974 at Pete Schoening's home before the Pamir expedition, and we didn't click. I finally received a rejection letter from Whittaker which was a huge blow to my ego. I was not going to K2.

About the same time, I heard from friends that Dane Burns of Coeur d'Alene, Idaho, was organizing an expedition to climb three peaks starting with the North Face of Mount Hunter, then Mount Huntington, and then Mount McKinley—during the same trip! I thought he was a dreamer. To climb any one of these peaks was a major commitment, but to try all three in the same expedition was insane. Burns called and invited me to go along with him, Oka, Momb and Dan Schnell. I knew everyone on the team except Schnell, but Burns assured me that Schnell was the strongest of all. I didn't hesitate to tell Burns that he was nuts. I said I would like to go, but I suggested concentrating on attempting just one peak. Burns was undaunted by my skepticism.

Denali, the highest peak in North America, (most climbers at the time already referred to McKinley by its local Athabaskan Indian name) was always on my short list of peaks to attempt, so I agreed to go on the condition that I would team up with one of the individuals on the team to attempt Denali. Among the world's greatest mountains, Denali had the most colorful history including attempts and failures by sourdoughs, sled doggers, and the first ascent of the high point, the south peak, by the son of a trapper. I didn't know Burns well, but I was friends with Momb and Oka and figured one of them would be well enough after whatever they had climbed to attempt Denali. Schnell came over to meet me at my house, and my first impression was that this man was Spokane's own Sir Edmund Hillary. At 6 foot 5, with the muscles to match his lanky frame, I figured if he couldn't climb it, then I couldn't either.

With the team in place, we began final preparations with gear and food in the spring of 1978. Burns and Momb left in the first week of June to attempt the first two peaks. Schnell and I continued to package all the necessary food, gear, and hardware at my centrally located home on 18th Avenue. Just a few days before we were to leave at the end of June, Oka had to cancel, leaving me to take a huge gamble. I had no familiarity with Schnell's capabilities and temperament, yet I was heading into a major expedition with him.

One afternoon several days before Schnell and I were to depart for Anchorage, I saw a man coming down the street toward my home on a motorcycle. It was Dane Burns! I was tongue-tied and thought I was hallucinating. Burns was supposed to be ascending Mount Hunter or Mount Huntington at that time, but there he was right before my eyes. He was disheveled, unshaven, and in obvious stress. His eyes were wild with excitement, and he started talking like a wound-up chatter box.

"Chris, the mountains are totally out of shape, too much snow, too much avalanche danger!" he said, blurting out one dire warning after another.

I listened dumbfounded to the rant about the terrible mountain conditions. Burns had clearly underestimated the scale of the Alaska wilderness. He was a basket case.

"Where is Kim Momb?" I asked. The answer was even harder to believe. Burns had left Momb on the Kahiltna Glacier to fend for himself. Burns had flown out with the first available bush pilot, leaving Momb to sit there all alone waiting for another plane. My morale puddled in my shoes as I watched Burns ride off. Schnell was just as stunned when I called to fill him in, but he agreed to go ahead with the expedition. It was now two against Denali.

Dan Schnell on the North Face of Mount Assiniboine, Alberta, Canada.

TALKEETNA

Talkeetna in 1978 was a fairly typical wild Alaskan village where the year-round population equaled one mouthful of teeth. True Alaskans, independent free spirits, lived here, and many of them lived in huts without electric power.

However, this berg some 100 miles from Anchorage had a notable distinction. On the opposite end of the human rainbow from the moss feet, the finest bush pilots in the world called Talkeetna home. This was the staging place for Denali expeditions from the south, and all the mountaineers hired professional bush pilots from Talkeetna. Don Sheldon was the most famous of a continuous string of great flyers. Cliff Hudson, Kitty Banner, and Doug Geeting were all flying out of Talkeetna when Dan Schnell and I got off the state-operated train station in Talkeetna to begin our adventure. We pitched our two-man tent right in front of our pilot's log home on the airstrip.

There was little to see on main street. A boardwalk, the hardware store, a tavern, and a couple of houses. When you walked to the end of the street, you were looking at a river. One local fisherman told us, "Don't go down to the river's edge without a fuckin' gun," as the salmon were running, luring in the bears. The hubs of occasional activity were the airport and train station. Only a few cars drove down the dirt streets.

Unfortunately for Schnell and me, the weather was socked in and foggy and planes were grounded. We had to wait a full seven days wandering around trying to keep from going nuts. We hung out in the one tavern, which had a sign "Hippies use side entrance." The wooden building had no side door. With nearly 21 hours of daylight, the pool games would last all night. Here we met Ray Genet, the most famous mountain guide on Denali. His nickname was "The Pirate," and based upon word of mouth in the village, he owed everyone money. Genet was a wild-eyed man with a jet-black beard. He commanded a striking presence of authority when you talked climbing. He was the most successful guide on Denali, and he knew the mountain better than the ravens that catch updrafts to soar over the upper slopes.

Our pilot was Kitty Banner. She owned a cabin next to the airport with a huge stack of uncut wood that Dan and I volunteered to split for her just to keep active. We spent a good three days splitting wood that probably lasted for several winters. Finally, we got a report that the weather was going to clear, and we should be able to fly out in the morning.

It's difficult to describe Denali even after you have seen it with your own eyes. The view from the north side near Fairbanks displays the Wickersham Wall, one of three highest mountain escarpments in the world. The mountain rises from the plains at 1,000 feet above sea level to the highest elevation in North America in one long graceful vision of shimmering white crystalline ice and granite, set against the cobalt Alaskan sky. From the southern side of the mountain the foothills rise from meandering salmon-filled streams and rivers through the forest and tundra of the McKinley Range. The undulating hills rise dramatically into jagged glacier-draped peaks of 15,000 to 17,000 feet. Set behind the huge granite and ice spires of Mount Foraker, Mount Huntington, and Mount Hunter, Denali dwarfs its impressive neighbors and reigns supreme. My first thought was a scientific question. How could this earth produce such a huge block of granite? The entire range was granite, not sedimentary or metamorphic rock. As you stare at the upper reaches of the peak, the vertical rise can trick your brain into thinking you are looking at high altitude clouds.

The elevation of Denali was measured at 20,320 in 1953, but US Geological Survey climbers re-measured the peak using GPS and other instruments in June 2015. Later that summer, on Sept. 2, the agency revised the elevation 10 feet lower to 20,310 feet. The announcement came on the same day President Barack Obama officially renamed Mount McKinley as Denali to reflect its cultural history. Most climbers, including me, had long referred to the peak as Denali rather than the name a prospector dubbed on the mountain to promote his favorite candidate in the presidential election. William McKinley was later elected the 25th president of the United States. Denali, in the native language, means "The Great One, " and that's no exaggeration.

Schnell and I first saw Denali as the clouds parted while we flew out of Talkeetna. I had never seen any landform that was more inspiring and beautiful. Schnell was fiddling around with his gear and had his back turned to the view ahead. I told him to turn around and take a look. His long wide-eyed stare spoke volumes.

Confused at first, and at the same time amazed at what he was seeing, Schnell said, "Chris, are those clouds, or is that the mountains?" I affirmed that he was looking at one of the greatest mountain scenes on earth.

"Is that Mount Hunter in the foreground?"

"Yes," I replied.

"I am going to kill Dane Burns; I have no business trying to climb that mountain, let alone the North Face."

Right there I knew I had a solid partner to climb Denali. Schnell knew his limitations and wasn't embarrassed to say so. Ahead of us was one of the most inspiring mountain ranges in the world, and Dan was unashamed to voice his fears and apprehension. He had already proven to be a solid mountaineer of high character, and I now felt confident of success.

Banner flew us between two granite spires and then descended into the huge Kahiltna Glacier and the ice landing strip. We stepped out of the plane near several tents of climbers from all over the world. Noticeably perched high on an ice hump, in full view of everyone, was the toilet, sitting directly over a small crevasse in the rather flat glacier.

A woman walked over to the plane and gave us a big hug and welcome. Her name was Francis, known as the "Queen of the Kahiltna," and her reputation of hospitality preceded her. Francis welcomed every climber that evening by playing her violin. She was famous in Alaskan mountaineering circles, friendly and self-effacing, and had a small evergreen tree set solidly in the ice in front of her small tent. She was one of six people on the mountain born in Avery, Idaho, and every summer she worked for the bush pilots as the landing strip manager on the ice sheet she called her summer home.

Upon our return three weeks later, she handed us a cold beer. She was one of a kind.

THE CLIMB

The Dynamic Duo Denali Expedition was underway, and we pulled our plastic sleds loaded with more than a hundred pounds of food up the Kahiltna. Striding on skis with skins, we sweated copiously to gain elevation. Youth was on our side, and after 12 hard miles of uphill drudgery, we were viewing most of the Kahiltna Glacier and the Alaskan Range below us from 10,000 feet.

There is a saddle at the base of the long west ridge, and when you crest the high point the view opens up to the expanse of the plains to the north. In the saddle, we dug a four-foot deep hole in the ice to put four days worth of emergency food for our return down the glacier. We buried the food deep to protect it from ravens notorious for flying up the slopes of an icy-white world to steal food from climbers. (When we returned, I was astounded to find the ravens had dug down 4 feet into the ice with their beaks and feet to reach the top layer of our cache!)

From the saddle at the upper reaches of the 35-mile-long Kahiltna Glacier, the route turns 90 degrees east and up. We reached another pass called Windy Corner. and then at the end of four hard days of pulling sleds we arrived at the

14,000-foot level basin below the west face. We pitched our tent in time to be treated to the first big snowstorm of the trip. In one night the clouds dumped 7 feet of snow. In the morning, after shoveling all night, the top of our dome tent was below the surface level of the snow in the basin.

We cached the sleds at this campsite and loaded gear into our packs. Our plan was to make one carry to establish another campsite at 17,000 feet before continuing up the West Buttress route to the summit.

We headed up with only 10 days of food remaining for the final assault. The seven days of food we'd consumed while waiting in Talkeetna wasn't with us on the mountain. We lacked extra supplies for the fairly common hitch of getting pinned down by a storm. We didn't have the luxury to take rest days, even though the packs biting into our shoulders weighed about 100 pounds apiece.

The slopes to gain the West Buttress are moderately technical with some exposed and steep places, but overall it's a straightforward climb to gain the ridge above. We had the benefit of using fixed ropes placed by the Denali guides while ascending the 2,000-foot headwall to where we crested the West Buttress and straddled a knife-edge of rock and ice. From here the West Buttress delivered a surreal feeling of floating between heaven and earth as we climbed another thousand feet to the campsite above. The weather was brilliantly clear and on both sides of the buttress the granite and ice fell steeply away to form the glaciers that continued to sculpt the mountain. Glaciers on the northern side of the ridge cascaded steeply down to the flat savanna north toward Fairbanks, offering a striking view of the serenity on the plains below.

The altitude began taking effect. In bitter subzero temperatures, we struggled with our heavy loads to reach the icy platform for our planned Camp Four. Clouds were moving in with fog and high winds, but we lucked out and found an abandoned ice cave with a banquet-size living space for cooking, sleeping and waiting out the weather. Snug inside the ice cave with the wind tearing at the mountain outside, we huddled for three full days, diminishing our food supply to seven days.

During the height of the storm, we were awakened by a voice. "Chris, listen; what is it?" Dan said.

A woman was singing, and not just any glee-club wannabe, but someone with an operatic voice that resonated through the thick ice walls. Genet and his six clients had pushed through the gale and were pitching their tents. One of the clients was a ballet dancer and singer from New York. Above 17,000 feet, she impressed us with her pipes as she sang Beethoven's Ode to Joy in German—an angelic respite in the storm.

As the weather broke, the high cirrus clouds and sun rainbow told me the storm wasn't over. We quickly packed and climbed under the load of the heavy packs to a headwall and ice ramp leading toward a platform for another camp at 18,000 feet. We wanted to get one step closer for the final summit push. The calm spell was brief and soon the wind began to howl and tear into all that was living and dead.

The Crux

Viewing Denali from the south, the western shoulder of the mountain forms a broad expanse of ice between the main summit and the north summit. This saddle between these two summits was to be our final campsite. It was just 2,000 vertical feet below the summit but more than seven miles across the open shoulder. The climb to the summit was not technical from there, so ropes, ice pitons, and climbing hardware—everything other than ice axes—were not needed.

The wind raged again as the sun sank lower in the sky. The shoulder was totally exposed to weather from any direction, and our tent was not designed to hold up in 70-mile-per-hour gusts. The only viable option for shelter was to dig an ice cave as deep as possible into the slope.

We climbed over to a corniced area on the granite ridge and began chipping away and digging with ice axes, a shovel, and our mittened hands. In an hour of hard labor we had carved only a few feet into snow that had been wind-compacted to the density of cheap concrete. We fruitlessly searched for other locations, finding nothing but wind-scoured ice. Soft snow for digging a shelter was as scarce as warmth.

With evening upon us, going back down the headwall was out of the question. It was a couple weeks past the summer solstice, and Denali is only a few degrees from the Arctic circle, so the sun set for only 30 minutes before resurfacing. At that low angle near the horizon the sun provided light but little warmth. The temperature was 25 degrees below zero, which is fairly tolerable when it's not turbo-charged by a ferocious wind. A couple more hours of hacking to get a small cave started was all but futile. The deeper into the slope we dug, the harder the ice. Swings with our puny ice axes sometimes made little more than a scratch. Instead of going deep into the slope, we had to enter the cave entrance and angle horizontally. After many hours, we had the bare minimum shelter for survival—an opening into a cave just large enough for two climbers to lie down out of the wind. The shelter was about 3 feet wide, 2 feet high, and 7 feet long. Flat on our backs inside, the ice roof was only inches above our faces. Dan, the tall one, crawled into the cave with his head toward the outside. Five inches shorter at nearly six feet tall, I crawled into the cave with my head toward the far end where there was no opening. Faced with an immediate problem for fresh air, I used an ice screw to bore a small breathing hole through the ice directly above my face. The solution for the next major problem wasn't so simple.

I had never experienced claustrophobia. Nothing I'd heard or read about the human psychological condition prepared me for cramming my body and mind into an icy tomb. Dan was just as miserable, too. We barely had enough room to start the cooker and melt ice for tea. Bivouacking high on glaciered peaks is rarely a pleasant recourse, but this was the worst of the worst overnights in my mountain experience. Even though we were fully clothed, including down parkas, inside our sleeping bags for maximum warmth, the unabated winds invaded every crack into our cave to chill us to the bone. We tossed, turned, groaned and moaned through the night vainly trying to maintain body core temperatures.

I was on a journey from unbridled confidence toward discovering my mortality. We were slowly freezing to death.

In a mad flash, I awoke from a brief doze disoriented, scared and unaware of where I was. My lungs were screaming for oxygen. Cheyne-Stokes breathing had blindsided me. At high elevation, the body works overtime to produce more red cells. Breathing becomes accelerated and laborious one moment, then relaxed and slow as the mind tries to convince the body it's still at sea level. In a sudden panic over suffocating inside an icy pipe, I sat up with a lurch, shoving my head and shoulders through a foot of hard snow and ice and popped out like a ground hog into the full force of the weather. The blistering wind slapped my face and brought me to my senses, but the damage was done. I had opened a gaping hole in the end of the cave rendering it useless as shelter. I sat blinded by spindrift and doing mental gymnastics trying to decide what to do next as my upper torso was exposed to the brunt of the storm. I had to make a quick decision. It had to be the right one.

The ice pipe could shelter only one man now, and I had no choice but to layer up with my remaining clothes as quickly as possible and try to find Genet's tent about a quarter mile away through the storm on the ice shoulder. In a brief visit the previous day, Genet had mentioned he would have room in his big dome tent in case of emergency. Genet's reputation as "The Pirate" may have been true in the village, but on the mountain, we found him to be a gracious man.

I yelled at Dan through the wind and told him I was going to take all my gear and try to make it over to Genet's campsite. I had no compass bearing and started out blindly in the whiteout. Fortunately, the winds parted the fog temporarily so I could occasionally glimpse Genet's tent. This was going to be a one-way journey. The gale was quickly erasing my tracks with spindrift ice. Occasionally, I would lose sight of the tent, but I could orient through the fog to the noise of flapping fabric. A quarter mile never seemed so far, but finally I was standing outside the tent like a zombie in a Gumby suit.

'JUST A BREEZE'

Ray Genet, a legendary climber in Alaskan circles, had climbed Denali more than 30 times to the summit, one of those climbs being in the middle of winter with a reported wind-chill temperature of 148 degrees below zero Fahrenheit. When I yelled, "Hello Ray" and opened the zipper, Genet was awake, and stared with his black eyes and black beard as though he had been expecting me. Earlier, I had conversed with Ray about being in death storms in the USSR Pamir Expedition, the Alps, and Canada. Genet was unimpressed and assured me that Denali storms are in a league of their own.

"This is a horrible storm!" I blurted.

"This is just a breeze," Genet said.

"What do you mean by that? It's a gale out here at 25 below zero! It snowed 7 feet in just one night down there!

Genet said again, "This is just a breeze."

I came back in 1983 to climb Denali with Spokane outdoor writer Rich Landers and survived a real wind and snowstorm that swept Landers and his 40-pound pack off his feet and slammed him onto the ground and into an ice-axe arrest at Windy Corner. That moment enlightened me to what Genet meant. The winds on Denali gust to more than 100 miles per hour, enough force to blow you off into space.

Genet did not have to let me inside the tent, but he did, and for the next four hours I rested with his six clients and slept in a half sitting position. With the storm showing no sign of losing steam, I offered to buy any extra food Genet had so Schnell and I could get a meal before going down, as we were down to our last crackers and cheese.

About 8 a.m., the wind faded and became tolerable. I got out of the tent and scrambled back to Dan's precarious bivouac. The wind and blowing spindrift had erased most evidence of the cave except for a small hole. Peering inside, I saw Schnell's face, weather-beaten and stressed, but in answer to my prayers, he was still alive.

We staggered back to Genet's tent site with our gear and erected our tent. As the wind continued to mellow, we ate a good, hot freeze-dried dinner that replenished our spirits.

About 2 p.m., Genet came outside the tent and stood rigid and in total concentration, perusing the horizon, his body feeling the air temperature and pressure with the sensitivity of a lizard's tongue. He had a sixth sense for the weather on Denali like no other man living or dead.

"You see those clouds over on the Pacific Ocean to the west?" he said to his clients in a commanding voice. "That storm we just went through has blown out to sea and it will be coming back with a vengeance! We have 18 hours of calm, that's it! Let's get hydrated, eat dinner, pack up and leave at 11 tonight for the summit!"

Suddenly, in lieu of retreat, I felt we had a shot. Genet knew the weather patterns here better than professional Alaskan weathermen. We prepared our summit packs, and at 10 in the evening on July 8, we began breaking trail ahead of Genet's group. The final 2,000 feet to the summit was a long slog. Climbers negotiate some ice slopes as they're buoyed with breathtaking views of the Alaska Range below to the south and west with the Pacific Ocean in the distance, and glaciers flowing down 19,000 feet to the north to terminate in the savanna surrounding Fairbanks. According to Genet's portable thermometer, the temperature was 35 below zero, the coldest any of us except Genet had experienced. After several hours, Schnell and I reached Archdeacon Tower, and then climbed the final 1,000 feet from the shoulder to the summit ridge in the even more bitter cold as the sun began its short dip below the northern horizon. Neither of us had ever been so cold, despite wearing seven layers of thermal clothing, including down pants and down jackets. The cold was affecting our movements. Another bivouac would be fatal. But our doubts melted in the chill as we crested the rise and the summit of Denali came into full view directly ahead of us along a friendly ridge. We would make the top!

Although my fingers were nearly frozen, I took one blurry picture of
Dan Schnell kneeling on the summit of Denali placing a small flag.
The temperature was 35 degrees below zero.

We climbed the final few feet to the summit by 3 a.m., July 9, 1978. We were too cold and exhausted for any celebration, other than placing a tiny wand on the tiptop of the south summit and congratulating each other for surviving the storms. I managed to snap one blurry black and white photo of

Schnell kneeling on the summit. My fingers were numb and I was shivering too much to hold the camera still.

ZOMBIE MARCH

As we started down we could see Genet and his clients cresting the summit ridge several hundred yards below us. We climbed down to the group, and Genet explained that his French songbird from New York was very ill with high altitude hypoxia. She was very lethargic, swaying and losing her balance, and nearly losing consciousness. This is a common occurrence at extreme altitude, and combined with the cold, hypoxia can be fatal. Genet approached us and asked us if we would consider taking his client back down the mountain so he could continue to the summit with the rest of his group. Without hesitation, we agreed. That would be the least we could do for his hospitality.

Neither Dan nor I realized the ramifications of the task we just agreed to. The woman, I'll call her Dixie, was nearly comatose from the altitude and cold. She needed to reach a lower altitude as fast as possible, but we had a 7-mile descent across the huge plateau of the western shoulder to get her a couple thousand feet lower. After a few steps, it was obvious that she could not stand upright on her own, so Dan and I locked arms, and with Dixie held up between us, we staggered forward. Schnell and I were in a weakened state anyway, from several nights of no sleep, and diminished further from our all-out summit push, so the addition of carrying a climber took all of our combined strength and fortitude.

We began our march like three drunken zombies in the horror movie "Night of the Living Dead." We sang together, made up fantasy stories, talked to ourselves—anything to keep Dixie awake and on her feet. The only other alternative was to carry her down, which we couldn't physically handle. In the mountaineering history of Denali, a dozen instances had been recorded of descending climbers taking breaks and falling asleep in similar circumstances, and they turned out badly. We were determined not to become another frozen tragedy.

Genet's group reappeared, disjointed and in a weakened state. Some of his clients stumbled past us trying to make it to the high camp. Hour after hour the March of the Three Zombies continued until as though out of a dream the tents appeared below. We crawled into warm bags for a couple hours of needed sleep and temporary safety. Genet arrived and reclaimed his French songbird for the remainder of the journey down the mountain.

In a few hours the wind began to flap the tents. Just as Genet predicted, the storm was upon us again, prompting us to jam gear into our packs and set out wearily on an urgent descent early in the morning of July 10. Going down is infinitely easier with lighter loads, and we descended through the 14,000-foot basin camps to a camping area at 11,000 feet and relative safety from the winds pounding the mountain above.

The final day of descent was done on skis, and when we reached the Kahiltna Glacier landing site, Francis greeted us holding up two cold beers! It was a great moment to be alive.

Words from the Wild

- Find a job you love, and you will never work a day in your life.
- You can't shake hands with a clenched fist.
- Build bridges, then you can cross them for the rest of your life.
- Ninety nine percent of success is showing up 15 minutes ahead of time.
- If you are not prepared, you have prepared to fail.
- A man's nature determines his fate.
- Nature rules.

SEVENTEEN

MAKALU

The West Ridge of Makalu.

THE 2002 AMERICAN ALPINE JOURNAL, an annual report distributed around the globe, included a special tribute to the "World's Most Significant Climbs." The "bible" for history and documentation of world alpinism looked back at the 21st century and chose to commemorate "Ten Significant Climbs of Historic Proportion and Inspiration." The club's editorial panel reviewed thousands of outstanding expeditions and narrowed the list to 10. The Spokane-based 1980 Makalu Expedition made the cut. For that achievement we would never earn a gold medal; no endorsements, and no parade or Wheaties box cover shot. Certainly we didn't solicit such fanfare, however, we are proud to be remembered as four who dared, and succeeded.

To reach maximum athletic expression a mountain climber must be dedicated to climbing hard routes to hone skills and reach top physical strength. It's also important to be consistent in making good decisions to stay alive. When mountain climbers feel close to their physical zenith, they look for the most challenging route up a world-class mountain. Climbing can be as competitive as any sport and as subjective as dancing. For example, a mountain's size isn't what really matters. Few top alpinists would rate Mount Everest as the greatest climb on earth even though it's the tallest. Many mountains have tougher, more demanding, more aesthetic routes to the top.

The base of Makalu, the world's fifth highest mountain, is in Nepal about 15 crow-flying miles from Everest's summit. Composed mostly of hard, crystalline granite and metamorphosed quartzite, it rises from the plains of Tibet to the north with the jungles of Nepal on its southern exposures. Makalu means "The Steep One" in Nepalese, and it rises heavenward in a triangular shaped pyramid to 27,825 feet above sea level. The geology of Makalu compared with the neighboring giants is as unique as its chiseled shape. Everest is composed almost entirely of limestone, a sea deposited sedimentary rock, right up to its 29,035-foot summit. Makalu is a pluton—a huge granite intrusion—making the rock considerably harder to erode by ice, wind, and water. That translates into sharper rock ridges and steeper mountain faces.

Of the 14 peaks in the world taller than 8,000-meters (26,000 feet) Makalu yields the lowest success rates for alpinists attempting to reach the summit. The reasons for failure vary starting with the remoteness of the mountain, which presents logistical problems. From Nepal, climbers must travel a hundred miles on foot and cross 14,000-foot Shipton Pass, then drop into the Arun Valley before starting back up the long and steep route toward the valley's headwall to reach the base camp at 17,000 feet. From Tibet, climbers travel to Lhasa and then via truck to the town of Tigri, where they set out on foot up the long, steep, and brushy valleys.

Makalu's steepness is impressive even to case-hardened mountaineers. The easiest route up this mountain takes great technical skill. I was immediately impressed when I read about Makalu in the book by the French mountaineer Lionel Terray, who made the first ascent. It's a mountain of daunting huge proportions with inviting light-tan colored granite and sculptured ridges. Seductive climbing lines dare climbers to try and reach its pointed summit. To me, it was the perfect mountain—one to dream about—and I placed Makalu on top of my list of peaks to scale.

RECONNAISSANCE

Kathmandu monkey temple.

I met John Roskelley in 1964 and within two years we had immersed ourselves into climbing to the point that we were both talking about someday going to

Makalu. By the end of the '60s, we were going our separate ways, but we never lost touch with the mountains or each other.

In 1978, I was working full time, supporting my family with my construction job, and Roskelley was climbing almost full time, trying to make a living from his passion. But the time was ripe to schedule our first serious attempt to get to the base of Makalu to do a reconnaissance of the long trek into the base and scope out what mountaineers considered to be the greatest ridge climb in the Himalayas, Makalu's West Pillar. Roskelley was climbing Nanda Devi in India that summer, and he planned to go directly to Kathmandu, Nepal, to meet me after his climb. Roskelley and Jim States succeeded in climbing Nanda Devi, but John contracted spinal meningitis on the trip out from the mountain. He had no choice but to fly directly back to Spokane for care. Unfortunately, I had already flown 12,000 miles with my gear prepared for a month-long stay and didn't know of his illness.

I was a sponge in Kathmandu soaking in the culture as I waited for my traveling partner in the world's most picturesque ancient city. I kept checking in with Elizabeth Hawley, an American woman who ran the office of Mountain Travel, looking for any sign of Roskelley there at our designated meeting place. On the third morning, Holly gave me a telegram with a terse message:

"Kop, can't make the trip and had to go home. John."

The words pierced me like a dagger. Roskelley and his telegram left me livid as I imagined what lame excuse he'd have to abandon me. I threw a tantrum nasty enough to frighten Hawley. This was not the first time I had wanted to throttle Roskelley. On the mountain, he's unequaled as a partner, but in life situations he could sometimes be self-absorbed and uncompromising. At great expense, I was halfway around the world from my home, and alone. Continuing a solo trek to Makalu was out of the question. I had heard of too many stories of bandits and the young Maoists, who would kidnap wayward trekkers, some of whom disappeared forever. I gathered my composure and chalked up another bitter life lesson.

I believe people are generally good and a person is more successful if he knows when to trust people. However, when planning a serious expedition into the wilds, you must be prepared to be your own pilot, navigator, porter, cook, dentist, doctor, and Master of your soul. When respect prevails, the chemistry is perfect, and everything goes as planned, an expedition can be a dream trip, but more often than not, things happen.

I moped around Kathmandu in a daze for two long days, riding a rented bicycle through town and chastising myself about getting into this position. Should I try the trek alone? The journey to Makalu entailed more than 200 miles of hiking from the jungles of Nepal, over Shipton Pass, and descending into the Barun Khola. While brooding over this decision, I pedaled to the city's most popular sites, including the Royal Palace, the Swayambhunath or "Monkey Temple" as tourists call it, and the greatest Boudhanath, where Buddha's bones are supposedly entombed in the construction. I also visited the local trade shops. One day I bicycled to the city of Patan, which I found to be far more culturally interesting. The local form of transportation was the rickshaw, a man-pulled type of wheelbarrow. Rickshaws were everywhere in 1978, when Kathmandu and Patan held about 250,000 people. A Nepali man would work slave labor all year to earn the equivalent of $100. The towns were ancient, quaint, romantic, and undisturbed by the modern world. (When I returned in September of 2004, I was stunned to find the Kathmandu Valley holding five million people, all pushed into the city by the political warring of the Chinese Maoists. The city as I first knew it was essentially destroyed, as was much of the old culture.)

After two days of pedaling and deliberation, I concluded a solo trek to Makalu would be too risky. With three weeks left in Nepal, I mulled over the options and bought a bus ticket for Pokhara, the world's ultimate hippie hangout, about 100 miles west of Kathmandu. The main attraction was that it is nestled below two giant Himalayan peaks, Dhaulagiri and Annapurna. I had been mesmerized when reading the book "Annapurna" by Maurice Herzog, and wanted to see and absorb the greatness in both of these 8,000-meter peaks.

Pokhara was far removed from Western culture, which made it a magnet for hippies who didn't share the work ethic instilled in me. Pokhara attracted the rebellious, the wealthy jet set, the spoiled rich brats, the dropouts, and jilted lovers. These utopian, drug-pushing, dope-smoking no-goods, in my estimation, gathered here to profess their ultraliberal political views and whine about everything wrong with the world. The 1960s produced millions of these dropouts. To me, they were the ultimate losers. Thousands of them were in this

Shangri-La of the Himalayas where they could legally stoke up on heroin, hash, and whatever drug they wanted and spread their Western germs to the poor local people without fear of being busted. The cancerous scene was sickening to witness.

I departed Pokhara as fast as I could gather the bread, nuts, and raisins to fuel me through a week or more of trekking into Dhaulagiri and then the Annapurna Sanctuary. I had made the rookie mistake of not bringing tennis shoes, so I trekked the countryside in heavy leather mountain boots, while wearing woolen knickers. I packed my own cooking pots, stove, utensils, and a small tent, plus a huge down parka that I never used. The trails in Nepal are worn from several thousand years of barefoot traffic, and I didn't see any motorized vehicles once I left the village. It was refreshing to get back to what I considered a "natural" setting.

To call it beautiful is an understatement. To the north rose Dhaulagiri and Annapurna to the astounding heights of more than 26,000 feet above sea level. When it was clear, the scene was like looking at heavenly clouds rising from the deep lush green hillsides of Nepal. I trekked between heaven and earth for the next 10 days, going to Ghandrung and Ghorepani Pass at 9,500 feet, then down to the Kali Kandaki River to Tatopani. From the deepest part of the gorge, I went up the river for several miles toward Jomsom, and then turned around to backtrack to Ghorepani Pass. This took two full days, as the drop into the river is one of the deepest gorges in the world. From Ghorepani Pass I found a trail that stayed the same elevation to traverse around the next mountains to the Annapurna Sanctuary. I slept one night beneath the South Face of Annapurna, and then hiked back to Pokhara.

From Pokhara, I took the bus back to Kathmandu, and bought another bus ticket to the small village of Batar Bazar, where I could begin the trek to the Langtang Valley. Taking the bus was the cheapest way to travel, but it was a grueling all-day bus ride over another steep mountain pass, then down thousands of feet to the Lenda Khola Gorge. The bus was crammed with motion sick Nepalese people pushing and shoving me out of the way so they could puke out the open windows. Nepal is a vertical country; the roads wind upward thousands of feet, and then twist and drop for thousands of feet. Every hour or so, the driver would stop at a hairpin turn carved into a cliff, hook up his water hose to established hose bibs, and wash the vomit off the side of his bus. Even while stopped, people could feel queasy just looking up and down at the situation. Many vehicles have driven off these roads while loaded with passengers. The accidents and deaths are acknowledged with little more than a small notice in the newspapers.

From Batar Bazar at the bottom of the valley, I set off on foot for another three days of steady uphill trekking into a huge valley to see the great peak of Langtang and the cheese factory built into this beautiful setting between Nepal and Tibet. The Langtang Valley of Nepal was the Shangri-La that I had read so much about. The pastures were full of longhaired yaks, which the herders pushed right up to the base of the glaciers that spewed from the monster peaks above. Nowhere in Nepal during three different expeditions did I witness such serenity.

After camping in the valley one night, I backtracked to the pits of Kathmandu. And then, the night before I left the city, I celebrated by going out to a restaurant for a cooked meal. Famished for greens, I foolishly ordered a huge salad. Right after the dinner, my insides turned upside down. I started vomiting and had severe diarrhea that kept me on the toilet all night. The ordeal left me so pathetically weak, I had to call a porter the next morning to carry my bags down from the slum room barrack that I had rented. I was barely able to shuffle to the taxicab taking me to the airport. Although I managed to keep my composure for the 30-hour flight back to the USA, I brought stool samples to the GI lab in Spokane for three months before confirming I had a severe case of giardiasis, caused by a single-cell parasite that looks like a male sperm with eyes and teeth. The giardia swim into the small intestine, bite through the wall to lay their eggs, and rapidly reproduce. For unknown reasons, the lab assistants couldn't see the parasites at the right time. I lost 10 pounds before a four-day hospital siege of Flagyl and antibrine treatments finally wiped the bugs out of my system.

My month of reconnaissance in Nepal left me seasoned, wiser, and ready to tackle Makalu. I determined I could safely climb the mountain, that is, if I didn't die from eating the food.

Left to right: Me, Kim Momb, Dr. Jim States, John Roskelley.

LIKE THE STONE MASTERS

The Stone Masters was the name given to the 1970s Yosemite Valley elite rock-climbing athletes who had mastered virtually all known pitches below 15,000 feet worth climbing on planet earth. They were the toughest of the toughest, with chiseled lean body mass and high V02 max, dedicated to climbing harder and steeper routes. They were fiercely competitive, which was the driving force to climb seemingly impossible rock walls.

In many ways, the four climbers who committed to climbing Makalu sized up like a high-altitude Stone Master team. We were crazies who dared to take the Yosemite big-wall technique to the Himalayas. We were in the prime of our physical lives, ranging in age from 24 to 34, yet freaks of the times, with no tattoos or pierced ears. None of us had ever taken drugs. All Makalu team members had calluses on their hands from manual labor, and intense personalities developed by years of demanding mountain training. All four were dedicated to pioneering the Stone Masters trade on rocks above 20,000 feet. We took the preparation seriously, going so far as to drink water in lieu of booze at parties. It's worth noting that some women were still attracted, perhaps to the novel approach of sober men with something intelligent to say.

Athletes come in different sizes. We ranged from 145 pounds to my weight at 175, but all four of us contained the common denominator needed for big achievement: mental toughness.

KIM MOMB

One day I arrived at Minnehaha Rocks in Spokane Valley and, while looking up at the cliff for any sign of climbers, I noticed movement in a large pine tree. At first glance, it looked like an orangutan, but upon closer inspection, it was a man doing one-arm pull-ups on a dead tree branch—not just one or two one arm pull-ups, but a dozen or more! "Who the hell is that guy?" I asked.

"Kim Momb," I was told. One of his nicknames was "29-44" which meant his waist was 29 inches and his chest 44 inches. First impressions tell you much, and I was impressed. This was no ordinary man; his body was sculpted from years of competitive gymnastics and professional motocross racing. Later I learned that Momb was also an accomplished musician and competitive freestyle skier. At 24, he would be the youngest Makalu team member. His integrity and aptitude for perfection was partly inherited from German ancestry, and partly self-trained. He was one of the finest all-around natural athletes I have ever been around. I figured that with all the God-given talent he had, he must have been pretty bored one day to try rock climbing.

DR. JIM STATES

Raised on the East Coast of the United States, Jim States is a graduate of Bucknell and Temple University. He was already into climbing when he found his way to Wyoming, and then, realizing the central location to the mountains that Spokane offered, he landed a medical internship at Deaconess Hospital. He later opened his practice specializing in adolescent and young adult medicine. States was an anomaly. Most doctors face a huge workload and buckle to demands after prolonged education. Dedication to the Hippocratic oath takes a physical toll on them. Not States. He was obsessed with tip-top fitness. Born with flat feet, he quickly overcame this "handicap" by mental desire to become a high-achieving mountaineer. If ever there was a man who genuinely loved the mountains and the solitude of the mountains, it was States. He lived to run and climb in the wilderness and made the most of the Spokane outdoor environment. He loved his medical practice, but I often thought his practice was only a vehicle to get him to the climbs he had on his wish list. A type of Henry David Thoreau loner his entire life, States was "married" to nature. He loved and cherished the time spent alone in rugged outdoor environments more than any person I have ever met.

JOHN ROSKELLEY

A freak of nature—I don't mean that in a slanderous way—John Roskelley was born with large hands, large feet, long toes for incredible balance, and the natural athletic talent and stamina to conquer all the greatest alpine routes in the world. Smart and a good student, he graduated from Washington State University with a degree in geology. His British ancestry infused him with the genetic code for mountaineering and world exploration. His stamina and mental toughness as an athlete developed over years of tenacious and bold mountain pioneering. Climbing some of world's highest mountains didn't come easy; he worked his ass off for all the international attention he garnered. Reinhold Messner, acclaimed as the world's greatest mountaineer, once said, "The American Roskelley is stronger than I." Among his many awards, Roskelley was the first non-traditional athlete to be inducted into the Inland Empire Sports Hall of Fame. His talent was recognized internationally in 2013 as he became the first American and sixth person given the Golden Ice Axe Lifetime Achievement Award by the French magazine Montagnes and the Groupe de Haute Montagne. His abilities in leadership on Makalu were admirable, although we sometimes fought with his decisions. In the end we all had mutual respect.

TRAINING

Even though the four of us had climbed together, only Roskelley and I had talked and planned for years to attempt Makalu. While on a climbing expedition the previous year, Roskelley had already secured the permit to climb

Makalu from the Nepal government for the spring of 1980. I believed the two of us could climb the mountain without support, but a team of four would add extra security. When Roskelley invited Momb and States, the expedition congealed, and we stepped up the training to include distance and elevation running. The four of us took climbing seriously. We already were scaling real mountains on the weekends and doing two- and three-hour mid-week workouts at Minnehaha Rocks. Now we could focus the effort on a lofty goal. Our running routine involved driving to the base of Mount Spokane at Linder's Lodge, then running up the old side logging roads while gaining 3,000 vertical feet to the mountain summit. Our goal was to run this route in under an hour.

On one late fall training run, I learned first-hand the dangers of hypothermia. States and I had driven to the top of Mount Spokane and left our bicycles on the summit. We then descended via car to Linder's Lodge and began our run, reaching the top in a driving rain and hailstorm clad only in cotton shirts and shorts as we descended on our bikes. Drenched, our body core temperatures dropped quickly. We staggered off our bikes at the Mount Spokane campground and a husband and wife saved our butts when they fed us a quart of hot tea. The conditioning runs weren't always so dire, but we routinely pushed ourselves to the limit.

Our training routine was a form of madness driven by competition. Up to this time in the Himalayas, all 14 of the "Eight-Thousanders," the giant mountains above 8,000 meters, had been climbed by huge expeditions sponsored by nations. Some of these expeditions included up to a thousand Sherpas and climbers. I was determined, as was Roskelley, to prove that a small team could climb one of the big Himalayan peaks without Sherpa support, and without supplementary oxygen. I have always believed a man's nature determines his fate, and I for one didn't like to get beat at anything. The four of us were competitive to a fault, and we all had the common thread of mental toughness. We were game for proving something to the mountaineering world.

THE EXPEDITION

The challenges of an expedition in a foreign country start long before the climb. You must deal with the politics of securing necessary permits, prepare the food and equipment lists, figure out a realistic schedule, plan the logistics, and hardest of all, raise funds. Once the permit was confirmed from the Nepal Kingdom, we were faced with assembling nearly two tons of food, rope, pitons, extra boots, and clothing. The permit required us to bring new tennis shoes, socks, and jackets for our planned 60 porters in Nepal. Since my home was centrally located in Spokane, we made my driveway the grand central station where the four of us met every week to pack gear for a planned three months in the wilds of the Himalayas. We solicited major equipment suppliers, food distributors, camera companies, and rope manufacturers and managed to get donations for most of the food and gear, including film from National Geographic. Ultimately the gear and food were bundled into 23 burlap feed bags.

We planned on fixing rope on the rock and ice pitches, and bought exactly 9,517 feet of the highest quality climbing rope varying in thickness from 7 to 10 millimeters, all sent to us in spools from the Mammut Company. We boxed the rope and hardware along with the food and gear, and shipped it to New Delhi, India, and then on to Nepal. My wife Sharon was an amazing fundraiser, and when it came time to leave Spokane, she had single-handedly raised more than $12,000 in cash! This was a huge boost that enabled us to purchase all the remaining rope, pitons, stoves, and extra items for our porters. From my diary notes on the morning of February 27, John and I left Spokane for San Francisco with $12,980.56. I paid $4,041.45 for airfreight for the group gear plus we had another 1,615 pounds of personal climbing equipment. The remaining dollars would go to pay the porters we hired, plus our Nepal liaison officers and porter foreman.

The next day Jim and Kim arrived in San Francisco and we boarded the plane for the long trip to India. States and I stayed in New Delhi for nearly a week before finally getting the customs clearance to ship the gear forward. On arrival in Kathmandu, Kim and I went to the National Bank of Nepal and exchanged $5,590 US dollars for 65,926 rupees. The bills had to be in small denominations to pay our porters in cash at the end of each load-carrying day. The stash of cash alone nearly filled my backpack to the lid. When you consider that the average male wage earner in Nepal in 1980 would make only $100 a year, I was a walking fortune. Momb was the expedition's designated "Sergeant-at-Arms" and he performed his duties like a professional. Everywhere we went in Nepal, Kim was close to my side.

The four of us were fanatical about avoiding germs, especially around meals. Each of us had a shiny silver spoon. Before eating, I would use my butane pocket lighter and carefully run the flame all over the spoon to burn off any bacteria that might have attached. This sounds bizarre, and perhaps a bit paranoid, but getting sick in the wilderness of a Third World country could be the kiss of death. I had visited the one-and-only hospital in all of Nepal and found it filthy. Chances of recovering from an illness might be better in the jungle. While on the three-week trek into the base of Makalu, all of us made sure our cook boy, Tez, had thoroughly cleaned all our pots and pans, and completely boiled the potatoes or rice. Our obsession with cleanliness paid off. During the entire three months in the foreign country, none of us got sick (except for one lapse of caution on my part, to be explained later).

On March 8, our last day in Kathmandu, we repacked some of our gear in gunnysacks, which were limited by regulations to no more than 65 pounds each. We had to hire 61 porters to carry our 55 full bags, plus six other bags of miscellaneous gear. In addition to the 65-pound load, each porter carried his or her own sleeping bag, clothing, and any other food and personal items for the three-week journey to the base camp.

We left early on March 9 for a 24-hour road journey, stopping only for short breaks. After spending the entire night jostling about in the truck, we euphorically jumped from the cab to the dusty ground in the small village of Dharan, where the adventure of traveling across Nepal to the base of Makalu began. We would be on foot for the next three months.

The first order of business was to sign up and organize porters for our journey. This job of hiring and firing was given to our government liaison officer, Mr. Mukia. A very experienced expedition officer, Mukia was a good man who knew how to pick the right people for the work.

From the get-go, Jim and I disagreed with the way John would treat some of the porters; being stingy about giving out sunglasses for example, but after a few days of arguments that are common with strong-minded individuals, we settled into a welcome peace zone for the remainder of the expedition.

Each day, depending on terrain, we would whittle five or 10 miles off the 150 miles we had to walk just to get to the Makalu Base Camp at 17,100 feet. At the end of the day's march, camp was usually made in a farmer's field. Tents were pitched if it looked like rain, otherwise we would sleep under the stars next to the campfire. I always slept with the money backpack under my head for a pillow. Kim kept his knife and machete handy in case of an attack that luckily never came. Both Kim and I were trained fighters, me in wrestling, and Kim in Jujitsu, and we probably appeared tough. Maybe that's why no one challenged either of us, even though it was common knowledge among the porters that I carried a small fortune on my back. Every day was a different experience and a delight to be in a country where money, power, and material things meant little to nothing. Day-to-day survival was all that mattered. Physically, the people are small, and everyone in Nepal had parasites or intestinal worms. I remember one vivid episode in the midway town of Tumlingtar looking down into a typically primitive wood outdoor toilet dug into the ground and seeing the entire bottom moving and crawling with huge tapeworms and grotesque intestinal worms that had been excreted from countless Nepali bowels. In 1980, according to the one doctor I met, the entire population of the country was infested with some type of worm or parasite. They simply had to live with their medical problems, as doctors, dentists, and medicines were basically unavailable.

Leaving Dharan, our trek took us over hills in the Nepal lowlands, through the villages of Dhankuta and Hile, then up the Arun River to Tumlingtar. The trail went up to Khadbari and along beautiful highlands before dropping back down into the village of Num in the Arun River Gorge. After crossing the suspension bridge over the gorge, we began our climb into the wilds of the Nepal jungle. It took two days of clawing our way uphill on steep, wet, and slippery trails to cross Shipton Pass at over 14,000 feet. I was stunned to watch the porters walk over the ice and snow-covered pass without boots or shoes. They were used to trekking and climbing barefoot. They were saving the tennis shoes we gave them for very special occasions. Shortly after cresting Shipton

Pass, the trail began to wind downward through a magnificent rhododendron forest in full spring bloom lit with white and pink blossoms, enough to supply every flower shop in the world. The trail continued nearly to the bottom of the Barun Valley, where we began the uphill challenge to our goal.

We camped under huge ancient pine trees near the bottom of the deep valley and woke to begin the last three days of trekking to the Makalu Base Camp. The trail wound through pines that gave way as we climbed to smaller brush and grass, and finally to bare rock. Occasionally, we would see a Tibetan sheep and goat herder along the trail. One herder offered me a whole bag of soybeans in exchange for a Hershey chocolate bar. Always eager to try the local food, I gulped in a mouthful of soybeans and, a few hours later, nearly paid the ultimate price. Approaching 13,000 feet, too many soybeans and the high altitude combined to wrench my intestine into knots, causing the most intense physical pain I had ever experienced. Frankly, I began to write out my will. After the eternity it took to reach our campsite, I spent the entire night withering in pain, getting up with diarrhea and vomiting. Exhausted and dehydrated by morning, I told my mates to travel on without me, as I would bring up the rear with our liaison officer, Mr. Mukia, and States. My mind and body slowly recovered, but never would I be able to look at soybeans without thinking of those wretched hours. It dawned on me as life trickled back through my veins that I saw the natives pop only one soybean at a time into their mouth, waiting hours between bites. My American "Big Gulp" mentality nearly killed me before reaching the mountain!

The slow, always-upward climb to the Base Camp was one of the most beautiful foot journeys I had ever taken. The rock of Makalu is clean, pristine granite, so the glaciated valleys expose huge blank vertical granite canyon walls. The trail from the bottom of the Barun Valley was like climbing through Yosemite Valley to reach an elevated plateau and terminus of the Barun Glacier. Next to the lateral moraines was the relatively flat Base Camp area at 16,000 feet. We camped one night and then continued across the tumultuous Barun Glacier with Makalu's West Pillar looming above. States continually monitored our progress of adaptation as we climbed higher. If even one of us were to get sick from exertion or altitude, our small team would be in trouble. On April 1, we established our true Base Camp in the rocky glacier at 17,100 feet and said goodbye to our crew. This would be our home for the next two months. Except for a mail runner scheduled to check in every two weeks, the four of us from Spokane were on our own.

The West Pillar rose directly above us in one sweeping glorious knife-edged ridge to the pointed summit of Makalu more than 2 vertical miles above our tents. Our mission was to climb it, and we soon began the laborious task, without the help of porters, of ferrying 35- to 50-pound loads every day to gradually move 1,500 pounds of tents, cooking fuel, ropes, and food to our four planned campsites on the ridge. The four of us were faced with three stress adjustments: The change from real fruits and vegetables to the marginal freeze-dried meals, the extreme altitude, and the extreme cold that dropped into sub-zero temperatures. Slowly, we all adjusted to the conditions and remained healthy to push on. John was the only high-altitude veteran amongst us, with his summit of Dhaulagiri under his belt, and his strong leadership kept us moving ever higher.

INTO THE DEATH ZONE

The climbing workdays on the West Pillar began at dawn as each of us would begin the loop of carrying six or seven loads to Camp One at 19,500 feet. From there, the technical ridge climbing began in earnest. We took turns leading and fixing thousands of feet of climbing rope from Camp One to Camp Two, which we located at 21,500 feet. We had brought 13,000 lineal feet of climbing rope for installing fixed lines, and we eventually used every foot. The climbing rope varied in thickness from 7 to 11 millimeters, the thickest rope being placed over the sharp rock leads. From Camp Two to Camp Three, the ridge rises dramatically skyward, and the work to install the lines from this point onward tested our resolve to the mission. At 23,500 feet, a huge cornice overhung the sharp ridge like a frozen wave of ice. There was just enough headroom under this ice wave to place a tent. The ice cornice offered protection from the possibility of falling rocks, and the relief from the certainty of severe wind. The rock fall on the Makalu West Pillar turned out to be virtually non-existent, as the dense, crystalline granite was a technical climber's dream. From Camp Three, the ridge became nearly vertical. To avoid the vertical gendarmes, we forced the route onto the South Face. John and I led several long pitches that we collectively named The Terrible Traverse because the rock was near vertical and technical, leading diagonally rightward on small friction holds with tremendous exposure looking straight down 8,000 feet of the South Face. From the top of The Terrible Traverse, we had to ascend 70- to 80-degree cracks and dihedrals for several hundred feet that led back to the knife-edged ridge and a small ledge that bit up against the large overhanging bulge in the ridge.

Here we were confronted with the actual West Pillar. From below, the Pillar appeared to be 600- to 800 vertical feet with no cracks. Indeed, the rock directly above us was blank and devoid of any weakness to climb. But off to our right 30 feet on a ledge, we could see a crack system on the South Face that was vertical for about 100 feet, where it bulged again into an overhanging block. John and I traversed over to the base of this wall, and upon closer inspection, we found a tiny, wired aluminum ladder that draped over the overhang! This small-wired ladder was left by the French expedition that had made the first ascent of this ridge. John led this incredible vertical pitch, then tested the wires and was able to ascend the overhanging wall with the ladder's aid. Once above this, we anchored our 11-millimeter fixed line. As tough as this pitch

Roskelley on The Terrible Traverse.

was to install, we still had 300 nearly vertical feet of line to fix to reach our Camp Four site, a perch situated dramatically on the ridge at 25,500 feet. The day John and I established this camp, I felt strong enough to go for the summit that evening, but Jim, who was at Base Camp resting, deserved a summit bid too. John and I decided to descend all the ropes to Base Camp, rest a couple days, and begin the long climb back to this place so all three of us could make a summit bid together.

Establishing the high camp had us working six days a week for five weeks. I stopped writing in my diary on April

17, more from fatigue than any other reason, and it was many days after our summit bid on the mountain before I was able to collect my thoughts about the ordeal. After April 17, the work of hauling loads higher and higher up the peak required every ounce of physical and psychological effort our bodies could muster. It was grueling work, carrying from 40 to 50 pounds daily over technical terrain, all at altitudes from 19,500 feet to 25,500 feet. Despite the incredible surroundings of the natural setting we were climbing in, our minds went into a state of numbness, mixed in with Divine Madness, trying to blank out the stress we were demanding on our bodies. We all began to lose weight, and none of us came to Nepal with any fat to burn. Our muscles began to atrophy.

As a direct consequence of the unusual stress and workload at the extreme heights, Kim began to complain of severe knee pain early in May. His knee problem may have stemmed from the atrophy we were all experiencing from the altitude and the climbing stress. In the first couple days of May, he was finished from further load carrying up the ridge. My own diagnosis was Kim's injuries were a result of his youth and exuberance. Kim was the youngest man on our team. From the outset he had worked daily with fury and unbounded energy. Something had to give, and his knees became his body's sacrificial lamb. Kim's summit bid and climbing were essentially over, and he had to return to Base Camp for recovery. This was a bummer for Kim, but not a crippling factor to our expedition, as he had already contributed his share of the workload leading and fixing the lines.

As John and I made our last haul and descended our fixed lines from 25,000 feet, I felt confident of our success. We rappelled, down climbed, and returned to our little Base Camp about the 10th of May. Our summit bid was slated for May 15, and we rested a couple of days before attempting the long, final climb to reach the summit of Makalu.

Victory

Our final assault on the summit of Makalu began from our Base Camp the morning of May 12. Jim, John, and I climbed past Camp One and slept at Camp Two. The next morning, we climbed to Camp Three at 23,500 feet and arranged our personal gear for the climb to Camp Four. The morning of May

Roskelley on crux at 25,500 feet.

14, we began the very technical and exposed climb up the West Pillar with John in the lead. I carried my own pack, as well as Jim States' pack up this vertical section. My diary makes no notes as to why I did this, but I wrote extensively on how doubling the load exhausted me. It's not uncommon in teams for one man to be stronger than his climbing partner on a given day. I woke that morning on my game, feeling my oats as they say, and Jim was not. Keeping the team together seemed important. Jim is one of the strongest mountaineers I had ever climbed with, but his weakness was over technical terrain, and the overhanging buttress was more than he could handle that day. I carried both of our packs on the jumars up and over the overhanging wall to 25,200 feet. The following excerpts come from my diary written on or about May 25, 10 days after our summit:

"Before summit day Jim and I carried our personal gear up from Camp Three with John. At the overhang (25,100 feet) I hauled both packs and totally underestimated the weight of my pack pulling back on my shoulders and arms. When I felt the full weight of the rope, my lungs almost burst from gasping for oxygen. Finally, I got my pack up and over. With Jim's pack, I played it more cautiously—however, the strain nearly finished me on the spot. My lungs burned, my arms ached, muscles cried for strength from lack of oxygen—but there seemed to be none there at 25,200 feet!"

Jim and I slowly made our way up another 300 vertical feet over two hours, reached Camp Four at 6 p.m., and crawled into the tent exhausted. Lucky for us, John had arrived two hours earlier, cut a platform in the snow and ice and erected our essential shelter from the elements. John's years of experience always paid off in time saved.

"We tried to sleep, but just lay there resting from 8:30 onward," I wrote in my diary. "At 11 p.m. we aroused ourselves from the groggy state and started the cooker to melt ice for water and hot tea. Conditions with three people were tight in the tent, and soup was the only thing that went down well as food just didn't taste good at 25,500 feet. At 2 a.m., May 15, we crawled out of the tent and laced up our crampons. We guessed the temperature to be about 25 degrees below zero. John led out, then Jim, then me, up the face and ridge, which was surprisingly steep. After four hours of climbing, we stopped for lunch at 6 a.m. We had gained only 900 feet over rock and deep snow. My body had been very cold those first four hours. My two-piece down suit didn't seem to help."

My feet were so numb I feared frostbite. I furiously wriggled my toes each step to no avail. States was in bad shape, complaining of cold and laboring. We continued slowly up the steep ridge, with vertical drops on both sides, to the south "shoulder" where the ridge levels and is horizontal for several hundred feet at elevation 26,750 feet. The ridge joined the southwest ridge at a small col. The snow was deep, in some places up to our waist. John took the lead again climbing up the southwest ridge, veering right, and eventually gaining the ridge crest at 27,000 feet. Only 807 feet remained to the summit!

Although the sun had been up for several hours, the temperature had dropped to about minus 30 degrees Fahrenheit. Jim said he was exhausted and "needed a nap," which prompted a heated argument about whether we could afford a break. It was late considering what was left to do. Looking up we saw the final knife-edge ridge to the pointed summit. John led up for one and a half hours and gained only 300 vertical feet. He yelled back to me to take the lead, but try as I might, I couldn't catch him. He never stopped until we met up at the final vertical rock step on the ridge, the last technical barrier to the summit. (Years later I studied detailed topo maps, and surmised we were at 27,450 feet, nearly 400 feet below the top.) The actual summit was hidden from our view at this point behind several cornices—so very close, yet a matter of life and death away.

Physical and mental exhaustion won out, and we decided to try napping for 10 minutes, which turned out to be 30 minutes. At 12:20 p.m. John woke us, and we talked about which way to go. To the left was a steep snow slope, and near vertical rock, but it looked climbable. To the right, the slope was steep, but looked climbable in snow to the ridge. The way to the right seemed to be easier for all three of us, so I began to lead out and off the knife-edged ridge until John pointed upward at a slightly different course. I balked. The snow looked much too deep and loose to me. After another heated discussion, I began to lead straight up the ridge crest. "Just let me take a look from here," I shouted down.

After about 50 vertical feet, I looked back down and to the right and saw John and Jim traversing farther right to the far side of the ridge. "Come down here and lead this," John commanded. I dropped down 50 feet and began breaking trail where he wanted, but the snow was exactly as I suspected—up to my waist and very loose. After about 200 feet of vainly floundering in powder that packed against my chest as the route steepened, I still hadn't gained the ridge above me. I turned and yelled, "No good." John and Jim agreed. This way was hopeless. I sat in the deep snow dismayed. We had drained my strength and wasted a full hour on this false lead. It was 1:30 p.m., and in my mental clock, we needed to be on the summit no later than 2 p.m. to ensure a safe journey back down this technical ridge. The numbers didn't look good. We had reached 27,450 feet, and our maximum speed at that stage was 200 to 250 feet per hour, which added up to a late afternoon summit, and almost certainly a bivouac. No moon would grace the sky that night. When the sun went below the horizon at 6:30, ink-black darkness would be close behind.

I slowly climbed back down from the false lead to the cupped basin where I started and tried to mentally address the task of heading up the left side of the ridge over steep snow and near-vertical rock. I looked at my watch and then over to see John and Jim straddling the ridge crest. As I climbed back up 50 feet to their position, I calculated the time and logistics in my mind and made my decision. I told John I was going down. I felt no emotion. I thought of my family, Jon, Jae, and Sharon. If I continued to the summit, it would mean at best frozen toes and hands. John knew exactly what my reasoning was without me saying a word. We had been climbing together for so many years; we could practically read each other's minds. Going up the remaining short, but technical terrain would take all three of us two to three hours. Jim was not an adept technical climber, and that would certainly add to the time, virtually assuring a bivouac at minus 30 degrees. We would not survive the night out. These grim factors were in John's mind, too, and the choice became obvious.

However, Jim, to our astonishment, blurted out, "I'm going up!" (Jim told me after the expedition, "I was going to go up, no matter if I died!" Such was his state of mind at that point.) Obvious to John and me, Jim was extremely lethargic, suffering from hypoxia, acting like a drunk. I laughed, and then John laughed out loud, and made the sharp and clear command. "Jim, as leader of this expedition, I am directing you to go down!"

"I'm going up to make a success out of this expedition," John added as he quickly untied the rope and started climbing upward heading directly to the rocks above. I knew John well from 15 years of intense climbing together, and unhindered, he could reach the summit safely, and return alive. Jim wept like a baby at this point, which made me cry, too. I pulled out my camera and snapped a photo of John nearing the rock on the crest of the ridge.

Jim began the descent first. As I belayed him down the first pitch, I could feel the full dead weight of his hypoxic condition. He was totally wiped out. My body strained to hold my position as he slid his limp 200 pounds of body and pack down the mountain to the end of the rope. I had no anchors to set in the rock, only my legs straddling the ridge. I had to wedge my ass into the slope as tight as possible to give a static belay. This procedure was repeated over and over and over for the entire 2,000 feet back down the stairway to heaven. As hour after frigid hour went by, I began to think of a bivouac around 26,000 feet. The sun had set, it was cold beyond description now, and the potential for a bivouac that I so wanted to avoid was staring me in the face.

It was after 8 p.m. when in the waning soft light I looked over to my left and spotted our small tent on the ridge crest! It was a dream come true for me, but Jim had slipped into a hallucinogenic state and didn't believe anything I was telling him. I had spotted the tent, but he insisted it was still below us. This set off one of several arguments Jim and I had on the way down owing to his altered mental state.

As I was belaying Jim down the ridge, I heard John yell my name. He seemed close. I yelled back, "John, is that you?" Later, John told me my answer removed all the pent up tension from his descent, as he had to laugh when he thought to himself, "Who does he think it is?"

I yelled again, "Jim and I are at the fixed ropes!"

There was no reply, and we would not hear from John for nearly three hours. He was resting only a couple hundred feet above us, which turned into a two-hour nap.

At the high camp I fired up the cranky stove and climbed into the tent with Jim as our arguing continued. It was pitch black now, and I'd had it with Jim. I continued to yell up to John, but he never answered. The wind was beginning to blow hard. I feared that if he was going to bivouac he would be dead by sunrise.

Relief arrived at a little past 11 p.m. as John reached the tent. He had made it to the summit, but he was exhausted—as we all were—and barely alive. One look on John's weather beaten face told the story. Emotionally weakened, as we all were, we lay there for a few numbing moments. We knew we needed to rehydrate, but the stove wasn't burning properly to melt ice, leaving us to give in to exhaustion zipped into our sleeping bags with thin nylon tent walls shedding the elements. During the frigid night, the wind roared. By dawn, we were in an all-out gale.

We needed to hydrate before attempting the difficult descent, so we coaxed the sputtering stove and melted enough ice for a quart of liquid apiece, which we got down our throats before breaking the campsite at 2 p.m. We rappelled slowly down to Camp Three at 23,500 feet, where we spent another miserable night. The next day we descended to Camp Two, where we had two tents, and a reasonable night. Jim and I slept in one tent and John in another tent. At one point, we all broke down and cried from pent up emotion and stress. The ordeal was concluding.

On May 18, the day Mount St. Helens erupted and sent a plume of ash around the world, John and Jim descended from our Camp Two all the way to Base Camp. We would not learn of the volcano's blast until our return to Spokane in mid-June. I remained in Camp One with our cook boy and Ang Nema, who had returned and had come up to help. The next morning, Tej and I climbed back up to Camp Two, and we brought down the tents, stoves, and some personal gear. We both carried 75 pounds back down the ropes. On

May 20, Tej and I returned to Base Camp where we were warmly greeted by Jim, John, and Kim. The climbing mission was over, and the next morning we broke camp and began the weeklong trek into the lowlands and green pastures of Nepal.

As our team returned to civilization and to Spokane, we found that we left more than emotion on the mountain. Each of us had dropped 15 to 20 pounds, and all of us were lean machines at the start. For me, it would take more than a year to recover physically and gain back the muscle lost to the stress of the climb. Kim Momb would meet a tragic death in a 1986 avalanche while guiding heli-skiers in Canada. Jim States would continue his climbing and adolescent medicine practice. John Roskelley would continue his profession of mountaineering, becoming an author as well as one of America's greatest mountaineers. I would go on to climb Mount Everest and the remaining highest points of the seven continents, but nothing, short of raising my children, would ever come close to the victory of Makalu.

MAKALU

For almost 15 years I had dreamed of climbing Makalu. Each individual on our four-man team gave everything he had emotionally and physically. We hauled all our gear off the mountain. For me, the dream to reach the summit of what I considered to be the world's greatest peak came up just short, but John touched the top, so we all celebrated a team victory.

We were recognized as a climbing team for the ages because we accomplished our goal without supplemental oxygen, and without Sherpa support. We succeeded because we respected each other's individual talents. We embarked on the expedition as friends, and we returned as friends, a rare outcome in Himalayan expeditions. We had proven that a cohesive team of four climbers could accomplish the same goal of the previous multi-million-dollar expeditions that included a thousand men and women.

I recognized that success was in the journey, not the destination. The American Alpine Club later rewarded us with the distinction as "one of the 10 most significant climbs of the past century."

Eighteen

Everest

Sunset on Everest from near Base Camp

My interest in Mount Everest goes way back to a shallow sea near the continent of Antarctica 325 million years ago, when tiny sea crustaceans died and dropped to what geologists have named the Tethys Sea Floor. Centimeter by centimeter the crustacean sediments turned into limestone a thousand meters thick on what experts believe was a supercontinent called Pangaea. As 100 million years passed, stress deep within the earth's mantle called plate tectonics caused the Pangaea to slowly split apart and "drift" like huge platters. The Indian Plate split from the Antarctica supercontinent and slowly drifted northward. In a collision that lasted for millions of years, the northern edge of the Indian plate was forced upward over the top of the Eurasian Plate forming the Himalaya and the Karakoram mountain ranges that rise to outlandish heights.

The lower rocks of Everest are composed mainly of metamorphic rocks, which intruded into the base of the massif from the earth's mantle. On the East Face of Everest, one can see these schists, which are coarse-grained and crystalline. They split easily into thin layers. Among the schists are gneisses and migmatites, all strongly metamorphic, bearing witness to having been wrought under profound heat and stress. Higher up, there is a huge intrusion of granite called the Makalu granite formation, which is strikingly evident on the lower part of the Nuptse-Lhotse wall. It is light-colored and characteristically it erodes in blocks. Above this are sedimentary rocks, which were laid down under the Tethys Sea and were only weakly metamorphosed. The clays, silts, and chalky remains of marine animals were transformed into pelites, shale, sandstone, and limestone. Everest climbers know this as the famous "yellow band." The summit of Mount Everest, at 8,850 meters or 29,035 feet, is the bottom of a huge fold in the sedimentary rock, called a syncline, meaning thousands of feet of sedimentary rock have been eroded away from above. In other words, Everest is much lower than it once was, or could be if there was no erosion from wind, ice, and water. Contemplating the geologic history of Everest takes a leap of imagination but seeing the mountain with your own eyes and thinking you will try to climb it requires an even greater leap.

Sir George Everest, the retired British Surveyor General of India, was embarrassed to learn in 1865 that a special mountain his countrymen had called Peak XV would be renamed in his honor. Although he'd traversed rugged terrain in mapping the region, he'd likely never set eyes on his namesake. But the mountain's destiny had already been mapped in 1852 when surveyors announced they had enough triangulation information to declare the peak as the highest on earth. The news spurred the dreams of climbers to touch the top of the world. Everest would become a symbol of conquest. In China, Everest is called Chomolungma, "The Goddess Mother of the Earth." In Nepal, they call it Sagarmatha, "The Goddess Mother of the Sky." There are enough stories and histories of the attempts, failures, and success on the exploration of Everest to fill a modest library. The elevation of Everest fascinates the human race, but for me, the geology was part of the hook. Not only did I want to climb it, I wanted to see for myself the tiny fossils at 28,000 feet in the famous limestone "yellow band." Scaling Everest would be my ultimate science project.

My dreams to climb Everest began as a teen fantasy after I'd climbed Mount Rainier. Thousands of mountains with beautiful names and romantic locations offer as much challenge and more difficult routes, but in the end the highest point on earth struck me as the peak of climbing achievement. I had engraved 'EVEREST' into the hickory shaft of my ice axe as a teenager so my goal would stare at me every time I went climbing. The Everest-sized problem of getting onto an expedition took me 18 years to solve.

Throughout the 1970s, John Roskelley and I had often discussed Mount Everest as we added to our climbing resumes. The subject came up again during the winter of 1980-1981 while on a climb of Cascade Waterfall near Banff. I was particularly passionate about wanting to try a two-man expedition to climb Everest without using supplemental oxygen. I had just turned 33, and felt my athletic peak was behind me, so if Everest was in my future it had better be soon. John, on the other hand, was more focused on doing new and untried Himalayan routes. He did not share my urgent ambition for a two-man Everest attempt. Our connections with other American alpinists were handicapped by Spokane's considerable distance from major mountains. The closest alpine peaks to our hometown required at least a hundred miles of driving. Most climbers selected for Everest expeditions hailed from coastal mountain areas like Seattle, California's Sierra-Nevada, and the Rockies of Colorado. Spokane was known as a "redneck" town in the scablands, and not noted for its mountaineers. Therefore, whenever we presented our resumes to an expedition leader, mentioning our home environment was a handicap for expedition solicitations. How could anyone from a place so far from big mountains be any good at climbing?

Roskelley always had his radar locked on what was happening in the world of mountaineering. During our down-time chat, he mentioned an American Medical Expedition was forming to try Everest in the upcoming post monsoon season. It would be led by Dr. John West of La Jolla, California, and the climbing leader was John Evans. Roskelley said Evans had already turned down his request to join this expedition, and he was clearly hurt by this rejection. Apparently, Evans didn't feel he could "control" John Roskelley. Evans told John that he was "too independent and opinionated." After my own rejection by Jim Whittaker for a shot at K2, I knew politics infused human interactions. An invitation for a Himalayan expedition would require a constitution for getting along with all types of personalities.

I knew Evans from the 1974 Pamir Expedition, so upon returning to Spokane from the Canadian Rockies, I called him in Boulder, Colorado, where he and his wife operated Outward Bound. Hundreds of men and women had already submitted their resumes, but I felt a good vibe over this phone conversation, our first contact in six years. I expressed my keen desire to go to Everest and sent him my updated climbing qualifications. Any expedition to Everest was a high-profile prize for a mountaineer to covet. The last successful expedition to get an American on top had been in 1976, sponsored in part by the US Army. As of 1980, only eight other Americans had climbed to the summit.

The climbing route up a mountain is an important consideration, based on a variety of logistical factors and, in the case of Everest, international relations. Mount Everest is on the border between Nepal and Tibet. During the Cultural Revolution, the People's Republic of China had invaded Tibet, claimed it as an integral part of China, and barred foreigners. (The Tibetan government-in-exile maintained that Tibet is an independent state under unlawful occupation.) The political situation changed in the spring of 1981 and, with little notice, entry was cleared for climbers to visit the Himalayas from the Tibetan plateau. Californian Richard Blume, the husband of then-mayor of San Francisco Diane Feinstein (later a US senator), had jumped at this opportunity and secured a permit to attempt the Kangshung Face of Everest. Blume contacted the American Alpine Club, which in turn chose Dr. Jim Morrissey of Stockton,

California, to lead the first expedition to the unclimbed route during the post monsoon season of 1981. Morrissey was the best mountaineering expedition leader of the time, having succeeded on the first American ascents of Dhaulagiri, Gaurishankar, and Trango Towers. The Kangshung Face of Everest, also known as the East Face, had not been approached since George Mallory and his expedition trekked up the valley to the huge face and deemed it "impossible." Getting invited on Morrissey's undertaking would be a BIG deal for a mountain climber. No expeditions had been to Everest from the north side since before World War II, including the ill-fated 1924 British attempt by Mallory and Andrew Irvine on the North Ridge.

I received two of the most prestigious calls in my climbing career in close succession. To my astonishment, the first call was from Louis Reichardt, one of four Americans who had summited K2 in 1963. Reichardt, chosen by Morrissey to head up the climbing team, invited me to join the first attempt of the Kangshung Face. This was the last "great problem" on Everest, as the two other sides had been climbed. I was elated. At long last I was pegged to challenge the world's highest mountain.

The second call came just a week later, from Evans, who invited me to go on his expedition, which would approach the peak via the Khumbu Icefall and Southwest Face. The American Medical Research Everest Expedition, or AMREE as it was called, was a pioneering expedition in the name of science to study the heart and lungs at extreme elevation. Suddenly I had two different Everest expeditions from which to choose: one would advance the science of human physiology, while the other would pioneer a rare shot at a new climbing route. The hard part was yet to come, but I was already walking on top of the world.

After much soul searching and consultation with my good friend Joe Collins, I decided to go with the AMREE expedition, first, because it was completely sponsored. All expenses would be paid for the climbers, including their airfare. Leaving my family for four months would be a financial concern I hadn't had to deal with on previous expeditions. I was the sole breadwinner for Sharon and our two kids. I would have to save enough cash for them to survive without me for an extended period. Playing the odds was my second reason for going on AMREE. The south side of Mount Everest was known, and with Sherpa support we had a good chance of success even with the added task of carrying scientific instruments strapped onto our bodies. My heart raced as I picked up the phone and called Evans to accept his invitation. Then with a heavy heart I called Reichardt and thanked him enormously for inviting me, but I had chosen to boost science in lieu of his pioneering attempt of the East Face.

AIMING FOR EVEREST

The differences between the strategic plans of the AMREE expedition and the 1980 Makalu expedition were comical. On Makalu we hired 60 porters, no Sherpas, one cook, and carried no supplemental oxygen. The Makalu team was comprised of four members, and our entire budget was $40,000. On the other hand, AMREE hired 900 porters and 53 Sherpas, 12 "professional" climbers, additional climbing doctors, and a dozen cooks. AMREE would prove to be a typical supplemental oxygen-fueled Himalayan siege of Hollywood proportions with a budget of more than half a million dollars.

Evans, our climbing team leader, was careful to choose personalities conducive to working together as a team. His extensive mountaineering background included the first ascent of the highest mountain in Antarctica, Mount Vinson, possibly the most remote mountain on earth. He had been on an ill-fated Everest expedition that theoretically had the "best" mountaineers in the world, but that "international all-star team had failed miserably, mostly because of the prima donna attitudes. Evans knew that team chemistry was important. Picking the right men with the right stuff was his leadership forte. His picks for the AMREE expedition included Jeff Lowe, the only "superstar" professional climber on the team, and the most humble. Others had PhDs and masters degrees framed on their office walls. With my lowly bachelor's degree from WSU, I had the least education beyond high school of the 18-man team. That's not to indicate these guys weren't accomplished mountaineers; they were, and all had sterling credentials of international climbing accomplishments. It was a pleasure to be adding my muscle to this mass of brain power on the world's highest mountain.

HIMALAYAN ODDS

From my early days of climbing, I learned that speed on big mountains was directly equated with survival. Dilly-dally climbing was reserved for outings with your mother. When the reality set in that I was going to attempt Everest, I felt that my training schedule had to be a step above whatever I had previously accomplished physically or achieved in athletics. Training for my previous expeditions, including Makalu, required discipline and dedication to squeeze in workouts and climbs between my full-time construction jobs. Physical training was critically important, but it's the mind that controls the body. The decisions you make in the wild are critical to success, which includes coming home alive. Having the body of Superman was just not that important, but having super speed was a major asset. Once I knew I was going to the highest mountain on earth, my first goal was to be the fastest man on the planet above 17,000 feet.

Pioneering expeditions in the Himalayas, some supported by more than a thousand porters and helpers, were successful if one or two team members reached the summit. I had learned from my research, that through 1979 more than 2,200 men and women including support Sherpas had made serious attempts on Mount Everest since 1921. Of all these attempts, only 107 men and two women had reached the summit. A climber's chance of reaching the top was 3 percent or less. You wouldn't bet your life savings on those odds in Vegas. The last two Everest summiteers were Swiss-born American mountaineer Ray Genet and Hannelore Schmatz of Germany. Both Genet and Schmatz reached the summit late in the afternoon, but they froze to death on the descent of the Southeast Ridge. By my count, 53 climbers had perished and were frozen in the icy slopes of Everest. The odds of dying on Everest or any other 8,000-meter peak were about 10 percent. In other words, a climber's chances of dying were more than three times the odds of reaching the summit. An expedition climber had a 97 percent chance of NOT reaching the summit, one way or another! These odds improved in the 1990s with the guided, fixed-rope commercialization of climbing on several Himalayan peaks including Mount Everest.

I was curious: Why did these climbers have so much difficulty reaching summits? Re-reading every account of ascents by Himalayan mountaineers on the big peaks, I calculated the feet per hour it took for successful climbers to reach the summit from their campsites above 8,000 meters. Ascent rates varied dramatically. All of them used supplementary oxygen except for Reinhold Messner and Peter Habler, who teamed up without supplementary oxygen in 1978. Even more interesting to me, Messner and Habler, at 375 feet per hour, clocked the fastest speed per hour above Everest's South Col. In comparison, Roskelley and Ridgeway went 208 feet per hour on the final day to the summit of K2. The slowest rate of ascent was logged in 1976 by Americans Bob Cormack and Chris Chandler, who made the first Everest autumn ascent at a snail's pace of 182 feet per hour. The fastest climbers were Tom Bourdillon and Charles Evans, who climbed in 1953 to the South Summit of Everest at the rate of 483 feet per hour. Three days later, Edmund Hillary and Tenzing Norgay completed their historic first ascent to the summit of Mount Everest at the rate of 220 feet per hour.

In my calculations, I deleted the slowest and highest speeds, and averaged the speeds per hour of about a hundred successful summiteers of the 8,000-meter Himalayan peaks. The average came out to be 276 feet per hour using supplemental oxygen, and 236 feet per hour without using supplemental oxygen. Considering the oxygen cylinder with the face mask weighed 21 pounds, using oxygen saved brain cells, but it gave the climber only a slight edge in speed. On summit day on Makalu the previous year, Roskelley, Jim States and I averaged 285 feet per hour for the first thousand feet, and only 190 feet per hour after that, so our average speed was right on the mark of 236 feet per hour. This was the reality of climbing into outer space.

Weight as well as speed was part of the equation for boosting high-altitude climbing success rates. Wrestlers know that lower body weight can translate into increased strength per pound as long as it's only water weight loss and not muscle mass. Runners and climbers know that putting on just a few ounces can add minutes of time to a long-distance run or difficult climb, and the body demands more calories to feed the added blubber. Bottom line: if you're lighter you go faster and with increased energy. The effects of excess weight are magnified in the thin air above 8,000 feet. As I readied for Everest, I weighed

172 pounds with about 7 percent body fat according to the pre-trip baseline tests conducted by scientists in La Jolla. All the AMREE climbers were honed lean of body fat.

I weighed every piece of gear and clothing that I used on Makalu, including boots, boot laces, socks, crampons, ice axes, gaiters, hats, jackets, underwear, gloves, climbing harness, carabiners, goggles, scarf, wristwatch, and camera. The days of ultra-light gear were years away, so much of our gear was improvised. For instance, Kim Momb and I bought two new pairs of Scott ski boots, took them to my father's cabinet shop, and cut off the top ankle supports to make them into lightweight climbing boots! Just a few years later, Koflach would come out with a lightweight climbing boot that was nearly identical to our self-modified boot. We used the same principle for other climbing items. When weighing and preparing my gear for Everest, I managed to whittle a total of 117.5 ounces (7 pounds) of needless weight from boots and clothing without sacrificing safety. Some of the gear was tailor made, including my one-piece Gore-Tex jumpsuit with an inner jacket of premium down. On my titanium axe, I cut off the rubber sheath and substituted lighter weight webbing. The "minimum weight equals maximum success" equation boiled down to tackling Everest in a Gore-Tex shell over down-insulated clothing while carrying a couple pieces of beef jerky.

INSANITY SAND BANK

I stepped up my hill-running and climbing program to tone my legs into hickory. The training program of Reinhold Messner, the greatest climber of all time, included steep uphill trail runs gaining 3,000 vertical feet in 30 minutes. The Austrian had a huge advantage as he lived in the Alps and he could focus full-time on climbing. It was his job. Nevertheless, his cardiovascular workout was very impressive. I set my goal to match it. Living in Spokane, the drive to a steep mountain with 3,000 feet of elevation to ascend was hours away. I made do with daytime workouts on a remnant of Pleistocene floods—a sand bank. It rose from Latah Creek 500 feet in a steady 40 percent grade to a road called High Drive. I hacked out steps in the sand and rock from the creekside to the top. My training regime involved plunge-stepping straight down the hill to the creek and running back up as fast as possible. Six continuous repetitions totaled 3,000 feet of elevation. My respect for Messner grew even higher after months of effort. My best times leveled off at 35 minutes—good, but five minutes inferior to the greatest.

On weekends, for variety, I would run the 3,000 feet up from the base of Mount Spokane to the summit and ride my bike down, or run from the base of Tower Mountain up and over the top and back, about six to seven miles. During the winter of 1980 I made the first winter ascents of Mount Ball and the Southeast Ridge of Mount Cascade, both near Banff. All of this climbing and training had to be done in the off hours from my construction job. The stress began to mount in my family life and marriage. I occasionally ran into people while training and told them what my routine was. More than once, they politely said I was crazy.

My diet was a joke for the AMREE science team. I had the gastronomical preferences of a bear. Whatever came before my eyes or on my plate was consumed with vigor. A true omnivore, I was never a picky eater. But training for Everest was a new nutritional world. Expending from 6,000 to 8,000 calories a day served up a reckoning with the pathetic eating habits I'd developed as a teenage wrestler. A typical day's diet included eggs, steaks, pancakes, beans, greens, oatmeal, a ton of peanut butter, mixed nuts, a loaf of bread, gravy, pretzels, candy bars of all types and sizes, cookies, doughnuts, and pounds of bananas, apples, oranges, raisins, and anything else that looked like food. I'd top it all off with an entire bag of corn chips and salsa. People were jealous that I could chow down so indiscriminately while holding steady at 172 pounds, but for me it was sometimes a curse. With apologies to educated foodies, I must note that I was paid for a time to write about my, ahem, training diet, which nutritionists would label as "macrobiotic." I wrote a couple articles, and referred to the richness of foods in Nepal, which were mostly wheat chapatis, rice, and vegetables served on a plate in a heap that challenged the angle of repose. At the time I never even knew what macrobiotic meant. In my nutritional universe, eating orbited around the simple requirement that calories in had to equal calories out.

SCIENCE IN LA JOLLA

In the spring of 1981, the Everest team gathered in La Jolla on a California coastal bluff overlooking the Pacific Ocean at the home of physiology professor John West. For three days we underwent complete physical, physiological, and psychological testing at the University of California, San Diego. AMREE would become the gold standard expedition for studies of human physiology of man at altitude, thanks to Professor West and his scientists. The impressive data they collected on human endurance tests were recorded in West's book, "Everest, The Testing Place."

Performance of athletes in any type of endurance sport is linked to their VO2 max, the number defining a person's ability and efficiency to absorb and utilize oxygen. For me, the volume of air the body can efficiently absorb was just another number, although I was pleased to find out my VO2 was right up there with the top athletes. Of course, other factors contribute to success in alpinism. In addition to VO2, the researchers studied our physiological profiles, maximal exercise output, and hypoxic ventilator response to exercise performance. All the baseline testing, hematocrit blood tests, and psychological testing was done in La Jolla while pulmonary specialist Dr. Brownie Schoene conducted the high ventilatory response tests in Seattle. The science team was impressive. PhDs included West, Duane Blume, Sukhamay Lahiri, plus James Milledge, a hospital physician with special interest in respiratory diseases. In 1960-1961, West and Milledge were part of the nine-month Silver Hut expedition, co-organized by Sir Edmund Hillary to study the physiology of acclimatization as they made an unsuccessful attempt to climb Makalu. Rounding out the AMREE expedition's science personnel were nine climber medical doctors. These gifted brains spoke in another language of medical terminology. The five of us on the team who were just experienced climbers found that our vocabulary increased just hanging around them as we donated our bodies to science. During the expedition, they would draw blood from us daily and subject us to follow-up psychological and VO2 max testing to further human knowledge of the heart and lungs. It was a climb of discovery and I was bursting with pride to be a member.

The morning before my flight out of California, I woke at sunrise, grabbed my camera gear, and climbed down the couple hundred feet to the beach. It was such a beautiful morning, I decided to take a long hike north to explore and photograph. Wearing long pants and a rain jacket to fend off the chilly breeze, I walked for miles up the beach without seeing a soul, content in myself and the ocean fog. At first just a few people trickled in as the beach stretched on for miles, but as the sun rose hundreds of people came walking in the opposite direction toward the secluded stretch where I had just been. I made several brief attempts to climb a sheer cliff that bordered the beach—a wall of river-washed conglomerates of mud, sand, and gravel—but deemed it much too dangerous.

John Evans performing the VO2 max tests in La Jolla.
From L-R. Dr. Dave Graver, Evans, Glen Porzak, Dr. John West,
Dr. Brownie Schoene.

Returning to the isolated section between the cliffs and surf, I noticed the hundreds of people had turned into a thousand or more, and as I walked closer to the crowd, it became evident they were all nude. Jumping, playing football and volleyball, lying spread-eagle on the sand bare-ass naked! It was a startling sight for a self-conscious Spokane boy. I was fully clothed, my big Nikon camera with an 80-200mm zoom lens hanging down at my waist like a big phallic symbol wagging in a permanent erection that I couldn't conceal. I didn't have sunglasses to hide my eye contact, which was unavoidable. Some of the women's bodies were magnets to my gaze no matter how hard I tried to look away. To get through all the bare skin occupying the beach I sometimes had to tiptoe around and in between bodies lying on towels. It was like a reverse nightmare of being naked in the crowd, only I was the one fully clothed. In a field of tits, I was the boob with the camera. For the record, I didn't take a photograph! When I got back to the house, I told West of my travail. Blushing a bit, he smiled and acknowledged that he knew about "Blacks Beach," but had never been there.

TREK TO BASE CAMP

For most people who get the chance to trek to the Everest Base Camp, it's the realization of a lifetime dream. For climbers, the trek also is a good way to stay in shape for the mission ahead. After arriving in Kathmandu over two days, the team departed on the morning of August 7 for the 175-mile walk. We started hiking from a small village just south of Kathmandu, which, like all small villages in Nepal, had a river running through it. The streams serve as the local source of drinking water and the sewer, thus making hygiene a constant concern for the expedition. Three years of planning had come to fruition. Twenty tons of food, equipment, and science tools, including a pre-molded fiberglass hut, were loaded on the backs of 900 Nepalese porters to carry for the next three weeks over some of the roughest mountain terrain in the world.

I joined with different team members to do daily workouts during the journey. They usually started right after a breakfast of eggs, chapatis, tea, and nuts. The routine for the climbers and climbing doctors was simple: hike, climb, and run to the next day's destination. The daily trek would range up to 12 miles and include 3,000 to as much as 5,000 feet of elevation gain, along with a similar range of elevation drop as we were crossing the grain of the Himalayan foothills. We were like pampered athletes, greeted at a lunch spot with chapatis, eggs, peanut butter, cookies, and tea prepared by our Sherpas and cook boys. Despite all the exercise, no one gained or lost weight during the trek into the base.

For the first couple days, the expedition was like a dream—a celebration of life among the world's greatest mountain scenery. For the first time in my life, I felt like an elite athlete in a professional sport, where the lifestyle is to work out, eat, sleep, and get up and do the same the next day—without the constant worry of how the bills will be paid. The dream got a little less comfortable when the porters went on strike. Even though it was something expedition leaders had expected, it was a problem to fix. With no labor unions in Nepal, each expedition at the time had to deal with how much more to pay a striking porter. We had already given them tennis shoes, but they preferred to save them rather than wear them. (However, the Sherpas, seemingly being of a higher "class" than the Nepali, would wear their shoes. They were always extremely grateful for the traveling expeditions because of the high wages, which afforded an increased standard of living for their families.) The romantic era of trekking this traditional way into Everest was on its way to ending in the late 1980s and early '90s. Future expeditions would bypass the hassle, as well as all of this glorious hiking and climbing, by flying to Lukla and hiking only the final seven days to the Everest Base Camp.

THE STING

On the third day out, I was running full tilt through a jungle of brush, with Dr. Steve Boyer ahead of me, just a mile from the village of Kirantichap, when I felt a sharp slap to my deltoid as though I had been shot in the shoulder with a bullet. The pain was excruciating. What hit me? Were we under attack by the notorious Maoist bandits that were known to hide in these jungles? I stopped and looked around. Seeing no one, I traced my tracks back down the trail. Examining the dense branches with broad leaves that hung down from the jungle canopy, I discovered a huge green and yellow-striped caterpillar with two massive horns protruding from its head. I carefully broke the branch the culprit was hanging on and carried it into the village. As I walked, the entire right side of my body began to ache. My arm went numb.

Usually, when entering a Nepali village, the barefoot children run up to you in joy and wonderment, but as they crowded up to me the kids spied the creature I was guarding and scattered like buckshot with terror in their big brown eyes. I got the message that I might be doomed. When I found Dr. Boyer waiting at a rock bench in the village center, he looked at the horned caterpillar and took my pulse and temperature. We discussed the options for an antidote, but Steve had no idea what to use. Some nearby adults explained in our best interpretation through the language barrier that this was a deadly bug. The entire right side of my body was numb and throbbing with pain. My heart was racing. I figured I should devote what could be my last minutes to dictating an update to my last will and testament to make my untimely death easier on my family. Dr. Boyer was accustomed to grave situations and stayed calm as he took notes for me. The pain started to creep into my entire body, but it gradually began to feel less potent in my nerves as I lay there over the next couple of hours. Turned out, it wasn't my time. It was after sunset before I felt good enough to continue hiking to the next campsite, which was 2,000 feet higher in elevation. The doctors at camp were extremely curious about the creature that stung me. I was simply thankful to have survived learning a lesson about situation awareness in the jungle, with no apparent ill side effects.

Leeches.

For the next 20 days we trekked across Nepal, navigating up and down deep gorges. Blood-sucking leeches lurked wherever there was water, which was everywhere. Springs trickled out of the ridge tops and flowed to the bottom of the jungle in the gorges. It seemed as though every leaf and willow held a leech waiting for the next warm leg to brush by. The porters would save the tennis shoes we gave them for a celebration or "rainy day," but never used them even when crossing the ice-covered passes. Being barefoot rendered the leeches easy for the native people to remove. The AMREE expedition, being typical Caucasian American white men, wore boots, which we found full of leeches when removing them at day's end. They were essentially harmless, but still hideous parasites when attached to your ankle or between your toes. A leech would wriggle into a boot, find its way to flesh, gently bite and flood the wound with an anticoagulant. Then it would quietly feast, gorging on blood and expanding its body two or three times. One leech that had been small enough to work its way through my shoelaces into the gap between two toes measured three inches long by the time I found it.

Lying in sleeping bags at night, it was impossible to keep the lice and fleas from biting. Glen Porzak counted more than a hundred flea welts on his body after sleeping inside one of the stone hotels in a village. Of all the discomforts we endured traveling the jungles of Nepal, getting bit by lice every night was the worst.

Despite the trials of the trail, the three-week cross-country tour of Nepal was an indulgence of scenery and culture that few Westerners understand or appreciate. I came to truly love the people. Not once did I see them raise their voice in anger or hit another person. Kind, gentle by nature, the people of Nepal had lived in relative peace and sheltered from the world's wars that raged outside their rugged country. Few were likely to have heard of the bomb dropped on Hiroshima. It was refreshing and nerve-calming to temporarily live with such gentle souls. They were masters of family life. In most villages outside of Kathmandu, the parents, kids, grandkids, and grandparents all lived together under one thatched roof. These people endured with no hospitals, no assisted-living facilities, no doctors, no medicine, no mental institutions, no unions, no health care, no cars, no electric appliances, no indoor plumbing, no heat except for wood stoves and fires, and no jails. In America, research has been devoted to determine that it's healthy for children to eat dinner every night with the whole family. This has been a way of life for the Nepali and Sherpas for centuries.

NAMCHE BAZAAR

On August 18, we arrived at the bottom of the V-shaped gorge called the Dudh Kosi, the river that flows directly from the Khumbu Icefall, which hangs on the side of Mount Everest 17,000 feet above our elevation. The Dudh Kosi gorge is similar to America's Grand Canyon. I had read of the tranquil beauty and remoteness of our next stop, Namche Bazaar, the small village tucked in a forested bowl three days of trekking below the first glimpse of Everest. The village is built into the steep mountainside high above the Dudh Kosi River at elevation 11,300 feet. The pictures I'd seen from the turn of the century presented Namche as Shangri-La, with stone homes and hotels tucked into a forested cirque and separated with terraces of rice and wheat below the Himalaya's mighty glacier-clad peaks. Sherpas made their home in Namche centuries ago after crossing the 17,000-foot Nangpa La Pass from Tibet. The isolated village is at least 700 years old, and before the eventual onslaught of trekkers and the commercial business of climbing began, it was more or less unknown to the world.

However, by 1981 about half of the forest around Namche had been cut down. As in all small villages in Nepal, wood was the fuel source for cooking and home heat. The growing population had taken a toll on the surrounding forests. Our expedition team straggled into Namche on August 20. Because of their strike, our 900 porters were spread out up to three days behind us in smaller villages. Namche had become more like a shopping mall with raw meat, vegetables, and bags of beans strewn out on the ground for shoppers. Virtually nothing in Nepal was refrigerated, so most of the cut yak meat was either bought the same day as the slaughter or hung out to dry. We never bought any of the meats, which always had flies crawling on them. We felt safe eating a dhal bhat, a huge plate of rice, small potatoes, and celeries covered with a rich tomato sauce. The drinks were always boiled tea or cocoa. This was the main meal of the day, every night, and the plates were heaped with as much as one could eat. Of course, everyone's appetite varied, but I always supplemented the meals with a couple candy bars.

I was able to take my first hot shower thanks to an old woman who would build a fire under a holding tank. When you stepped into the wood-walled shower, she would turn a lever so the hot water would flow over your head for a minute or so. After two weeks of trekking, it was heaven.

The Thyangboche Monastery 1981.

Refreshed, the team left Namche ready to attack. We hit the trails and made our way to Thyangboche (also spelled Tengboche), one of the most famous Buddhist monasteries in Nepal. The structure is built atop the huge terminal moraine debris of the Khumbu Glacier, which had reached down to that point some 400 years ago. Each team member was given a prayer scarf blessed by the Dali Lama's appointed holy man. Regardless of the religions we had grown up with, we all took the Buddhist blessing seriously. We treasured our prayer scarves and protected them as though they were gold. As we walked into Everest Base Camp I realized I had viewed Nepal from east to west. I found the last three days trekking to be as scenic and beautiful as anywhere in the country.

CO2 vs. VO2 Max

The mission of AMREE was to study the hearts and lungs of climbers as they ascended to the highest point on earth. Just to climb Mount Everest is a major achievement. Attempting to reach the summit with medical equipment strapped to your body is even more ambitious and risky. The science mission essentially had four categories:

1. Maximal exercise at extreme altitudes.
2. Physiological profiles of world-class high-altitude climbers.
3. Relationship of hypoxic ventilator response to exercise performance.
4. Control of ventilation in climbers to extreme altitude.

Psychological profiles and blood sampling were done in San Diego, on the mountain, and after the expedition back in San Diego.

In addition to the official science, I had a personal experiment I intended to conduct in secret. The last two people to climb Everest, Ray Genet and Hannelore Schmatz both died as a result of exhaustion near the summit in 1979. If I were to be fortunate enough to get a summit bid, I didn't want to risk being known as having run out of energy on the way down. Ninety percent of mountain climbing fatalities occur after the summit has been reached. I had met and climbed with Genet and knew first-hand that he was a powerful mountaineer. How could a climber with so much experience succumb to the mountain? This was on my mind before the climb as I tried to prepare for every possible scenario I might face. I convinced myself that I needed to experiment with "maximal exercise at extreme altitude." This would involve pushing myself past complete exhaustion to passing out. Only then could I experience what the preliminary symptoms of hyperventilation and fainting felt like. In La Jolla, and on the side of Mount Everest, we peddled the exercise bike to "exhaustion" every time we had to perform the VO2 max test, but never had I seen anyone pass out. In my seven years of wrestling, I had come close to blacking out during intense workouts, but never had I pushed myself beyond my limit.

Test pilots undergo this type of evaluation in a decompression chamber where the atmosphere is removed until the subject slowly passes out. At the University of Washington, I performed a similar test under the supervision of Dr. Schoene. The shortfall with a test chamber is that the environment is "faked." You are inside a steel tube at sea level sitting on a bench, doing little or no exercise. I felt that I had gained minimal insight to what true exhaustion would be like in extreme field conditions.

Marathoners who deplete their body can "hit the wall," but usually they're still standing. My theory was that if I could learn the symptoms from experience I could react in time in the field to control the fainting or hyperventilation by quickly putting a coat over my head to breathe my own oxygen and CO2, and recover. My goal was to be in control of a potentially dire situation.

Pacing itself in the last few days to acclimate to the elevation, the expedition stopped in Pheriche. This was my opportunity. The atmosphere at the summit of Everest is only one third that of sea level, so staying alive at 29,000 feet is one of the miracles of human adaptation. Pheriche, located at 14,200 feet beneath Everest has about half the atmosphere of sea level. I figured that if I ran straight up the mountainside in this rarified air for 3,000 feet, I could push myself past my previous physical extremes of exhaustion. You can see why I kept this plan a secret. Teammates would have thought I was nuts.

The 3,500-foot rocky mountainside rising behind Pheriche would be my natural treadmill. After completing my expedition work in the morning, I set off alone in early afternoon to climb and run to the ridge above. Going alone was not rational or recommended, but I learned early in my life that if it's going to be, it's up to me.

I took candy bars and a quart of fruit-flavored beverage and set off as fast as my legs would take me. I bounded, climbed and clawed, pushing myself as hard as I could, reaching the ridge at 17,500 feet in about 45 minutes with my lungs bursting and sweat pouring off my body in the cold air. I was lightheaded as I straddled the ridge and checked my pulse. Suddenly, as I started to descend, my entire body felt as though a billion pins were sticking into my flesh. Pain was the first sensation, and then I had the feeling of floating out of my body. I couldn't move. The extreme altitude and the rapid ascent had left me oxygen deprived to my limit. Dizzy with little spots floating in front of my eyes, I was close to passing out. I collapsed flat on my back between two boulders and wrapped my coat over my face tightly to trap my exhalations of oxygen and CO_2. I was barely conscious as I tried to relax and breathe. I felt I was at the point that if I didn't re-breathe my expended gases, I would pass out. The air we breathe at sea level is 21 percent oxygen, and mostly nitrogen. Exhaled air is 15 percent oxygen, and 4 percent carbon dioxide. Even above 17,000 feet, recycling my breath was enough to refresh my body! Gradually, the floating spots disappeared, my vision was restored, and my mind became clear. I slowly ate my candy bar and drank a liter of Kool-Aid. My experiment succeeded in building the neuron connection in my memory for dealing with conditions beyond exhaustion. I felt more confident about controlling my survival high on the mountain. I felt ready mentally and physically to climb the highest peak.

THE KHUMBU ICEFALL

The trail from Pheriche winds along the dry rocky lateral moraine of the Khumbu Glacier, climbing 3,000 vertical feet to the last "civilized" goat and yak herders' outpost called Gorak Shep. Adjacent to the settlement is the huge glacier and above that, the famous Khumbu Icefall cascading off Mount Everest. From Gorak Shep, we climbed onto the ice and began building stone markers for our yaks and 900 porters carrying 20 tons of our equipment to follow up the glacier. On August 30 at 10:30 a.m., after 24 days and trekking 175 miles, Pizzo, Porzak, Boyer, and I found a relatively flat place on the glacier that we would call Base Camp. There was no cause for celebration. The real work was just beginning.

The first day we laid the base stones for what would be a covered cooking shelter and community gathering hall for a total of 75 Sherpas and climbers. Our personal tents and equipment would be placed outside, but the Sherpas would also use the community hall for their sleeping quarters. The preformed fiberglass igloo was erected solely for the science experiments, including the exercise bicycle for determining and monitoring our VO2 max.

The climb up the icefall began the next morning, August 31, at 6:20 a.m. Boyer, Porzak, Pizzo, and I led the way into the jaws of death, as I called it, as the infamous Khumbu Icefall had claimed so many lives. It was the scariest place I have ever been in the mountains, and I dreaded every minute we were in its teeth. As the Khumbu Glacier flows off the southern side of Everest, it is squeezed between the mountain's massive west shoulder and the near-vertical Nuptse shoulder and ridge on the south side. The ice is twisted into a mass of jumbled, jagged, tumbling blocks, some as big as skyscrapers. Moving between two to three feet a day, the glacier drops 2,000 feet to the valley below. The tumbling ice had to be climbed directly because each side of the ice is walled in by huge cliffs. Unlike Makalu West Pillar, which was arguably the safest but one of the most difficult routes in the Himalaya, the Khumbu Icefall was statistically the most dangerous place. Thirty-four men previous to our journey had lost their lives in the icefall while trying to climb Everest.

Climbers love difficulty but abhor natural hazards they can't control. The only way to gain any sway over the danger on the route through the icefall was to get up in the middle of the night and be climbing into the icefall by 4 or 5 o'clock in the morning. You always wanted to be out of the icefall by 11 a.m. Most of the movement of icefalls occurs in the afternoon direct sunlight and rising temperatures, but not always. In the Khumbu Icefall, it seemed to me there were serrac collapses during the night as well as the afternoon, so one could never predict when an ice tower or crevasse would break.

With emotions strung tight on the first day of route finding, Boyer and I had a disagreement with Porzak and Pizzo. Porzak wanted to take a route that went right under the west shoulder. I instinctively knew that course would not work out just by visual observation and experience. I convinced Boyer to go with me up the center of the icefall and we broke away from Porzak and Pizzo. The icefall was no place to linger. Over the next two hours Boyer and I strung our line up and through some tumbling blocks for a thousand feet, and then found a relatively safe way to proceed above. Meanwhile, Porzak and Pizzo appeared to be floundering on their route as we could see them far below wandering between huge crevasses. They eventually climbed to the top of a jagged serac, a dead-end. Boyer and I, having placed all our fixed line, began to descend. As we neared the two stymied climbers, Porzak started berating me at the top of his lungs for leaving them. I lit into both Porzak and Pizzo about their incompetence and yelled that I wasn't about to waste my time and life on a route to nowhere. To make myself clear, I added that I was not about to follow anything they led, not through the icefall anyway!

Porzak, a famous trial lawyer in Boulder, Colorado, stunned by my audacious response, displayed visible emotion, which prompted all four of us to cry. We had buckled to the stress of dangerous technical climbing, and we spent the next few minutes apologizing to each other for our words of anger.

When the four of us approached Base Camp, we could see our teammates and Sherpas gathering outside and slowly walking up the ice to meet us. They'd heard our screaming match and feared that someone had died. Evans, our climbing leader, was very concerned and demanded that each of us explain exactly what had happened. The tension would not go away during the next two months on the mountain, as the competition to get to the top had begun along with the political jockeying for position.

During the first five days of September, our climbing team composed of me, Porzak, Pizzo, Boyer, Mike Weis, Jeff Lowe, and Peter Hackett, took turns finding a route through the icefall, over huge crevasses, and up vertical cliffs of ice. Except for the lower portion of the icefall, we strung fixed rope of 7 to 11 millimeters thick for a hand line that would be used for carrying our loads back and forth during the next two months. We placed long aluminum ladders over some big crevasses, and also used ladders for some vertical pitches after a lead climber had installed the fixed lines. Once Camp One was established at the top of the icefall at around 19,500 feet we could begin shuffling tons of gear up from Base Camp at 17,700 feet. When gear could be staged at Camp One we would begin establishing Camp Two seven miles away at the head of the Western Cwm. This staging process would be used to shuffle our campsites all the way up to a high Camp Five at 26,400 feet at the South Col. This was the process of expedition climbing. By the end of the trip, all of us would schlep loads up and down through the icefall at least seven times.

My sketch of Everest from above Gorak Shep.

BLOWN AWAY

On September 5, Boyer and I rose at 2 a.m. and started into the Khumbu Ice-fall at about 3 a.m. Our mission for the day was to string the last 600 feet of fixed line to our proposed Camp One. As we made our way, the sky darkened and snow began to fall. This suggested that even more snow could be accumulating above us on the huge West Buttress of Everest that formed the northern boundary of the Khumbu Glacier. At some point as snow built up, avalanches would rush tons of snow down into the icefall. It was not a good day to be there, but we were obsessed with getting the last safety lines tied in so we could advance the entire team to the Camp One location. Since the expedition had lost four days during the porter strike a month earlier, we always felt pressure to make up time. Fog rolled in as we reached the end of the fixed lines. Our rope was in spools, so the lead climber could just tie the rope on his body and start "spooling" out the line as fast as he could climb. Boyer and I switched leads and rapidly ascended the last few hundred feet to the Camp One site by early morning. We slapped each other on the back in a brief celebration and hightailed it back down and out of the icefall.

We dubbed one section of the icefall El Camino Real, "The Royal Road," a name the Spanish used to designate a special trail while pioneering California. This stretch was like climbing a snowboarding half pipe for several hundred yards. No safety line was strung here—the only relatively safe area of the entire route through the Khumbu Icefall. Boyer and I had just entered the top of El Camino Real and started climbing down the top of the "half pipe" when we heard a huge CRRAACCCKK coming from high above on the dangerous slopes of the West Buttress. Visibility was only 50 feet through fog and snowfall, but we instinctively knew what we heard was the start of an avalanche coming our way. On the verge of panic, we both ran down the ice as fast as our legs would move with packs on our backs and crampons attached to our mountain boots. With no safety line to clip a carabiner into, we were running scared. The roar of a thousand trains was coming right behind us. I thought my life was over.

Suddenly we were airborne, flying through the fog weightless with arms and legs flailing like rag dolls. My mind was racing. I couldn't determine if I was dead, dreaming, or hallucinating. The wind blast that rushes in front of the snow debris of an avalanche had swept us off our feet like dry leaves. We were flying down the half pipe at what felt like 90 miles per hour on a cushion of air several feet above the ice. Finally, the wind blast spit us out the lower end of El Camino Real and deposited us abruptly on a big fan of ice half the size of a football field. Totally unnerved, I looked at my arms, then at my legs and feet to see if they were still attached to my body. Boyer had been in front of me when the blast hit us, but he ended up several yards behind, sitting with a stunned expression. As quickly as we could compose ourselves, and with just a couple words spoken, we started descending out of the icefall as fast as we could.

The audience at Base Camp listened with rapt attention as we described our ordeal. Our brush with death was food for anxiety as we hunkered in camp the next four days while storms continued to build. One avalanche after another slid off the West Shoulder, wiping out half of our fixed lines so laboriously installed through the icefall. One avalanche was so large that the wind blast from nearly a mile away lifted some of our individual tents off their pegged foundations.

CAMP ONE TO CAMP TWO

Successful climbers can be egomaniacs, big risk takers by nature, and aggressive high achievers. The answer to "Why?" we climb a mountain isn't just "Because it's there." More likely it's "Because we're competitive." Climbers who attempt Everest believe they can get to the summit even though the success rate is very low. Reasons for climbers reaching or not reaching the summit are as varied as their personalities. Relationships can play a role as cliques develop quickly. They might band together based on political beliefs, or similar technical expertise, or educational background. While it certainly wasn't my cup of tea, some bonded over the temptation to smoke pot to relax. AMREE teammates had a common connection in the pursuit of science.

John Evans, who knew he didn't acclimate well above 23,000 feet, concentrated on the leadership of the expedition. Porzak had vast experience, but he already had his climbing buddies from Colorado: Weis and Lowe. David Jones had all the experience but was a true loner. I just couldn't communicate well at all with Hackett, and even less so with Pizzo. I was the last man chosen for the AMREE team, and consequently struggled to bond with anyone except Boyer, and our leader, Evans. The team chemistry just wasn't cohesive, as it was on Makalu. We were all good athletes, but extremely independent. This was a huge expedition with 53 Sherpas and ambitious science goals. Evans had a mammoth job in keeping the group pulling together.

After two weeks of cowering to avalanches, we finally were able to get all the fixed lines replaced and repaired through the icefall and Camp One was established on September 12. No power plays or cutthroat tactics occurred while climbing the icefall as everyone focused on getting through it as fast as possible. But, in the safety of Camp One at the Western Cwm of Everest, gamesmanship among the cliques and Sherpa groups began to surface like a huge poker game, with no one else wanting to show his cards for how he planned to reach the top first. My cards were on the table early, however. I had teamed up with Boyer while on the trek in, as I felt he had the best chemistry and chance of making the summit with me. Boyer shared my vision that speed is safety. He had the leg strength, endurance, and strong lungs. We felt confident of our success if we stayed together.

Six of us, including myself, set out from Camp One to establish Camp Two at 20,700 feet on September 14. The Western Cwm is a huge gently sloped valley between the massive 10,000-foot-high South Face of Everest and the mile-high northern wall and buttress of Nuptse. Of all my mountain journeys, the Western Cwm of Everest was the most serene. For seven miles, the cwm provides a temple of solitude with low-angle slopes of snow and ice that inspires the soul. There were no dangerous crevasses. Avalanche paths were too far away to be a threat. Some of the team went on snowshoes here. I had hauled up my skis, which proved to be pure joy when gliding the seven miles back down to Camp One after depositing my daily load of gear. Once the porters hauled the science equipment, including a pre-molded science hut, up the icefall and onward to Camp Two, the science testing and experiments kicked into gear.

LITTLE SHOP OF HORRORS

At Camp Two, Weis and I cut big ice blocks out of the glacier to build a rect-angular shaped structure with an ice block roof to house the medical laboratory supplies for various experiments. Here, Dr. Duane Blume, Dr. Frank Sarn-quist, and Dr. Schoene, would take weekly blood samples from all of us. The vials were stored in the ice to ship back to La Jolla at the end of the expedition. We also erected an aluminum frame laboratory with a pre-molded fiberglass floor and insulated walls for the EKG and VO2 max performance testing.

At night in the high-altitude tranquility of the Western Cwm at Camp Two, one could see every star in the universe over a horizon featuring a good share of the Himalayas. One could get the feeling of being on another planet in a clear, calm night with the temperature around minus 20 degrees. However, we would quickly return to earth as we took our turns walking into the science laboratory. I would open the door of what I came to call the "Little Shop of Horrors," unzip my coat in the 50-degree temperatures and watch as another climber rode an exercise bicycle with a face mask strapped tightly over his face, and EKG wires pasted to his bare chest while a doctor screamed, "Faster, faster; come on push it all out!" The exertion took an especially high toll on the body at 20,700 feet, in the lower end of The Death Zone with thin, extremely dry air. The subject would complete the VO2 max test with a group of doctors looking on and collapse virtually devastated to the ground while another doctor bound one arm with a rubber tourniquet to extract a blood sample. When it came my turn to be tested, I nearly vomited when they ripped out my chest hairs while removing the EKG nodes. My fear of needles added to the stress. To avoid watching the needle stick into my vein I tried singing or thinking of anything I could to turn off my mind. We were asked to perform to exhaustion every other day, and we were exhausted to begin with! The science testing up there between heaven and earth was like a scene out of a science fiction movie in which the climbers were the victims. To top it off, our mission was to carry the exercise bicycle all the way to the South Col to perform VO2 max tests above 26,000 feet!

CAMP TWO TO CAMP FIVE

Evans had been on the failed International Everest Expedition in 1971 and was well-acquainted with the south side of the peak. At his home in Colorado, he worked with Lowe to design an aluminum platform that would anchor on the side of a cliff enabling us to attempt a new route up the Southwest Pillar. Attempting a new more direct route was a bold but wise decision as it would bypass the long first-ascent route that zigzags up the Lhotse Headwall. The climbers were excited to be pioneers in science and pioneering a new course. And we were relieved to begin the technical climbing, which meant a respite from the needles and performance testing.

The climbing above Camp Two that started on September 19 required another level of skill. The first obstacle was to cross the gigantic bergschrund that separates the Khumbu Glacier from the Southwest Face of Everest. We would have to employ our ice tools, screws, and pickets to roll out another mile and a half of fixed lines that would eventually go all the way to the South Col. On the route up the Southwest Pillar at the sites for Camp Three and Camp Four we would install a couple of the ingenious tent platforms that Lowe had tested in Colorado. They worked exactly as planned. The Camp Three platform was erected at 23,800 feet under a cliff that we hoped would protect the tents from any avalanche sweeping the Southwest Face.

Mount Everest Camp Three.

Boyer and I were assigned to move up to Camp Three and begin installing fixed lines to Camp Four. I had just run out line to the end of our 600-foot spool when I noticed that Boyer had begun to climb very, very slowly. He was normally a powerhouse, so something had obviously happened. He was barely moving. "Something's wrong with me," he said as he slogged heavy-footed up to my belay stance. "I think I have pulmonary edema." I put my ear to his back, listened to the breathing, and sure enough, the unmistakable gurgling sound of rales. His lung membrane had fractured and fluid was flooding inside. Our only immediate option, while he was still able, was to go down as quickly as possible all the way to Base Camp. We were both stunned. My notion that Steve was my best partner for a summit attempt was suddenly dashed as fate was making us take a U-turn at 24,000 feet. We started rappelling to Camp Three. Going down with pulmonary edema was infinitely easier for him than going up, and we made it to Camp Two in just a few hours. I stayed at Camp Two and watched as Steve, breathing easier, continued his descent toward Camp One and eventually back to base.

On September 25, Evans, Jones, and I moved back up to Camp Three to begin three days of fixing ropes up the solid ice slope to 24,500 feet where we hacked out a flat spot on the ice and erected a tent platform for Camp Four. None of the climbers liked Camp Four, as it was exposed to ice and avalanche from above. It was to be used only as an emergency overnight stay between the long and strenuous climb from Camp Three to the South Col. Sleeping and movement on cliff sites were planned very carefully. Anything dropped could tumble over 2,000 feet into the cwm.

Pizzo, Schoene, Lowe, and Porzak climbed up from Camp Four and continued where Jones and I left off fixing the last 1,500 feet of rope to Camp Five, which was eventually located at about 26,200 feet, under a rock cliff and deep ice well. Even though the vertical distance between these two camps was only 1,500 feet of elevation, more than 2,500 feet of fixed line had to be anchored because of the slope angle and the distance.

Jones and I were back at Camp Two on September 28 as the upper reaches of the mountain were being scoured by high winds. Judging by the ice plume and a deafening noise—like a blast furnace—we guessed the gusts were well over 100 miles per hour. Everest would be plastered for three days by a storm we would all remember. As it peaked on the 29th, winds ripped out some of our tents and buried others completely in unrelenting blasts of horizontal snow and ice. We were all seasoned mountaineers, but this was the worst storm any of us had experienced. Everest reaches high enough in the atmosphere to snag the low end of the wandering jet streams. The ferocious winds can last for weeks. I was at Camp Two in relative safety compared to some of our climbers who were at Camps Three and Four catching the full force of winds threatening to sweep tents off the mountain—with people in them. That's no exaggeration. Climbers have been blown off Himalayan mountains, never to be seen again.

When the storm abated, our dejected teammates Porzak, Pizzo, Lowe, and Weiss climbed down from higher camps and Jones and I headed down from Camp Two and eventually made an unnerving descent through a rearranged icefall, where nothing was recognizable. We arrived at Base Camp on October 1 for much needed R & R. Upon getting weighed by Sarnquist, I was astounded that I was down to 166 pounds, a loss of about six pounds.

I've never been shy about food consumption, and I knew it was critical to pack in as many calories as possible even at high altitudes where appetite is curtailed. Breakfasts between Base Camp and Camp Three usually consisted of oatmeal with sugar, raisins, and honey, sometimes with pancakes and syrup. For daily hydration I drank four or five quarts of powdered drinks loaded with sugar. I snacked on about six candy bars a day, sometimes with yak jerky. Lunch usually consisted of chapatis rolled up with peanut butter and jam. In the afternoon I usually ate a whole can of sardines or kipper snacks with bread and a slab of cheese. I had the sardines virtually to myself as no one else on the expedition could stomach the smell of fish at extreme altitude. Dinners were usually tea or coffee with a generous serving of what we loosely called "Irish stew" consisting of yak meat, rice, potatoes, peas, and chapatis, with chocolate pudding and cream for dessert. I also had a shot of whiskey every night.

Regardless of how many calories are consumed, the body essentially rots at elevations above 15,000 feet. Boyer's goal was to recover from high altitude pulmonary edema at the lower elevation of Base Camp. Some climbers with HAPE reportedly recovered after three weeks rest, but none was known to recover at elevations above 17,000 feet. Boyer was optimistic about his recovery, but I felt his chances of healing were very slim, so David Jones became my climbing teammate.

From October 2 through 5, Jones and I rested at Base Camp as well as we could at 17,700 feet. Realizing that the body is in an accelerated condition of aging at this altitude, it's mostly a psychological and attitude adjustment to keep the body moving. I spent one day trekking down the Khumbu and up the side of a mountain the Sherpas called Kolipata where I managed to get some stunning sunset photographs of Everest. Once word got out that I was going to photograph on this getaway, my backpack filled with my teammates' cameras. I must have needed the time alone. In my diary I wrote that I was quite frustrated at this juncture with the slow progress of fixing the remaining lines to the South Col. Hackett, Graber and Porzak were planning to install the ropes between October 2 and 6 and then make a summit bid.

On October 7, Jones, Pizzo and I left Base Camp at 5 a.m. We climbed through the icefall in just two hours and continued another hour all the way to Camp Two. I spent the rest of the afternoon conferring with Evans by radio and convinced him not to install more fixed ropes above the col. We were already late in the fall season and the winter winds were upon us. I felt we just couldn't afford another week's delay. The slopes above the col were not that severe. On October 9, Jones, Pizzo, Sherpa Anu and I climbed to Camp Three. The next morning, the four of us joined by Sherpa Sungdare climbed all the way to the South Col where we'd make Camp Five. Buffeted by consistent 45 mile per hour winds, we labored several hours to chop ice to make fairly level platforms so we could erect two North Face VE-24 tents. We finally climbed inside the shelters at our highest and last camp at 6 p.m. It was a spectacular setting perched at what we estimated to be 26,400 feet. From this vantage we looked "down" on practically every other mountain within a hundred miles. As long as we could survive the minus 20-degree temperatures, gale winds, and lack of oxygen, the whole world was below our feet.

The next three days were miserable as we endured the never-ending windblasts that had accelerated to the range of 50 to 100 miles per hour. We prayed the tents would not shred to rags while we huddled in our down bags and garments trying to keep the stove going to melt ice for critical hydration. Jones began to deteriorate rapidly from either a lingering cold or possibly a severe chill he got while evacuating his bowels in the brutally frigid elements. People always ask mountain climbers two classic questions: "How do you go the bathroom?" and "How cold was it?" In a few words, answering the call of nature is very difficult in extreme conditions. Urination is easy for men, who can simply lie down inside the tent and empty their bladders into plastic "pee bottles." However, a bowel movement above 26,000 feet is exceedingly difficult, if not dangerous. Dropping your pants exposes a large vulnerable skin area to the elements and enables extreme weather to suck heat from the body core. This is what I believe happened to Jones. While outside in the frigid gale taking a BM on the evening of October 12, his body temperature dropped significantly. When he crawled back inside the tent he was shaking uncontrollably. He could not warm up. After hours of trying to rehydrate and recover, he was still shaking. He knew he was slowly dying, and that he would have to retreat down the mountain, which he eventually did—all the way to Base Camp. The expedition was over for Jones. Later he would tell me that even after returning home to Vancouver, he needed months to recover his strength.

My method of taking a dump was crude and perhaps offensive to the senses of my tent mates, but the art of survival should not be constrained by pride. I carried plastic bags to the South Col. When I had to go, I told my teammates to turn their backs, and then I would poop into a bag while inside the tent. It wasn't a potty joke when I tried to convince Jones that if he didn't use my method at high altitudes, he might die. He very nearly did.

The morning of October 13 dawned clear, but the winds were approaching hurricane force. Pizzo and I still wouldn't give up hope, so we piled on our gear and started out for the summit through the gullies above the col. But our immediate hopes were dashed by relentless winds of about 75 miles per hour. We struggled upward for only a few hundred feet before realizing we had to turn back. At the noon radio call with our leader, Evans gave the order to "hop on the ropes and make a retreat." Three miserable days at Camp Five had brought us no closer to the summit.

As we descended to Camp Two on October 14, we passed Porzak, Hackett, and Sherpa Topa as they were heading up the fixed lines to Camp Three to try for the summit. The next morning we could not hear any winds, and the weather looked perfect above us, but the trio at Camp Five reported they were too exhausted to move out of the tents. A day later they were ready to go, but as fate would have it, the jet stream had dropped again overnight and was blasting Camp Five and the summit slopes above. Our situation was becoming quite tenuous, as we were getting close to running out of time but closer to running out of energy. A human being's survival is on borrowed time in The Death Zone, and we were pushing our limits. The two-pronged mission of summit and science had taken its toll. The scientists had gathered almost all the data they had sought, except the alveolar gas samples and spirometer data needed above the col. Evans and West also wanted us to haul the exercise bicycle all the way up to the col to perform the VO2 max testing, but my climbing teammates and I managed to convince them that was impossible under the circumstances. We would have to compromise, sacrificing the VO2 max data for the lighter weight science tasks above the South Col.

Resting at Camp Two on October 17, I was in a quandary trying to figure out which teammate was healthy and strong enough to go back up for one more crack at the top of Everest. In conference with Evans, the plan was for me, Boyer, Lowe, and Weiss to go back up for a summit attempt and complete what science tasks we could. I was instructed by Evans to pick three of the strongest and healthiest Sherpas, so I chose Sherpas Sungdare, Anu, and Ang Sangbu. Lowe and Weiss were "purists" and wanted to try for the summit without using bottled oxygen. I had trashed my tentative plan of using no supplementary oxygen, as the past 45 days of hard labor in The Death Zone had me wanting to save whatever brain cells I had left. I knew from my experience on Makalu that in pioneering climbs such as ours the margin between success and failure as well as life and death is razor thin. Using oxygen on the last leg to the top would give me one more element of safety. Also, I already had experienced how the brain is damaged during prolonged stays at oxygen-poor high elevations. Following the Makalu climb I suffered short-term memory loss. My brain was able to recover through laborious, disciplined exercises that I didn't care to repeat. Going for the summit without supplementary oxygen wasn't worth the risk for me.

Boyer had only a little more than a week to heal his HAPE at Base Camp, so he was taking a gamble by making another ascent to the high camps. Sure enough, while ascending the ropes to Camp Four his lungs started filling with fluid again. Weiss, Lowe and I spent a shared miserable night with Boyer crammed inside the tent at Camp Four listening to his lungs gurgle as he labored to breath. The Sherpas had elected to stay below in Camp Three. In the morning, at about half strength, Boyer made his final retreat down the mountain, taking his dreams of the summit with him. We learned over the radio that two of our Sherpas also were too sick to continue, leaving only Sungdare, Weiss, Lowe, and myself in climbing condition.

After another miserable night of no sleep, the four of us got out of the Camp Four tent on October 20 and began ascending to the South Col. Sungdare and I were breathing bottled oxygen now and we made rapid progress to Camp Five, which had been ravaged by the winds. One VE-24 tent was in good condition, while the other tent was nearly destroyed. Both the tents were half full of spindrift. Hours would be required to chisel and chop enough of the ice out of just one tent to make it habitable. Weiss, climbing without supplemental oxygen, arrived about an hour later, and Lowe was nowhere in sight. Weiss mentioned that Lowe was moving very slowly that morning. I would find out later that he had developed a mild case of pulmonary edema and turned around.

Weiss surveyed the situation and said the only reasonable option was for him to descend with Lowe to Camp Four and leave Sungdare and me at Camp Five with a chance for the summit. I couldn't believe what Weiss had just said. He was essentially giving up his chance for the summit to give Sungdare and me the best shot. I argued that the VE-24 was designed for four in a squeeze. But with Lowe nowhere to be seen, Weiss concluded that if he continued without his buddy and without supplemental oxygen, he would slow us up. With his mind made up, Weiss reached deep inside his rucksack and pulled out a small carefully wrapped box and placed it in my hand. Inside were four large Grandma's Cookies that he had saved for the summit day. Of all the kind and generous human gestures I have had the good fortune to receive, this ranks number one. Weiss then turned around, clipped himself into the fixed ropes and began his rappels into the abyss below to find Lowe and continue down the mountain. Sungdare and I were now alone.

SHERPA SUNGDARE

The Sherpas are a special race of people. Only a small band of them lives around Namche Bazaar where they settled after coming over the Nangpa La from Tibet more than 800 years ago. The Sherpas I met spoke as much English as I knew of their language, which was very little, but Sungdare was more accomplished in English than his mates. He was 26, and about 135 pounds. Sungdare was his first, middle, and only name. That was as much as any of the American climbers knew to this point about the man we respectfully called Sherpa Sungdare.

He was the only Sherpa on our expedition who had summited Everest. He was with Genet and Schmatz trying to save their lives as they slowly died from exhaustion and exposure shortly after reaching the summit in 1979. On that fateful day, in a supreme, heroic rescue effort, Sungdare descended from just below the South Summit to the South Col, grabbed a full bottle of oxygen, and then climbed back up to 28,000 feet in a vain attempt to save their lives. In this astounding feat of strength, he froze his feet and fingers, eventually losing virtually all of his toes. Seeing his bare feet in Base Camp, one would assume his medical treatment had been done by someone using a dull axe, leaving raw scar tissue and calloused stump on one foot that ended at mid arch from which the rest of his foot and toes used to extend. He would stuff wool socks inside his boots to fill the cavities at the ends, and then he'd cram what remained of his feet inside. That Sungdare could walk and balance himself in delicate climbing situations was an astounding credit to his athleticism, will, and determination. His performance ranked with the world's top sports stars in my book, and certainly would earn him a page all his own in my version of "Ripley's Believe It or Not!" I couldn't fathom how he could climb rock and steep ice with no toes. The route above Camp V would have no fixed lines to hold for balance in the final 3,000 feet to the summit. There would be no belaying; it was each man for himself. Sungdare lived up to the Sherpa mystique and image. He was a real Tiger, and like most Sherpas, self-effacing. He smoked cigarettes like there would be no tomorrow. He drank alcohol heavily, a scourge that plagued many of the Sherpas. Any one of these vices is a handicap for high altitude mountaineering. But without toes, a normal man would have difficulty functioning even at sea level.

Regardless of how you summed up his personal profile, my partner for my dream of climbing to the top of the world revealed a troubling problem as we hunkered in the tent at Camp Five. In broken English he said he did not want to go any farther. He had summited Everest and had been a witness to tragedy. I could tell by his body actions and eyes that he was balking at going any higher. He didn't want to face more drama. Although the wind was raging outside the flapping nylon, I managed to persuade his thinking by offering money. He was already getting paid well as a team member of our expedition, but this was my last hurrah for Everest. This was my third trip to the South Col, my body was wasting, and to try soloing in these terrible winds would be suicide. I told Sungdare that if he would at least make an attempt with me in the morning, I would personally pay him $100, and also give him my prized Eddie Bauer down shirt, something he had been eyeing for weeks every time I put it on. The incentives seemed to work. He didn't say no but was still very reluctant and apparently didn't say yes, either. What he couldn't adequately communicate to me with his limited English vocabulary, arm gestures and acting, was that he would not budge out of the tent until the sun broke the horizon. For reasons unknown to me, he was superstitious about the darkness. Either his Buddhist faith or his own superstitions led him to be wary of traveling before the sun rose. He tried in vain to communicate, leaving me skeptical of his total commitment.

In late October, the sun would rise at about 7 o'clock. Leaving the tent that late in the morning was unconscionable from my experience. I wanted to get going by 3 a.m. at the latest, so I stubbornly refused to understand his words, and went about the business of getting our gear together for an early getaway. I was eager to escape the hellish conditions in the tent, which was buffeted by chilling winds on the outside while the not-so-cozy inside was still partially packed with snow and ice.

One of the key assignments of our science mission was to paste electrodes on my chest for an electrocardiogram test. The electrodes were to be connected to a device on my waist called a Medilog recorder, a slow-running four-channel tape. I needed the expedition's custom-built alveolar gas sampler bundled with six or eight small cartridges. Hackett had carried the science equipment to Camp Five and stashed it somewhere, but I didn't have a clue where to look. At sunset, I went outside the tent into the bitter cold wind and dug around in the likely places—such as the ice well and rock bergschrund—but came up empty. It could have been placed anywhere outside, but without knowing exactly where, I could have dug fruitlessly for hours. Returning to the tent, I gave up on finding the equipment and concentrated on starting the stove for hot drinks and oatmeal. I would be unable to make a summit-bid contribution to the science mission. (However, the gear showed up. It was discovered when Pizzo and Hackett came back up to the col for their summit bid five days later. Unbeknownst to me, Sungdare had been practically sitting on top of the science equipment while I'd been outside looking for it. The bag was buried "inside" the tent under a foot of neve—granular snow that had been partially melted, refrozen and compacted.)

As Sungdare and I sat cramped between billows of down sleeping bags and coats, I removed my boots to heat them up over the stove flame. They were a brand-new design made by Koflach, and the ankle supports were made of super-light soft plastic on the sides. Inadvertently, while trying to warm the inside of the frozen boot, I put the side of it too close to the butane cooker. In an instant the hot flame burned off part of the plastic ankle support including a couple of the shoelace eyelets. "Bad mistake!" I thought as I wracked my deteriorating brain for improvisations. I bored a couple new eyelets through the plastic with my knife so I could wrap avalanche cord into a type of shoelace tourniquet around my ankle to keep the plastic support from breaking off completely. I had learned to sleep with my boots on because the extreme difficulty of trying to put on boots at this altitude became an exhausting ordeal in itself. It's pretty uncomfortable to cram your legs deep into a mummy bag with boots on, but it was the only way to keep warm. The previous two nights, I hadn't slept but an hour, and this night didn't look like it would be any different. Sungdare made his living on these expeditions, and he seemed more comfortable with his boots off. With only half a foot, and the other one damaged, he had no more toes to lose!

We unceremoniously dined on hot tea and noodle soup that evening of October 20. To my astonishment, Sungdare also smoked a cigarette as we sat upright and tried to rest as best we could while the wind raged. Gusts would smack the tent walls as though a gang mob was trying to beat us with baseball bats. The tent was still substantially filled with spindrift preventing us from lying prone to sleep, so we huddled in a sitting position like two Peruvian mummies. I tried thinking of home, the paradise of fall colors in Spokane, the valleys of British Columbia. I fantasized about eating all the delicious foods I took for granted while in the comfort of civilization. I tried chanting the

Om of the Buddhist prayers to subdue the roar of the wind. My thoughts scanned for any diversion to the mental and physical discomfort. Sungdare, ever stoic, kept to himself the entire night. The only consolation for me was occasionally peering out the zipper where I could see countless stars in the ink-black moonless night. It was beyond human comprehension how many stars I could see at this position on earth with no dust, no city lights, and halfway to space. The sky was an astronomer's dream.

My mind was tortured by the slow passing of time. The uncomfortable sitting positions with no wriggle room made both of us stir crazy. Midnight was my long-awaited cue to start the stove to heat water. Sungdare wouldn't budge, adding much to my already elevated anxiety. He simply would not move! I exhausted my negotiation skills and all of the persuasion tactics I could invent. Nothing worked. He was not going to rally. So there we sat, me drinking and stewing in my angst. The only comfort was that we each had a bottle of oxygen to help us breathe more normally and stay warmer as we rested and waited for dawn. I had planned for this moment for years, and this was not the way I'd pictured it.

THE GREAT TEMPEST

The sky to the east began to show a different color at about 5:30 a.m., a hint that a clear dawn would eventually occur on October 21. According to our tiny thermometer hanging on the tent, the temperature was still 20 below zero. I estimated the wind at a steady 45 miles per hour. I had everything prepared except the rope, which was outside the tent, tangled and partially frozen into the ice. Sungdare said nothing while I prepared some oatmeal. As the sky continued to brighten, I prepared to make one last try for the summit, with or without my partner. Either way, the forceful winds dampened any prognosis for success. I crawled out of the tent and cut off about 50 feet of seven-millimeter rope, tying two pieces together from the hopelessly frozen tangle. This would be our climbing rope. Then I quickly crawled back inside the tent to get out of the wind. Sungdare began to stir. I promised him again that if he would try for the summit with me, he would get my coat and the bonus regardless of how far we got.

We packed a quart of water each, and a couple candy bars plus the cookies Weiss had graciously given me. By Sungdare's actions, facial expression, and movement, I could tell he would be up for the task and ready at dawn. Slowly, the sun's rays hit the tip of Lhotse just above us to the south. I bolted from the tent and tied on the rope. Sungdare, to my delight climbed out, grabbed the other end of the rope and tied on. He asked me if he should bring an extra bottle of oxygen beyond what each of us was already using. Yes, I replied, but only if he felt strong enough to carry it. If we didn't need it, we could place the bottle higher up the mountain for the next climbers should they make another attempt. I started climbing and he was on my heels like a puppy. It was exactly 7 a.m. We were off!

The winds were blowing west to east and the climbing was not difficult. I made a diagonal traverse upward into the large couloir that split the center of the Southeast Ridge. We were climbing off of our pioneering route and I knew from previous expedition photos that we could follow this gulley system all the way to the "bench" or shoulder of the Southeast Ridge at 27,600 feet. Sungdare let the full 50 feet of rope pay out between us as I upped the pace to my maximum. I had read horror stories of previous climbers who struggled mightily in waist-deep spindrift trying to ascend this couloir, but the snow conditions were perfect on this morning, allowing our crampons to cut into the ice as easily and securely as if we were climbing Styrofoam.

After gaining nearly 300 feet of elevation, I noticed the wind was beginning to subside. Violent blasts were followed by calm before the next blast. But the gusts were becoming less frequent as we gained elevation. I kept the pace up to the maximum speed that I felt I could sustain all the way to the top. Sunshine was flooding the valleys below as we were gaining on the summit of Lhotse, the world's fourth highest mountain. About 15 miles to our east, and in full view now, was mighty Makalu, the world's fifth highest mountain. Behind that on the horizon 85 miles away was Kanchenjunga, the world's third highest peak. All were bathed in glorious morning sunlight.

After 40 minutes of climbing the winds were gone! It was as if we had climbed out of hell directly into nirvana. I didn't dare lessen the pace, though. Experience had taught me well that surprises in nature know no boundaries, especially in the mountains. Sungdare tugged on the rope and signaled that the weight of the emergency oxygen bottle was too much for the fast pace. He had found a small notch in the rock to stash the tank and placed a flag for location upon our return. I didn't protest at all. He knew his limits. The bottle would still be in position to be a safety valve for us, or our teammates should they follow. After five more minutes of climbing, I felt another tug. Sungdare had stopped to adjust his gloves, and when I turned around to look, I saw both of his gloves tumbling down the mountain! Jesus, what can happen next! Fortunately, my partner had a spare pair of fabric-covered wool mittens in his pack ready to put on.

After an hour of climbing on a steady angle of slope, I noticed the horizon above us had color and a different shape from the grey black limestone. My first thought was that it must be a tent belonging to the East Face Expedition, as they had been working on that route for two months during the same time as our expedition. It could be Roskelley! The closer we climbed, the more perplexed were my thoughts. The shape was stationary, and right in the center of the couloir, an odd place for a campsite. The shock hit me as I climbed within 10 feet of the object. It was a human body! A recently broken off piece of ice was shading the head of Hannelore Schmatz, who, according to Sungdare, had died of exposure while crawling down the mountain on her hands and knees a little over two years prior. Sungdare, of course, was intimately acquainted with the tragic story and the deaths of Schmatz and Ray Genet.

Stunned, I made a Catholic gesture with the sign of the cross, a reflex of watching my cousins in church. Sungdare briefly recounted those devastating moments on the ill-fated 1979 German expedition. On his rescue attempt to save his rope mates, Schmatz was still crawling down the mountain on her hands and knees when he passed her going back up to try and revive Genet. Sungdare explained that as night fell the three of them had bivouacked just a few hundred feet higher because they were too exhausted to descend farther. They dug a small alcove into the ice to wait out the night. In the morning, both Genet and Schmatz were barely alive. Sungdare made his legendary effort to go down 1,500 feet to the South Col and get a full oxygen tank. Under any circumstances, performing this deed above 27,000 feet would be classified "superhuman," but Sungdare had barely survived the bivouac himself, and both of his feet and hands were already frozen. To climb down, then back

UP to this spot with 30 pounds in his pack and frozen feet was beyond my comprehension, a feat only a super Sherpa could pull off.

The body of Hannelore Schmatz lay where she died in 1979,
being covered and uncovered again by the blowing snows of Everest.

Unfortunately, Genet had died by the time he returned, and when he climbed back down to Schmatz, she was dead, too. Sungdare harbored emotions he could not explain to me in any language. But now I clearly understood why he'd been unenthusiastic about coming back up past this gruesome memory on the mountain.

I had to keep moving beyond this sobering moment and put myself back into gear. Within just a couple hundred feet of climbing as fast as my legs would move, we reached the spectacular ledge called the "Bench" at 27,600 feet on the Southeast Ridge. Remnants of several old campsites were visible; torn rags of tents flapped in the light breeze. This was the spot from which Ed Hillary and Tenzing Norgay launched the final leg of their 1953 first ascent of Everest. I knew what was ahead from here, but the reality is always much different than you've read or imagined. For a few steps along this crest of the icy ridge, the climbing views were magnificent. To the east rose Makalu and Kanchenjunga, and to the north were the brown plains of Tibet. The air was clear as crystal.

We were at the same elevation as my turn around spot on Makalu the previous year, and every step that I took now was a personal altitude record. Just a few feet higher, as we reached a shallow nook at the base of the steepening ridge, Sungdare climbed up beside me and said, "This is the spot where Ray Genet died."

GHOSTS OF THE PEAKS

In my formative years before I imagined that I could climb Everest, I had read of climbers having hallucinations at extreme altitude, seeing things, having ghost partners, and talking to imaginary companions that were very real to the climber. The most famous story was Edward Whimper's visions of four crosses in the sky right after the rope broke and his companions fell to their death on the first ascent of the Matterhorn. I had read of these things and brushed them off as more good stories for the Bible.

Sungdare on the "Bench" on the SE Ridge. Makalu in foreground,
Kanchenjunga on the horizon.

As we stood there over the spot Ray Genet had died at 27,700 feet on Everest, Sungdare just stared. I considered Genet a friend. Dan Schnell of

Spokane and I had climbed with him on Denali just a few months before he left for his fatal Everest expedition. Genet, a man of the mountains, was known for having a powerful body odor, probably from bathing only once a month or maybe even every six months. Suddenly, standing over his death bed, the oxygen mask strapped tight to my face filled with the smell of Ray Genet's body stench. In a panic, I ripped off the mask. Sungdare looked appropriately startled as I quickly bolted upward breathing heavily as I fled the scene. The odor I sensed whirling into my nostrils conjured up the notion that the ghost of Ray Genet was in my face and trying to take over my body. Years later I still recalled this experience as being very real in that moment of my life. Apparently it was a psychosomatic hallucination of some sort, brought on by the extreme stress we were feeling near the top of the world.

Above Genet's last bivouac was a thousand feet of Southeast Ridge, a rounded crest of ice and wind slab snow that led to the South Summit of Everest. During my teenage years of climbing, I developed powerful mental images of this opportunity. I had visualized myself climbing the last steps to the top of the world's highest peak. Now I was living that moment one step after another as I pounded my crampons and ice axe into the neve to make the best steps I could for Sungdare to follow. A couple spooky wind slabs of ice could have avalanched, but I managed to find safe snow by making diagonal traverses. We climbed together without hesitation for an hour before the South Summit gradually came into view. It was just a few hundred feet away. The air was still mostly calm, but with each step higher, the roar of the tempest above warned me that our calm was about to change.

TOP OF THE WORLD

First the frightening roar, and then the full force of the jet stream winds hit us as we climbed the last few feet to the South Summit at 28,750 feet. We had to anchor our axes and lean into the wind to stay upright as we gazed at the ridge ahead. Reinhold Messner, the most accomplished historical figure in mountaineering, said the final ridge of ice and rock leading up nearly 300 vertical feet to the summit of Everest was the most beautiful ridge he had ever seen. For several seconds I was horrified at the tremendous exposure. The reality of the scene caught me off guard. The ridge was crested on the east side by huge cornices that overhung the Kangshung Face, which dropped steeply, then vertically to the Kangshung Glacier over 12,000 feet below. On the west side of the ridge, the Southwest Face dropped 8,000 feet to the abyss of the Western Cwm. In the center of the ridge was the vertical Hillary Step, the final technical barrier to the summit. And then there was our enemy the jet stream, giving us the full monty. At minus 20 degrees with winds around 60 miles per hour, the only possible way to survive was to keep moving. On the positive side, the air was clear and the wind was steady, not gusty. We sought shelter from the wind for a few minutes in a small crevasse that lay just beneath the South Summit. We got out our belay devices, drank some water, and repacked our gear for the technical climbing ahead.

Descending the South Summit to a notch, we placed our feet on the final ridge. Our rope was only 50 feet long, so at the end of my lead, I would give Sungdare a boot axe belay. The ice conditions and exposure of the ridge had us carefully belaying each other all the way to the Hillary Step. I watched Sungdare carefully balance himself climbing along the knife-edged ice and was amazed many times over at his astounding poise and agility with no toes! The belays were mostly psychological. If one of us slipped, the chances of recovery were slim. From the base of the Hillary Step, a 40-foot vertical step in the ridge rock covered in ice, I tried the most obvious line of stemming between the cornice and the rock like Hillary did. The constant battering of the wind had rendered the snow so unconsolidated and grainy that it wouldn't hold my weight. I floundered for several minutes, thrashing my legs in all directions but couldn't gain any footholds. The ice seemed to turn into piles of sugar below my feet. I definitely couldn't make it up the step the way the first summiteers did.

I backed off a dozen feet or so and surveyed the situation. Sungdare was visibly shivering from the brief inaction, slowly freezing to death in the unrelenting wind. To my left about 40 feet the ice was blasted off by the winds exposing vertical limestone. I had never read of anyone climbing this rock cliff, but taking one look at it I was confident of success. The limestone here at the summit of Everest is horizontally banded and would afford good foot and hand holds. This was my way to the top. We traversed down a few feet and out about 50 feet on a ledge to get beneath the rock wall. I helped Sungdare plunge his axe deep into the ice next to his boot and told him to hold on tight as I started to climb this vertical section.

With two crampon points on each boot and heavy mittens grabbing the wrinkled rock, I managed to carefully inch my way up and gain foot after foot. I didn't stop until I felt the pull below, signaling I had run out of rope. In my concentration, I nearly failed one of the great philosophic rules: "First with the head, then the heart." I climbed the wall with my mind still trained like I was at sea level, forgetting the extreme elevation. At nearly 29,000 feet, even using supplemental oxygen, I failed to breathe properly, holding my breath too long as I focused on each stressful move up 40 vertical feet of rock. My heart rate increased substantially and my breathing was so out of control that I collapsed in a heap on an ice ledge, sucking air into my lungs in search of oxygen. My heart seemed to be jumping out of my throat as I struggled on my hands and knees to recuperate. I looked down and saw Sungdare doing a frantic jig trying to keep warm. As quickly as I was able to gain some composure, I anchored my axe and belayed him up to my stance. The severe wind was slowly doing its damage to both of us.

Sungdare and I huddled behind a cornice under the South Summit of Everest trying to avoid the wind. Hidden behind Sungdare's head is the Hillary Step.

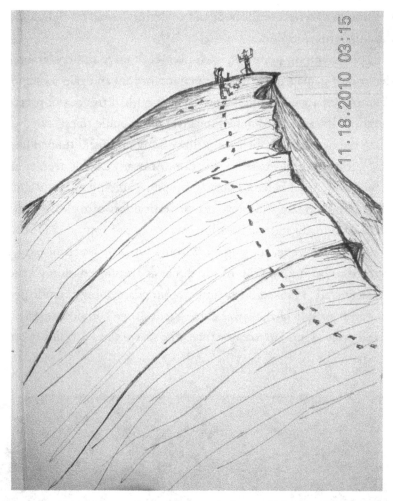

The only picture I have of myself on top is the one I sketched in my diary.

From this ledge, and for the first time, I KNEW we would make the summit. There was just a couple hundred feet to go, and I quickly led up the ice slope kicking in the best steps that I could. One ice hummock after another rose before us until I looked up at a sharp ridge that rose from the west and saw the deep blue above and nothing else. Without hesitation I chopped the last steps into the ice and pulled myself on top of the world! We did it! Three great ridges met under my feet, and above only the indigo sky!

As I stepped onto the summit of Everest I looked out over the plains of India and the savage landscape below me in all directions. My first thoughts scrambled to put it all into perspective. "How deep is the Pacific Ocean?" I pondered. "Over 37,000 feet; over seven miles down! What a planet we live on!" We huddled together and clutched the ice so we wouldn't be blown off our precarious perch on the needle of the summit. My mind was racing with the wonder of it all. Eons of forces lifted the ocean bottom to this height for me to experience for a few minutes! The world was ours to view, and no one, not even our teammates, knew we were here. We had no radio communication, no GPS, no nothing. It was just the two of us gasping for breath.

My watch read 11:23 a.m. Shocked, I thought maybe the watch had stopped and wondered if I should believe it, but shadows off Makalu were verification. We had climbed from the South Col in 4 hours and 23 minutes, nearly cutting the time in half from previous ascents.

Looking over the north side, I could see Everest's great North Face plunging straight down for two and a half miles. At the base of the face, the Rongbuk Glacier began its flow northward to its terminus in the chocolate brown hills of Tibet, which rolled off a hundred miles or more to the horizon. The air was so clear I could pick out a tiny village in Tibet although I didn't know its name. Sungdare suddenly jumped up and down in elation, grabbed me, and shouted, "Sahib! Sahib! Sahib! I can see my village and my home!" Sure enough, looking down into the mighty Khumbu Glacier, I followed the river of ice to the terminus and then traced the valley for miles farther until I could see a few of the tiny homes of his village, Pangboche, hanging on the side of the valley. It was nearly three vertical miles and 25 horizontal miles below us. For a few moments, I forgot about taking pictures as I slowly did a 360-degree visual survey. I was trying to burn this scene permanently into my memory cells. Makalu, Kanchenjunga to the east, and then turning north the entire horizon was the magnificent rolling hills of Tibet with the sacred Mount Kailash clearly visible far to the northwest. To the west rose Cho Oyu, Lang Tang Himal, Annapurna, Manaslu, and Dhaulagiri on the horizon. Looking to the south and far below were dozens of "smaller" 23,000 feet high peaks of Nepal that gave way to the plains of India. And then Sungdare grabbed my shoulder and shook me back to the reality of the situation. We had to leave this place of my life-long dreams and start climbing down.

Sungdare holds the flags of Spokane with Makalu in background.

DESCENT FROM THE SUMMIT

The bitter cold and unrelenting tempest with wind-chill factors around 40 below zero had taken a toll on Sungdare. He was freezing to death in his two-piece down uniform. I had learned my lessons well on Denali to wear a one-piece jumpsuit in extreme conditions. I was cold even with five layers of clothing plus my full-body Gore-Tex shell, but my partner was chilled to the core. He danced continuously to keep warm during the all-too-brief 20 minutes we were on the top. I desperately wanted to get a photograph of myself, but I felt the intense cold and wind made it too risky to go through the operation of taking off my gloves and giving instructions to Sungdare. One false move could mean severe frostbite or much worse. I did convince Sungdare to hold still for just a couple more photos of the flags of Spokane I had carried, and then I put the camera away and began the retreat.

The first steps off the summit seemed to magnify the exposure of this place. Ninety percent of mountaineering accidents happen on descent, and after 18 years of climbing, the neuron connections in my brain were hard-wired with the knowledge that the slightest lapse in concentration could mean death. I yelled at Sungdare, "Don't slip!" I was quickly reassured watching the Sherpa climb down as surefooted as a mountain goat, even without his toes. At the Hillary Step, I felt that going down between the vertical rock and the cornice would prove easier than the sheer rock wall we had climbed. I also figured I could kick steps into the vertical sides of the cornice where it was separated from the rock to make it easier for Sungdare to descend. On belay, I started my vertical descent spread eagle between the ice and rock. It was quickly obvious that the snow on the cornice wasn't going to hold my weight, but I was committed. It wasn't pretty, but I managed to wriggle my way down, clutching dearly to the rock. Sungdare, watching my struggle from his belay stance above, realized the safest way down for him was to traverse over to the top of the rock we had climbed up, and descend the same way. Carefully, and with ice axe in one hand and crampon tips piercing the wrinkles in the rock, he down-climbed the 40-foot section to my belay. From there we made a half dozen quick boot-axe belays in a row to down-climb the knife-edge ridge back to the South Summit.

We continued down the Southeast Ridge crest where the mountain above gave us shelter from the killer winds none too soon for Sungdare. All the pleasures of life started to flow back into our veins with every pump of our hearts. For the first time all day, we sat on our asses and soaked in the view of the savage landscape below our feet with great admiration and wonderment. It was as if we were sitting atop the crest of a gargantuan frozen wave sweeping over the brown Tibetan plateau. We were still higher than any other mountain in the world at our lunch spot, and we enjoyed drinking some fruit-flavored beverage and savored the cookies that Weiss had graciously given me. The air was eerily calm and soothing. Sitting at this tranquil spot, I searched every square meter of the great Kangshung Face trying to spy my friend Roskelley or sign of other American climbers below, but I couldn't see any tracks or trace of activity. Sir Edmund Hillary was on that expedition with Roskelley, along with George Lowe and an all-star crew. I learned later that Hillary developed HAPE upon arrival at the Base Camp and had to turn around and make the long trek out. Their pioneer expedition had succeeded in climbing the difficult lower buttress but got no farther. From his ascending perspective, Roskelley had deemed the expedition "leaderless" with "not one single leader in charge" that he trusted, and he returned to Spokane dejected. I took a good photo looking down the face that indicated the upper part of this route was very climbable. The seed was planted in me that if that team failed to climb it, I might return to try it myself.

It was tempting to pause longer at our sheltered lair for a much-needed nap, but we knew we couldn't stop. In five minutes we were on our way, continuing the descent past the ghost of Genet and the body of Schmatz. I was later asked many times why we didn't bring down her body. It's difficult to explain to anyone how razor thin your own existence is up there, and the effort required to safely move your own exhausted body down from extreme altitude. A rescue in this sort of terrain would be dangerous even at sea-level conditions. After hearing accounts about Sungdare and me viewing the body, the Nepalese government in 1984 commissioned our liaison officer Yogendra Thapa and another climber to remove Schmatz's corpse from the savage heights of the mountain. All I know for certain is that Thapa and his climbing companion both perished high on Everest in the vain body recovery attempt, thus doubling the tragedy.

When Sungdare and I reached Camp Five late in the afternoon, we were exhausted and again exposed to the full force of the winds. Neither of us was about to endure another night out in that tent no matter how tired we were. We gathered our sleeping bags, a stove, and some fuel and continued our descent. I had made a concentrated effort to get the tent cleaned and intact for the next climbers should they decide to climb up. From Camp Five, we had fixed lines to clip into for rappelling, which infinitely increased our margin of safety. Going down uses much less energy than ascending. As we were making rapid progress, I could spy several climbers heading up the ropes. The weather was still remarkably clear, but the winds had not abated. It appeared from what Sungdare and I had experienced that day, that if we had climbed just 500 feet higher into the gullies above Camp Five on our first summit attempt a few weeks prior, we might have climbed out of the fierce winds. I'll never know.

At Camp Four we crossed paths with the upbound climbers: Pizzo, Hackett, and Sherpa Young Tenzing. All looked fresh and ready for another try. As I approached Pizzo, I held my thumb up in the air in a victory signal. He was very excited to hear we'd made the summit, and he tried in vain to contact John Evans on his walkie-talkie. That was typical of the experience we had with the devices. Once the batteries were low, there was no communication. Our success buoyed our teammates and we filled them in as best we could about the conditions they would experience above. They were planning to bivouac at Camp Four, so the space was already taken. Sungdare and I had no choice but to continue down to Camp Three, which we were happy to do. Right after sunset we reached the elevated platforms hanging on the cliff. We had Camp Three to ourselves, and for the first time in three long days of virtually no sleep, we enjoyed the luxury of lying down and stretching out on a flat surface. Sungdare found a radio in one of the tents, and before I realized what was happening he was calling Base Camp or anyone else who was on that band. Bubbling with excitement he exclaimed to Sonnam Girney, our lead liaison officer, that we had reached the summit. Then Sungdare handed the radio to me.

"Kop! Is that you?" Evans asked.

"John, we made the summit," I replied as calmly as I could trying to keep my emotions in check.

The Base Camp radio was also tuned into this conversation, and I heard a huge, "HIP HIP HOORAY, HIP HIP HOORAY, HIP HIP HOORAY!" sung in unison by my teammates.

There was no way to communicate to my family half-way around the world, but from Base Camp a notice of our success was sent via Morse code to the BBC station in Kathmandu, and then over the wire to London and eventually the news was picked up by KJRB radio station in my home town. A disc jockey friend of mine, Gary Darigol, was getting to work at the station on Spokane's South Hill at around 5 a.m., and he saw the news coming over the wire that Sherpa Sungdare and I had just climbed Everest. Darigol called my wife, and then Sharon called my climbing mentor Joe Collins. She later told me that Joe was quite relieved. When she contacted my parents, they knocked the phone off the nightstand in their excitement. Sungdare and I didn't know any of this at our bivouac at Camp Three. We were exhausted, and more than ready to enjoy our last night out in the silence of supreme wilderness. The only other time in my life that I've slept that soundly was after climbing Mount Robson. It was like being in a dreamless, deathlike coma. When I opened my eyes in the morning, I had to remember that we were still at 23,900 feet on Everest. It seemed as though the first day of my life was beginning.

Climbing down to Camp Two took all morning in our still-weakened condition. In a debriefing, West recorded everything that was said, and most importantly, he was able to relay to Pizzo, Hackett, and Young Tensing useful knowledge about the winds on the upper reaches of the mountain. They reported back that they had found the medical gear buried in the tent at Camp Five, so our mission of science could be completed.

Sungdare and me. John Evans photo.

In the next two days, Sungdare and I climbed down to Camp One, then down through the Khumbu Icefall, which neither of us recognized. The tumultuous twisting of the ice and the glacier's movement of two or three feet a day had changed our route to a snaking course to avoid huge crevasses that had opened. Our expedition was fortunate to finish through our climbing window with no one injured or killed in the icefall.

We were met enthusiastically at Base Camp by our teammates, including the scientists eager to usher us away for a last round of testing. Soon I was headed one more time into the Little Shop of Horrors, where Sarnquist did several experiments on me. One pioneering experiment involved "a good bleeding." My hematocrit was extremely high, in the low 60s. That means my blood was so thick that with each pump of my heart the strain to get this relatively sludgy blood distributed throughout my body could greatly increase the possibility of stroke or an increased risk of aneurism rupture. This is nothing new to high altitude climbers. The only way the body can adapt to extreme altitude is for the bone marrow to produce red cells by the millions. Over long periods at altitude, the blood thickens causing some climbers to have serious problems such as blood clots in the legs or arms, or strokes that lead to death in some victims. When you descend from the mountains to sea level, the extra red cells gradually dissipate and, in most climbers,, the hematocrit percentages return to the mid-30s or lower 40s. And even though I'd been consuming from 6,000 to 7,000 calories a day, my weight from the first arrival at Base Camp to now had dropped from 172 to 158 pounds!

My final blood experiments inside the chamber of horrors involved removing two quarts of my blood from one arm and replacing it with two quarts of sterilized plasma in the other arm. This "operation" took all my concentration to get through mostly because I feared the double whammy of needles. Before I had the blood transfusion, I had to do the VO2 max test, and then right after the transfusion, I performed the VO2 max test again. My performance was much better after the transfusion, and I could physically feel a surge in energy with my thinned out blood. It was quite remarkable for the scientists to witness, but it proved what Sarnquist had predicted.

After two days in Base Camp, we got news over the radio that Pizzo, Hackett, and Young Tenzing had reached the summit on October 25. Pizzo also was able to perform the last of the science tests including alveolar gas samples taken right on the summit of Everest, noting the barometric pressure was 253.0. They had a much calmer summit day than Sungdare and I had experienced. Combining the science tests with the climb was another "first" on the world's highest mountain. Our expedition was a resounding success. We had completed our two-pronged goal of science testing and climbing. More importantly, none of our teammates was injured or killed, a claim few large Himalayan expeditions can make.

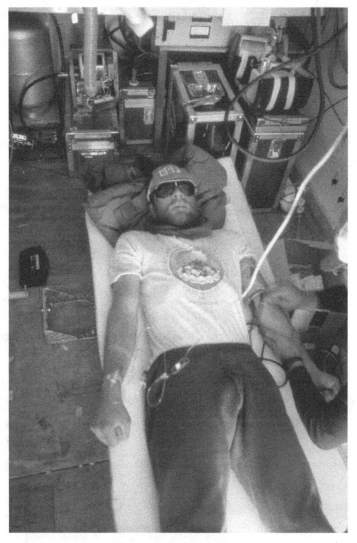

Me in Little Shop of Horrors.

FINAL FAREWELL

By October 27, several of us had completed our science work in Base Camp and could turn our backs to the mountain and return home after 51 days above 18,000 feet. After saying final goodbyes to West, I said more goodbyes over the walkie-talkie to my teammates still up on the mountain. Porzak, Sungdare, and I started the four-day hike down the mountain to the village of Lukla where an airstrip had been built on a surprisingly horizontal piece of ground, a rarity in Nepal. This airstrip was graded for small commuter airplanes out of a 20- to 30-degree slope. The challenging landings were for seasoned pilots only.

On the trek to Lukla, we went into Sungdare's home, which was built on a stunning cliff side between Pheriche and Pangboche. Here I received a warm greeting from Sungdare's beautiful wife and his mother. I did the customary Namaste greeting and then against custom, threw my arms around both of them complete with a big hug and a kiss on the cheek, and they seemed to enjoy it. I had given Sungdare gifts of my prized Eddie Bauer down shirt and $100 cash. This bonus alone was a year's earnings for the average man in Nepal. They were grateful. Sungdare celebrated by drinking glass after glass of Chang, a rice liquor. I sipped a glass of Chang along with eating wheat chapatis and rice cakes. As I stood at the doorway to say my final goodbye, Sungdare and his wife went into the back room of his home to discuss something. When they returned, she grabbed a stool, and climbed up to reach above the entry door where the family picture hung. Surrounding the frame was the traditional golden silk scarf that is custom in the Sherpa home, placed strategically to bless the family and all who enter. She carefully removed the scarf, held out her hands, and placed it in mine. I was tongue-tied, not knowing how to respond. They wanted me to have their sacred scarf as a gift for my home in America. I was very touched, and thanked them, hugged them and kissed them again, which they seemed to enjoy a second time.

My mentor and good friend Joe Collins often told me that if a man has three good friends who will come to his rescue when the chips are down, he's a lucky man. In climbing, you develop friendships with climbers sharing the "fraternity of the rope," but my final days climbing to the summit of the world with Sungdare were most special and life-changing. I had felt a strong bond with him unchecked by our language and cultural differences. We had gained each other's trust and confidence in a short time in a stressful situation. Sungdare didn't have to continue the climb to the summit that day with me, and I felt he had displayed uncommon bravery with his actions. I developed a deep respect for him and his people, and their way of life. I told him that when I had the means, I wanted Sungdare and his wife to come to America on my expense to see our land. This is a promise I dearly wanted to keep. Then we slapped each other on the shoulders and hugged one last time, and I walked away.

SAD ADDENDUM

Almost 10 years later, I got a call on the phone at my home in Spokane. It was Jonathan Waterman, the park ranger for Denali National Park in Alaska. The hesitation in his voice warned me that he was about to tell me something that was difficult for him to understand, let alone relate in words. He told me my Everest rope mate Sungdare, after an argument with his wife, went down the trail to the high suspension bridge that spans the Dudh Kosi River, and jumped to his death. I was numbed to speechlessness. After all the victories he had won, including his ability to conquer the world's highest mountain with no toes, he couldn't conquer his demons. His was a brilliant flame extinguished.

THE PERSONAL JOURNEY

I had trained as hard as any Olympic gold medal athlete to complete my goals to climb the North Face of the Eiger and Mount Everest. While I was the ninth American to reach the summit of Everest and return safely, I was the first American as far as I know to climb what many of my peers considered "the hardest, and the highest." The fact of the matter is, it mattered to no one but me. The feat was a struggle, and I survived. There was no Heisman Trophy to gain, no "Best Performance by a Climber" award. The local newspapers featured my Everest climb upon my return 16 days after being on top of the world, and Spokane Mayor Ron Bair declared it Chris Kopczynski Day. But like most climbers of the time, I had paid my own way for most of my personal journey. Truth is, climbing feats are upstaged regularly by someone faster and stronger, and blossoming stars doing a claimed "harder" route. As far as the typical American figured, I was just another nut.

So why do people climb mountains anyway? For me, the personal journey has been reason enough. With every climb I've been able to add a few more of life's truths and a bit more wisdom into my brain. That's not to say that climbing has ever left me ultimately satisfied. Home from the top of Everest I had a vision burned into my memory of looking down the great unclimbed Kangshung Face, and knowing that route up Everest could be climbed, and someone was going to do it.

Words From The Wild

- Climbing Everest gives you temporary relief from the prison of ambition.
- The world stands aside for you to pass, if you know where you are going.
- When you act more sensibly than others, people call you "lucky."
- There are two tragedies in life. First, not getting what you want, and second, getting what you want.
- Be aware of what the other guy is doing.
- Just be the best you can be.

NINETEEN

KANGSHUNG FACE OF EVEREST

Dave Cheesemond climbs the buttress at 20,500' on the
Kangshung Face of Everest. Photo by Jay Cassell.

"THE LONGER YOU ARE CRAZY, the longer you're crazy," Larry said, responding in the mid-1970s to my question about erratic and errant human behavior. He was a psychologist and partner in an Adolescent Medicine practice with my climbing partner, Dr. Jim States. Larry specialized in working with wayward teenagers to help steer them toward a productive direction in life. These young patients already had backgrounds in theft, drug abuse, assault and battery, rape, and even murder. Many of the kids Larry and Jim treated had already been in and out of jail before high school. If they continued their bad decisions, some were on a track toward the big house, maybe for life. Or maybe their lives would be tragically short.

The Adolescent Medicine practice sought to correct deviant behavior with a program that involved a lot of listening followed by long-term constructive actions and discipline. My question to Larry was, "How do you correct these kids so they can get back into society to lead productive lives?" He pointed out that most of them had the disadvantage of coming from disjointed family backgrounds. Most had huge anger problems. If a kid made destructive decisions for five years, Larry said it would take five years of intense personal attention and rigid programs to straighten out the behavioral problems.

Despite coming from a good family, I had been climbing for nearly 20 years and couldn't see myself committing to 20 years of therapy to correct this deviant behavior. So, my fate was sealed. When talking about my climbing objectives to "normal" people, I heard the words "you're crazy" more often than I cared to remember. And now I was having recurring dreams of the unclimbed East Face of Everest.

THE MYTHIC IMAGE

In 1779, Swiss geologist Horace Benedict de Saussure, often called the founder of alpinism and modern meteorology, offered a prize for the first ascent of Mount Blanc, the highest mountain in the Alps. A village physician, Dr. Michel-Gabriel Paccard, and Jacques Balmat completed that quest in 1786. De Saussure himself reached the summit the following year, and the "sport" of alpinism was born. When Paccard and Balmat came down from the top of the Alps they debunked cultural myths that people-devouring demons lurked among the peaks. Climbers such as Albert Mummery set their sights on even more ambitious mountain routes. One by one the great north faces of the Alps were pioneered until mountaineers pegged the Eiger North Face as "The Last Great Problem." As that challenge was solved in 1938, peaks were revealed as the next "Last Great Problem," which was initially identified across the Atlantic at Cerro Torre in Patagonia. Then it cropped up in Alaska at the South Face of Denali, and then the focus shifted to the Himalayas and, of course, to Everest, and then to challenges such as the South Face of Annapurna, and then to the South Face of Dhaulagiri, and on and on. Every time I opened a new issue of a climbing magazine some mountaineer was writing about conquering the next "Last Great Problem." Eventually, the concept became something of a joke.

"Imagery, especially the imagery of dreams, is the basis of mythology," wrote Joseph Campbell, professor emeritus of literature at Sarah Lawrence College, describing how idols and the mythic image developed in the minds of man through the millennium. By 1980, in the specialized world of mountaineering, the quest to scale the Kangshung Face of Mount Everest had reached a mythological realm. Average people don't bother themselves with visions of dangling from a thin rope in even thinner air. My dreams of climbing overhanging rock above 20,000 feet certainly weren't normal by society's description, but I wasn't alone in visualizing the challenge of the Kangshung Face and pushing through technical barriers at 21,000 feet. While other climbers were still coming up with "Last Great Problems," Everest remained the highest, and the Kangshung Face was the hardest. The central buttress that dissected the wall was the straightest way up to the top of the world, and if any crazy group of heretics and dreamers was going to rise to the occasion, it included me. I knew first-hand that the Kangshung Face could be climbed.

Everest is a triangular pyramid shaped by its Southwest Face, North Face, and East Face—also known as the Kangshung Face, which is entirely in Tibet. A prominent rock and ice feature in the middle of the Kangshung Face resembles a giant's backbone. The lower section of this buttress is vertical and looks like a rotten spine ravaged by scoliosis. Both sides of the prominent buttress are swept with violent avalanches, especially during the monsoon season. Looking at a photo of this face makes a knowledgeable climber shrink like a spider in a corner. The one relatively safe passage up this wall is only marginally sheltered from the 10,000 vertical feet of ice and snow that looms above. Because of the altitude, vertical exposure, and danger, not to mention the cost, the competition to attempt this enormously difficult face withered into a tiny fraction of the climbing community. The base of the wall begins a full 4,000 feet HIGHER than the top of the Eiger, then continues up almost vertically in a straight line another 12,000 feet to reach the summit!

The first white man to study the East Face of Everest was British adventurer George Mallory, who in 1921 dismissed climbing the mountain from that side. "Men less wise than us might try it, but emphatically it was not for us," he said. For years, climbers dismissed it as impossible primarily because of the avalanche danger. Climbing the route would require starting at 17,000 feet to scale a vertical face and then facing another 8,000 feet of exposed climbing to reach the summit.

By the 1980s, climbers were evolving through a revolution of lighter gear and competitive technique. Mythic imagery was alive as climbers reassessed risks and created new dreams. Science offered some positive factors to add to the equation of solving the Kangshung Face problem. Even though the lower third of the buttress is insanely steep—overhanging in places—the rock is composed of metamorphosed gneiss at the base, topped with some granite intrusions, which are part of the Makalu formation. Those rocks are overlaid by compact limestone sedimentary rock all the way to the summit. This rock mixture favors the use of pitons, which is a ray of hope in an otherwise dark scenario. Depending on who is looking at it, this face was either the most god-awful, dangerous, and intimidating piece of mountainside, or the most beautiful, awesome contortion of ice and rock on the planet. No one disputed that it was formidable. Indeed, the People's Republic of China would never have to patrol this naturally secured stretch of border. In a climber's eyes, it's the ultimate Great Wall of China!

In 1980, as China reopened its doors to the world, Richard Blum of San Francisco jumped at the opportunity to obtain a permit to climb Mount Everest from Tibet, and a team was assembled by the American Alpine Club to make an attempt on the "impossible" wall. Blum had political connections to secure this permit from China through his wife, Sen. Diane Feinstein. I had purposely studied the Kangshung Face from the top down when descending from the summit of Everest in 1981. I knew if the lower buttress could be climbed, the upper slopes on the buttress crest were not danger-free, but at least were relatively safe from avalanches IF they were climbed in a post-monsoon season. As in fishing, timing is everything. I began conjuring up dreams of climbing what I considered "the final line."

Just six months after climbing Everest in 1981, I corresponded with leaders of the East Face expedition. My friend, John Roskelley, had retreated in 1981 because of a "leadership vacuum", but deemed the route climbable with the right team. But the outlook was changing. The Japanese were rumored to be vying for a permit as well as a European team. Dr. Jim Morrissey was selected to lead the 1983 team to take advantage of his experience as a member of the unsuccessful 1981 East Face Expedition. Morrissey had begun to assemble pioneers from that effort, including George Lowe and Louis Reichardt, for a return. I had turned down Morrissey's invitation to join the 1981 expedition in favor of the medical research team that would tackle Everest at the same time from Nepal. Now, with even more experience to offer, I wanted a shot at the Kangshung Face.

INTO THE BELL JAR

Before author Sylvia Plath committed suicide at the age of 30, she wrote a classic novel. "The Bell Jar" chronicles the crack-up of Ester Greenwood, a beautiful, enormously talented, and successful woman who was slowly going under, maybe for the last time. The novel, a prose poem, describes the slow transition into mental illness that struck an odd chord with me. For the first time, I had begun to question my love for the mountains. Was I "now living my life as in the rarefied atmosphere under a bell jar" as Plath phrased it? Had I crossed the barrier from passion into a type of mental illness, like some of the cults I detested?

I had achieved my two major climbing goals—the Eiger North Face and Everest— and I returned to work in the winter of 1981-82. I managed commercial projects for my father's construction firm, but my mind still obsessed with that moment just a few months in the past, on October 21, when I looked down the Kangshung Face of Everest and saw for myself that it could be climbed. I was undaunted by the failed 1981 East Face Expedition that included Sir Edmund Hillary and my best friend, Roskelley, along with a stellar American climbing team. Morrissey, a renowned cardiothoracic surgeon, graciously returned my initial call despite his grueling work schedule. I detailed my promising observations of the route. He said Lowe had already committed and immediately invited me to join them for another try. That was the easy part: no letter campaign, no schmoozing, no waiting period. The hard part was telling my wife, my kids, and my parents that I was heading back to Everest. I didn't realize it then, but the stress inflicted by my decision to return would trigger the dissolution of my marriage. In my mind, my financial situation was always a struggle to balance family with climbing. I was in the prime of my "financial earning" years, and I chose to climb. At the time, I did not realize the magnitude and price to pay for my decision to return to Everest.

In any field of human endeavor, people learn from mistakes of previous generations. We have the opportunity to stand on the shoulders of pioneers to go farther and higher. Their experience dissolves our fear enabling our brains to rewire for different approaches to previous barriers. New horizons are revealed with new thresholds to conquer. That's how the human race has progressed to the standard of living that many of us enjoy. Mountaineering is rife with athletes who accomplished bold, magnificent feats. One of the most inspiring mountaineering achievements was Reinhold Messner's solo climb of Nanga Parbat, followed by going solo to the top of Mount Everest. Lynn Hill's all-free ascent of El Capitan is historic, and the Swiss climber Ueli Steck's astounding solo ascent of the Eiger North Face in just 2 hours and 22 minutes may never be equaled. Among thousands of inspirational climbs, I wanted to find my tiny niche in the history of mountaineering.

THE MIRACLE TEAM MACHINE

The USA hockey team's "Miracle on Ice" in the 1980 Winter Olympics has been ranked as one of the greatest sports achievements of the 20th century. An unlikely group of collegiate skaters took down the undefeated professional USSR team—the so-called "Mighty Red Machine," that had come to Lake Placid having won four consecutive Olympic gold medals. Then USA went on to beat Finland to capture the gold. The victories, attained without a recognized "superstar," resonated around the world.

1983 Kangshung Face team. Bottom row, L-R. John Boyle, George Lowe, Kim Momb, Jay Cassell, Geoff Tabin, Jack Alustiza. Top row L-R. Andy Harvard, Dave Cheesemond, Dr. James Morrissey, Carlos Buhler, Dan Reid, Louis Reichardt, Carl Tobin, David Coombs, Chris Kopczynski.

Morrissey knew that building a great team requires the right makeup of personalities starting from the leader on down. Morrissey was a dynamic, charismatic man of great talent as a climber as well as a surgeon in Stockton, California. He also had a storied reputation as a ladies' man. I had never met anyone who had such an understanding of human nature and a telepathic gift of physiognomy to judge good and bad character. He had a talent for choosing the right mix of personalities for either a surgery team or climbing team. Morrissey had successfully led the first American ascent of Dhaulagiri, and the first ever ascent of Gaurishankar and was on the first ascent of Great Trango Tower. In addition, he had been a team member of the first Kangshung Face expedition in 1981. Although that team failed, the effort had proven that the lower buttress could be climbed.

This 1983 team would be America's entry in an international competition for the stature of bagging the first ascent of the Kangshung Face. Morrissey was looking for the most competitive, dedicated, athletic climbers. The team would be limited to those who had no doubts that the route could be climbed.

With the commercialization and "business" of climbing still in its infancy, even elite mountaineers considered themselves lucky to break even on an expedition. For the most part, they paid dearly for their addiction. This would be no exception. The team Morrissey assembled was composed of men willing to lay on the line their marriages and their kids' livelihood to forge into a dangerous unknown in pursuit of a dream and an indelible mark in climbing history.

Everest from a 17,000-foot pass near Sakya on the Tibetan Plateau en route to the Kangshung Face. I am in the center wearing silver pants.

After months of training on our own—for example, I made time in my work and training schedule for a three-week spring trip in Alaska to climb Denali—we left the United States on August 11, 1983, flying to Japan and then to Beijing. We spent several days trekking around Beijing, visited the Ming Tombs, toured the Forbidden City, scampered over a portion of the Great Wall of China. I started my diary on August 15 in Chentu, China, where we boarded planes to fly over Himalayan peaks to the Tibetan plateau airport at 12,000 feet near Lhasa. We had two days in Lhasa, which was enough time to explore most of the 1,400 rooms of the Great Patala Palace, the last bastion of the Dali Llama. From Lhasa, the group traveled over road in two minibuses, one Land Rover, and a Chinese jeep, accompanied by two trucks loaded with our food and equipment. The dusty route passed through the towns of Chushul, Xigaze, and Lhaze, over a scenic 17,000-foot pass near Sakya, and down into the Bum Chu River gorge. In Xigaze, I climbed with Lowe and Carl Tobin to the Cliffside Monastery to see firsthand the impact that bullets and cannon balls had in destroying the Tibetan Empire. Thousands of monks and natives were annihilated here.

According to my diary, road travel ended at "Karta," although I have not found a town by that name on a modern map. Nestled in the Himalayan foothills, it was a typical Tibetan village composed of rugged, leather-faced men and women whose daily routine was focused on basic survival. Like a peaceful band of religious heretics, our group of 15 Everest climbers and five trekkers assembled backpacks and began the seven-day trek westward up the Karta Valley beneath the north face of Makalu. The scenic approach, a fulfilling trip in itself for trekkers, didn't distract us from the single-minded purpose of pioneering a difficult route up Everest. The team was a mix of professional climbers, scientists, engineers, contractors, doctors, professors, and attorneys. We had a range of personalities and mental toughness while everyone had a passion for relishing nature on its own terms. Morrissey had begun his team selection search from a circle of climbers he knew in the San Francisco Bay area, plus the list of climbers involved in the failed 1981 attempt—Dave Breashears, Gary Bocard, Nick Clinch, Susan Giller, Andy Harvard, Sir Edmund Hillary, Chris Jones, Scott Macbeth, Eric Perlman, Lou Reichardt, Drummond Rennie, and Roskelley. All these men and the lone woman were pioneers in their own right, and all had extensive Himalayan experience. The 1981 team had personality struggles, arguments about routes, and disagreements on logistics but still managed to find a way up the central buttress. Lowe and Giller climbed the vertical, overhanging upper buttress. With Lowe leading, they found a route to the ice-crested top of the buttress, but the expedition went no farther. (Breashears made an outstanding documentary film of this attempt that aired as a 15-minute segment on the ABC Sports network.) From this cast of experienced climbers, Morrissey assembled this team to join him for the second attempt.

- John Boyle, a banker and mechanical engineer hired by Morrissey to design and construct a winch system to help with load carrying on the lower buttress.
- David Breashears, a renowned climber-cinematographer for the major American television sports networks who had summited Everest the previous year. (Although Breashears accompanied us part way on the trek, personal issues back home caused him to abandon the expedition just a couple days into the trek and return to the United States.)
- Carlos Buhler, a professional mountaineer and guide from Bellingham, Washington.
- David Cheesemond, a petroleum engineer from Calgary, Alberta, who pioneered some of the hardest routes in North America, including the Emperor Face of Mount Robson and the East Face of Mount Assiniboine in the Canadian Rockies.
- Jay Cassell, an investment banker from Ketchum, Idaho.
- David Coombs, a business consultant from Spokane.
- Andy Harvard, an attorney from Fort Wayne, Indiana.
- Jack Alustiza, our hired cook, from San Ramon, California.
- Dan Reid, a cardiac surgeon from San Francisco.
- Geoffrey Tabin, an ophthalmologist from Burlington, Vermont.
- Carl Tobin, an entomology professor at the University of Alaska.
- George Henry Lowe III, a consultant who wrote a PhD thesis on cosmic ray physics while based at University of Utah. Lowe was our inspiration—the man who had proved the lower buttress could be climbed.
- Kim Momb, a journeyman carpenter and professional ski and climbing instructor from Spokane.
- Louis Reichardt, a PhD scientist from the Department of Physiology at the University of California.
- Me.

Additionally, we had five paying trekkers who helped defray the expedition expenses: Hank Bahnson, a surgeon from Pittsburgh, Pennsylvania; Carlton Dean, a neurologist from Golden, Colorado; Phil Osborne, a cardiothoracic surgeon; Ben Eiseman from Denver, Colorado; Jim Funk, a doctor from Atlanta, Georgia, and Jim Greenbaum from Kittaning, Pennsylvania. A Tibetan man named Kongur was hired to assist with cooking duties and arrange for local farmers to haul fresh vegetables to our camps. Other than Kongur, we had no additional porters to carry our loads.

After reaching the top of the Karta Valley on August 30, Base Camp was established on the north side of the Kangshung Glacier about six or seven miles from the bottom of the main buttress we planned to ascend. We shuffled loads of gear for a few days up the main stem of the Kangshung Glacier to Advanced Base Camp at about 17,200 feet in a pocket of bare ice below what we viewed as the Greatest Wall of China. From here, the climbing began in earnest on a task that involved establishing six more camps. Up, up, and away we carried loads on the steep metamorphic rock bands polished by glaciers during the ice age that preceded us by more than 10,000 years. Snow Camp was established at 18,800 feet on a small ledge. On September 3, 4, and 5, Coombs and I occupied this camp to lead and fix lines up the breathtaking "Mushroom Ridge" as we named it because of the overhanging cornices on both sides. Momb followed Coombs and me up and made the final two vertical leads to the Pinsetter Camp, at 20,100 feet, above a gully we called the "Bowling Alley."

The technical climbing started right off the Kangshung Glacier and never let up for nearly a vertical mile until we reached the top of the ice-covered buttress at 21,300 feet. It was like climbing the Eiger, but the base of the wall started at 17,200 feet, and the climbing was much more technically difficult. Speaking for myself, the fear factor was ever present, and the adrenalin was constantly flowing. Anchors often were long pickets driven as deeply as possible into snow and ice, although we used ice screws whenever we could find exposed bare ice. In the rock, we hammered pitons and wart hogs. As we climbed inch by inch, the exposure seemed to intensify the puckering view when we glanced into the abyss below. At the top of the Mushroom Ridge we had to traverse across a vertical, loose, overhanging sheet of ice-plastered rock into the Bowling Alley, an ice chute about 450 feet long and angled at a consistent 70 degrees, with some vertical rock bands interspersed. In the afternoon, rock and ice dislodges from above and hurtles full throttle down this gutter of demise. Early morning was the only sane time to travel through here.

The Mushroom Ridge.

David Coombs enters the Bowling Alley.

Pinsetter Camp located at the top of the Bowling Alley.

Kangshung Face of Everest showing line of ascent.

Pinsetter Camp was at the top of the Bowling Alley hacked out of ice on a small ledge just wide enough to hold two men and a pot of stew. At Pinsetter and Snow Camps we kept our body harnesses fastened and tied onto a rope that was short-tied to a couple of pitons anchored in the rock. We made sure we were tethered to the mountain for every move we made, even inside the tent. Sleeping was difficult with the harness and rope strapped to our bodies. A good rest was the most we could expect while hanging on a cliff. After several days of working in this exposure at Pinsetter Camp, around 20,100 feet, the mind started to adjust to the vertical world, but I never got comfortable in the dangerous surroundings and showers of loose rock and ice from above.

Above Pinsetter Camp, the technical climbing became even more demanding. The headwall continues up 1,200 feet of vertical rock with some overhanging horizontal bands of metamorphosed and loose sedimentary rock. At the top of this cliff looms the 800-feet thick ice cap of the Kangshung Glacier that hangs over the rock lip at a 60- to 70-degree slope. In 1981, Lowe with Giller belaying climbed this intimidating wall, and then continued up the ice all the way to the top of the ice cap. On the descent, they left about 500 feet of fixed line hanging on the most technical section. We could see through binoculars that the rope was still dangling in space, but we could only guess how much the rope had deteriorated from two years of exposure to solar rays, freeze-thaw cycles, rock fall, and avalanches.

After seven tense days of climbing, we reached the base of the upper buttress. Momb, Cheesemond, Tobin, and Lowe took the lead and climbed to the old dangling line. Momb being the lightest, hooked on his jumars and gently put weight onto the rope to test it. It held. He courageously eased his entire weight onto the old line until he was convinced it would hold. And then he proceeded to jumar up the free-hanging line all the way to the top of the rock buttress! This was a bold, gutsy act, or a foolish risk, depending on a person's viewpoint. I regarded Momb's confidence and bravery in awe. His high threshold for danger saved the expedition about a week of technical climbing and fixing lines above 20,000 feet. This move proved to be a psychological as well as a physical breakthrough. He not only ascended the headwall, but also managed to install a new rope for the rest of us to follow. Cheesemond and Lowe were able to ascend the fresh rope to the top of the buttress by 7 p.m. on September 8. The team had climbed the entire buttress in just eight days.

With fixed lines in place, we installed an ingenious aerial tramway with pulleys anchored into the rock at the top of the headwall. The tram was rigged with 2,500 feet of continuous 7-millimeter rope anchored from Pinsetter Camp to the top of the rock portion of the headwall. Once this was in place, we would attach a counterweight of 60 pounds on the line, then hook on and hoist a 60-pound sack of gear and food up the 1,200-foot vertical wall. This operation required two-way radio communication between two men at Pinsetter Camp installing the loads in a gunnysack and two men at the top of the headwall to unload and tie the bags onto the ice face above. It worked well enough.

We tried to hook up a similar tramway system all the way from Pinsetter Camp to the Kangshung Glacier below by shooting a "messenger line" attached to a rocket developed by the Kilgore Company for the US Navy. This system was the brainchild of our engineer and teammate John Boyle, who brought three "ship to shore" rockets and line. The operation was nearly successful, but after firing two rockets into the abyss from Pinsetter Camp, we learned the horizontal distance the rockets had to travel was greater than expected, and so was the friction of the messenger line piled on the snow. The combination of factors caused the rocket and line to fall into the face of the cliff long before it reached the glacier at the base of the wall. We temporarily abandoned the project at that point and descended to Snow Camp at 18,800 feet. From here, the third rocket was successfully fired. It reached the glacier below and landed on the ice a 15-minute walk from Advanced Base Camp. Now we could string rope into a taut line directly from the glacier to Snow Camp, saving 2,000 feet of load hauling. A small Honda engine power winch was anchored at the base enabling us to hook our loads onto a fixed carabiner and watch one bag at a time magically lift into space.

These tramways took more than a week to complete, but our well-spent time up front spared us from tons of back-breaking work hauling gear at extreme altitude up the steep face. It's debatable whether the lower winch system was worth the effort, but from my viewpoint, we could not have been successful on the mountain without the upper lift.

The route above the headwall involved about 800 feet of 50- to 90-degree snow and ice into the unnerving feature we called "The Jaws." The ice cap overhanging the top of the pointed rock buttress was serrated and fluted by sun and wind into sculptures resembling teeth. Once we put aside the notion that a giant's mouth was waiting to chew us up, we found the near-vertical upper part of The Jaws was delightfully technical and safe from falling rocks and ice. Cresting the top of the cap brought us to one of the rarest of features on the

Kangshung Face—flatness. A table of ice, the first relatively level section we'd enjoyed in 4,200 vertical feet of climbing, was a strange but welcome mental respite from vertical stress.

We erected two North Face VE24 tents on top of the ice dome, which resembled a hard hat over the buttress. Helmet Camp, as we called it, would eventually become Morrissey's leadership control center at 21,300 feet. Three camps were needed below this to accommodate the extreme climbing and work to fix lines and haul gear up the headwall. Helmet Camp allowed 7,735 vertical feet of unobstructed view all the way to the summit of Everest. That span would require three more high camps to stage climbers. Undulating ice and snow formed a poorly defined ridge that ran in nearly a straight line all the way to the "Bench" where Hillary and Tenzing Norgay in 1953 made their final high camp at 27,600 feet on the Southeast Ridge.

From Helmet Camp our route appeared to be relatively easy compared with the extreme climbing to that point, although caution would be required in negotiating the crevasses and broken ice blocks. Before climbing higher, we had to stock Helmet Camp with several tons of supplies that had to be hauled up the headwall. This was accomplished by a miracle of teamwork. No one on the team hesitated for even a microsecond to work all day and into the night. We would ferry 50- to 70-pound loads up the lower and upper winch systems. The loads were transferred at the top of the headwall to a pair of climbers who would make the carry to Camp One. This audacious and grueling undertaking was accomplished without Sherpa support.

The other miracle was that all 15 of us remained relatively healthy and physically strong. Nobody wavered from our single-minded purpose. Anyone with expedition experience knows it is extremely hard to keep a group this large pulling together through such stressful circumstances. No one even uttered a negative word. We all knew this would be our only shot at a first ascent of the fabled China Wall of Everest.

After seven days, Helmet Camp was stocked with more than 2,000 pounds of food and gear. From the top of the headwall, we could concentrate on trying to acclimate to the extreme altitude and keeping a physiological balance as we pushed upward. Every day was a new footstep into the unknown where no one had gone before. Those of us working at the top of the buttress didn't dare make the rigorous retreat down the headwall to rest at a lower elevation for fear of not having the strength to return. Over the next several days we hacked out ice platforms into the ridge for two camps en route to High Camp Three, which would be roughly at the same elevation as the Everest South Col, which I frequently eyeballed off my left shoulder as I climbed. We were pioneering the hardest and most dangerous route up the world's highest mountain. Inevitably our enthusiasm would gradually be dimmed by ever-increasing stress to body and brain aggravated by the low atmospheric pressure.

Everyone selected for a big expedition has visions of climbing all the way and standing on the summit. The cold reality is that only a small percentage of the climbers stay healthy and strong enough to even have the opportunity. On the Kangshung Face, we had an experienced leader as well as an exceptionally capable climbing team. Deciding who would be first up the Kangshung Face was done democratically with a vote over one of our daily 5 p.m. walkie-talkie radio calls. Each climber cast a vote for the person he felt was the strongest and most deserving to get the first summit bid from High Camp Three. The top three vote getters would be on the first team. This was the moment of truth for me. While I certainly wanted to climb Everest again, I knew this also was my chance to be the first American to climb the highest mountain twice. My competitiveness rose to the extreme height of the occasion when my turn came to offer a name. I voted for myself. Morrissey tallied the votes and relayed the top three results to us by radio: Cheesemond, Lowe, Kopczynski. I couldn't have cared less that Morrissey didn't detail the vote totals. I was pumped to be on the first summit team!

The strategic plan was revealed in the next radio call Morrissey made to a team that was scattered up the Kangshung Face from Base Camp to Helmet Camp. Cheesemond, Lowe, and I were to carry food, fuel, ropes, and one oxygen bottle each to 25,900 feet and make a cache for High Camp Three, the highest campsite. Our orders were to cut a platform into the ice for the VE24 tent that was to be carried up by the second summit team composed of Reichardt, Buhler, and Momb. This was a job the Nepalese Sherpas do in their sleep, but for us mere mortals, carrying more than 50 pounds in a backpack at this altitude was simply too much. At best, an average climber with a light load above 25,000 feet is capable of moving only about 250 vertical feet per hour without supplemental oxygen. Add a big load on your back and the going gets real tough and snail slow.

Having our marching orders, Lowe, Cheesemond, and I broke trail up moderately steep snow and ice over and around a couple huge crevasses. At 24,900 feet we cut in a tent platform and established what we called High Camp Two. The next morning we pioneered the route to 25,900 feet, dumped our loads, and descended back to High Camp Two, where Reichardt, Momb, and Buhler greeted us after climbing up to make a tent platform next to ours. The next morning the second summit team headed up for the highest camp. Their objective was to erect a tent, set up a stove, and ready the site for Cheesemond, Lowe, and me to make the first summit bid. But everything didn't go according to plan.

I don't know exactly what happened, but when Reichardt and company returned to High Camp Two, Momb blurted that while trying to set up the tent at the high camp, "Reichardt dropped the tent fly with the poles and it went sailing down the mountain!" They also reported that none of them had the energy to hack out a tent platform in the ice so they just dumped some more food and a couple oxygen bottles. Was this a reminder that no one is immune to the affects of thin air, or was it something else? I'm not sure what Lowe was thinking, but I was devastated. The perfect plan was changing every minute.

That same day, Cheesemond developed high altitude pulmonary edema and his lungs began filling with fluid. His only alternative for survival was to get down as quickly as possible. Lowe and I said our regrets as our teammate began his solo descent to the lower camps. Cheesemond had made giant efforts to get the team this far. Suddenly, his role in the expedition was done.

The summit team situation was reversed, and I found myself back under the bell jar. Morrissey ordered Lowe and me to dismantle our tent and haul it to the highest campsite. Morrissey felt the team's best chances of success were to have Momb, Reichardt, and Buhler follow us up after we cut a platform and erected the tent at High Camp Three, thus putting their squad in position to make the first bid for the summit. Lowe and I would have to do more grunt work and stay another night in The Death Zone before getting our shot. This jockeying was the beginning of the decline in my spirit. I had no control over my fate. My brain was wired for "timing," and I could feel my strength slowly ebbing. The "mental toughness" that had taken me to the highest level of sport was ebbing.

Fatigue was becoming a factor for everyone. The team had dwindled to half-strength. Alustiza and Breashears had left the expedition weeks earlier. Coombs was suffering from nausea and headaches, and Tabin was physically exhausted and not able to carry loads in the extreme altitude. Tabin also suffered from HAPE and was out of the picture for the high camp work. Morrissey, wise and always controlled, stayed relatively low and healthy. He ran the expedition like a pro from Helmet Camp, providing the glue for our success.

The next morning, October 7, Lowe and I made another carry to High Camp Three, where we pitched a tent and arranged the food and gear for our teammates. We then returned to 24,500-feet where Momb, Reichardt, and Buhler left a tent they had fetched from below for Lowe and me. Momb and company then continued up to 25,900 feet to be in position for a summit bid the next morning.

CURTAIN CALL

October 8 dawned cold and clear. The temperature at 26,000 feet was about 20 degrees below zero even though global warming was melting every glacier on the planet below us. Momb, Reichardt, and Buhler were off on their summit attempt by 2 a.m. We all felt confident of their success as the weather was ideal. They had 3,135 feet to climb to the summit of Everest from our highest camp, and once they reached the Southeast Ridge, the terrain was known. The biggest obstacle was the Hillary Step, but for anyone who'd ascended the Kangshung Face, it would be little more challenging than stepping across a crevasse. Winds were light, the snow conditions seemed perfect, and expectations were high as Cassel and Reid came up to High Camp Two to join Lowe and me. The four of us made our way up to High Camp Three where we would cram four big bodies into the single VE24 tent and attempt to prepare ourselves for the second summit attempt. Losing one tent was becoming a huge factor in my mind. We'd lost a critical margin of safety.

The plan called for Momb, Reichardt, and Buhler to climb to the top and then descend all the way to High Camp Two at 24,500-feet. This ambitious plan made some sense, as sleeping at the lowest possible elevation is much better on the brain than staying another night at 25,900-feet. The holes in this objective began to widen as October 8 dragged on. Momb, Reichardt, and Buhler had made an early start for their summit bid, so we all expected them to return to the high camp no later than 4 p.m. if they maintained even a cautious pace. (I had climbed the final 3,000 feet in 1981 in just over four hours.) Meanwhile, Lowe, Cassell, Reid, and I, ranging from 6 feet tall to Cassell's 6-foot-3, crawled one by one into a single tent designed for two mountaineers, or three in a pinch. It was like stuffing pork sausage into a casing. Not only was there a shortage of space to relax, there also was a dearth of oxygen to breath. Our bodies were trying to function in one-third the atmosphere of sea level while the oxygen level was even lower inside, where four men crammed into a two-man tent had to breathe and re-breathe expired CO_2 from their teammates' lungs.

We stayed warm, fully dressed in down jumpsuits and swaddled in our sleeping bags, but slowly the stress of labored breathing and not being able to move had my head aching. Migraines had plagued me in the past at extreme altitudes. Normally, the pain would pass in a few hours. This situation on Everest was abnormal, and my headache was getting worse. As the afternoon wore on, my head began to pulsate. I downed aspirin after aspirin and hydrated as much as possible, but nothing diminished the pain. I tried to focus on the favorable weather conditions as a distraction. Years of training, preparation, and dedication came down to these final moments of readiness. But the clock had become another major factor for our summit bid.

The glaciers were moving faster than the afternoon hours passed. The summit team was slower than expected, too. We could view about 1,500 feet up the final ridge of the "American Buttress" before it merged into the Southeast Ridge and we could see the final summit ridge, but the actual climbing route was hidden. At 4 p.m., the summit climbers were still nowhere in sight. Every minute seemed to turn into an hour for me. My head was throbbing, and it was obvious this was more than a regular headache. For the first time on the expedition, thoughts of descent began to haunt my mind. Five o'clock came, then 6 p.m. and the sun was setting. Still no signs of life from above. Stars began to appear in the crystal-clear sky and the "Bell Jar" was ringing loudly now. Lowe, Cassell, and Reid suffered silently inside the tent while I stayed outside pacing like a jaguar and growling about my misery. Lowe kept the cooker going constantly to melt ice and keep us hydrated and full of soup, which was about the only food that seemed palatable. We pondered the possibility that something had happened to our teammates above, otherwise why would they be so slow? My lifelong shortcoming for not cutting slack to slow people wasn't going to resolve itself on this night. It was like they were purposely sabotaging the expedition, and making my head throb all the worse.

Kim Momb on the summit of Everest. Photo by Lou Reichardt.

In the faint light from alpenglow reflecting off Makalu, we finally saw a figure descending about a thousand feet above. It was 8 p.m. and too dark to see a face, but soon I could recognize the swagger of Kim Momb coming down the footsteps from their early morning ascent. A broad smile beamed as he approached us. He'd just climbed the world's highest mountain, and we took turns hugging him in congratulations. Seeing the jammed quarters at high camp, Momb had no choice but to continue directly downward as planned to sleep at 24,900 feet. He wished us well. I was thrilled and proud that my hometown friend had climbed to the top, this being his third attempt to scale Everest. Momb seemed in good health and sprits. We knew he would be OK climbing down alone as we turned our concern upward for Reichardt and Buhler, who were still nowhere in sight. Lowe, Reid, Cassel, and I squished back into the tent like sardines in a can to try and keep warm and rest. We all knew this scene was not unfolding favorably. As more time passed waiting for their return, it became more obvious that Reichardt and Buhler likely would not be able to safely follow Momb down the slopes to High Camp Two. I couldn't imagine the prospect of trying to cram SIX grown, gasping, slowly dying humans into one two-man tent at High Camp Three! Reality struck at 10 p.m. when out of near darkness Reichardt and Buhler finally appeared. Fatigued and delirious, they stumbled like drunks. They looked gaunt and anemic as though each had lost more than 10 pounds to dehydration.

Reichardt and Buhler were in no condition to continue down to 24,900 feet. Without the warmth of the sun, the temperatures on the upper elevations of Everest had quickly dropped to bitter cold, so bivouacking outside at High Camp Three was not an option. We crawled into the lone tent, wedged with three heads one way and three the other in a convoluting, withering mass of 12 lungs gasping for oxygen.

My aching mind scanned my memory searching for words of wisdom and encouragement to surmount moments of despair. In "The Old Man and the Sea," Earnest Hemmingway wrote, "A man can be destroyed, but not defeated." Hamlet's speech seemed appropriate: "To be or not to be, that is the question, whether 'tis nobler to suffer the slings and arrows of outrageous fortune, or to take arms against a sea of troubles, and by opposing we say we end them." I finished the rest of Shakespeare's soliloquy in its entirety the best I could remember, and repeated it over and over as I had memorized the passage in high school. But my mood deteriorated. I vowed to myself that I would never again join a big expedition with no personal control of the outcome. Dante's Inferno would be a vacation from this torment. The relentless pain in my head was eating at my psyche. Something deep inside said, "Don't quit," but the changes in the game plan had affected my mind. Lowe, Cassell, and Reid were suffering, too, but they had one carrot in front of them that I didn't have: none of them had been to the summit of Everest.

Babbling and emotional, Reichardt recounted a harrowing incident on their journey to the top. After reaching the Southeast Ridge, their route merged with a Japanese team. Reichardt was near them when a Japanese climber slipped, fell, and pulled his Sherpa teammate off his feet on the vertical ice just before the Hillary Step. They both tumbled like rag dolls down the Southwest Face. Reichardt described the horror in the climber's face as he tried to dig his gloved fingers into the ice before disappearing over the cliff. Roped together, the pair most likely fell some 8,000 feet into the Western Cwm. I knew the exact location from my 1981 summit climb. The entire summit ridge offers no room for error. The commercialization of Everest and the plague of fixed ropes that would resolve such mishaps was a decade away.

That was the straw that broke the camel's back. I wasn't in the right frame of mind to take on the dangers I'd previously conquered while in a better mental and physical state. I was done with this climb. I had been to the summit and, thinking of my family first for a change, I had nothing to prove. At least that's the way I felt at that moment. My good friend Kim Momb had just summited. The expedition had successfully pioneered a first ascent of the East Face. My headache was worsening minute by minute.

On the other hand, Lowe and Cassell were determined to go for the summit, where they had yet to stand. I told George and Jay that I would not go farther and both of them tried in vain to convince me to climb. I was steadfast. I said I didn't need any oxygen and would leave at camp the bottle I'd carried up, should they need it. My decision didn't make it any easier to get even semi-comfortable with six men pressed together like sextuplets in the womb. The seconds became minutes, the minutes were hours, and each hour was eternity. It's a wonder that none of us suffocated that evening.

At midnight, Lowe and Cassell crept out of a stupor. Each climber hooked up an oxygen bottle, fastened a mask over his face, and climbed out into the freezing rarefied air. They roped up and began the upward grind into the darkness. I bid my friends goodbye and lay there sucking aspirin, trying to cope with my pain and my decisions.

Time passes ever so slowly in hell. But when dawn finally arrived, we were still alive. My body was rebelling from three nights of detainment at 25,900 feet. As much as I knew my only sane option was to descend, I also was aware that going down now was the end of my summit opportunity on this expedition. Slogging down the broken trail with Buhler and Reichardt was bittersweet.

Alone in my thoughts, the word "quitter" surfaced in my mind. I had turned around for good reason, but could I have gutted it out? Added to my misery was a sort of post-traumatic stress. I was still not 100 percent comfortable with my decision even though I knew it was the right one.

We bypassed High Camp Two, marched right by High Camp One, and continued down all the way to Helmet Camp, where, after 36 hours of misery, my headache diminished and faded away in the thicker air at 21,300 feet. I didn't just feel better, I was reborn. Celebration was underway for the expedition's success, and we soon heard by radio that Lowe, Reid, and Cassell had reached the summit. Rejoicing was tempered somewhat with the report that Reid and Cassell were suffering frostbite and exhaustion. In the end, both would recover.

An overnight storm dumped a couple feet of fresh snow. Nevertheless, a couple of climbers still wanted to make the expedition's final gasp for the summit. Feeling better, I instinctively joined them. The reverse magnetic field of Everest lured me out of my teetering relationship with good judgment. However, the weather did us in the next day at High Camp Two as another couple feet of snowfall smothered the already dangerous avalanche slopes above. Morrissey wisely made the decision for all to descend. The summit game was over.

The ascent of the Kangshung Face Expedition had been a resounding success. Momb, Reichardt, Buhler, Reid, Lowe, and Cassell had climbed Everest via the most treacherous way to the top. But the expedition still had to negotiate the critical hurdle of a safe descent. All of us were aware that 90 percent of mountaineering accidents occur when climbing down. Every step was made as though we were descending the face of a giant Mona Lisa painting. Extra care was taken to avoid dislodging stones or ice that could injure teammates below. We double-checked and triple-checked our ropes, anchor pins, carabiner links, crampons, and ice screws. From the top of the ice cap was a full 4,500 feet of rappelling down dangerous vertical terrain. It took a few days, but all of us landed safely in Base Camp. Except for some frostbite, none of us was injured seriously. A dream team machine was needed to conquer the Kangshung Face. That's how the "Last Great Problem" of the Himalaya was climbed.

As we packed our gear and began the week-long trek down the Karta Valley, I was alive like never before, but my killer instinct had died. I had traveled back to Everest with the goal of becoming the first American to climb it twice, and came oh-so close. For years afterward I suffered post-traumatic stress from my decision to turn around at the highest camp. I was 35, and putting my family first was the right choice, but it would take me years to convince my subconscious. Every man needs to come to grips with when to push forward and when to hold back. Things can happen. Dave Cheesemond and his partner, Catherine Freer, disappeared in 1987 while climbing the Hummingbird Ridge on Mount Logan, Canada's highest peak. Apparently they broke through a cornice, as their tent and bodies were found 10 years later below the ridge but in an area too dangerous for recovery. Another Everest team member, Dan Reid and his wife, Barbara, fell to their deaths in 1991 while climbing a technical rock and ice route on Mount Kenya, Tanzania.

The intensity of the game I was playing had taken its toll. To succeed in Himalayan mountaineering, your concentration must be 100 percent, 24 hours a day in the mountains and committed the other 300-some days of the year. That's the way I viewed it. On the Kangshung Face, my peak physical performance was a couple years behind me. On my personal list of greatest mountaineers is Walter Bonatti, an Italian who essentially walked away from the game at 35, and now I understood why. The strain of burning a candle at both ends, climbing in the Himalayas and supporting my family, was too much. It would be years before I could muster the drive to launch from my success on Everest to continue toward my next goal to climb the highest mountain on each of the seven continents.

Words from the Wild

- "The mountains will never disappoint you, but people will." — Walter Bonatti
- Visualize being in the moment and then take small steps.
- For every action, there is an equal and opposite reaction. For every decision there is a consequence with a price tag attached.
- Pioneers have fear like anyone else, but like the quest for absolute zero, they find heat in all things.
- A goal is a journey, not a destination, and each year you have to set new goals.
- There are no pockets in a shroud.
- If you have good health, you have everything.
- "Its hard to stay in Kansas, once you've been to Oz." —Kim Momb

TWENTY

VINSON

Antarctica's second highest peak,
Mount Tyree from near the landing strip.

Dick Bass expanded the perspective of exploring the world through climbing in the early 1980s. The developer of Snowbird resort in Utah joined in a bet with his good friend Frank Wells, who was CEO of the Disney empire. The pair would compete for the distinction of being first to climb the highest mountain on each of the seven continents. Bass spared no expense to eventually win the contest in 1985. Word got out that he spent some $250,000 just for the private expedition in Antarctica. Nevertheless, the idea caught the attention of mountaineers around the globe, including me.

Among the world's continents, Antarctica is the southernmost and, on average, it's the coldest, driest, windiest, and has the highest average elevation. The fifth largest continent, with a landmass the size of the United States and Mexico combined, it is covered with ice to an average height of more than 6,000 feet from storms of snow that never melts. The tremendous weight of all this ice depresses the underlying bedrock in some areas to below sea level. For mountaineers, the hardest part of the Seven Summits Challenge is reaching Mount Vinson. The highest peak in Antarctica, nestled in the center of the Ellsworth Mountains, rises to the elevation of 16,067 feet above a sea of ice. This lonely, isolated mountain range about 78 degrees south was first spotted at a distance in 1935 during a flight by American polar explorer Lincoln Ellsworth. US Navy aircraft discovered the highest peak in the range in 1957. That same year the mountain was named for Congressman Carl G. Vinson, an advocate for Antarctic exploration. These mountains are sculptured on all sides by nature's tiny instrument, the snowflake, resulting in peaks with classic pyramid shapes. Glaciers have no advantage in sculpturing these slopes of metamorphic rock. Six months of the year, sun shines almost equally on all sides of the mountains near the South Pole as the earth spins like a top. Each mountain has a chiseled, pointed shape unique to Antarctica.

Courageous explorations in Antarctica began early in the 20th century. They included the most famous adventure race in modern times as British explorer Robert Falcon Scott vied with Norway's Roald Amundsen to be the first to reach the South Pole. Amundsen won that contest on December 14, 1911. Scott reached the pole a month later, but he and all his men tragically starved and froze to death during their return. Ernest Shackleton, the century's greatest explorer in my estimation, led a South Pole discovery expedition that transformed into a two-year survival saga. Shackleton's book "Endurance" ranks number one in my library for heroic adventure. After reading this and other historical accounts of one gripping feat after another, I was intrigued if not obsessed with trying to climb Antarctica's highest mountain. I simply had to go for it before age 40 while I still had some benefit of athletic prowess.

The first ascent of Vinson, sponsored in part by National Geographic, was led by American Nick Clinch in 1966, nearly 200 years after James Cook circumnavigated Antarctica. According to the mountaineering records, 37 men had climbed the peak prior to the attempt I planned for 1988. The cold—that is the "mighty" cold—would be the biggest obstacle to success and the most unavoidable safety issue. My research indicated the warmest temperature would be about minus 25 degrees Fahrenheit. The record low, set in 1983, was minus 128.6 degrees, the coldest natural temperature recorded on the planet. The actual climbing was reported to be moderately difficult on rock and ice. The ascent would not be a fingernail-gripping cliffhanger, although climbers always must be alert for danger when traveling on glaciers. Climbing the steep ice cliffs to a plateau appeared to be the most dangerous section. Once a climber reached that final plateau between Mount Shinn and Vinson, the final 2,000 feet included some interesting ice and ridges to negotiate en route to the summit.

Vinson is the most remote of the Seven Summits, and from Spokane, traveling to the bottom of the world was expensive. The roundtrip flight from Punta Arenas, Chile, the southern-most city in the Southern Hemisphere, to the ice landing strip near the Ellsworth Mountains on West Antarctica would cost $15,000. You didn't want to miss the connections, as only one flight in and out was scheduled each season. Famed pioneer daredevil pilot Giles Kershaw was leader of a Canadian company called Adventure Network that flew a DC-4 prop aircraft that looked like it had gone through World War II, and perhaps it had. The plane's wheels were modified with super large tires for landing on rough ice. This was the flying tool of the trade for transporting crazies to the world's cold shoulder.

The flight from Punta Arenas to the unimproved ice strip was nearly 2,500 miles each way, a daring service provided by the loose-knit Adventure Network, which catered to the wild side of humanity at a semi-affordable price considering the logistics. Adding to the roundtrip flight from Punta Arenas were the costs of special gear, such as a new one-piece, tailor-made, ultra-lightweight Gore-Tex climbing suit stuffed with the finest goose down. Indeed, I would have to come up with a minimum of $20,000 cash to reach Mount Vinson and return. I also had to factor in the considerable costs of a month off work and no way to communicate with my construction crews or my family. It's no wonder my wife left me. Our marriage was on the rocks, and I knew it. My time away from home had two people growing in opposite directions. My climbing addiction soothed my soul, and the thought of traveling to Antarctica lifted my spirits. But achieving inner peace wasn't going to pay for this trip.

The problem with money is that it's always a problem! I solved some of the equation by redeeming the $15,000 in cash value built up in a life insurance policy. My insurance broker was flabbergasted when I called. It was useless trying to explain this to anyone, as I was sick and tired of being called crazy. I solved the other major issue—finding a climbing partner willing to shell out $20,000—as my planning began to take shape in 1987. I would go solo. The mountaineering world is small, and climbers always seem to know what other climbers are doing by word of mouth. I'd heard that Seattle-based international guide Phil Ershler was planning a trip to Antarctica. I contacted Ershler, who said he had a paying client who wanted to be guided up Vinson. So, I knew there'd be at least one person who spoke English on the flight to the Ellsworth Mountains.

Once I knew the insurance check was in the mail, I began to plan and pack. At this point of my life, my diary is thin on meat and details because of the chaos in my personal life. I left Spokane on a mid-November day in 1988 with an airport send-off from Sharon and my good friends John Roskelley and Joe Collins. The flight took me to Florida, where I had the loneliest feeling of my life, sitting in the Miami airport with not one other person in the waiting area at the end of a long gate for the flight to Santiago, Chile. It was at the airport, sitting alone for hours, that the weight of pursuing my climbing dreams threatened to crush my soul. Far from the mountains, I felt unbearably lonely and isolated from within. What was wrong with me?

ANTARCTICA

Once the flight departed, the excitement of the adventure eased my qualms. Everything I had read about Antarctica captured my imagination, but when the dream turned to reality, the reality was better than the dream. The flight across the equator over South America to Santiago offered stunning aerial views of the Andes' peaks and glaciers. The weather was clear enough on the next flight to Punta Arenas to see the wild, golden granite spires of Patagonia—The Fitzroy, Cerro Torre, and Torre Egger were piercing the blue sky. I was greeted by an Adventure Network employee at Punta Arenas, where I assumed the unfamiliar role as a paying client. My excitement was fanned on the drive into town as I could see Tierra del Fuego, the islands at the tip of South America, across the Strait of Magellan. This is the narrow strait that posed so much difficulty for Ferdinand Magellan in 1520 as he sailed his ships into the violent winds while navigating passage to the Pacific Ocean.

My euphoria reversed into anxiousness when I visited the Adventure Network "office" to see how they operated. I met Giles Kershaw, who took me into a tiny rented downtown hotel room crammed with transmission amplifiers, receivers, and other electronic gear wired to a transmitter and dish on the hotel roof. Everything looked jury-rigged and disheveled, like a movie scene from a 1930s Chicago police office. A lone employee wearing a headset sat at a desk in front of a microphone stand communicating by radio with a man 2,500 miles away and surrounded by ice. "How's the weather?" the office staffer said. A speaker allowed anyone in the room to hear the garbled, static voice transmissions that would fade and amplify depending upon the atmosphere in between. This span between Punta Arenas and the ice landing strip included the Drake Passage off the southern edge of Tierra del Fuego and Cape Horn. The Drake was known as a graveyard for ships that sailed into these infamous seas. This section of the Southern Ocean on to the northern tip of Antarctica's Palmer Peninsula is known as the "roaring forties" for the sustained winds and brutal storms. High winds and cyclones generate from the Andes and whip the seas into a constant froth of 30- to 60- foot waves. These seas are relatively shallow causing a fast-moving undercurrent that accentuates the ocean forces and turbulence from the winds above. The equipment they had in place offered little information on the weather between take-off and destination, with the potential for the in-between to be rougher than hell! But at least we knew it was clear at the ice landing strip. That's more than polar pioneers knew a hundred years before us.

Eighteen adventurers and crew climbed the gangway into the DC-4 at the quiet airstrip. A party of three from Europe was going on a long ski expedition. Three Chinese included two mountaineers selected to be their country's first to climb Vinson while the other was a geologist looking for ore and minerals. Ershler and his client, Hall Wendle, me, and another team of five mountaineers from various points on the globe made up the load. We sat on metal seats next to about a dozen 50-gallon drums of aviation gasoline. If we made it to Antarctica, these barrels would be carefully lowered to the ice so the fuel would be pumped into the plane tanks for the return journey. Everyone had been warned to be dressed for maximum cold. I wore my one-piece down jumpsuit. The plane was unpressurized, so we would be flying at an altitude of 10,000 feet for nearly 10 hours. On a wing and a prayer, we took off for Antarctica.

The flight took us south across the narrow Strait of Magellan and over the huge island of Tierra del Fuego, the "land of fire," so-named by Magellan because of the small camp-fires natives used to keep warm. Expecting to see some hills and valleys, I was surprised to observe that most of Tierra del Fuego's terrain was relatively flat and lifeless. Passing over Cape Horn, the aircraft entered the open seas and the Drake Passage. Winds buffeted the plane and the ocean raged below for hours before we saw our first glimpse of Antarctica. The Palmer Peninsula is the land feature first seen in 1820 by US sealer Nathaniel Palmer, who is credited with discovering Antarctica. In the same year, British and Russian whalers also claimed discovery of the continent. The DC-4 flew over land for another 1,300 miles along a jagged mountain range. We could see countless glaciers flowing into the Weddell Sea. Few words were said as everyone on the plane was awestruck by mile after mile of pure ice and rock that stretched below us to the horizon in every direction. For all we knew, there were no more footprints below us than on the backside of Mars.

The DC 4 leaves us in the middle of Antarctica after the pilot
promised to return "if weather permits."

The landing site dubbed Patriot Hills was a huge, flat slab of ice that the
wind had blown clean of snow. After a couple passes over the base camp,
Kershaw picked his line and skillfully touched the DC-4's fat tires down on the
washboard surface like a gentle kiss.

Stepping out the door of the plane, minus 35-degree temperatures greeted
me like a kick in the teeth. The pilot and co-pilot were the only ones on the
plane who were fully braced for the wallop of cold. With just a small amount
of humidity, ice crystals formed by the billions and floated in the air. It was as
if sparklers were drifting before my eyes.

The sun was shining 30 degrees above the horizon in late November, and
the sky was clear. For the next six months the sun would not drop below the
skyline. This would be my first experience in 24-hour daylight. I was on a path
to new respect for what the human body can endure. With every breath my
body had to instantly deal with flesh-freezing air flashing in at 35 degrees below
zero and warm it to body temperature so the oxygen could be extracted inside
the lungs. It was amazing to just be standing and breathing and living in such
a savage environment. For two years I planned for this challenge. My body

felt ready and strong, but I knew that my survival here depended on my gear. Something as simple as a faulty cooking stove could spell doom.

Kershaw and his co-pilot immediately went to work installing huge insulated doughnut pads around and over the four engines to help retain heat for the plane's brief stopover. Everyone stepped in to help the crew transfer the aviation barrels down a steel gangway to the ice, where the pilots installed a pump and hooked up a fuel line to the wing tanks above. This operation was done without hesitation because they did not want the engines to freeze up. Afterward, I walked a long way out on the ice looking for a good vantage for a photograph of the plane taking off. Attracted to a thoroughly wind-polished spot, I got down on my belly to gaze deeply into the crystal-clear ice below me. I could see maybe 20 feet down before the light faded to black. The ice sparkled with tiny air bubbles as though it was a gigantic frozen slab of champagne. I raised my ice axe with my right arm and thrust the adz down. Instead of penetrating the ice, it bounced back! The ice was so old and dense, my axe splattered only a few tiny shards in several hard blows. Comfort is rare here, but wonderment abounds.

We bid Kershaw a bon voyage, and as he climbed back up the extension ladder into the DC-4, he turned to us and said that if weather was good he would return in three weeks. We were not left alone, however, as the company had a Twin Otter shuttle aircraft parked near a large, steel reinforced tent. The other pilot would stay at the company's landing strip camp with a couple of assistants while the rest of us went on our adventures. I never took for granted the skills and bravery of pilots who fly to remote places. Kershaw is regarded as one of the most accomplished pilots in Antarctic aviation history. While safety was his top priority, especially with others on board, he was a pilot driven to test limits. He was killed in 1990 at age 41 while flying an experimental aircraft called a gyrocopter over the Jones Ice Shelf in Antarctica.

The 10 climbers and one geologist boarded the Twin Otter for the 100-mile flight along the Ellsworth Mountains. The climbers viewed out the windows like kids peering into the Willie Wonka Chocolate Factory. Nearly every peak we saw was unexplored and unclimbed, mountain after mountain. Finally, the pilot circled and landed on a flat snowfield below Mount Tyree, Antarctica's second highest peak.

I pitched my tent outside the established base camp shelter and alongside the American team of Ershler and Wendle. Sleep came fast as we had been up for 48 hours straight, running on adrenalin. It was strange to prepare for sleep with the sun staying up to traverse around the pole at the same elevation. Only the shadows on the mountains changed.

After eight hours of rest, I started my daily Antarctica routine. The first order of business was to pull the stove out of my backpack, set it up on the solid ice, and start melting ice for water. I had brought more than 3 pounds of dried food per day to last 30 days (allowing for the possibility of weather delaying the DC-4s return). Being able to melt ice and snow was vitally important. I checked every working part of my cooker as I set it up. Then I did what any experienced mountaineer would do at that moment in Antarctica. I prayed that it would light. Gasoline's flash point—the lowest temperature at which volatile fluid will evaporate enough to form a combustible concentration of gas—is minus 45 degrees Fahrenheit, so by the laws of physics this refined camping fuel should light even when it's so cold your breath falls to the ground. After pumping several times to pressurize the tank, I watched the gas trickle into the heating bowl. Oddly, the fuel seemed to be on the verge of freezing, and I was almost surprised to touch the lighter flame to the fuel and see it ignite. The flame heated the burner and the vaporized gas burst into a small orange fireball that settled into a familiar roaring blue flame of joy and well-being. I was transformed.

The lighting of a stove is such an insignificant exercise on other continents, but in Antarctica it sparked euphoria. The fact that I could create BTUs while standing on thousands of feet of solid ice and thousands of miles from civilization was more satisfying at the moment than the flames of passion. No fine restaurant could serve hot tea and oatmeal that tasted better than what my cooker brewed. The meal was hot, and that's really all that mattered for sustenance and morale. My breakfast consisted of two packs of oatmeal, two packs of hot chocolate, instant coffee, and a granola bar. Lunch was string cheese, whole wheat crackers, peanut butter, Buffalo Jerky or sausage, and dried fruit. Dinners became a ceremony, as I could boil water for ramen and then dump that hot water into an aluminum packet of freeze-dried spaghetti, mashed potatoes, and bacon bits, or maybe chili. I would top off the feast with a mug of Knorr soup. In between meals during the day I'd snack on Snickers bars, Clif bars, hard candy, and handfuls of mixed nuts and dried fruit. I had planned for taking in 7,000 calories a day, and I ate it all. I had accurately calculated that one liter of fuel would last three or four days for melting ice and cooking meals. My traveling load amounted to 125 pounds of fuel, food, tent and extra hardware split between my backpack and the plastic sled I would hook to my climbing harness and pull the first seven miles to an advanced base camp.

The most common questions the public asks mountaineers are, first, "How cold is it?" and, second, "How do you go to the bathroom?" The first answer in this case is "Colder than I've ever been before." The second answer is more involved. When nature called in Antarctica, urinating was chilling but fairly easy. I would crouch on my knees inside the tent or lie down inside my sleeping bag and go into a quart Nalgene bottle designated for pee. Evacuating my bowels was much more problematic. I got the nickname "Gumby" for wearing a one-piece down jumpsuit that made me look like a down sleeping bag with a head sticking out. I had designed this suit with no butt-end zipper, and I thought I was being wise in having it custom-made with only one zipper running down the breast and under my crotch, ending at my buttocks. Zippers are escape routes for warmth. Having no zipper in the back translated into more BTUs of body heat staying inside my garments. This design had worked on other climbs, but I quickly learned the alarming difference between 20 below zero on Everest and 40 or more below on Vinson. In Antarctica, this one misjudged detail turned out to be a huge mistake. In order to facilitate a bowel movement, I had to unzip to my crotch, take my arms out of the suit, and drop the top half, which exposed my torso to the elements. That wasn't my only mistake. My chosen base layer was one-piece angora underwear, which also had to be peeled down. I found the tiny zipper pulls in factory-made butt-zip long johns to be too small for my fingers, and half the time they were cheaply made zippers that got stuck. It was faster to pull the underwear top off. Exposing bare skin while standing on ice in minus 40-degree weather with a wind blowing is a recipe for disaster. Unprotected skin can freeze very quickly. Every time I got the urge I would have to find an ice block or some sort of hollow for wind protection. I was thankful that my ass was relatively small, measured in square inches and not square feet of extra surface area that would be exposed! Undressing was painful and extremely dangerous to private parts. As we climbed higher up the mountain speed and regularity became a matter of life and death.

The climbing of the mountain is the easiest part, and the reward for two years of preparation. The thought process and meticulous planning of minute details before setting out is every bit as important as the muscle power on the slopes. Calculating how many calories to eat, gathering the right type of food, the right kind of stove and fuel, the boots, crampons, clothing, tent, sled, harness, and other gear was tedious. Assembling all this equipment sounds simple, but it's sobering to read account after account of men dying on expeditions because of one miscalculation. I was stuck with a bad decision on clothing. I would have to be extra careful to make sure it came out all right.

Adventure Network's base camp was at 6,000 feet, leaving the climbers 10,000 feet of elevation to gain over about 17 miles of rugged glacier and ice travel to reach the summit of Vinson. I introduced myself to the two Chinese climbers, who were young men in their early 20s, about half my age. They were traveling with a pioneer woman geologist, Gin Quingman. The two young men, Li Zhi Xin and Wang Yong Feng, were sent to Antarctica with all expenses paid by the Chinese Mountaineering Association. This was Quingman's second government-sponsored trip to Antarctica. Her job was to map and record the mineralogy of the Vinson Massif. At the end of the trip she would describe to me how the rocks in the Ellsworth Mountains are loaded with iron deposits. A Chinese iron mine in Antarctica? I cringed at the thought. When there's money to be made, mankind has no boundaries.

Once we set off from base camp, I was in my element. The rhythm of climbing transported my mind into a pleasant space between heaven and earth. Every foot gained expanded the horizon. The nature of the terrain was not dangerous, as the ice at the base of the Ellsworth Mountains was relatively flat and compact with no glacier movement, but hazards lurked. Twenty-five years of glacier climbing taught me to pay extra attention to soft shadows and slight undulations on the surface that might be clues to hidden crevasses. Reaching a pass after a long day, we pitched our tents on a narrow cornice of ice with magnificent views in all directions. I would leave my sled here before traveling the dangerous, undulating glacial terrain. After setting up camp, I prepared a cache by using my adz to chip a hole in the ice big enough to stash food for several days. I marked it with a flagged wand. Since the average snowfall in Antarctica is only six inches a year, there was no worry of this cache being buried. And there was no threat from hungry bears or wolves. After repacking my rucksack, I would still have more than 100 pounds of food and equipment on my back as the real work was set to begin the next day.

After descending a thousand feet to the Branscomb Glacier, we ascended the middle of the river of ice and through a headwall of ice cliffs to gain a high plateau where we would place our high camp. I had carried an extra rope just for this glacier. Ershler graciously allowed me to tie in with his client for safer travel through dangerous crevassed areas. From this high camp at nearly 14,000 feet, the summit was five miles away and up more than 2,000 feet. The high camp was easily achieved in three days, although I was still learning to deal with the elements. Even in temperatures of minus 30 to minus 40 degrees, I was amazed that my wonderful down suit was too hot while I was moving in still or light winds. Every so often with exertion, I would start to sweat, forcing me to unzip to my waist, take the top half of the down suit off and tie the arms around my waist. Without the insulation I would chill quickly and have to put on the top again. This off-again, on-again hassle became part of the ordeal of ascent. It was the only way I could keep from soaking my down suit with sweat.

The high camp was located on the 14,000-foot plateau between Vinson Massif and Mount Shinn, Antarctica's third highest mountain. The danger of climbing Vinson increases here, with the threat of horrific storms coming out of nowhere. As the air cools over the South Pole, where atmospheric pressure is lower, it descends rapidly and rushes outward at ferocious speeds. My friend Glen Porzak had described a storm he endured while trying to climb Vinson that lasted seven days with 100 mile per hour winds, and wind-chill factors as cold as minus 120 degrees! One of America's greatest mountaineers, Yvon Chouinard, wrote an essay about this storm and how their perfectly designed tent saved their lives. After reading about the killer winds, I bought the same tent, a North Face VE24. I had used the same type of tent on Everest, but I didn't want to put it to the test of an Antarctica storm. At 14,000 feet, few ice blocks or good wind shelters were available, so I chipped down in the ice just a few inches to set the tent, and fastened it with ice screws. Complete protection from the wind was impossible.

The ritual of cooking and melting snow for water had become more intense every day as the temperatures got colder the higher we climbed. My big nose was a standout liability especially when the winds picked up. In the past I had tried to use masks made of down or plastic to keep my face warm, but these masks compressed my huge nose and restricted my breathing. I gave up on them and resorted to sunglasses with a leather nose flap that helped to protect the top of my nose from sun and wind. However, the sides of my nose and cheeks were still exposed, so as I climbed in the bitter cold, I had to pull my suit's down hood completely over and cinch the hood strap tight around my face. I had to turn my head slightly downward and to the side to keep the wind from freezing the small remaining spots of bare skin. Maintaining clear vision—very important—was tedious at times. The sunglasses were enough to keep the surface of my eyes warm, but occasionally the lenses would fog up. I removed the shades and exposed my naked eyes with utmost care.

COLD AND COLDER

The two Chinese climbers were healthy and ready as soon as high camp was established and so were Ershler and Wendle. I was also ready, although I was having some issues coping with the elements. Even inside the tent my exhalations would instantly freeze into tiny ice flakes that would drift around inside looking like a million miniscule floating lamps. It was a constant battle to keep semi-warm. The Vinson Massif summit area is a broad, high plateau with eight peaks of elevations ranging from 14,000 feet to more than 16,000 feet. South from our camp, the two highest jagged-rock peaks stood about a mile apart and about five miles from our campsite. None of us knew which one of the two was the tallest. The highest summit appeared to be the one to the east. The map I had was poorly detailed, simply showing the highest point as "Vinson Massif." I hadn't read any articles about difficulty in finding the highest summit, so I assumed the eastern peak to be the highest. The Chinese team had presumed the same thing.

Early in the morning on December 2, I crawled out of my tent into the elements—about minus 30 degrees with a nasty 20 mile per hour headwind—to try for the summit of Vinson. My first steps were awkward as my crampons barely scratched through the ancient ice. I probably looked like the hunchback of Notre Dame, rucksack on and bent over into the wind as I shuffled upward. Fighting the unbelievable cold and the headwind required a commitment to staying alive rivaling any of my career's hardest rock climbs. The weather left no margin for error. I left my rope behind to save weight. I had my pockets crammed with candy bars. Two full quart bottles of lemonade were snuggled inside my breast pockets next to my chest. If they froze next to my heart, I supposed that hydration would be needless. Each step upward boosted my heart rate, increased my warmth, and soon my veins were pumping with the euphoria of heading for the summit of Antarctica's highest point!

At first, I stayed close to Ershler and Hall who were roped together, but shortly I could see they were going much too slow for my liking. The young-stud Chinese climbers, Li and Wang, dressed entirely in red down suits, had climbed off like rockets, so I tried to catch up to them. The ice was so hard in some stretches that crampons hardly left a scratch, and in places it was so clear I could peer into the soul of the continent. The terrain presented a gentle grind up this frigid fortress of peaks. The wind was steady and the only way to fight the cold was to keep moving and nibbling on candy for energy.

Eventually, I gained on the Chinese as they were climbing directly for the east peak, which still appeared to be the highest on the plateau. We had less than a thousand feet to go as the slope steepened to about 45 degrees and transitioned from ice to hard-pack snow. I needed to up my concentration a notch and keep focused on balance. After about 500 feet of this steep climbing I crested a sharp, corniced ridge and began traversing southward following the tracks of Li and Wang. This was technical terrain and the two Chinese were belaying each other but still moved swiftly along the ridge for another several hundred yards to where it crested with another ridge rising from the north. The Chinese were only a couple hundred feet ahead of me now, belaying each other up the icy ridge to the top of the peak. Being solo, I had to put the ever-so-close summit out of my mind and go slowly with extreme caution. I could not afford the slightest misstep. With every move I made I had to check the snow for ice underneath. A slip here would be fatal.

As I gained the final ridge to the top, the north peak came into view and, to my dismay, it was clearly higher. We had climbed to the wrong summit! The

Chinese immediately came off the crown and I knew they had just realized their mistake, too, so I cut a platform and waited as they down-climbed the ridge. They were very quick, competent climbers, and soon we were all huddled on the little ice platform for an international summit.

"Mr. Wang, Mr. Wang! How many meters high are we!" I said as I pointed my finger to the altimeter he was holding in his hand. "Weee hunng go neh, ha ha ah!" Of course that's a very rough stab at what he said, but it's how the Chinese language sounded to me. Not understanding one word, I pointed to the summit they had just climbed. "Uhn mee songoong," Wang said, as best as I could tell, waving his hands downward and pointing to the altimeter. I could see that the peak we had climbed was lower than the peak to the north, and Wang was confirming this with his gestures.

Out of my pack I pulled a two-pound package of fudge that Sharon had made and broke off a couple of ice-cube-size pieces. "Here! Have some of my homemade fudge! It's good, good, very good American food! Mmmm good." I chomped on a piece of frozen fudge as an example, trying to chew it as my heart attempted to pound out of my chest in the thin air. I put a piece of fudge in Wang's hand and he put it to his nose, carefully taking a sniff before chancing a tiny bite.

Li pulled out a brightly colored Chinese designer thermos adorned with a fine lithograph of a pagoda etched into the metal. "So, leeh tooo muk sa, ha ha ha," Li said as he pushed the thermos over to my face for a taste. It was the most sublime swallow of hot tea ever to warm my lips. New life seemed to flood down my esophagus and into my veins with each sip.

Bug-eyed, waving my hands high, and rubbing my stomach, I said, "Thank you, thank you my friends!" with the biggest grin I could stretch into my freezing cheeks.

We were fast friends now with a mutual problem. We all wanted to climb Vinson, but the summit suddenly seemed farther off than when we started more than six hours ago. The marathon, if we chose to finish it, was just starting. The only comfort was that there was no nightfall. We had about 700 feet to descend on steep, icy slopes to a saddle between the real summit of Vinson and the subsidiary peak we had just climbed. Visualizing our route, we pointed to an ice depression that led across the col, and then we could climb over and up the rock and ice of the West Face of Vinson. It looked steep but safe from avalanche hazard. Looking down the valley, we could see Ershler and Hall climbing up at a steady pace.

Down we went to the ice saddle between the two peaks, where we began the Quasimodo shuffle hunched into the wind toward the main peak of Vinson about a mile distant and a thousand feet higher. In a couple more hours we gained a vertical rock ridge that I knew would lead directly to the summit of Vinson above. We finally could put our gloved hands on the compact metamorphic greenstone that made up the summit block, although physically and psychologically, we were nearly exhausted. Before beginning this final ascent, I broke out more fudge squares. Even the second time around, my newfound Chinese companions smelled the chocolate confections first, and then nibbled cautiously before taking a real bite.

Climbing just a few meters up the rock rib, we crested a slanting ice field that led directly into a gully of hard-pack snow over ice at a 40- or 45-degree angle—perfect conditions for front-pointing. This gully would be our ticket to the top, and the climbing here would go much faster than climbing the rock rib. I started out first, kicking in steps as deeply as possible for my new mates, who followed roped together. I was very comfortable on this slope without a rope, and with the newfound energy from the fudge squares, I was feeling a surge of adrenalin. The gully ran straight up the West Face of the summit block, and for the first time during the day we were fairly sheltered from the killer wind and blowing ice shards. Moving in a steady climb, it took about an hour to reach the top of the gully where the angle gradually eased off.

Climbing along the final steps to the ridge crest I checked my watch. It was nearly 6 p.m. We had been going steadily for 12 hours but the fatigue was overcome temporarily by achievement in a few more steps when I crested the ridge and found myself looking down the southern exposure of Vinson. We had come so far, and now were so close—just another 500 vertical feet. There was no need to hurry, as the sun would just hang over the horizon at the same elevation all day and all night. The climbing was much easier here on the ridge crest, and together we continued for another hour until we came to the steep summit cornice. Li chopped his way through the vertical ice first, and when he stood up, he threw his hands in the air. "Oooeeeetooo!" he yelled.

Whatever that meant in Chinese I didn't know, but he was clearly thrilled! I climbed through the cornice and looked over a hundred feet to a point of rock and ice with nothing but blue sky all around it. This was the highest point in Antarctica. Momentarily we were impervious to the brutal wind. We climbed up to the summit together as tears flowed down my cheeks and froze. We slapped each other on the back hard enough to hurt, but it hurt so good.

In 25 years of climbing the world's greatest mountains, I had never felt such ecstasy. I was thrilled to be able to share it. Li, Wang, and I wanted to photograph each other with our flags. In preparation for this moment, I had bored a hole through the adz of my ice axe to place a tiny bolt for a camera mount. I set the axe soundly in the ice, screwed on the camera, set the timing device, and managed to snap a good photo of all three of us on the top. I had two flags, one USA flag as well as a Norway flag to pay respect to my Norwegian father-in-law who graciously purchased new boots for me before this expedition.

L-R. Li, me, Wang on the summit of Vinson.

Below our feet were unclimbed, unexplored mountains in all directions. Glaciers cascaded down into gentle valleys terminating into the flat, timeless expanse of blue-green ice that went across the continent. Ice, ice as far as we could see. On this clear day, standing 16,067 feet above sea level, I imagined that I could see 750 miles to the South Pole.

The summit of Vinson is thousands of miles from civilization and being there felt like reaching nirvana. Even on the top of Everest you can see a tiny village below. Standing on Vinson's summit was the closest I would come to being an astronaut and the feelings of infinite space. The time seemed to stand still until Li and Wang wanted to leave the summit after five minutes. I wanted to stay, so I watched them begin their descent carefully following the footsteps we had made coming up. I sat on top of the world at the bottom of planet Earth for another half hour as though I were lounging in my living room at home soaking in the view out the front window. I had friends back home who were very religious, who had preached to me about the "glories of heaven" after you die. Looking down at the world from Vinson, I couldn't picture heaven being much better.

The view from the summit of Vinson.
Our base camp was above the upper left corner of this photograph.

As much as I wanted to stay, my desire to live snapped me back to my senses. The time was nearly 8 p.m. and the cold was penetrating my premium down suit. As I climbed down off the summit cornice and gained the ridge crest, I could see Ershler and Wendle climbing up the final 500 feet below me. Li, Wang and I were the 38th, 39th, and 40th humans to reach the summit of Vinson, and in about an hour, Ershler and Wendle would be the 41st and 42nd. The cold only seemed to get colder with each step of my descent. It was a blessing that the wind had died down to almost nothing. The technical terrain seemed friendly to me now. After five miles of descent to the high camp, I plunged into the tent and warmth of my sleeping bag. It was nearly midnight.

The weather was stable and clear that night, and we still had time to do more climbing the next day, so I asked Ershler if he was game to try and climb Mount Shinn, the foot of which was right across the big ice saddle from our campsite. He was enthusiastic about the idea, so we slept in late and started out at mid-morning. It was another glorious day, with some moderate ice and rock climbing that made the route interesting all the way to the summit.

After the climb of Shinn, we packed, climbed back down, and reached the landing site in just two days. In two more days the DC-4 aircraft that had flown us in landed in perfect weather at Patriot Hills and took us back to Punta Arenas. Vinson was not the highest peak I'd climbed in my life, but it was the most remote and dangerous expedition I'd ever completed. When I stepped off the plane onto terra firma, I got down on the ground and kissed the dirt and grass, not caring how much of it stuck to my lips.

Words from the Wild
- "Inaction breeds doubt and fear. Action breeds confidence and courage. If you want to conquer fear, do not sit home and think about it. Go out and get busy." —Dale Carnegie

Twenty-One

Aconcagua

Immediately after kissing the dirt at the Punta Arenas airport, I joined Phil Ershler, Hall Wendle, and the three Chinese adventurers for a shuttle into town to celebrate our success on Mount Vinson. The warm breeze drifting through the small Chilean fishing seaport felt like Miami Beach after being to Antarctica. With spirits lifted, Ershler, Wendle, and I befriended several attractive local girls who wanted to party all night. The ladies were much younger than we, but they knew every swinging dance haunt in town. We traveled from one rock-and-roll venue to another, hitting every corner of the small city and dancing until our feet were sore. Punta Arenas is the southernmost city on the planet, so in the South American summer, being a party animal was within reach of a social lightweight such as myself. The span from sunset to sunrise was only a few hours. This was one of the few times in my life that I actually "partied all night."

Trying to call home was useless, as I felt Sharon was giving up on me and our marriage, so I drifted back into a state of mind that had always saved my soul: dreaming of wilderness. The thought crossed my mind that I could solo Aconcagua while here in South America to save expenses in my quest for the Seven Summits. I still had nine days until my scheduled flight back to the USA from Santiago, so why not try? In 1974, John Roskelley and I had managed to climb the Eiger North Face in a seven-day extension to our expedition in the Soviet Union and the Pamirs. Tacking on an extra climb that was just a domestic flight and a bus ride away seemed like a doable plan.

Aconcagua is the highest peak in the Southern Hemisphere. It's also the highest peak outside of Asia and the second highest of the Seven Summits, below Everest. It rises to 22,841 feet above sea level just a hundred miles from the Pacific Ocean Chilean Trench that dives to 24,000 feet below the sea. This is the biggest wrinkle on planet Earth with an astounding 46,000 feet of elevation difference in such a short span. The geologic history of the Andes includes hundreds of volcanoes, large and small, poking up all along the 4,000-mile spine of the mountain chain. Shaped like a huge wedge, Aconcagua is not a volcano, but rather the remains of layer upon layer of volcanic intrusions pushed from deep within the earth like a giant bowel movement. The result is a high blister of rock peak that stands above them all on the border of Chile and Argentina despite millions of years of wear from wind, ice, and water. Located south of the equator, the mountain's erosion is the opposite of mountains in the Northern Hemisphere. Ice and glaciers gradually formed and chiseled away on the cold south-facing shadow side, creating one of the three largest vertical escarpments on the planet, the great 10,000-foot South Face of Aconcagua. Perhaps no other great mountain on earth has such a dramatically contrasting display of geology. The relatively gentle sloping North Face rises up and up to the summit, while the South Face plunges from the summit nearly straight down for two vertical miles! The highest mountain in our solar system, Olympus Mons on the planet Mars, was formed in a similar fashion and is more than 90,000 feet high. I would be content with Aconcagua for now.

Bidding farewell to our Adventure Network pilot Giles Kershaw and my climbing friends, I took off from Punta Arenas and flew north for Santiago. Except for Phil Ershler, I would never see any of these people again. The Chinese returned to their country and Kershaw would crash and die a few years later while flying an ultra-light aircraft over the ice in Antarctica.

Santiago, Chile's capital city, had a wonderful mix of people. The small Spanish dictionary I carried was of some help in poking through the language barrier, but mostly I acted like a deaf mute in crowds. I wandered about the city's main strips trying to enjoy the displays of jewelry, food, and beautiful women, and there was an abundance of all three. The main tourist attractions were of historic significance, as the city is centered on the parliament buildings where the latest dictator Augusto Pinochet ordered dissidents to be tried and hanged for speaking their minds. Everywhere in Chile, and Santiago in particular, I ran into military men and women guarding roads and byways. I was amazed to see so many old structures that dated back to the Spanish conquest from 1540 to 1810. Traveling is always a wakeup call to realize how young the United States is in comparison to the rest of the civilized world.

With only one overnight in Santiago at a low-rent dump of a room, I managed to read just enough Spanish at the bus station to purchase a ticket to Puente del Inca, the station at a scenic viewpoint on the top of the 8,000-foot pass on the main road across the Andes from Santiago to Mendoza, Argentina. The pass is the staging site for Aconcagua expeditions, and a 2,000-year-old gathering place for the Incas who were attracted by the area's natural hot springs. My personal fascination with the Inca Empire was enough reason to make the trip, as they had been climbing the Andes a thousand years before Columbus discovered the New World. The Incas were drawn to the wild mountain summits for religious reasons. Many artifacts including remains of small children sacrificed to the gods have been found on some of the highest summits of the Andes. It's not inconceivable that Incas could have climbed Aconcagua long before the first recorded ascent by the Swiss guide Matthew Zurbriggen in 1897.

Ershler, who had had climbed Aconcagua, told me to contact Senor Fernando Grajales at the pass. Grajales was known as the mule king, the organizer of porters and pack strings to usher climbers into Aconcagua base camps. With my 100-plus-pound pack on my back, I stepped off the bus at the top of the pass and ended up standing next to a couple of steel industrial-like buildings, one of them apparently a police station. I hiked to an old hotel sitting right on the pass that looked over a bridge into a deep vertical canyon where hot springs bubbled out of fissures and a huge cave. Countless trickles of mineral-laced water had painted the rocks and cliff walls every color of the rainbow and more. The journey was already worthwhile just to see this ancient attraction.

While hiking back along the road, I spotted a corral full of mules, and behind it, a tiny office where I met Grajales. The first words out of the entrepreneur's mouth were music to my ears, because he spoke broken English that I could understand. Grajales was a rugged looking man, about 6 feet tall, leather skinned, with large, wild eyes, a full head of hair, and dressed like a gaucho. But a businessman he was to the core. I needed a mule to carry my pack and food 25 miles up the Horcones Valley to the Plaza del Mulas base camp. This of course could be accomplished for a fee, but I was mildly stunned at the charges. The cost was nearly double what I had expected to pay, perhaps because Grajales knew an American face with cash in hand on first sight. As hard as I try to blend in like a local in all my travels, I stick out like a Damn Yankee to every vendor. Grajales was not to be bargained down. He had the mule, and so, reluctantly, I pulled out my cash and bought a one-way ticket up the valley. I would just have to eat all my food and hope that my pack would be light enough to hike out on the return journey.

Aconcagua attracts climbers and trekkers from around the world, a linear mass of traffic that had left an eyesore of trash, and lots of it! Every major stopping area had big stone walls built like house basements to hide the paper trash and cans piled many feet high. Toilets were nonexistent, so I would climb around a bush or big boulder to find out that many people before me had the same idea. It was sad to see such a beautiful wilderness so unkempt. The problem got so severe that since my visit the governments and the national parks of Chile and Argentina eventually stepped in to establish a mandatory trash haul-out program that reportedly has made a huge improvement.

The Viento Blanco.

The two-and-a-half-day trek to the Plaza del Mulas base camp, elevation 13,875 feet, leads through a high-desert land of extremes. A windless summer day in the low humidity would become terribly hot and uncomfortable. Shortly after sunset, the temperature would plummet to the range of 15 degrees or lower, freezing small streams and dripping water in minutes. The high arid valleys were full of bushes and grass and a few sand dunes much like the desert in central Washington, but virtually devoid of visible wildlife. Occasionally, a few wildflowers dotted the landscape with color among sand and rocks. The puma hunts in this desert, but I saw no tracks, and just a few small birds picking through trash. The largest flying bird on earth, the Andean condor, inhabits this area, but I didn't see any of them soaring in the thin air. The journey was essentially like hiking through Death Valley in California. I had read about the deadly wind known as the Viento Blanco, or "White Wind," that could blow for days at hurricane forces, making travel impossible. Indeed, a climber has to keep in mind that death lurks around every corner for the unprepared in these extreme environments. Sanitation was a human-caused additional concern. I over-boiled my water every day as though I were trying to kill every pathogen known to man.

The biggest obstacle to safely scaling Aconcagua is acclimatization. Most climbers have the transportation means to go from sea level to high altitude in just a couple days. You have to hold yourself back and be patient, taking time to let the body adjust to the altitude. I knew from experience that many climbers get in a hurry and then fail and endanger themselves and others by going up too soon and too fast. Speed kills when going to altitude. My climbing philosophy calls for taking the time necessary to adjust to nature. But I thought I had an advantage going into this climb. Having recently climbed to 16,000 feet on Mount Vinson, I felt that I should have residual acclimatization for Aconcagua.

Arriving at Plaza del Mulas base camp, I was appalled at the trash heap left by countless expeditions before me. Mounds of garbage including mule bones were thrown into the confines of a huge basement-type foundation wall of stones. There had to be a better way for a national park to welcome visitors and handle their impacts. I called the camp "Plaza del Trasho." I fetched my gear from the muleteer who would turn around and head down with his animals as I set up my tent next to the big trash pit on one of the flattened dirt platforms dug out of the mountainside. Capturing my attention was Aconcagua, which stretched to the sky in one giant swoop of multiple rock-and-ice ridges. The original ascent, which has become the standard, went up a vertical mile of zigzag climbing to reach an enormous col on the north side called Nido del Condores (the condor's nest). If I could reach the col in decent shape, and the weather was good, I would have a chance for the summit.

The next morning after my standard breakfast of oatmeal, granola bars, coffee, and hot chocolate, I loaded my pack with enough freeze-dried food for five days. I lumbered off and upward, passing two stone shelter huts on the well-traveled climbers' trail. The first shelter, at 16,000 feet, was named "Canada," and the second, at 17,100 feet, was named "Alaska." The trail was steep in places, and openly exposed to the winds, but the view of the wild Andes to the north was a just reward.

Viento Blanco

The wind began as a whisper from the south while I was climbing to the col and gradually built into a steady roar of maybe 50 miles per hour. The dreaded Viento Blanco was waging an assault on the relatively decent weather I'd been enjoying. On a route with no wind protection I might as well have been a boxer getting pummeled inside a ring, waiting for a bell that would never sound. At about 19,000 feet I reached the Nido del Condores, a col that seemed more like a barren, unprotected landing strip for 747s. Not a soul or living thing was in sight on the rocky expanse as I searched for a sheltered spot to erect my tent. I could see a large stone shelter of some sort in the distance far above me on a broad ridge of rock and ice. I assumed it was Camp Berlin located at 19,520 feet. Above that the climbing still looked easy over rock for another 2,000 feet all the way to the Canaletto, which had been described to me as a 1,300-foot chute of terribly loose boulders stacked at a high angle leading to the summit ridge.

Left to themselves, my legs were trained through years of mountaineering to keep climbing one step after another. But voices of reason rose to the occasion in my brain. I commonly talked to myself when I was alone in the wilderness when needing to work things out. My pack had been feeling heavier and heavier, and I'd already ascended far enough or maybe too far for the day. I had to find shelter from the badgering wind. Camp Berlin was too high to get to that day. I could see a rock outcropping below that looked like it might provide some protection, so I scrambled down and found it to be only about two feet high, but it would have to do.

I unfolded my tent being as careful as possible to not let the wind catch it like a kite and pull me off the ridge. Shortly, I was inside, and as I fired up my cooker to heat water and a freeze-dried dinner, I began to second-guess myself. The wind wasn't just whipping my tent; it was also rattling my brain. I had carried 20 pounds of water and fuel on my back, and I started to wonder if that was enough. My inner voices seemed to be joining the wind to beat me up. Maybe I wasn't as smart as I thought or as strong as I imagined. I had tripped on my ego, violating my own mantra of slow, deliberate pace. Still fatigued from the three-week ordeal in Antarctica, climbing so soon up to 19,000 feet was perhaps too much. My body needed more time for normal oxygenation to create more red cells from the bone marrow to reduce the alkalinity in my blood. My normal resting heart rate at sea level is 48, but now it was 100 beats a minute. Climbing in Antarctica may not have been a boon to such a quick turnaround trip. That success may have given me false confidence that going another mile higher to the top of South America would be a cakewalk. I got to thinking how much danger I was in being solo should something go wrong so far away from any help.

As I looked outside the tent door zipper watching the sun set over the lower peaks of Argentina, stars began to appear over a cloudless horizon. The temperature had dropped to near zero. With the tent flapping in the gale, nothing looked pretty to me. I wanted to climb this mountain, but the cards seemed to be stacked against me as I braced for a long, dark, moonless night. I tossed and turned, drinking as much water as possible between intermittent sleep, nightmares, and worries about having a stroke. A pulmonary embolism would be a terrible way to go. If I were to have a stroke, I might not know where I was, and certainly anybody finding me would not know WHO I was. On any other climb, I could amuse myself by trying to figure out the geologic history of the stones, whether they were sedimentary, igneous, or metamorphic, and their age. On this miserable night, all the rocks looked like colorless black marbles littered among miserable larger stones. The wind increased to a deafening roar and time seemed to drag on minute by agonizing minute. Reaching midnight sometimes seemed unattainable. My madness steamed until finally I let out a scream that resonated from my core. For an instant I felt relief from my woes—until I realized that my cry was totally drowned out by winds that were letting me know who was boss. Trying to explain my passion for mountaineering to non-climbers had always been difficult if not impossible, but now I found myself struggling to explain the foolishness to myself.

After what felt like an eternity, the horizon to the east began to lighten, confirming that the world was still turning. I reached my cold hands out from the flapping tent fly and lit the stove to boil water for an early breakfast. Descending was the easiest way toward safety but a sure path to self-loathing. "Give it all you've got," a voice said. Maybe the wind would stop blowing and give me half a chance. Crawling out of my down bag, I slowly pulled up my one-piece super down suit. My boots were frozen like big bricks, and since my fingers were already chapped and split from weeks in Antarctica, I had to tighten the boot laces with clenched fists and teeth. After a second cup of hot chocolate, I loaded my pockets with candy bars, a brick of frozen cheese, and a block of frozen salami. I boiled enough hot water to fill two quart bottles and placed them inside my suit into breast pockets. The hot water near to my heart seemed to give me a jump-start. The Viento Blanco was still raging and the sun was still below the horizon when I trudged off with no rope and no pack, carrying only my ice axe, what was in my pockets, and a small camera.

I climbed like a robot with the batteries dying. The fitful night coupled with weight loss from Antarctica had compromised my strength. The horizon was bright with the sun about to burst over the edge of a jagged peak below, but nothing felt right. My surroundings were fuzzy, and though I was still driven to climb, the effort seemed meaningless. I continued for another hour placing one leg in front of the other as the sun flooded some warmth into my body. The jagged Andes spread out like a smorgasbord. To the left and to my dismay only slightly below me was Camp Berlin. I hadn't even made it to 20,000 feet. The summit was still about 2,800 feet above. If I continued, I was sure I could make the top, but in my weakened condition, I wasn't so sure I could survive the descent. Passion, emotion, and purpose were overruled by rational judgment. The peak was too much for me to safely handle at this moment, especially through the teeth of the unrelenting wind. Whatever victory could be gained from this insanity would not be won today.

Even going down, each step took concentration that didn't seem to be there. Cramming more chocolate into my mouth didn't provide a surge of energy. When I reached the tent, I collapsed inside and tried to get some sleep, but it was no use, as my heart was still beating much faster than normal. I had to get farther down. Talking and cursing to myself I struggled to dismantle the tent and pack my heavy gear into the rucksack. My legs were feeling like rubber. I had to pause frequently to rest. The descent to the Plaza del Mulas took me the entire day and into the early evening. Too tired to pitch the tent, I simply found a small flat spot next to what I thought was the garbage pit, rolled out my bag and mattress, and collapsed into a coma-like sleep.

The next thing I remember was the smell of animals and seeing Aconcagua flooded in morning sunlight above me. In my stupor the night before, I had bedded down on a variant of the walking trail. Trekkers and climbers were stepping by, gazing down at me like I was in a coffin at my own funeral.

"Buenos dias," I said in my best Spanish as though nothing was unusual. Exhaustion had evaporated my self-respect. My goals had deteriorated to simply surviving the trek out and getting home. As I pondered the slow, agonizing death march of carrying my pack another 25 miles to the trailhead, I looked down the mountain trail and saw a mule team snaking up the mountain toward me.

"Grajales!" I hollered as his pack string neared.

I had no money to pay him. I was down to my return bus and airline tickets to get me back to America, but I convinced Grajales to take my word that I would pay him back. I couldn't tell if he was just taking pity on my condition, but he grabbed my pack and placed it on his mule. I quickly dressed and headed down the trail. Two days later we reached the Puente del Inca, and the next day I caught the bus back to Santiago. With my debt to Grajales embedded in my mind during the flight back to the United States, I began planning my next attempt to climb Aconcagua.

NO SECOND CHANCE

My love for wilderness continued to grow from the time my parents first took me to the mountains. Perhaps the dopamine chemical neurotransmitters in my brain were scrambled early in life to instill a long-term relationship with rocks and ice. I understood and obeyed the rules of the outdoors, but when it came to understanding human nature, any class dunce could score higher marks than me. Planning, thinking, and dreaming of climbing overruled other considerations. The terrible price I paid for wanderlust was that my family life suffered. Back in Spokane, climbing to the top of a faraway mountain dominated my thoughts. I kept visualizing the last steps to the summit. Construction work became just a means to provide money for the next expedition.

My home on the lower South Hill on 18th Avenue was a little brick house, picture perfect for a Three Little Pigs postcard. The bricks were laid in 1927, and when Sharon and I purchased it in 1976, we were the proud second owners. With youthful exuberance, Sharon and I remodeled the bathroom and kitchen and installed shiny new appliances. With the help of my genius engineering friends, we squeezed a prefabricated 40-by-15-foot swimming pool into a 10-foot-deep hole between giant old-growth pine trees in the back yard. The pool was bigger than the house and was the favorite attraction to every kid within a four-block radius. Pictures of our kids graced the inside walls of the house, and the refrigerator. The American dream was alive and well on 18th Avenue. I routinely had a bowl of homemade soup and bread for lunch.

My kids greeted their wandering, smelly, knuckle-dragging dad at the Spokane airport with open arms and big smiles when I returned from the Antarctic adventure, but the smile on Sharon's lips was noticeably terse. There would be no homecoming party this time, as Sharon had little love left for me. Cashing in the life insurance for the Mount Vinson expedition was the beginning of the end for our relationship. I loved my family and tried to show it in many ways such as being a good provider, but another truth in life came to light—as my mentor and friend Joe Collins had warned: "Relationships take a lot of work and nurturing."

Sharon and I were growing apart. Vainly, I tried not to admit failure to myself and attempted to keep our relationship patched together, but it was too late. She had lived with my marriage to mountains for 17 years and that was enough. Her cold greeting said it all.

Still obsessed with staying at the top of my game, I started a training program of weekend mountaineering. On one memorable occasion, I came home early Sunday afternoon from a weathered-out climb. I drove around the corner to 18th Avenue and saw a colorful display in our front yard. Driving closer, I distinguished the splashes of color as clothing—MY clothing! Sharon had removed all my garments and dumped them in the front yard. Her car was not in the driveway. No one appeared to be home. The doors were locked. It was pretty clear that I wasn't wanted here anymore. I glanced around the neighborhood. Normally, on a Sunday afternoon the street would be as lively as a dancing scene from West Side Story. But today it was quiet as a cemetery. The neighbors were aware of Sharon's temper, and curtains were drawn tight in the houses directly across the street. I suppose the neighbor wives were holding their breath wondering how I would react. I got the message and began picking up my clothes and neatly folding them to place in the back of my 1979 Dodge Ram Charger.

Thus began a period of off-and-on homelessness that left me frequently camping in my vehicle at different spots from Mount Spokane State Park to wayward dirt roads that the Department of Transportation didn't visit. It was a brutal adjustment involving a tumultuous breakup that would carry on for years. I increased the hours in my work schedule to financially support my family as I vainly tried, with lots of flowers and chocolate, to patch together an on-again, off-again romance. Trying to be a dad to my kids, to attend their activities between work assignments, became an exhausting blur. The guilt for how I'd disrupted my family would haunt me every day of my life. Jae, my oldest daughter, was going through her teenage years and personal trials without much guidance and support, and my son, Jon, was struggling with schoolwork.

Dreams of high mountains were my emotional rock through all of this personal drama. During the spring of 1989, I nixed the idea of another solo trip to Aconcagua. Advancement to age 41 had a way of adding some rational thinking to my climbing madness. This time I'd seek strength in numbers. A strong group of six would offer physical and mental support. Dan Schnell signed on and we rounded up four more experienced climbers who committed to the expedition. I wrote to Grajales in Argentina to tell him I was coming back to try the peak again, but this time with a team. He wrote back and said he would be waiting. That was the extent of the advance planning. Done.

We would leave the day after Christmas and take the entire month of January if necessary. After Schnell committed to the expedition, other climbers seemed to come out of the woodwork. Word of mouth in the climbing community always traveled faster than the phone system. Soon, I was saying no to people who wanted to sign on just for the trek to the base camp. The final team was made up of Spokane athletes and friends: Schnell, Phil Camp, Dawes Eddy, Dr. Henry Crowley, Dave Yadon, and Bill McElroy. All these men were in great physical shape on their own, so there was no organized training to be done. We all pitched in to buy and sort the equipment and food during the summer. I knew Schnell's climbing capabilities well but did not know the strengths and weaknesses of the other four members. I chose the moderately difficult Polish Glacier route for our line of ascent thinking this would be a challenging but safe climb for all. We would take things slow and steady and acclimate properly. How could we fail?

We left for Santiago by way of Miami on December 27 and took the next available flight to Mendoza, where we found out that Yadon's gear was still sitting at the Santiago airport. Yadon would have to wait for his gear to arrive and then catch up to the team at the pass near the border where vehicles drop off Aconcagua climbers and trekkers. After overnighting in Mendoza, the rest of the team took a 120-mile truck drive up to the Puente del Inca and met Grajales at his office.

"Ah-ha, Pollocko, I remember you," Grajales exclaimed when he saw me. Of course, he remembered I still owed him $100 from last year's expedition, which I paid him with five US $20 bills. Now we were square. Aconcagua Expedition II could begin, with the team referring to their leader as "Pollocko."

From Puente del Inca, we backtracked nine miles down the highway to Punta de Vacas, where we began a three-day trek with the mules carrying our loads up the Vacas Valley. The trek was 30 miles over desert and then up the Relinchos Valley to Plaza Argentina base camp at 14,000 feet. On the second day we were delighted to see two huge Andean condors circling overhead. We watched them glide effortlessly for nearly an hour searching for dead animals to scavenge. When the giant birds landed on a cliff about a thousand feet above the trail, we scampered up the mountain like little boys to get a photograph. This of course proved to be futile, as the condors were much too wary and were gone by the time we breathlessly reached the ridge top. However, our effort was rewarded with a great view of the valley and mountains all around our camp, and an even better view of the giant mountain we had traveled all this way to climb. Its name, it is said, translates from the Quechua word "Akon-Kahuak," which means Stone Sentinel. From this approach, Aconcagua stood mighty and proud of being the highest mountain of the Southern Hemisphere.

We celebrated New Year's Eve with a bottle of Cognac that Camp had carried from Spokane. The dangerous river crossings were behind us, and we were below the base of the mountain's eastern shoulder. The mules had performed their duty, and from this point the human grunt work began. Each of us had about 100 pounds of food and gear, which we would shuttle on our backs in two trips to a camp at 19,000 feet. An enjoyable trek had suddenly transformed to an endurance test of will and grit. Since I was used to concentrating on my own climbing needs, I quickly proved inept as a guide. I hadn't realized that we were climbing too high and too fast for Crowley, Camp, and Yadon. The desert environment, the altitude, and maybe the trek wasn't as forgiving as group members had expected, and some of them started to question their decision to join the expedition. Teamwork is imperative for attempting a major summit like Aconcagua, but my selected group began to fall apart like a stone hut built without mortar on unstable ground.

The Viento Blanco began to buffet our bodies as we climbed to a camp at 19,000 feet. Setting up our tents against the jet-stream-force wind on the mountain's exposed eastern shoulder, I noticed a black bag that looked like a long, rumpled rucksack behind a rock just a few feet from one of our tent sites. I shrugged it off as a cache of food or gear left by another expedition. After getting everything inside the tents and setting up for cooking, I strolled to view the mountain and the terrain above until I nearly stumbled on the big bag, which was actually several pieces of plastic used for tent ground cloths. It was cinched together tightly with one-eighth-inch nylon cord. Carefully, without ripping the plastic, I pulled back a piece of the tarp far enough to stare into the empty eye sockets of a man's mummified face. The skin was barely hanging on and I guessed the person had been dead for a long time. Obviously, this poor soul did not have a family with the money to retrieve him; nor did the park service have the wherewithal to remove the corpse. Although it was bizarre to have a body next to our tent, it's not unusual for people to die in mountains like these. Aconcagua accounts for two or three deaths a year.

Removing a body from high elevations can be difficult and dangerous. The public is aghast that some bodies are not recovered and left to slowly decompose for years in the thin, dry, cold air. The public, of course, has no idea that it's all you can do to move your own body safely up and down the mountain above 19,000 feet, let alone to carry a body off the rocky, icy slopes. Many rescuers have died trying.

So, here we were on the high slopes of Aconcagua preparing for the final summit assault with a disheveled team sobered further by the proximity of a decomposing corpse. "I've had it; I am turning around and heading home," said Crowley, who I'd judged to be one of the strongest men on our team. I could hardly believe my ears.

As I was trying to digest that statement, Camp blurted out: "This is as far as I am going; I will head back with Dr. Crowley."

They assured me, or tried to assure me, that their decision to leave wasn't my fault, but I felt bad that I had pushed the pace. This was an emotional and logistical blow to absorb. Every expedition should have a competent doctor along to help with potential medical emergencies. All of us were prepared for minor cuts and bruises, but if a cardiac arrest or a pulmonary embolism occurs far from medical attention, it helps to have a doctor in the group. Nevertheless, I admired and defended their decisions. Sometimes it takes more guts to know when to turn around rather than continue up, especially after you've come so far toward a goal. None of us wanted to end up like the man in the body bag.

The morning broke clear with below-zero temperatures and tame winds. While we planned to take two or even three full days of rest here at 19,000 feet to properly let our bodies adjust, Schnell and I left camp to check out the Polish Glacier by climbing 1,000 feet in elevation above camp. We started up the lower part of the glacier, climbing 500 feet of low-angle, hard-packed snow that gradually turned into ice ferns and wind-sculptured ice cubes. As we climbed higher, we were disappointed to find the slope transforming into a solid sheet of glare ice. It was summer in South America and we expected the glacier ice to be consolidated in a Styrofoam-like texture that is ideal for cramponing. Apparently, a light winter and spring had left the mountain unusually dry, so the glacier was melted all the way down to a hard, plate-glass ice that afforded little grip even to sharp crampon points. This section of the glacier, if we were to climb it, would require careful belaying with fixed ropes and dozens of ice screws to pass up and down safely. Schnell and I climbed another 500 feet, but as the glacier steepened, the exposure magnified the dangers of a fall. Another 2,000 feet of this ice had to be surmounted to reach the relative safety of a ridge crest. The route was simply too risky with our team. Splitting into pairs was out of the question, as everyone deserved an honest attempt at the summit. As we down-climbed, I swallowed another bitter pill. I had dreamed for a year of climbing this beautiful, classic ice line on the Polish Glacier. It was a dream that wouldn't come true.

That evening we decided to change our course and traverse horizontally across the North Face of the mountain to join the standard route of ascent from Camp Berlin. I knew that a traverse could be made to the standard route from our campsite, but it would make at best for a long, grueling day. I guessed the traverse would take an additional four to six hours, one way. We'd likely have to start and end in darkness. We would take one more rest day at this camp at 19,000 feet to let our bodies prepare for what was certain to be at least a 24-hour climbing marathon to the summit and back.

Of more urgent concern was Dave Yadon, who was experiencing symptoms of high-altitude sickness with stomachache and nausea. This was the expedition of a lifetime for Yadon. He had trained hard to make this journey, and to get this high on the mountain and get sick was devastating. We could only hope that his problem resolved with another day of rest.

Earlier in the afternoon, an expedition from Australia climbed up to our campsite and erected their tents near ours. The Australian group was made up of four men and one incredibly attractive woman, who also was their team doctor. Her name was Ann, and she was dressed in a bright red mountain jumpsuit that was insulated for warmth, but the design could not hide her curves. She instantly became a magnet for our team. Every Australian I had ever met was a likeable, self-effacing human being, and this climbing team of Aussies was no exception—laughing, telling jokes, making fun of one another, and generally having the time of their lives. This was in stark contrast to Yadon, who, even the next morning, lay immobile inside his cocoon of a sleeping bag, still lethargic and not showing any visible signs of improvement. He also was emotionally upset, knowing that going up farther appeared to be out of the question. As the leader of the expedition, I was upset, too, but I had no magic potion. As a last resort, I decided to visit the Australian doctor. Her tent was several hundred feet back down the mountain, so I put on all my gear to make the trek. Arriving at her solo tent, I announced my name with difficulty due to the cold's grip on my face and cheeks. When she answered with the unmistakable Australian accent, "Come on in," I took a big breath of rarefied air. Up close she was even more beautiful, with light red hair, strong facial features, and piercing green eyes that kept me hypnotized.

"Ann, I know you have your own team to take care of, but could you possibly help some wayward American who has no doctor? We had a doctor, but he decided the mountain was more than he had anticipated and turned back."

She just stared back at me, and I imagined her thinking, "What kind of a line is that from this American nut case?" I started to twitch nervously while waiting for an answer.

"Well, what's wrong?"

I explained that it wasn't me, but one of my teammates, and he had symptoms probably related to high altitude sickness. "Nausea, but no vomiting. Headache, but no retinal hemorrhage that we can detect. Overall lethargic attitude." And then out of the blue I blurted, "Dave has just gone through a nasty divorce, and I think a lot of his sickness stems from that emotion. I think a woman's advice to him would be well received at this time and would make him feel better. Would you mind just talking to him to see if there's anything you can do?"

Ann stared at me until that pesky nervous twitch kicked in again. I have no idea what else I said, but she graciously suited up with an additional layer of outerwear and followed me to Yadon's tent. Perhaps because of whatever she said, along with whatever medicine she prescribed, he soon began to recover. I didn't think any man could be sick in her presence. My hunch seemed to play out that just sitting and talking with this woman would be an effective therapy.

Now the rest of us could turn our attention to getting a few hours of rest for the tall task ahead. Yadon would hang back in his tent while the four remaining climbers would leave camp at 10 p.m. and climb through the night in a bid for the summit. At 8 o'clock, we started boiling water for drinking and for freeze-dried chili-mac dinners that tasted like rehydrated cardboard. Nothing seemed to be delightful to our taste buds on this trip. Maybe it was the low humidity in the air and dust from the desert. Two hours later we were off with our headlamps beaming ahead into the black night. We took only one rope and carried two quarts of water apiece, along with minimal extra clothing and emergency gear. The summit team included Dawes Eddy, Bill McElroy, Schnell, and me in the lead. We had to travel about two miles across a side-slope of steep ice and rocks, with no hint of a trail. My only guidance was an 8-by-12-inch contour map of the mountain and a few aerial photographs.

Within a couple hundred yards from the tents, we had to use the rope for crossing the toe of the Polish Glacier. Travel was fairly easy on this section until we climbed off the glacier onto the rocky ridge crests that made up the lateral barriers of the ice. The side-hill travel became more difficult with each step. One sprained ankle here would end the expedition.

Our chorus of grunting, groaning, and whimpering seemed almost irreverent in contrast to the perfect weather. The breeze was cold but light and the moonless sky was bursting with stars. Otherwise our world for the most part was narrowed to the shafts of light cast by our headlamps. Each step had to be planted on unstable rocks with utmost care. We didn't encounter hazardous terrain that required a belay; that is, we didn't think so. It was impossible to see far enough into the inky darkness to judge the slope—or how far we would fall if we fell! Climbing through the night is a head game. You must force the body to move while the brain screams for sleep. The sensation of climbing at 20,000 feet through a black tomb was like we were the only humans on the planet.

I had no idea where we would join the standard route up Aconcagua. It's a path trampled each year by the boots of hundreds of climbers, so certainly there would be signs of human passage. We just couldn't afford to miss it in the dark. Eddy, Schnell, McElroy, and I had traversed for hours, and we had definitely rounded the shoulder to the southwest side of the mountain. In the early dawn light, I could make out the shadow line of the Camp Berlin stone-wall wind breaks below me. I also could make out the giant Nido del Condors saddle farther below, so I knew we had to be getting close to my high point from the previous year's solo summit attempt. The relief of finally casting a headlamp beam onto the unmistakable worn path of the standard route was like getting weight off my back. For a few moments we could relax, eat, and drink. From this point onward, we should have no problems staying on course to the summit.

The sun was still an hour from rising, but the light was increasing every second. We were at about 20,000 feet—with only 2,800 vertical feet to go—but from the route description, we were still seven to eight hours from the summit. The climbing was not technical. The crux would be everyone's ability to adjust to the altitude. We moved well as a team, gaining the next 1,000 feet in just two hours. Everything seemed to be falling in place when we came upon a makeshift bivouac site with some well-placed stone walls to provide shelter from the wind. McElroy, who had been the strongest of the group, saw this as his opportunity. "I can't go any farther," he said.

"That headache still bothering you, Bill?" I asked.

"Yes, and I just can't go any higher: I'll wait here while you guys go for the summit and return to camp with you."

McElroy had been suffering from a migraine that had started almost immediately after leaving the tent. His entire body was feeling the pain. The stress of climbing the mountain was enough, but as the leader, I felt another jolt of responsibility for a man's life. On the chance of a situation like this, we were carrying an emergency tent, which we pitched behind the stone wall for shelter from winds that had picked up to 25 or 30 miles per hour. McElroy, ever the stoic, climbed into the emergency sleeping bag he had the forethought to bring along. He still had a quart and a half of water, which would be plenty for the day, except that it wouldn't wash away his disappointment. With just 1,000 feet to go, he had to step out of the game.

From this bivouac site, Schnell, Eddy, and I donned crampons to climb diagonally across an ice field to reach the bottom of the infamous Canaletto, a dangerous couloir of large and small loose boulders hanging precariously on a steady slope of 35 degrees. I was thrilled no other climbers were in sight. Any disturbance above that could cause deadly rockfall, especially since none of us had helmets. The gully lived up to its reputation. Boulders were stacked at the angle of repose and looked like sleeping giants ready to slip, slide, and tumble down on a hapless climber. The rocks seemed to cling together by magic. Luck seemed to be the ticket for getting through. Step after step, we climbed at half-speed with extreme concentration, taking care against dislodging even one stone that could release a rockslide onto a teammate.

We were still in full-caution mode when the Cresta del Guanaco—the summit ridge—started coming into view 100 feet above under the indigo sky. Just a few feet from cresting this knife-blade ridge, which bridges the lower south summit to the true summit, I was overcome with a tingling sensation. It suddenly felt like billions of pins were sticking into my skin on every square inch of my body. Doubling over with the pain, I recognized this as the first symptom of hypoxia, that is, low blood oxygen saturation caused by high altitude. I sprawled out on the flattest rock I could find as my insides seemed to be on fire. The air temperature was probably 20 degrees below zero, but I was burning up. I frantically ripped my balaclava and down hood from the top of my head and then zippered off my parka. I even pulled down my thermal underwear, exposing my bare chest to the elements. I lay on the rock, face up, half naked, panting like a wild beast, feeling faint with mild hallucinations. The deep blue sky faded to grey as though I were staring at a wall of death. Still coherent, I knew exactly what was happening. I responded by drinking the remainder of my water, eating a PowerBar, and panting with concentration to stay awake. After a year of stress—the family breakup, the strain of work—even my long-anticipated climbing expedition was falling apart. I was just 300 feet below the summit of the Western Hemisphere, and I couldn't move.

"Kop! Are you all right?" Schnell shouted.

"What's happening?" Eddy asked.

"KOP! Put on your parka!" Schnell screamed in my face. "You're going to freeze to death!"

I was lucid enough to realize the sensation of burning up was caused by electrical shorts in my body chemistry, but I could barely react. I slowly pulled my thermal underwear over my exposed upper torso, and then zipped up the parka. I blinked my eyes and gasped for breath. My heart felt like it would break through my chest. I often had wondered where I would die. The rock I'd chosen to crap out on was hard and uncomfortable, but the view was unbeatable.

Squinting upward, the dazzling sun was just to the left of my climbing partners' heads. With their faces in shadow, and wearing ski goggles, Schnell and Eddy looked like aliens staring down on me as I lay on my open casket.

"KOP! Drink some more Gatorade. DRINK IT!" Schnell ordered, handing me his own bottle. I swallowed a few more gulps and fell back again panting.

"Drink more! DRINK IT!"

"So, this is how it all ends: overdosing on Gatorade," I thought.

"Please go on you guys; I can't move," I said, trying to make it sound like an official command. Schnell and Eddy stood their ground as an hour passed with little improvement in my condition.

It was 9:30 a.m. and we should have been on the summit. I repeated my command as forcefully as I could: "You guys both go on without me. I can't go any farther." Schnell and Eddy didn't budge. They told me later that they weren't about to leave me, partly because they welcomed the chance to rest.

The situation was nightmarish. As leader, I was supposed to be the strongest, but I was a mess. However, with a little more time, the sweating and the feeling of piercing needles began to ebb. My spirits were lifted a bit by the sensation that my arms and legs were attached to my torso, and I started to feel my fingers and toes, too. I tried to make light of my embarrassing situation. "Soooo," I commented to my partners, "this is what people mean by "born again."

Schnell and Eddy had no reply, so I said, "I'm feeling better; can you guys just leave me?" For the next 90 minutes I lay on the rocks in a semi-comatose state looking up at Schnell and Eddy staring back at me. Miraculously, there was no wind.

"Kop, sit up!" Schnell insisted.

I did as he said, and then stood on wobbly legs, breathing hard but definitely feeling new life from the potassium drink replenishing my electrolytes. Moving my legs was a victory of sorts. Creeping cautiously across the boulders for a few more feet, I reached the Cresta del Guanaco and looked two miles down Aconcagua's South Face. It was approaching noon, and I felt that including me in the attempt for the ever-so-close summit would jeopardize everyone's chances of making it back down safely.

"Kop, the wind has died down a little," Eddy coaxed. "Let's see if you can make it to the top."

Looking down the South Face from Cresta del Guanaco.

283

I couldn't afford the energy to argue. At his urging, I dug deep for the strength to get going. Starting with small steps, I resumed climbing, but at a snail's pace. I was talking to my body as though I were a parent persuading a child beyond his comfort zone. I set mini goals: "Count 100 steps, then stop, rest, and breathe." My pace was torturously slow, but my partners stayed with me. The counting helped me ward off thoughts of climbers who'd perished after continuing up when they should have turned around. At 12:30 p.m. we still had about a hundred feet to climb. "...98, 99, 100." Stop. Breathe. Rest. Repeat. That's how I got to where I raised my head from looking at my feet, gazed

The Southern Hemisphere was below my feet.

past one last boulder, and there it was. Bawling like a baby, I climbed to the aluminum cross marking the broad summit of Aconcagua at 22,841 feet. The cross had been blown over nearly on its side from the last Viento Blanco, but calm winds greeted us at the top where my tears marked perhaps my slowest-ever march to a mountain's peak. It was 1 p.m. and I had only three things on my mind: briefly soaking in the view and the accomplishment, finding some way to express appreciation to my partners for their patience, kindness, and even sharing their precious water with me, and, finally, getting off this mountain safely.

Last Man Standing

The Vacas River starts as a trickle from the northern slopes of Aconcagua. We had come to the mountain days earlier by trekking 33 miles up the Vacas Valley to Plaza Argentina, while enjoying beautiful starry nights and warm, sunny afternoons with the small stream gurgling nearby. Then the arduous climb. Then the top. And then we relished the satisfaction of our upstream journey for just 10 minutes on the top of the Andes before heading down toward warmth, river valleys, and air rich with oxygen. We moved steadily but in a sort of survival mode. Descending the Canaletto was extremely slow, as being safe going down a steep slope of boulders is even more taxing than going up. We traversed the ice to the bivouac site where we found McElroy alive but cold, and ready to go down. He had patiently waited in that tent more than 10 hours for our return. The four of us continued down and into another round of darkness before stumbling at midnight back into our camp at 19,000 feet. We'd survived a 26-hour effort!

After a much-needed rest day, we descended off the eastern shoulder and started down the Vacas Valley for the three-day trek to Punta de Vacas. Two weeks earlier when we'd hiked up the valley, the Vacas River was easy to ford in bare feet with water only up to our knees during the three crossings. Now the stream, swollen with glacier melt in the South American summer, was at least two feet higher, and raging. The first two crossings weren't dangerous, as the river split into a half dozen or so braided sections on a relatively flat valley floor. We banded together arm-in-arm for stability as we waded. The current wasn't too fast, and, generally, it was no more than thigh deep. The final crossing would be more challenging.

We made our last camp just above the last crossing five miles from Punta de Vacas so we could get on the trail a couple hours before sunrise to take advantage of the lowest flows of the day. More feeder streams had added to the river's volume, and even before the sun started bearing down on the glaciers above, the rushing water roared as the valley narrowed. Here the river split into two raging torrents. The first channel was going to be the deepest and looked positively frightening. At first glance, I feared we might have to stay three months to wait for fall flows. The river was very swift. We would have to belay each other across and have another safety rope ready to throw just in case. The Australian climbing team was right behind us, and one man who was 6 foot 6 volunteered to be the first to cross. We tied him onto a tight belay, and he entered the water carrying two tag ropes. By the time he reached the middle of the first channel, he was chest-deep, and the power of the flow nearly swept him down the river as he gingerly inched across. On the other side, he tied the ropes to a tree while we tied off to a tree on our bank to form a safety line. One by one we would clip into the line with a carabiner and cross, leaving our boots on for more traction and protection.

Dawes Eddy is a powerhouse—one of the strongest mountaineers to join me on a climb—but he is a lightweight in stature. Standing 5 foot 6 and weighing 125 pounds soaking wet, which he soon would be, Eddy was about to face the test of a lifetime. He sat on the bank watching everyone flail, thrash, and pray his way across the dangerous, icy-cold torrent. It became clear that height mattered on this ford, and Eddy didn't have much of it. I was to be the last man across, so I watched Eddy fasten the belay rope tightly and hook his carabineer to the safety line. Like the rest of us, he was lugging a 70-pound pack on his back. As he reached the deepest section of the river, the water was up to his neck and he was struggling to keep his balance. He was valiantly probing for the next foothold when a pressure wave leveraged his backpack, ripped his feet out from under him and sucked him underwater. Eddy was swept downstream a good 10 feet before the safety rope stretched tight like a piano wire. With each pounding wave, we could see him thrashing to get a breath of air. The pack waistband had been left unfastened so the load could be jettisoned in an emergency, but Dawes couldn't seem to release the shoulder straps.

Schnell and the big Australian jumped back into the river to help. Schnell had the shallowest section of the stream to wade and got to the middle first still holding the belay rope that was hooked onto Eddy. I watched helplessly as the two rescuers pulled with all their might on the belay rope trying to hoist Eddy up and out of the relentless current, but the frantic struggle wasn't enabling him to get his head up to catch a breath. They were pulling so hard I feared his back would break. It seemed like he was underwater for a minute and I was getting frantic that he would go limp, but Eddy finally gave a last-gasp effort, thrashed wildly to gain a foothold, and pushed upward to expose his face. He was able to catch a breath now and then, buying time for Schnell and the Aussie to change tactics. They were within 10 feet of each other, all three of them connected to a safety line that couldn't be expected to hold if they all were overcome by the flow.

Chest deep, Schnell shimmied closer and changed the angle of the safety line enough to allow Eddy to scoot his way. A few inches more and Schnell and the Aussie were able to grab the top of Eddy's pack and pull his face out of the water. Miraculously, Eddy hadn't drowned or lost consciousness in the frigid glacial melt. Locking arms, they struggled to the far bank. I joined them both about 20 minutes later after my own struggle to cross the rising river. Eddy was shivering uncontrollably from hypothermia, so with the Aussie's help, we stripped off his wet clothes, quickly built a plastic tent shelter and started two cookers. Eddy spent a couple of hours recovering while sitting with his feet in a pan of hot water as he consumed cup after cup of hot tea to re-warm his core. We counted our blessings, and then we marched on.

Of the seven-man team that climbed Aconcagua, Dan Schnell was the last man standing on solid legs. All of us were exhausted as we marched down the trail toward Punta de Vacas and the resort inn near the viewpoint of Puente del Inca. Along the trail, I warned my friends about one last danger: the perils of overeating after so much stress to the body.

"You guys, listen up," I said during a break. "I'm the last guy who should give this lecture, but after what our bodies have been through, it's imperative that you eat lightly. The stresses of the temperatures, climbing to extreme altitude, the physical exhaustion of one marathon day after another, along with the weight loss add up. It will take weeks of light eating to get back to normal. You need to take it easy with the food intake."

Judging from their blank stares, I drew from years of expedition experience and repeated the advice. More blank faces. At this juncture of the expedition, I was herding deaf cats.

Arrival at the trailhead usually marks the end of an adventure, but the biggest ordeal of the expedition was just beginning for Dawes Eddy. A food vendor set up at Punta de Vacas was waiting for the next busload of tourists on the main road between Mendoza and Santiago. Dawes, being understandably famished, bought two huge pork sandwiches, loaded them with condiments and ate them with all the restraint of a starved dog being served its first meal in weeks. After a brief rest, we hired a ride to the pass at Puente del Inca, where we rented a room at the Inn for the night. Dawes might be small, but he can pack away the grub. He continued to gorge himself on beer, steak, spaghetti, and whatever was put in front of his face. The rest of us were amazed at how much food this man could eat! Regardless of my lectures, Dawes had the ill-fated combination of being hungry and stubborn. As midnight approached, we were celebrating in the main lobby when I realized that Dawes had left. I went into the bunk room to find him on his back suffering with terrible stomach cramps.

"Dawes, are you OK?" I asked.

"Uh, well, uhhh, not feeling so good right now."

He vomited through the night, and when dawn broke, his stomach was distended. He moaned and contorted in vain attempts to find a comfort.

"Uhhh, I'm not doing so well," Dawes said, stating the obvious. "The pain is really uncomfortable, and all I can do is urinate."

We needed help, so I ran across the highway and up a half mile to the Argentine border military base. Inside the building were half a dozen soldiers who seemed bored and oblivious to any goings on. I waved, and with an obvious look of distress, said, "I've got an emergency across the street in the inn! I'm the leader of an American expedition and one of my men is suffering and needs the attention of a doctor quickly."

I knew very little Spanish and the Argentine soldiers were blank with emotion. A man stepped out from behind a curtain and said through a deadpan interpreter. "We have no doctor here." The closest doctor would be at the Mendoza hospital, he said, and the cost for getting a patient there by ambulance was $250.

This was the only choice. While the rest of the group would head into Chile to Santiago, Dawes and I would depart for medical attention in Argentina. I paid the military officer, and we boarded a modified pickup with a canopy bolted over the top of the back where Dawes could lie down and find some comfort. We drove 125 miles on a winding road with the siren blaring the entire way.

SIX LITER MAN

Mendoza is one of the most beautiful cities in the world. Before the city was founded, the indigenous Huarpes people dug canals from the Rio Mendoza to irrigate their crops spread across the large valley at the foothills of the Andes.

As the valley developed and population increased, the canals also were used to water 100,000 planted trees that lined wide streets graced by wide sidewalks. In 1861, the city suffered a huge earthquake that inflicted massive damage, prompting a rebuilding plan in which new downtown buildings, set in oversize squares, could be no more than two stories tall. Driving in Mendoza is like traveling through a beautiful, manicured forest with well-maintained buildings hidden behind the trees. I had figured that such a beautiful city would have nothing less than a first-rate private hospital. It was early afternoon when we arrived, and Dawes appeared to be in his second trimester of pregnancy. His stomach's acidic gastric juices apparently had churned the pounds of food he had consumed into a soupy mixture that wasn't being passed into the intestines so he could relieve himself. His gut just continued to bloat. I was worried that his stomach would split open.

"I'm a gringo from America," I said waving my hands to the hospital receptionist. "My friend needs his stomach pumped, and immediately!" The private hospital of about 150 beds served the Mendoza elite. Negotiating the hospital procedures was to become a nightmare. After taking a $200 deposit, the clerk emphasized that I would have to pay in cash for any treatment. After a couple hours of waiting, two young doctors came into the exam room. With the aid of an interpreter, I explained that Eddy had eaten a half dozen pork sandwiches, spaghetti, a gallon of beer, potatoes, salad, and he'd vomited through the night. The doctors agreed his stomach needed to be pumped, and they handed me a list of the medical supplies needed. I was told that I had to go downtown, purchase the items on the list and return to the hospital before the doctors could help my suffering friend.

I was dumbfounded. There sat Dawes with his guts ready to explode, and the protocol had me running errands to find medical equipment on a list that was scribbled in Spanish! When I questioned this procedure, the clerk said that if I wanted to gamble with Dawes' life, I could go to the public hospital.

I hailed a cab. The first stop was an American Express office to get more cash. Then it took an hour to find the medical supply building where I waited in a long line for yet another hour until, finally, I was able to hand the slip to the clerk. He went back to gather the supplies and came back with a box of needles, surgical tubing, bags, nose plug devices, blood drawing syringes, rolls of tape, and several small stainless-steel bag hangers. I knew hospital equipment was expensive, and my background as a contractor told me that I was buying maybe $100 of supplies.

Two uniformed clerks approached the counter and one calmly said, "That will be 450,000 Astrals." The exchange rate was one US dollar for 1,200 astral. I knew I was being swindled. That amounted to $375. My friend might be dying in the hospital and the clerks were cashing in on my urgency. I had no recourse. The nurse had said this was the only medical supply company to deal with. As I pulled out my money, a man back in the line yelled, "Hey! Hey! Hey!" He came ahead to the counter by me and gave the two clerks a tongue-lashing, but they remained calm and poker-faced. I paid the bill. As I walked out, the man said they had taken advantage of my situation.

"I am married to an American consulate, and here is my card," he said in perfect English. "If you need more supplies, call me and I will go with you to get them. This behavior is an atrocity in this country, and it makes me sick. We at the government are trying to do something about this."

I got back to the hospital after three stressful hours and ran down the halls to Eddy's room. He was alive, thank God, but he was sitting with his legs hanging over the side of the gurney and his belly looked as though a huge medicine ball had been crammed inside.

"Dawes, I'm sorry but you are a month overdue with this baby," I said trying to add some levity to the situation. "It looks like a 15 pounder and we are going to induce labor!"

"Uhhh, man, this is really uncomfortable."

The doctors came in, took my box of items, and got to work. I watched anxiously as they forced plastic tubing down Eddy's nostrils and all the way into his stomach. Brownish-green bile rushed up the tubing as though they'd struck oil and started to fill a liter bag that I had purchased. During the next 45 minutes I watched in amazement, as did the doctors, as another five full liters of bile were evacuated from Eddy's stomach. A college football linebacker might be able to hold four liters in his gut, but pint-size Dawes had his stomach stretched to hold six liters—about 11 pounds of fluid!

After three days in the Mendoza hospital, Eddy's problems weren't over. The fluids continued to build and drain from his stomach. I had to purchase another box of medical equipment, this time with the help of my newfound local friend. The doctors were stumped. Dawes and I had maxed out our credit cards and were out of cash. Eddy would have to travel back to the United States with a catheter taped to his side and the surgical tubing from his nose running down to a plastic liter bag strapped to his belt.

We flew to Santiago, changed planes, and then began a nightmare 10-hour international flight with Dawes in great pain flat on his back in the aisle where passengers had to step over him. The situation on the plane was dire, as the tubing that was supposed to drain his stomach wasn't working, and his abdomen started to enlarge again. The flight attendants didn't need any convincing that this was a medical emergency, and the pilots radioed ahead. When we landed in Miami, an ambulance was waiting to rush us to Jacksonville Memorial Hospital, where emergency room doctors performed another evacuation of four liters. They shook their heads in disbelief when I told them his stomach gave up six liters at one session in Mendoza.

After three days, Dawes' family took over and had him flown to Sacred Heart Hospital in Spokane. Doctors determined that his pyloric sphincter muscle had seized up because of the stress of the climb coupled with the near-death experience of drowning and hypothermia. To be more precise, the peristaltic waves that churn and aid in the digestive process of his stomach failed to work, and the pyloric sphincter muscle in between the stomach and the duodenum (the first part of the small intestine) closed tightly, and failed to let any food or fluid pass through. He had elevated levels of the hormone gastrin causing high hydrochloric acid levels, and increased volume of stomach secretions. This caused grotesque abdominal distension and discomfort. He would need another three weeks of hospital recovery in Spokane.

I went home just happy to be alive.

Several years after this expedition, Dr. Henry Crowley was hit by a lightning bolt while riding his mountain bike on a clear day in Colorado. He would later die of his injuries from this freak accident of nature.

Dawes Eddy recovered from his intestinal ordeal and, 20 years later at age 66, he would climb Mount Everest. At the time, he was the oldest American man to climb the world's highest peak.

Words from the Wild

- "Many a good hanging prevents a bad marriage"
—William Shakespeare
- If mama isn't happy, no one's happy.
- If you travel to South America, learn the word "help" in Spanish.
- Eat less.

Twenty-Two

Elbrus

Mount Elbrus from the north.

Sitting on my butt with my arms draped over the white porcelain bowl, the little round pool of water stared back at me like a one-eyed monster. The whole room was rotating. I seemed to be in the water swirling down the drain in Hitchcock's horror movie "Psycho." Every few minutes my guts would wretch into a spastic convulsion and more goulash would hurl out my mouth. Flush. Repeat.

Through the door in my peripheral vision, a dozen people were laughing and eating dinner at a huge, hand-carved wood dinner table decked out with fluted candles warming the scene. Inlaid china bowls were sitting on an embroidered tablecloth. The good times were on the outskirts of my personal nightmare as I clutched the toilet in the washroom next to my Soviet host's dining room in the village of Kislovodsk, Ukraine. My pathetic gut-wrenching performance was the center of attention and the source of hearty laughter as though I was a circus side show freak. This was not what President Dwight D. Eisenhower had in mind when he established the People to People program in 1956.

"Can't handle a little Russian vodka, eh Chris!" Dr. Jim Morrissey said while my Russian hosts roared with laughter. Morrissey, his son David, and the local family with names I couldn't begin to pronounce went about eating their dinner while relishing the entertainment value of my misery. Having never acquired a taste for hard liquor, the vodkas that my hosts insisted I drink were poison to my body. The Russian family had graciously welcomed us into their home, and I hadn't wanted to seem unappreciative of their hospitality. Rather than taking a chance of insulting my hosts, I assaulted my body by drinking vodka that went down with all the taste, smell, and pleasure I would expect from shots of kerosene. For lack of the courage to say, "No thanks," I seemed to be looking death in the eye.

GLASNOST

In the fall of 1989, while telling tales of my mountaineering expeditions during a local YMCA banquet program, I mentioned my quest to climb the Seven Summits. A man came up to me afterward and introduced himself as a local organizer for People to People in Spokane. President Eisenhower had founded People to People to promote cultural understanding and world peace through direct interaction between ordinary citizens around the world. The man said he could arrange everything I needed for climbing Mount Elbrus, the highest peak on the continent of Europe, and he really caught my attention when he added, "We will pay all your expenses." The man had connections in Moscow with Alexei Khoblov, president of a national sports organization. "The USSR will sponsor your expedition," he said.

I was speechless. This new Russian outlook of openness, or "glasnost" was the brainchild of Soviet Union leader Mikhail Gorbachev, as he promoted "perestroika," or "restructuring," in an attempt to hold together the hundreds of separate cultures and ethnic groups that composed the USSR.

The bearer of such encouraging news in Spokane went on to another climbing-related topic regarding a famous Ukrainian climber named Missilav Gorbenko, who had been on the 1990 "International Peace Climb" to the Chinese North Face of Mount Everest with American expedition leader Jim Whittaker. On that expedition, Missilav, who lived in Odessa on the Black Sea, told of the medical issues inflicting his one-year-old son. Young Rustem was born with four congenital heart defects requiring an operation to correct the defects, but the surgeons in Moscow at that time were having a survival rate of only 50 percent in procedures dealing with this type of heart problem. Doctors in the United States were scoring a 90 percent survival rate for the same operation. When the Spokane-based charity Healing the Children heard of Rustem's plight through the grapevine of the mountaineering community in Seattle, they agreed to arrange medical treatment if Missilav could raise the money for airfare.

Later, after my Elbrus expedition was planned, People to People started searching for a host home in Spokane for Rustem and his 29-year-old mother, Lylia. This was no small order as the total stay at the host home would be six to seven weeks. Drs. Wes Allen, Jack Leonard, and Leland Siwek would perform the surgery at no cost while Deaconess Medical Center also offered to write off its charges. Rustem would be the first boy saved by Healing the Children. I was contacted by Jim Whittaker, the first American to climb Mount Everest, and asked if the boy and his mother could be accommodated in my home. My family agreed to rise to the occasion. Lylia and Rustem landed in Seattle and were flown to Spokane on July 17, 1990, by the wife of Scott Fisher, the founder of Mountain Madness, a Seattle adventure company. Fisher's wife at the time was a commercial airline pilot who was able to shuttle the Russians to the Spokane airport in a jet aircraft. Scott and his wife arrived by taxi at our doorstep with Lylia and Rustem. (Scott would die tragically in 1996 while descending from the summit of Everest in a terrible storm immortalized in Jon Krakauer's book "Into Thin Air.")

Lylia had platinum blonde hair, a petit, curvaceous figure, and blue eyes open wide to the cultural differences she was suddenly experiencing in America. Rustem also was fair-skinned, blonde, blue eyed, and as handsome as a spring flower.

I would be leaving for the Soviet Union to climb Mount Elbrus a week later. Sharon, as always, would work overtime in my absence to make the Gorbenkos feel at home while keeping Jon on track in school, and holding our family together.

The language barrier was the first challenge to overcome as a host family, followed by the difference in food, and, not the least, the cultural differences of American excess. Rustem did not like the American diet. All he wanted at first was borscht, the beet soup staple in his Russian diet. In the Ukraine, the Gorbenkos enjoyed privileged status, since Missilav was a USSR "master of sport" and was paid by the government as a full-time mountain climber. However, a comfortable four-bedroom flat in Odessa was a pauper's shack compared with our Spokane home equipped with all the modern conveniences, two cars, the largesse of a lake cabin for family escapes, and a construction business complete with an office all my own. For Lylia, just walking around the streets of Spokane and visiting the local supermarkets was a fascinating journey. You could see the wonder in her eyes everywhere we took her. She drooled over all the merchandise in the downtown stores and was especially amazed at the bounty of food in the supermarkets. She saw with her own eyes the difference in wealth and creativity produced by free enterprise versus communism. While walking through the local Rosauer's, she commented that the experience was like "spending a day at the museum." On one shopping trip. Sharon was dismayed that Lylia was fascinated by products labeled as "sanitary napkins." This was a foreign concept to someone from a country with no Kotex factories. Where Lylia grew up, menstruating women used old shirts or rags. I knew this from having walked the back streets of Moscow, but Sharon was shocked.

THE EXPEDITION

"Hello Jim, this is Chris; let's go climb Mount Elbrus!"

That's about all the persuasion needed to get Dr. Jim Morrissey away from the operating room and to commit to a three-week expedition to climb Europe's highest mountain.

"Chris, count me in for this expedition, and I want to bring my son, David."

"Great! I will get the tickets and make hotel arrangements. We will fly to Norway, and then arrive in Moscow on August 6. The next day we will fly to Mineralny Wody, north of Mount Elbrus, and be hosted by a local family. Then we will travel to Kislovodsk and on to Pyatigorsk and then to a mountain village called Djili-Su. From there, we will have seven days to climb the mountain before returning August 15 to Pyatigorsk and our host family, and then back to Moscow for our flight home on August 17. Sounds easy, eh, Jim?"

Morrissey was a successful man, driven to perfection as a nationally known heart surgeon, and similarly driven to distinction in climbing mountains. Eight years since our Everest Kangshung Face expedition, Morrissey was still in top physical shape. Standing 6 foot 2 and looking more like the quarterback for the New York Giants than a heart surgeon, Morrissey commanded respect in the mountaineering world as well as the hospital. He worked hard and played hard. With a charismatic personality and sheer will he organized the funding and led the American Dhaulagiri Expedition to success in 1972, and subsequently led expeditions to Garishanker and Great Trango Tower. When the permit was secured to attempt the last unclimbed face of Everest, the Kangshung Face, Morrissey was the leader and driving force for success. A commitment for Elbrus from Morrissey and his son was like striking climbing partner gold. I looked no further.

Revisiting Moscow resurrected suppressed memories of my 1974 experience and the mountaineering tragedies in the high Pamirs. Sixteen years had passed, but the loss of life on that international expedition had left a scar on my soul. This time around I'd have to be mindful of the region's new issues. The Union of Soviet Socialist Republics was breaking apart. I was somewhat nervous about traveling to an increasingly violent, ethnic war zone and a land of fusion between East and West. I devoted long hours at night to reading everything I could about the history of the region. Chechnya, Georgia, Azerbaijan, and Armenia had fought with themselves and against their political masters to the north in Moscow for centuries, with varying degrees of success. Terrorists in this part of the world routinely kidnapped foreigners at will. I was no stranger to being ripped off in my travels, so I had to force myself to believe I would be greeted with handshakes rather than bullets. The People to People staffers were reassuring. The connections I'd made seemed to be working. But I was about to learn that sticking out like a red flag at a Russian dinner party would be my trademark.

The two Morrisseys and I began our adventure with a sight-seeing day in Moscow, where I paid homage to composer Peter Ilyich Tchaikovsky at one of his former studios. We traveled south to Kislovodsk where we were welcomed by a local family that was eager to make us comfortable in their home. I've never had a bad experience in social interactions anywhere in the world by adhering to the universal wisdom of avoiding the topics of politics and religion. This discipline paid off in fine evenings of positive communication in Moscow, Kislovodsk, Pyatigorsk, and all the hamlets in between in the remote Caucasus Mountains. Regardless of their ethnic background, the folks of the old USSR were friendly and nice to us.

People to People had facilitated my complementary travel package to climb Elbrus with hopes that I would engage in positive social and cultural intercourse with the locals. I was determined to make a good impression and not screw up my welcome. So, when dinner time came around with our first host family, I stepped out of my comfort zone and into the ceremonial tradition of belting shots of vodka. I didn't want to offend my gracious hosts. Down went the vodka and I immediately felt ill. I held it together at first, but my lightweight status as a drinker apparently was obvious, especially when I was egged on to throw back another shot.

"You are just a novice, Chris." I heard someone say. "Russian vodka will put hair on your chest. Have another!"

"I have plenty of hair on my chest already," I said, pulling down the neck of my shirt. "Take a look."

Not impressed with my attempt at humorous diversion, the whole family in chorus insisted I down a third shot in celebration of our new international friendship. I would have felt less pressure if a loaded gun was pressed against my temple. After I choked down the third drink, the gathering finally shifted to the dinner table for food—but not before the customary fourth glass of vodka. Not understanding more than a couple words of Russian, I made a valiant effort, but couldn't finagle the body language to say "NO WAY" politely. They wouldn't take "nyet" for an answer. My hosts wished nothing but happiness for me, and there was no better catalyst for goodwill than alcohol. Gradually, the room began to rock and the food in my gut churned. That was the end of my socializing with our hosts and the beginning of my intimate relationship with a Russian toilet. After an hour of vomiting I was ready to crash, but the party was just getting started as darkness fell. Undaunted by my pale face and pitiful posture on the bathroom floor, the head of the family came in and said, "Mr. Chris! Mr. Chris! Arise and follow me outside, as we are going to continue our celebration on top of the mountain!"

What more could I do to embarrass myself? I thought. We all crammed into a car fuming with tobacco smoke and drove to the top of the local mountain to view the lights of the city below. My guts were still swirling, and I sealed my reputation as a drinking patsy by bolting out the car door to hurl some more. I was glad that my parents had migrated west from Poland and not to the Ukraine. I never would have survived in this culture of wild all-night parties fueled with vodka and cigarettes.

LONG AND WINDING ROAD

People to People had set a strict itinerary that had us travelling by 5 a.m. to a small village called Djili-Su, where we bought food to last for eight days and hooked up with three Russian guides who would escort us to the base of the mountain. They preferred to go by English nicknames rather than their Russian names while in the company of language-challenged clients, so we obliged their suggestion and called them Alex, Fred, and Jerry. They hired a taxi to drive us up a dirt road that had not seen a grader or improvement of any kind in years. After an hour of rough going the road condition worsened with ruts and cobbles. Our driver began to scowl and smoke one cigarette after another. Suddenly, as Mount Elbrus came in sight on the horizon, he stopped the car and insisted that we all get out. He communicated in Russian to our guides that he was not going any farther and began unloading our gear onto the ground.

The mountain, we estimated, was still 17 miles away—a long overland hike just to reach the base. But this was as far as the driver would take us, and he wasn't open to negotiation. He didn't care how far we'd come for this climb.

Elbrus rises in the Caucasus Mountains on a land bridge between the Caspian and Black Seas. The now-dormant volcano erupted during the

Holocene period over one million years ago and evolved into a twin-summited peak in Southern Russia near the border with Georgia. The peak's west summit rises to 18,510 feet. A mile away, the east summit is only 68 feet lower. In modern times, the fascinating ethnic and cultural diversity in the Caucasus region is renowned for its human longevity, where centenarians are common on rolling farm and goat pastures on the far edge of civilization.

The prospect of hiking an extra 17 miles carrying all our gear didn't make the guides happy, either, but we did have the extra food and water. So, we shrugged it off and set out for what would be a two-day overland approach through treeless but beautiful green rolling pastures. The driver had unwittingly done me a favor, as I never would have soaked in the feeling of the Caucasus while bouncing in a taxi. With a hundred pounds on our backs, we moved at a pace that allowed us to experience goat herders, farmers, and old timers all along the way. Except for the language difference they were just like us, except that in this section of the world, people were known to live longer. Scientists attribute human longevity to many factors but being happy while laboring hard every day in a beautiful environment apparently contributed to their enduring health. Their diet, we learned, included a lot of mutton fat and vodka, which made me ponder the price one must pay to live a long, happy life.

Elbrus rose abruptly before us from our base camp at 13,000 feet. The route up the mountain is not nearly as steep as one would tackle to climb Mount Rainier, but Elbrus is more than 4,000 feet higher. A summit bid from our base camp would involve climbing more than 5,000 feet, and then returning. While it looks fairly easy by big-mountain standards, Elbrus is a sleeping giant volcano notorious for an average annual death toll of 15-30 people. Sudden, vicious sub-zero snowstorms and violent winds created by the rise of upwelling moisture currents from the Black Sea to the west and Caspian Sea to the east play a role in most of the deaths. The evening before we would begin our ascent the air was perfectly clear, crisp, and cold. Of course, we knew this calmness could change without much warning. Our guides had done their duty, as they were not assigned to climb the mountain, so our team of three Americans said good-bye before bedtime and organized our gear for our climb.

Jim, David, and I left camp just after midnight wearing crampons to begin our ascent of the mountain. We climbed roped up through fresh snow on a gentle glacier at first, negotiating crevasses by the light of our headlamps. The route to the saddle between the twin summit craters was nearly a straight line but slow going because the snow was knee-deep in some areas. Except for the slogging, we encountered no technical difficulties in a six-hour uphill endurance test. Upon reaching the saddle between the east and west summits, I double-checked the mountain map to avoid making the mistake I made in Antarctica of climbing the lower of the twin peaks. After re-confirming the west summit was the highest by 68 feet, we started up ice slopes as steep as 35 degrees. The crevasses were behind us now, so we coiled the rope into a pack and began free soloing. However, Jim and David were getting slower and slower. Looking back at them, I could see that something was wrong.

"Jim, you OK?" I called.

"Well, no. David and I are feeling the effects of altitude."

A short way farther, just beneath the summit crater rim, Jim yelled, "Go for it alone, Chris! David and I will wait here for your return."

Altitude sickness can affect almost any person at any elevation above 10,000 feet. We were at nearly 18,000 feet and I felt super fit and driven to finish the climb, but the summit was not in sight. Should I go solo? My heart rate accelerated. I tried to convince Jim and Dave to keep going, but they had made up their minds and were staying put. I refocused on the mission and continued the ascent alone, picking up the pace. In about 500 feet I gained the crater rim and could see the summit less than a half-mile to the west. Beyond the summit, however, I could also see huge clouds beginning to billow into thunderheads at lower elevation in the direction of the Black Sea.

Suddenly I was in a race against the oncoming storm, and the potential for a decision to turn back. I quickly unlaced my crampons, threw them into my pack, and began to run as fast as my lungs would allow at that altitude. The crater rim here was nearly a level swath of black rock laced with ice; nothing technical. I briefly considered dropping my pack, food, and everything except a pint of water to make a quick-as-possible dash to the summit. It was past noon and the approaching storm clouds and wind were beginning to whip spindrift into the air. Horror stories of climbers dying in storms on Elbrus ran through my mind, but I balanced my anxiety with my experience. Judging by the feel of the air, the humidity, and the wind direction, I made a quick mental calculation that I had a 75 percent or greater chance of success IF I ran up and back as fast as possible without hitting the wall from the exertion. At 18,000 feet above sea level, the mind and body are out of sync when running. I had no crowd in the stands to cheer and shout encouragement. I wasn't going to set any track records while wearing heavy boots, backpack, and down parka. But I wasn't running for glory. I just had to beat a storm.

I settled into a comfortable running pace that I knew I could sustain over the moonscape of rock and ice on the crater rim. In about 20 minutes I reached the final 100-foot slope to the summit. My pace slowed to accommodate the incline, but my heart was racing as I climbed onto the summit where I was greeted by astounding views in all directions. No chemical high can match the pure unadulterated joy that climbing unloads on my neurons in a moment such as this!

Self-portrait on top of Mount Elbrus, highest point of Europe, 18,510 feet.

Elated and proud of my accomplishment, I held a camera over my head and snapped a self-portrait standing on the top of Europe. I touched the summit rocks with my hand, keeping with my tradition, and that was all the celebrating time allowed. I downclimbed and then settled into a run again along the rim.

With the storm chasing my tail, I reached the lip of the crater and was relieved to see Jim and David about 1,000 feet below me. The clouds were swarming around, and the wind was picking up, so after strapping crampons onto my boots, I jogged downhill with the metal teeth on my feet biting into solid ice. From the rendezvous with my teammates in the saddle between the two craters, we immediately began down-climbing with visibility limited by clouds and snowfall. Luckily, the tracks from our ascent were still showing, which enabled us to travel quickly even through periods of thick fog all the way down to the comfort and safety of our camp.

MORE GLASNOST

When Missilav Gorbenko found out that I was climbing Mount Elbrus, he arranged enough free time to make the journey from Odessa to our camp on the North Face of Elbrus. Before the days of cell phones, wireless Internet, and the magic of instant communications, word of mouth was still remarkably fast. Elbrus is a huge mountain, but Missilav made the contacts to learn our itinerary and pinpoint where we were. While Jim, David and I climbed exhausted into our tents late in the evening, Missilav was hoofing across the highlands en-route to greeting us the next morning at 13,000 feet. Stirring from our sacks at sunrise, I noticed a lone fit figure running up the mountain below us toward our camp. When the man approached our tents, I recognized from photos that he was the father of Rustem, who was resting peacefully at that moment a half a world away in my home in Spokane. Missilav had hiked and run for more than 17 miles, after being dumped off by the same taxi driver, just to thank me for hosting his son and wife. This was the new "glasnost" in action and my image of the old Soviet Union of 1974 evaporated before my eyes. He brought a present of tea and chocolate and some biscuits, which we devoured for breakfast while a glorious sunrise unfolded.

The foot journey off the mountain and back down through bergs in the limestone hills was a cultural immersion. We stopped in a small village situated on a stream that poured off the mountainside. A turbine made of wood and metal plates that resembled a Mississippi river boat paddle wheel was turning by the force of a small waterfall to generate electricity for a group of farmers.

We marveled at the simplicity of this effective power station. The locals were deservedly proud of their ingenuity. Jim, David, and I also were invited to go target shooting, a popular local entertainment. To my relief, it didn't involve drinking vodka, and soon we were aiming rifles at bottles placed on rocks across the valley. The Russians were all very polite, making us long for a world of people as peaceful and welcoming as the farmers and goat herders of the Caucasus Mountains.

Returning to Spokane I faced a new challenge with my home guests. Rustem had survived the operation and was well on his way to a full recovery from heart defects that would have eventually ended his life. Lylia, however, had been spoiled by her new "opulent" surroundings. She had fully embraced the American dream, including the electric appliances, cars, boats, and food stores that came with it. A few days before her scheduled departure, she approached me and said, as best as I could decipher, "Chris, it's very difficult for me back in Odessa, very, very difficult. Could I find another husband here in America? I do not want to leave."

This is what I understood her to say, but I didn't know how to adequately respond to her question through the language barrier. I called the People to People office and told them to get out to my house immediately with a Russian interpreter. Three of the staff including a woman who spoke Russian came to our house, picked up Lylia and drove her around some of Spokane's lower-class neighborhoods to show her that living in America didn't necessarily mean a life of luxury. They explained that defecting to America was impossible. I was sheltered from the hours of discussion, but the People to People personnel told me that she became very emotional in the moments of departing from the Spokane and Seattle airports. However, Lylia wrote letters to us in the coming years that described a healthy, happy Rustem growing up into a strong boy with a wide smile on his face.

Words from the Wild
- "Paradise is here or nowhere: You must take your joy with you, or you will never find it." —O.S. Marden

Twenty-Three

Kosciuszko

Kosciuszko, highest mountain in Australia.

At 37,000 feet somewhere above the South Pacific Ocean, my son, Jon, and I peered out the jetliner windows over cirrus clouds and an endless expanse of the blue water. My head has always been in the clouds, one way or another. Hanging out in high places fuels my dreams. Cruising at 600 miles per hour over such mind-boggling openness for hour after hour sent my imagination into overdrive. How did the Polynesians get the guts to launch their hollowed-out log catamaran, with little more than a couple chickens for food, and row and sail from the Gambier or the Marquesas Islands some 2,000 miles to Easter Island? Who were the first brave—or desperate—souls to sail to Hawaii? Was it just a game of hit and miss or were they the greatest sailors of all time? Some archeologists say the Polynesians may have mastered a natural form of radar as they learned to identify waves that had been created by bouncing off an island perhaps a thousand miles away! Being able to read these waves helped the pioneering people navigate daunting ocean expanses to distant island destinations.

Looking out over the universe of water below our airplane in late December 1990 reinforced my notion that human spirit has no limits. I pictured Captain James Cook's Endeavour sailing over this blue water, centuries or perhaps thousands of years after these natives had colonized remote atolls and islands. Cook was amazed to find inhabitants on such widely scattered islands, but then, he too was pushing the barriers of discovery in a wooden ship powered by up to 28 canvas sails operated with 18 miles of rigging. Cook was probably the greatest "white man" sailor of the time, but he marveled at the earlier prowess of the Polynesians, Maori, Tahitians, and Hawaiians. Cook "discovered" Australia after the aborigines had been tramping about the continent for more than 40,000 years. While mankind travels farther, faster, and more reliably nowadays, the sense of discovery is still alive for those who seek it. The nearly 8,000 miles we'd fly one way on this trip would be just a warm-up to the 20-day adventure involved with climbing to the highest point in the "Land Down Under."

Jon and I could not overlook, nor did we take for granted, the leaps and bounds transportation has made since Cook sailed the seas below us. During our long flight, I tapped one of the Qantas Airlines flight attendants on the shoulder and asked if I could show my son the "pilot house." With a big smile, she pointed to the spiral staircase and said, "Go on up." We climbed the stairs to the loft where the first-class passengers were being served like kings and queens, and walked down the aisle to the open door of the flight deck. The pilot, co-pilot, and navigator were sitting casually at the controls of the 747. The massive metal airship, obviously on autopilot, was streaking past the clouds faster than anything can fall from the sky, yet the crew was remarkably relaxed with their hands folded as though they were in a parlor. The pilot turned to us and said with a huge grin across his face, "Beautiful day to fly to Australia, don't you think?"

Jon and I were mesmerized by our surroundings, speeding to another continent while standing in the cockpit of a ship the likes of which Cook couldn't even have dreamed up. We could barely hear the noise of the jet engines. These were the days of no barriers and little fear of extremists or hijackers. People actually trusted one another. It was a wonderful feeling.

"Well Dad, you see one, you've seen 'em all," Jon said, staring straight ahead with a calm, confident demeanor, as we continued our walking tour in Sydney at a "scenic" tourist destination. Bondi Beach, world famous for dousing inhibitions among locals and visitors alike, was alive with young topless women running, frolicking, and opening our eyes to volleyball being a captivating spectator sport. Acres of surrounding sand were graced by other bare-breasted beauties soaking up the heat like lizards, although that's admittedly not a perfect simile. My 15-year-old son also was soaking it all in, too, seeming in love with every moment of discovering the differences between the USA and a more relaxed and uninhibited culture. This was going to be a great expedition. We even made time to wander around the bustling city, which we found to be well-endowed with marvelous architecture. Everything seemed to be well-built here.

As in most great adventures, the city was just the starting point. Before long we were off in a rented car and headed into the outback. As we drove into the desert, I was eager to share some of what I'd learned from pre-trip research about the land we were visiting.

"You realize, Jon, that Australia rifted from Antarctica in the Cretaceous Period. The formation of our mountain, Kosciuszko, was in the Triassic-Cretaceous granite, and was once a high plateau on the edge of the continent. When the continents separated from the single landmass called Gondwana, this slow splitting apart was much less radical and violent than the continental collision that forms the Himalayas and the Swiss Alps."

"Uh-huh," Jon replied in noticeably less interest than he allocated to his learning experience on the beach.

To me, geology is as fascinating as contemplating the size of the universe or trying to figure out how the first sailors found Hawaii. "This plateau of granite where Kosciuszko is located wasn't high enough and cold enough to host a commensurate share of the glacial ice that engulfed and carved most of the planet including Australia in the recent Pleistocene Epoch," I continued. "The Australian continent isn't a worn-down landmass like many people think; it was simply created by slow continental splitting."

Silence. I was trying my best to sound smarter than anyone else; and even if I was not, I tried my best to impress my son. "This continent has incredibly old rocks found in the metamorphosed sandstone conglomerate in Western Australia, and near these rocks geologists have discovered fossil microbes in the Strelley Pool dated to be 3.4 billion years old! Isn't that amazing?"

"Uh-huh."

"The rounded nubbins of hills and valleys you see out here are crawling with poisonous snakes, spiders, and unique indigenous animals like the kangaroo, platypus, and koala," I said, advancing to juicier subject matter.

"Uh-huh," Jon said, staring straight ahead.

It's conceivable that my teen companion was working through a hormonal surge that was rendering his brain chemically incapable of comprehending Kosciuszko, ancient rocks, or how life formed in the Strelley Pool. His forebrain may have been overloaded with educational images of the natural and "au naturel" shapes and formations he studied while wearing sunglasses on Bondi Beach. My lessons in geology and fauna passed through his consciousness like neutrinos in space. However, that didn't stop me from talking to myself, as I was amazed at what we were seeing around every turn in the road.

Kangaroos, which resemble handsome giant mice with muscular tails, seemed to be everywhere. "Kangaroo crossings" were marked with signs along the roads similar to deer crossing signs in America. When we pitched our tent at the first campground, the kangaroos hopped out of the bush to greet us. Seeing Jon's delight in feeding a buck from his hand, an Australian in the adjacent campsite said, "If he wanted to, he could gut you in an instant with his hind claws."

Indeed, kangaroos appear so calm and cute, but up close one can see their quickness and power. A grown buck can stretch up 8 feet tall and sport muscles hardened by years of sparring. Their front paws have clawed "fingers" and amazing dexterity while their rear feet each sport a dagger-like middle claw. If provoked, they've been known to box, kick, slash, and kill grown men, the Aussie said. Behind their endearing eyes, they are wild animals with wild instincts to survive. I warned Jon to be extremely cautious.

Driving east on the two-lane paved highway toward the Snowy Mountains of New South Wales, we traveled from the desert-like environment to the high moorland rolling hills, to 4,500 feet above sea level at the ski resort of Thredbo. From the base of the Snowy Mountains a popular trail gains about 2,800 feet in a seven-mile hike to the top of Mount Kosciuszko, Australia's highest point. The lower portion of the trail winds up 2,000 feet through dense pines with ferns blanketing the forest floor. The pine forest eventually transitions to eucalyptus trees. Black cockatoos serenaded us with songs as we hiked up the trail and out of the trees into waist-high native snow gum bushes. We were told at the visitor center for the 1.73-million-acre Kosciuszko National Park that it's not uncommon to see a wombat or even a dingo in this habitat, but our eyes spotted none during our trek.

From the high vantage of the ridge crest, we looked over an otherworldly landscape of dry plains giving way to one blue ridge after another to the horizon. Views were unlimited to the south and the north as we walked an old road on the Snowy Mountains crest toward the highest point on the horizon. The long-abandoned road was mostly a dirt rut en route to the last upslope, where snowfields were still clinging to Kosciuszko's rounded sides. The weather was perfect for hiking—cool, crisp with no wind—and I wondered if the aboriginal natives ever ran to the summits of the surrounding hilltops thousands of years ago seeking respite from lowland heat to relax in the pleasure of nature on the rim of their world.

"Which way do we go, Dad?" Jon looked at me with a smile on his face. We were hiking the final 200 yards to the summit of the highest mountain in Australia. With zero technical challenge to worry about on this expedition, I made a challenging suggestion.

"Jon, let's be real bold and take the direct line to the summit, right up these big boulders in front of us. It will be fun!"

Tossing caution to the Australian wind, we boldly started running up the huge granite rocks that made up the summit block of the mountain. For a moment here on Jan.1, 1991, we were kindred spirits with Tadeusz Kosciuszko, a Polish army officer and statesman of the late 1700s who came to America to help win the revolution before returning to Europe with his pioneering passion for freedom to fight for the liberation of Poland. Meanwhile, Jon and I were passionately leaping from one boulder to another to the top of Australia with a warm breeze and no more conflict than some biting bugs in our faces.

Mount Kosciuszko, elevation 7,310 feet, was named in honor of the revered freedom fighter by Paweł Edmund Strzelecki, a Polish geologist, while he was exploring Australia in 1840. Strzelecki said at the time that the top of Australia's highest mountain resembled the Kosciuszko Mound, an artificial "mountain" built in Krakow to commemorate the statesman Kosciuszko. History aside, I was moved to be on top of yet another continent with the feeling of emptiness and the expanse of the universe above and below my feet.

Jon and I were comfortably scanning terrain hunted by Aborigines long before white men first laid eyes on the summit in 1824. Our survival didn't depend on gathering seeds or bagging a wombat. The day was fine, and we were amazed to be the only people on the summit in an otherwise crowded national park. Our solitude didn't last long, as we spotted a couple trekking up toward us on a trail from the back side of the mountain. The man was whistling "Waltzing Matilda" as though the unique country Down Under had orchestrated a concert just for us. I flashed back to Tibetan prayer wheels spinning in the breeze as Jon and I just sat and listened on top of the Australian Alps.

Words from the Wild

- "Life isn't about finding yourself. Life is about creating yourself."
  —George Bernard Shaw, Irish playwright

Twenty-Four

Kilimanjaro

Mount Kilimanjaro with the Breach Wall and Heim Glacier
in the center of the photo.

Mountains have played a major role in mankind's never-ending search for knowledge, enlightenment, and inspiration. In the past several hundred years, the English in particular were dogmatic in this search, especially in the realm of conquest and adventure in faraway lands.

In 1802, the Great Trigonometric Survey of British India was begun with an objective to determine the names and locations of the world's highest mountains. The British survey started from the Indian Ocean and moved north. Each team of surveyors carried a 1,100-pound theodolite, a complex surveying tool. Twelve men were needed to carry it as well as building platforms and stretching chains in between to record and observe each sighting over the flat land of India. Twenty-eight years later, the surveyors moved within visual observation of the Himalayas, but Nepal was unwilling to allow the Englishmen to enter the country because of suspected political aggression and possible annexation. The British were forced to continue their observations from Terai, a region south of Nepal parallel to the Himalayas but still 240 miles away from the mountain tops.

Kanchenjunga, in Sikkim, was thought to be the highest mountain in the world, but in 1849 Andrew Waugh, the British Surveyor General of India, made several conflicting observations from Sawajpore station located in the eastern end of the Himalayas. Waugh noted a peak beyond Kanchenjunga some 140 miles to the west. This was the first "white man" sighting of the top of the world as Waugh noted that the mountain appeared to be higher than Kanchenjunga. The taller was tentatively dubbed using Roman numerals as Peak XV. The calculations of light refraction, barometric pressure, and temperature over the vast observation distance continued until March of 1856 before the survey announced to the world that Peak XV was "most probably" the world's highest mountain. The official height was listed as 29,002 feet above sea level, a calculation astounding in its accuracy considering the triangulation was done from 200 miles away! In 1865, Peak XV was named Everest by the Royal Geographical Society after George Everest, the first Surveyor General of India. On May 29, 1953, Edmund Hillary and Tenzing Norgay became the first to climb to the top of Mount Everest and return.

At the same time back in Great Britain, amateur astronomer Patrick Moore was engaged in the British tradition of exploring the heavens. Moore observed over time that an already-identified geologic feature on Mars wasn't just big, but also, as he put it, "extremely high." The top of this huge mountain, named the Nix Olympica, could be seen clearly when surrounding areas of Mars were engulfed in dust storms. In 1971, the Mariner 9 spacecraft arrived in orbit around Mars during a global dust storm. The tops of the planet's volcanoes were above it all, and scientists were able to calculate the height of Nix Olympica. It was re-named Olympus Mons by astronomers and is known as the highest mountain in our solar system.

Olympus Mons is nearly three times as high as Mount Everest, standing

16 miles above the surface of Mars. The summit of the mountain has six nested calderas (collapsed craters) that are 50 miles wide forming an irregular depression that is two miles deep. In other words, the crater on top of Olympus Mons is as long and deep as the Grand Canyon. Geologically, Olympus Mons is a shield volcano. Its base is the size of Arizona, with five-degree slopes similar to Mouna Loa and Mouna Kea in Hawaii. Unlike any shield volcanoes on Earth, however, Mars has no drifting plate tectonics to "float" the crust over a hot spot. Thus, Olympus Mons just continued to grow higher and wider with successive low viscosity lava flows. In my fantasies of climbing the highest peaks, Olympus Mons has been intriguing. Which robot will claim the first ascent?

AURA OF THE MOUNTAIN

The highest peak on the continent of Africa is Kilimanjaro. At 19,340 feet above sea level, it's in the league of the top 100 highest mountains on earth and isn't even close to the height of Olympus Mons. Yet it still intrigued me beyond being just one of the mountains I intended to climb in my quest for the Seven Summits. I did not want to climb it by the regular trekkers' route. Kilimanjaro stands alone above the African plains. As much as it dominates the landscape, the mountain is sometimes overshadowed in the eyes of visitors by encounters with wildlife such as elephants, African buffalo, and eland on the north slopes, black and white colobus monkeys, Sykes monkeys, plus the tropical boubou in the forest belt, and hundreds of other bird species.

Kilimanjaro's summit zone has resembled Himalayan 8,000-meter peaks complete with the raw beauty of hanging glaciers draped with 300-foot icicles dangling over the breach walls. However, the resemblance is changing as the massive ice cliffs and the summit ice cap on Africa's giant mountain are rapidly melting. Climate change is likely to erase the glaciers sometime before 2033. When the ice melts, Kilimanjaro will look like just another huge, barren, windswept conical rock, and the romance and character will live on only in old movies, novels, narratives, and our imagination.

The aura of the mountain is the background for Ernest Hemingway's novel "The Snows of Kilimanjaro" that features Harry, a writer on safari in Africa who develops an infection in a wound from a thorn puncture and braces for his slow death. Harry realizes he had spent his entire life living in the moment with no regard for the future. In a dream shortly before he dies, Harry sees a plane coming to carry him to the top of Mount Kilimanjaro.

"Then they began to climb and they were going to the East it seemed, and then it darkened and they were in a storm, the rain so thick it seemed like flying through a waterfall, and then they were out and Compie turned his head and grinned and pointed there, ahead, all he could see, as wide as all the world, great, high, and unbelievably white in the sun, was the square top of Kilimanjaro. And then he knew that was where he was going."

This beautiful passage by Hemmingway prompted me to leave Kilimanjaro as the last climb to complete in my pursuit of the Seven Summits. The highest mountains are known and climbed, but the spiritual mountains of the mind are harder to conquer. Every dedicated mountaineer eventually climbs Kilimanjaro, either in dreams or by actually hoofing up its slopes. I envisioned a plane taking me to Africa, but I wanted to climb a difficult route.

Hatching a Plan

I called on another dreamer and pioneer mountaineer, David Coombs, to join me. Coombs, an intellectual with a voracious reading habit, was a talking encyclopedia on the history of every major mountain. He was raised in Spokane by his parents, Barbara and Richard Coombs. Richard was dean of the Cathedral of St. John the Evangelist (Episcopal Church). David had taken to mountaineering in his early teenage years and developed a passion for the sport. He would search out unclimbed mountain routes and traverses that wouldn't enter the mind of a normal climber. His climbing resume would fill a book, and I was most impressed with the success of his four-man expedition to climb Alaska's Mount Fairweather, the earth's highest coastal mountain. Coombs once taught at a private school, then was a professor at the University of Idaho, and then a business manufacturing consultant. Talking with Coombs was always an education.

"David, this is Kop. I want to climb Kilimanjaro next spring; would you be interested in climbing with me?"

"I would love to go. "I've always wanted to try the Heim Glacier route on Kilimanjaro, are you game for that?"

"Frankly, David, I've never heard of it, but knowing how your mind works, I assume it must be one of the routes less traveled."

"Yeah, that's right. The Heim Icefall is seldom climbed, and I'll tell you it's a tremendous challenge for ice climbers, as the glacier tumbles down the south side next to the great Breach Wall. All the way up you look directly onto the wall. A bit of trivia for you, Kop: Heim Glacier was first climbed by a couple of Brits named David Goodall and John Cooke. Take a guess who the third climbing partner was."

"I'm not up on any of the mountain's history except for what Hemmingway wrote in the "Snows of Kilimanjaro," and other fictional accounts—Stanley and Livingston, and the African Queen come to mind."

"Their climbing partner was Anton Nelson, or the name you probably recognize, Ax Nelson."

"Ax Nelson? Wasn't that the guy who pioneered the direct Lost Arrow Spire in Yosemite Valley with John Salathe? That's one of the hardest and boldest rock climbs ever done!"

"Yeah, Ax Nelson. And get this: Salathe was 47 when they climbed the Lost Arrow. And that was after he and Nelson had done the first ascent of the Northwest Face of Half Dome in a 20-hour ascent. After all that pioneer climbing in Yosemite, Nelson ended up working in Africa for the poor and downtrodden. How's that for a bit of trivia?"

"OK Coombs, we'll have plenty of time to talk history on this expedition; tell me about climbing the Heim Glacier. I'm excited now to try it."

"The Heim Glacier begins with gentle slopes right off the top of the south side of Kilimanjaro, then makes a dogleg turn westward and tumbles right next to the vertical Breach Wall, and then turns again cascading over more cliffs down to the terminal moraine at 12,000 feet. It's a gorgeous sight!"

"Man, I've seen this photo of the Breach Wall where Messner climbed the huge icicle that hangs off the top."

"Kop, the best part is the trek up through the jungle just to reach the toe of the glacier. From what I've read, the route starts just above 1,500 feet elevation, meanders through the savannah, and then goes into the jungle and follows a ridge top with deep canyons on either side. There are lots of monkeys, birds, and insects to see. You'd better start reading about what you are going to experience! May is the best climbing season there, so if you are planning for next year, we had better get going quick with the logistics. By the way, our family is on a first-name basis with Dr. Richard Leaky, the anthropologist. I will write to see if we can arrange a personal meeting with him at his museum in Nairobi."

"Jeez, Coombs, who don't you know in the world? Most people are content just to see Dr. Leaky on TV, but meeting him in person? Man! That would be an education. OK, I will get the gear prepared for Heim Glacier, and let's plan on next May!"

I hung up the phone more excited than ever, thinking this adventure would be like no other. I knew no one else who dreamed of climbing the Heim Glacier, and this would be a real exploration. The possibility of meeting Richard Leaky was amazing enough, but to see Africa from the top down had my adrenaline spurting out my body pores.

Of course, then I had to deal with reality. I was nearing the end of a nightmare divorce from an 18-year marriage with Sharon. Our communication had deteriorated to parting glances on the way to and from the attorney's office. The kids were suffering terribly as the innocent victims of our arguments. The gravity of my financial condition got worse every day. My house was mortgaged; the construction company property was double mortgaged to keep my bank loans for payroll. Could I manage this expedition without the company going bankrupt? Could I jump ship yet another time? The strain started eating at me, but the dream of being at 18,000 feet climbing the last steps to the summit of Kilimanjaro seemed to keep my life together.

AMERICAN IN AFRICA

In April 1991, Coombs and I headed to Africa to begin the adventure of climbing a peak that, in my view, had created more intrigue and fantasy for poets and writers than any other mountain on earth. From Spokane we flew to New York, and to Mecca, where I had time to walk around the airport and, with bleary eyes, gaze into the early morning light and wonder why so many pilgrims wanted to come to this place for anything. It seemed so dry and barren.

The last flight took us to Kenya where we landed in Nairobi, an expansive city known as "the cradle of mankind." European influence was especially evident in the architecture.

"Kop, let's hail a taxi and go see the marketplace," Coombs said. "We only have one day in the city." Indeed, we had only three weeks to see this sliver of Africa and climb its tallest mountain. The taxi took us on a wild ride through much of the modern section of Nairobi, and then down side streets to an area loaded with street vendors in an open market, where we roamed on foot.

"Hey mister, you American?"

The short black man in a white shirt with black pants waved at me to come into his store. How could he tell I was American?

"Look around, look around; there is many African artifacts here in my store for you to see!"

Everywhere I traveled the natives could pick me out of a group as the American. "OK, OK, but how could you tell I was American?" I asked as I walked inside his store and proceeded to wander from one side of the room to the next gazing at colorful blankets and shields, as well as carved wooden spears and tridents that looked like they were hand-made by the devil himself.

"The curious look on your face told me that you are American."

"What curious look?" I asked. The man only smiled. Maybe it was my whiteness, or maybe the smell of cash in my wallet.

We slinked past stereos, radios, glassware, chairs, tables, colorful vases, and mannequins dressed in native clothing. I followed the shopkeeper back through a corridor to an older building that was attached to his storefront. The room was dark, dingy, and permeated with the musty smell of oldness. The floor was made of wooden planks that appeared to be hand-hewn with still visible knots from tree limbs. "Here mister!" he said. "This is what you search for."

Truth is, I wasn't searching for something horrific, but there it was anyway: an African witch doctor voodoo doll. It appeared to be very old. Painted stripes were faded on wood so dry it had check marks. The figure was about 2 feet 6 inches high and was decorated in excruciating detail with engraved tattoos, and black, red, and orange war paint. Real black hair exploded out the top of the doll's head and fell down all sides of the face to partially conceal the nose, eyes, ears, and mouth. The grotesque, misshapen facial features would give

Edgar Allen Poe nightmares. I was mortified, frozen in place. I couldn't utter a sound. Normally, I try to take a photograph of unusual items I come across in my journeys, but I was unable to move. All of my body's energy was converted into blood pressure pulsing in the sides of my head. I had to gasp for air. Never in my life had I seen something so painfully real and horrifying that I felt faint and transfixed at the same moment. Numerous tiny knives were plunged deep into the doll with slashes of red paint around the "wounds." Daggers were impaled into nearly every inch of the naked doll, including the chest, crotch, arms, back, legs, feet, and ass. Everywhere except the face, which was carved into a tortured mask of death. It was creepy enough that the shopkeeper knew I was American, but was he psychic? Did he know I was going through a divorce? For an instant, I felt the doll's pain.

"Kop! Kop! You OK?" Coombs said. "Let's get out of here quick!"

I bolted out of the shop and back to the street to hail a taxi. "This is enough of Nairobi, Coombs. We leave in the morning, so no more tourist stuff."

INTO THE COUNTRY

A tentative plan we had to meet Richard Leaky fell through as he had important museum business to deal with and had to leave Nairobi. That was fine as we were ready to hit the road. John Mchaki of the Chahnga tribe, who worked for Lion's Safari, drove us out of the city toward Kilimanjaro National Park. Joining us was Nikos Nguma, our government-assigned guide. The road to Arusha was much like going into the countryside in central Idaho, and we started to relax from the stress of the crowded, busy urban experience. After about an hour of driving along the two-way highway, we spotted ostriches feeding, some Marabou storks in the trees, and a puff adder on the road. Then through the dense brush alongside the road I spotted the bodies of two large animals with long legs. Looking higher, I saw the bodies were connected to 10-foot-long necks topped with a head. They were real live giraffes!

"Stop the car! STOP THE CAR!" I yelled so urgently that I frightened our driver. I saw his wide eyes in the rear-view mirror. Visibly shaken, he eased the car to the side of the road. "Let me out here," I said. "I need to get a photograph of those giraffes!"

The petrified driver looked at me, then at Coombs, then back at the giraffes still standing right next to the road, and started to laugh, flashing a huge white toothy grin. He sighed deeply in relief.

"Kop, listen to me; you have to calm down a bit," Coombs said. "I know the voodoo doll was a bad experience, but don't throw knives at the rest of us in the car. It's stressful enough just hoping we stay on the road."

"How many times do you see a couple giraffes standing next to the highway back in Spokane?"

I walked right up to the wild giraffes. As in Australia, there were no barbed-wire fences, no cattle guards, no manmade barriers of any kind in sight. About a hundred yards behind the two roadside giraffes were another 10 grazing on tree leaves. Behind those giraffes were a couple dozen zebras feeding on the wild grass. The animals were free to escape across the road to the open range beyond, but they stood their ground and looked at me as though I was the one in a pen. It was like a storybook fantasy come true to see these wild species—animals I'd associated only with zoos, books, and movies—roaming freely in their natural habitat.

The road was almost void of vehicle traffic as we continued. Most people were walking, including many Maasai tribesmen dressed in dark maroon garments. Women seemed to be the only ones carrying water jugs or tools.

"Hey Coombs, why do those young boys wear the head feathers?"

"Well, Kop, as you know, or maybe you don't know, that means they have just been circumcised. Do you want some head feathers?"

"Actually, another circumcision would do me in."

Around mid-day we stopped for lunch and feasted on lamb stew, which we washed down with a Tusker beer. Across the street from our lunch spot was a sign saying, "Welcome President Jimmy Carter." As we continued in the car, we saw thousands of people walking, including children in uniform headed for schools, and locals going to seminaries, missions, and other destinations. Coombs and I were the only two white men among masses of black people.

On the second day we had an early breakfast and were picked up by a different driver named John Mkwene in his Land Rover for the trip to Moshi. We stopped at an outdoor market where we walked through tables of dried fish, trinkets, and farming tools. Goat meat was hanging from old wooden beams.

Everything was buzzing with countless flies. Many of the people were dressed in Muslim garb, and we noted that the market was next to a mosque built of wood with classic Arab features. Coombs also pointed out a Jain temple.

"Do not take pictures of the local people," Mkwene advised. "There are many more of them than you."

"What does he mean by that remark, Coombs?"

"I haven't got a clue, Kop. I assume it must be something to do with not wanting us to steal a part of their personality."

Nikos bought plenty of oranges for Coombs and me as well as a huge load of food that he had bundled in plastic bags for our two hired porters. After loading the food into the Land Rover, we met Gaspara Damiani and Joachim Oto, who would carry all of our gear plus their own food and clothing for the 10-day expedition. The thousands of people we saw along the dirt road from Moshi up to the Umbwe mission village area gave us the sense that a large population lived hidden under the thick forest canopy perhaps all around the base of Mount Kilimanjaro. At the mission village we saw banana, coffee, and acacia trees, as well as a lot of slippery red mud and moss. Mold seemed to be growing on everything. The villages were close to the roadway, with a lot of men sitting around. They generally were dirty and appeared to be extremely poor. In a dirt clearing at the end of the road, we parked and did our last-minute packing while kids were popping out of the brush from all directions to watch us. As we hiked up the trail, a woman ran across ahead of us with some lumber in her hands. She was followed by a man who also was carrying lumber. Both quickly melted into the forest. Nikos said he could turn them in to the authorities, as taking lumber in the national park is illegal.

Where the track narrowed and steepened with lots of undergrowth, we had the good fortune to encounter a wild troop of monkeys going crazy in an open grove of trees.

"These are the colobus monkeys, and their name in Swahili is mbega," Nikos said. "They are very rarely seen!"

The bush was very thick in places as we climbed through a wild diversity of plant species, but not much in the way of flowers. The forest canopy became very high, some 150 to 200 feet above us, with several intermediate levels in-between. Any exposed skin became laced with scratches from rose-like thorns.

A bloody cut on Coombs' ear appeared to be from a leech that had latched on and was brushed off undetected.

Just before nightfall, we arrived at what Nikos called "Forest Caves Camp" somewhere around the elevation of 9,000 feet.

"Look, a clear pool of water," Coombs said.

"Pretty fetid looking to me, Coombs. I wouldn't drink any of it if I were you. Just look at all the animals around here. No telling what amoebas they carry."

"I'll treat some water with purification pills and give it a taste."

Meanwhile, Nikos, Gaspara, and Joachim gathered wood and, even though everything in the forest seemed waterlogged, they built a nice campfire. Coombs and I simmered a big pot of soup as the sun set and the sky went black. Screeching ripped out of the cloak of darkness as we huddled around the dancing flames. "Hyrax monkeys," Nikos told us. As the evening wore on, they sometimes jumped down onto the ground and played around us while countless other weird noises emanated from the jungle. It sounded like a bullfrog swamp on steroids.

Heavy rains drenched camp during the night, and we rose in a drizzle to begin the long hike to Barranco Hut. The route headed steeply up through jungle on a rocky ridge covered with tree roots. The path was interrupted by short cliffs we had to scramble up in the rain. An overgrown drop-off to our east fell some 2,000 feet into the Barranco Gorge. Clouds shrouded the views, but we could hear the rushing torrent of water at the bottom. Hands-on rock climbing was required in several spots, where we helped the porters with the monster duffle bags they carried on top of their heads. Our world changed abruptly when we broke out of the jungle into the heather forest above the steep ridge. Before us in all its glory was Mount Kilimanjaro.

The view through the trees would make angels weep. Towering 15,000 feet above us, the summit of the world's most romantic mountain was bathed in morning sunlight that highlighted mists gently swirling up its slopes. "Then, ahead, all he could see, as wide as all the world, great, high, and unbelievably white in the sun, was the square top of Kilimanjaro," Hemmingway wrote. "And then he knew where he was going."

I said to Coombs, "That's the whitest snow I have ever laid eyes on."

"I have to agree with you, Kop."

Starting from the top of the mountain and cascading directly toward us over high cliffs was the Heim Glacier. It was rugged, steep, and masculine looking, almost like the rippled, muscled arm protruding off the mammoth shoulders of a giant body builder. The route we came to climb looked steep and challenging, but nothing I saw on the mountain instilled fear, or at least nothing close to the degree of fear one suffers while staring into the face of a voodoo doll.

We continued ascending through trees and brush covered with hanging moss for two more taxing hours to the Barranco Hut at 12,930 feet. We were feeling very sluggish from the altitude as we arrived at 2 p.m. in a downpour. The octagonal hut looked like a stubby farm silo of galvanized sheet metal, with a sloped, pointed roof capped with a small vent. It was probably brought up in pieces by 20 or 30 porters as a prefabricated unit and assembled by national park workers. The area surrounding the hut was denuded by firewood seekers—a micro example of Third World deforestation—and our porters had to walk a half hour downhill to pick up soaked heather logs for a fire. The earthen floor of the hut was filthy with dried grass, dirt mixed with ashes, and littered with sheets of old cardboard and other disgusting garbage. Interior walls were stained black from smoke and the air was musty. Our porters had dropped the food, including tomatoes, a few bundles of spinach, and chunks of beef still on the bone, on the ground against the wall. The hut had been built with a wood floor, which apparently had been dismantled board by board by previous campers and used for firewood. Coombs and I made the easy decision to pitch our tent outside on the grass. We were rewarded later when the clouds dissipated and the moon illuminated Kilimanjaro so we could see the huge looming presence of the Breach Wall and Heim Glacier directly above us.

WRESTLING WITH REALITY

The next day was devoted to resting, reading, and organizing our gear for the technical climb. Rain and drizzle all morning at 100 percent humidity made it impossible to stay dry. Nobody had worn a rain jacket to this point even in a downpour because temperatures were too warm. We just devoted a layer of clothing to muggy wetness. However, we had one good reason to look up into the gloomy skies as Nikos spotted a rare 15-pound scavenger soaring near our tent. He seemed pleased to see the Lammergeier (bearded vulture), which lives only among the tallest peaks of the Eastern Hemisphere. Indeed, as the Audubon Society notes in its "Sketch" series on birds, "The Lammergeier is... the most extraordinary scavenger in the world. Like other vultures, it feeds solely on the dead—yet it feasts on bone rather than flesh. After spotting a fresh carcass from (the sky), the bird silently dives in, regardless of whoever else is waiting in line. The vulture then makes off with bones, swallowing the small ones and dropping the femurs and ulnas down hundreds of feet to break them up on rocks and liberate the marrow—the most nutritious part of any bone-based diet. Meanwhile, the harder shards are easily turned into sludge by the Lammergeier's stomach acid, which is more caustic than lemon juice."

The rest day at the Barranco Hut allowed the emotion of my situation back home to catch up with my getaway. Depression and exhaustion were creeping in as I wrestled with the reality of divorce. I felt like my physical and mental health was deteriorating. My usual altitude headaches began, and I withdrew into my shell of silence zipped into my bag in the tent. I tried to drift away from the stress by drinking mugs of hot tea. Coombs, too, was suffering headaches from the altitude. Given this state of mind, perhaps it was therapeutic that I was about to confront a significant distraction. While emptying and sorting the gear in our bags, to my horror, I discovered that I had not packed a waterproof anorak. I rationalized away my concern by convincing myself the temperatures would get colder as we climbed higher and any precipitation would be in the form of snow that would be shed by my down parka.

As the day passed, the porters hauled more logs up the hill and built a huge fire outside the hut. Nikos, Gaspara, and Joachim were adept at getting the soaked wood to burn. They nestled their pots right on the fire to fry beef and onions and make a spinach stew. They also cooked a thick porridge by dumping several handfuls of maize flour into a pan of boiling water and then pushing it around athletically with a huge wooden spoon. The result was the consistency between mashed potatoes and bread dough.

"Coombs, do we dare ask them for a taste of that? It sure smells good."

"Considering how hard it was to haul all of that up here, I think not. We've got our freeze-dried crap to eat."

We were comfortable huddled around the fire, and just before darkness the clouds cleared so we could see some of the African plains below, with an outstanding view of Heim Glacier and Breach Wall above us.

"Kop, compared with the photos I saw 15 years ago, it looks like a lot of ice has melted up there," Coombs observed. "Look at that rock band that traverses the entire icefall."

"Yeah, but Nikos says it has a way through, and the only way to tell is to climb up there."

Twilight on the equator is brief, and within a few minutes, we could see the lights of "Moshi Town" 8,000 feet below. Nikos, Gaspara, and Joachim were giddy with excitement to see their hometown from this eagle's perch.

The Heim Glacier and Breach Wall.

The Heim Glacier was seldom climbed at the time of our trip in 1991, and our guide Nikos had traveled up this way only once. Back in Umbwe, Coombs and I made a game plan for a bold traverse of Kilimanjaro by a difficult route. We would climb up and over the summit at 19,341 feet, continuing down to

Kibo Hut at 15,520 feet. We were equipped with a rack of ice pitons, two ropes, climbing harnesses, carabineers, a two-man tent, and cook stoves for our task. We reviewed our plan with Nikos, Gaspara, and Joachim. Their assignment was to carry our "luggage," as they called it, all the way around the mountain to the south circuit-Karanga Valley, and meet us in four days as we descended to the Horombo Hut at 12,155 feet on the standard Kilimanjaro climbing route.

On the fifth day of the expedition, we did a final sorting of technical gear while the porters packed for their trek around the mountain. Coombs and I started with Nikos about 8 a.m. on the contours of the Great Barranco, a huge cwm leading from the base of the Breach Wall, with low-growing plants scattered among the lava rocks, all the way down into the timber. In the low point was a clear-running stream, a rarity on Kilimanjaro. Despite the vast amount of rainfall at the middle elevations and ice above, surface water is scarce.

"I think the gravelly pumice and lava base here is so porous that the water just soaks into the groundwater," Coombs said.

Just beyond the Barranco stream, we passed a huge overhanging boulder with cave-like shelter for climbers who didn't want to stay at the hut, and then we continued up for an hour or more on a track up the steep side of the Lower Breach Wall. The rocks were reddish brown, igneous lava, with a gritty texture that made the climbing a sure-footed delight. The trail, like all official routes on Kilimanjaro, was marked with occasional daubs of red paint. It led back and forth, up ledges and over steep cliff bands that sometimes required hands-and-boot climbing.

"Kop, take a look at the sky above us. What do you think?"

"That's a high mackerel cloud pattern, Coombs; lots of turbulence and high moisture."

"Looks like we are in for more rain. That's my forecast."

"I hope you are wrong, Coombs."

We crested out from the basin over the Lower Breach Wall and took a break on an open rock outcropping. Winds were gusting and high clouds were building. Sunglasses went on even though the sunlight was not direct. The route wound up and down through towers of the lower Window Buttress, with some plant life still visible here and there. The trail was gone, but we could see occasional suggestions of previous passage. The solar heat bore down on us through the clouds at 14,500 feet feeling like a hot lamp beaming on our skin. Just below the first ice of the Heim Glacier we hacked out a tent platform on steep moraine rubble. This was as far as Nikos would go with us, and Coombs and I said goodbye with high hopes that we would meet up in four days on the other side of the mountain. Nikos climbed down the rocks and into the valley to regroup with Gaspara and Joachim.

BREACH OF RESPONSIBILITY

Before daylight on the sixth day, we shouldered 70-pound packs stuffed with gear and food for five days. We had planned for three days to reach the summit, plus food and water for two more days to get us back down the Ubberagua route to the hut on the western side of Kilimanjaro. It was a lot of weight to carry over technical terrain, but we felt up to the task. My mountaineering mantra is "speed is safety," and "it's what you DON'T bring along in the mountains that makes you successful." However, I mismanaged that wisdom this trip.

"Belay on?" Coombs yelled.

"Belay is on, climb away."

The first pitch off the rocky, loose moraine was a treat, with our crampons biting soundly into solid ice. We climbed foot by foot with our ice axes and ice screws for protection as the mist began to swirl below us, obstructing the view. All morning we climbed over a combination of ice mixed with rock cliffs that required caution. Gusting winds slashed us with blasts of horizontal rain. My down coat, which was doing the job perfectly to this point, was getting drenched. Nothing I had read about the mountain mentioned temperatures so warm at 15,000 feet! "So warm" is a relative term. The thermometer was just above freezing, ideal conditions for hypothermia as water began soaking through my clothing to my skin. This was supposed to be the dry altitude and May the dry month! Maybe it was the curse of the voodoo doll.

The consequence of forgetting my rain parka began to haunt me. I started cursing and talking to myself. I missed Sharon, who more than anyone else in my life had believed in my mission and helped me rise high. She had always assisted in packing my gear; she had been my support system, and my best friend. Now she hated me, and it felt terrible. Maybe this rush of emotional anguish was simply preparing me for the painful task of telling Coombs that despite all my mountaineering experience I had forgotten an essential piece of equipment. I hammered two ice pitons into the solid ice, tied myself off to the mountain, and yelled down, "Coombs, come on up to my belay stance!"

I could hear his crampons crunching as I belayed him across the ice while wind gusts blasted rain into my face. My parka had been reduced to two layers of wet nylon with egg-sized clumps of soggy goose down in the baffles. Perhaps I would be better off removing all my clothing and climbing in my bare skin, I pondered. My pack was soaking wet, too. I felt my body core temperature start to drop. My mind was becoming sluggish from the combination of cold and the lack of oxygen at 16,000 feet.

"Coombs, I'm freezing to death," I said.

"Well it's no damn wonder, you idiot. Your parka is soaked, Kop. Put on your rain parka! NOW!"

"Coombs, I didn't bring a rain parka. I forgot it, and then shrugged it off. I didn't believe we would have any rain at this altitude."

Coombs' face turned beet red. I could see the veins in his eyes. He moved up close and screamed into my face from the end of my nose. "How the hell could you come all the way to Africa to climb Kilimanjaro without a rain parka?"

I felt the knife piercing the voodoo doll. "Look David, with the divorce on my mind, I couldn't even get to work some days until noon. I'm just not all here, but other than that, I don't have any excuse. None!"

Coombs, even more than I, wanted to climb the Heim Glacier route up Kilimanjaro. I felt lowly as a worm.

The rain abated as we continued upward, belaying each other the next 500 feet of 50-degree ice to a small ridge crest that overlooked the canyon of the Breach Wall. The clouds parted briefly so we could see the entire upper section of the glacier. All the difficult climbing was below us as the upper section looked like much easier ground. Then, just as suddenly as the sky had opened, the mist, wind, and fog engulfed us again complete with wind-driven sheets of rain. I was soaked and shivering like a willow switch.

At twilight we found an area big enough to make a platform to erect our small tent on the small ridge crest. I furiously but futilely chopped at the ice with my axe. I had no power. I couldn't seem to get blood flowing through my veins to warm my body. Coombs had said no more than a couple words since I confessed about forgetting my parka, but I knew what he was thinking, and I deserved it. The rain pounded all night long as I shivered inside my bag in a silent hell listening to myself talk. Alone in my misery, I beat myself up. I'd let my family down; I'd let Coombs down; I'd let myself down.

I was awake as the first light of our seventh day began to show inside the tent. Outlines of our bags were silhouetted against the tent walls. Heavy mists engulfed the ridge, but the rain had stopped, at least temporarily. After a restless night of soul searching, I finally said, "I am freezing to death. If I go up, I feel I will die. I've got to get down."

Coombs stayed snug in his bag, pretending he hadn't heard me. Whatever the reason, he chose not to answer. Would he solo the rest of the route? That thought crossed my mind. Maybe that was the solution. I would rappel down and hike around the mountain to catch up with Nikos.

"Coombs, I really can't continue to go up. I'm terribly sorry, but my body has failed me. I'm getting more hypothermic. Are you thinking of soloing the rest of the route to the top? The hard climbing is already done."

"Jeez, have some hot tea. That will warm you and maybe you'll feel better."

Indeed, the liquids helped, but not much. My body core temperatures were low, and my energy level was sunk, all because of one missing piece of critical gear.

Coombs unzipped the tent fly and gazed up through a gap in the mist at the Heim Glacier. The icefall appeared much easier than the slopes we had climbed the previous day, but there was only one choice for me: go down.

Muttering no more than a couple words, Coombs began to stuff gear into his pack while I dismantled the tent. I was still shivering as I began down-climbing the brittle ice. We belayed each other one pitch after another, taking frequent rest stops. The shivering had taken a toll on my mental toughness, and the whiteout of fog and mist added gloom to the misery of my failing to reach a goal. Descending gives climbers a different perspective of a route they had climbed. As we rappelled down the vertical rock cliff bands, we were surprised at the exposure. Finally, the crampons came off our boots when we reached the toe of the Heim Glacier. I was bushed, but I also felt much better at the lower altitude. We decided to camp where we picked up the trail. The afternoon sky appeared to be having mercy on me by parting clouds enough to reveal small patches of blue sky.

At the dawn of our eighth day, I still hadn't reconciled with my melt down. "David, I've had many failures in my life, but I will never forgive myself for this mistake. We had the route climbed. I don't know how or what to say. All the planning, all the effort to get here...."

"Forget it, Kop. We move on from here, we've got a long day ahead of us to hike around the mountain to Horombo Hut. Here, take a look at the map. We've got miles and miles to hike before we sleep."

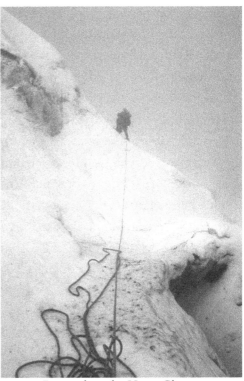

Descending the Heim Glacier.

"Yeah, and to add to the challenge, we have to hike the trail in our mountain boots, because the porters took our sneakers."

New Beginning

The trail to Horombo was well-maintained, clear of any brush or rocks, and easy walking. When the sunshine burned away the clouds, everything felt better; even the heavy, ridged, plastic mountain boots were bearable. After marching for 12 hours, we reached the hut late in the afternoon, greeted with big smiles by Nikos and Gaspara.

"Mr. David," Nikos said, "we were getting very concerned, and Joachim has climbed up to the Kibo Hut to see if you are coming down yet."

We spent the night at Horombo and rose early to make the hike to 15,520 feet and the Kibo Hut, which is the last stay on the main route before the final ascent of Kilimanjaro. It was another long but gentle uphill trudge in the mist as the heath gave way to tundra and scree. We were in the expansive saddle between Kibo and Mawenzi, a 16,000-foot satellite peak. The trail was fine red sand and gravel that would be a joy to ride on a mountain bike.

As the trail got steeper, winding through rocky outcrops, we looked up to see a wheeled rescue stretcher coming down fast in the hands of several guides and porters. The rescuers wore orange shoulder harnesses attached to the stretcher. Nikos jumped in with the men to get the details as he supported them down the trail for a quarter mile. The patient had been stricken with high altitude pulmonary edema at about 17,000 feet. He had been assisted to the Kibo Hut, where he was put into the stretcher to be wheeled down the mountain. The only treatment for HAPE is getting to lower elevation.

"Pretty sobering to watch this, eh Coombs? Could be you or me tomorrow."

"Let's hope not!"

Rain returned just after noon and we made the last few steps to the Kibo Hut in a whiteout that was belching sleet. Joachim made rice and sauce, bread, butter, and tea for all of us. I felt like a new man right away, and I watched in relief as the air turned colder, and snow began to fall. A good 4 inches of snow accumulated in the afternoon as we rested. For dinner, Nikos and Joachim cooked a traditional beef goulash with potatoes, carrots, peas, and a bit of spinach. "This is the best, most excellent recipe for climbing Kilimanjaro," Nikos proclaimed in Swahili and English.

After dinner, we sat and tapped our guides for information about the Kilimanjaro region. According to Nikos, the area has a long history of missionaries and schools resulting in 75 percent of the local people being Christian. Missionaries liked to settle here, he explained: "Good food, good weather, and little or no disease." On the other hand, the coastal portion of Tanzania is 95 percent Muslim, he said, yet there seemed to be no resentment toward the Christian missionaries. Coombs brought up the work of Albert Schweitzer in West Africa. None of the men, including another local guide sitting with us had ever heard of the Nobel Peace Prize recipient.

In Tanzania, a brewery worker earned 1,000 schillings a day (about $5), and a desk manager in a hotel made $10 a day, Nikos said. A basic transistor radio cost $2. As we talked, lots of static and calls were coming in over his national parks radio. "Roger. Roger. Over." He answered calls in several languages including Swahili and Changha. It was soon obvious to listeners that Nikos was the man in charge of the Kilimanjaro guides.

I tried my best to keep engaged in the conversation, as I was still filled with remorse about the failed Heim Glacier attempt. Coombs, ever the intellect, continued to sponge up information about these men and their homeland long after the sun had set.

We crawled into our sleeping bags about 8 p.m. The new game plan was to rise at midnight and go for the summit. We didn't get much sleep. Coombs suffered from Cheyne-Stokes respiration, a symptom of high altitude that leaves the victim gasping for air between normal segments of breathing. Meanwhile, I tossed and turned for most of the four hours until we all rallied for tea at the stroke of midnight, and Day 10. The good news was that the climbing gods were greeting us with billions of stars flickering in a cold, clear sky. Soon, by the light of our headlamps, we headed up into the 4,000 vertical feet of Kilimanjaro that loomed above us. From here the ascent was merely a matter of one step in front of the other with no technical ground to navigate, no route-finding decisions, no stress beyond dealing with the cold and altitude. The final leg of my Seven Summits Challenge was reduced to a mundane march. I started counting steps in my head, and to pass the time I tried to estimate the paces needed to gain the rim above us.

I was still counting several thousand steps later, when the crater rim was coming into view, or so it seemed. We crested one false ridge after another until suddenly we were staring into the massive collapsed volcano crater. My boredom evaporated. Neither Coombs nor I had seen anything that compared with the scale of this crater. When we had looked up from the plains below, the square-topped summit of Kilimanjaro looked relatively flat. From our position on the crater rim, we could see the true summit far off in the distance—the goal at the end of a circuitous route for at least another mile around the massive hole in front of us. The crater appeared to be a stadium large enough for a hundred football fields with room to spare for bleachers to seat millions of people. As with every walk in nature, the size, scale, and miracle of the early morning light caused Coombs and me to stare in humble amazement.

Nestled inside the collapsed crater was an expansive ice cap, or in other words, a stationary glacier. The sun had melted some areas on the southern exposure of the ice cap into vertical walls of ice that were hundreds of feet high in places. On the far northern end of the cap, the ice was melted into 50-foot high steps, like a giant frozen stairway to heaven. All the ice cliffs were glistening as dawn still simmered just below the horizon. The feeling was other worldly, as though we had made it to Mars!

The sun had yet to show, but more than enough light had gathered so we could turn off our headlamps and continue our march albeit slower in the thinner air at 19,000 feet. The journey became surreal moving through such remarkable surroundings. My brain seemed to be gasping for oxygen as we climbed higher and higher over one false summit after another, until there was nothing above us but sky. The summit of Kilimanjaro, 19,341 feet, the end of my quest for the Seven Summits, was marked by wooden poles bearing three small flags that barely fluttered in the whispering wind.

As the sun rises on the summit of Kilimanjaro, the mists begin to form.

Coombs, Nikos, and I stepped onto the summit, just as sunshine streaked over the horizon. As the mists swirled and started to block the sun another weird cloud formed below and behind us. These spooky, weird clouds forming all around us were capturing our attention when Coombs erupted with excitement and exclaimed, "THE BROCKEN SPECTRE!"

I wheeled around to witness three long shadows appear from our bodies, stretching out in an odd triangular shape into the center of a gorgeous circular rainbow that seemed to pulsate with brightness. Coombs, from his deep memory bank of knowledge, explained the spectacle to me and Nikos as we stood riveted to the image.

"The Brocken Spectre was first witnessed in 1789 on the Brocken, a peak in the Harz Mountains in Germany. For many years people thought the sighting was imagined, as it can only be seen in perfect circumstances. You have to be looking down from a peak into the fog bank like this when the sun is at the perfect angle."

The Brocken Spectre from the summit of Kilimanjaro.

Mesmerized, we bowed in humility to another wondrous vision of nature. The ground under my feet would have been no more hallowed if it were Olympus Mons on Mars, and I felt like Hemingway's Harry had arrived with me, too. All the troubles of the world vanished in that moment, and as I climbed off the mountain, everyone and everything was beautiful.

Words from the Wild

- "Imagination will often carry us to worlds that never were. But without it, we go nowhere." —Carl Sagan

Twenty-Five

Carstensz

The Carstensz Pyramid, 16,024 feet, Irian Jaya.

"PRAYER DOES NOT USE UP artificial energy, doesn't burn up any fossil fuel, doesn't pollute," said Margaret Mead. "Neither does song, neither does love, neither does dance."

Fifty thousand years before the birth of this famous anthropologist, who studied the primitive tribes of Papua New Guinea, people migrated from Southeast Asia across land bridges all the way to Australia. Aborigines were isolated to the continent by rising oceans. Nearby, some 500 tribes were scattered over two countries, Papua New Guinea and Irian Jaya, on what is now known as the world's largest island. The tribes that made this island home are vastly different in appearance and culture from societies that moved in later from "civilization." They thrived in an inhospitable dense jungle where even King Kong could roam undetected.

In the 19th century, the first missionaries who sailed into the Pacific Ocean and laid eyes on the Hawaiian natives were appalled at their nude bodies. Missionaries who met the tribes of New Guinea saw a much more exotic form of nakedness as some of the tribesmen painted their entire bodies, some were tattooed from head to toe, some had boar tusks pierced in their noses, and some were clad in nothing more than eye-catching penis gourds. One missionary reported 10,000 skulls in a long house, indicating that proselytizing here was a high-stakes game. If things didn't work out, missionaries might have their heads cut off for a headhunter's necklace, or be eaten if they chanced to engage with a cannibalistic tribe. The existence of people who called this island "home" was not documented until World War II aircraft spotted clearings in the jungle while flying from Australia to Indonesia.

Oceania, also known as Australasia, is a geographical region of islands identified as a continent that includes 14 countries: Australia, Micronesia, Fiji, Kiribati, Marshall Islands, Nauru, New Zealand, Palau, Papua New Guinea, Samoa, Solomon Islands, Tonga, Tuvalu, and Vanuatu. The highest point of this land is in the middle of the jungle of Irian Jaya. In 1623, Dutch explorer Jan Carstensz first recorded seeing the sawtooth horizon of glacier-clad mountains in central New Guinea only 4 degrees from the equator. When Carstensz returned to Europe to report his sighting of ice in the tropics, he was ridiculed and not believed until 200 years after his death. This unlikely range of high country was news to me, too.

I was pleased with myself when I completed my climb of Kilimanjaro, the last of the true "Seven Summits" in my global quest to step on the top of all the continents. However, there's nothing more humbling than gloating to somebody as well-read and well-versed about mountains as my good friend Bill Fix. I was visiting his home, which housed the most extensive mountaineering library in the West, when the subject of Kilimanjaro came up. I was stopped short of a chance to recount tales of the climb when Bill interrupted and said, "Chris, you climbed the wrong one! You climbed the wrong seventh summit." I felt like a burglar who'd just been busted. "For mountaineers, the recognized high point for that 'continent' is Carstensz in Irian Jaya, and it's a real tough one."

"OK Bill, I've been reading the debate about the true Seven Summits according to mountaineers, and I have to agree, Kosciuszko (Australia) wasn't much of a challenge, and I've kept Carstensz on my list, but getting there— man, that would be a tough trip even if it wasn't through headhunter country. It scares me to death! Besides, I finished the continental Seven Summits; it's just another game to play."

"Well, you're going to have to climb it, Chris. At 16,024 feet, it's the real high point of Australasia and the highest mountain between the Andes and the Himalayas."

My main climbing goals were completed after Everest in 1981. The competition to climb the Seven Summits was an encore to a contest that began after my original goals were set. Having such a good start on bagging the seven, I jumped into that game and became the 12th man in the world to complete the Seven Summits Challenge. During the quest, my divorce from Sharon became final. With the emotional see-saw stress of the divorce and trying to run a construction business, I wasn't exactly living the dream. I was simply trying to survive the dream. But I could not resist the temptation. At the least, it was a grand way to see the world from the top down.

I drove away from Fix's house with my tail tucked firmly between my legs. Shit! The idea of NOT climbing Carstensz was untenable, especially since I knew the quest was also on the mind of my Everest climbing partner, Glen Porzak. He had worked for years trying to secure a permit to climb Carstensz, and he called me one day elated that he'd received permission from all the agencies. He invited me to join his expedition.

Saying yes was easy, but how the hell would I explain this to Michelle? I had met her in 1985, and when we met again in 1992 after my divorce was final, we grabbed each other, and the next thing I remember we were expecting our first child. Would I lose her, too, if I told her about this longing to attempt a wild mountain in the middle of Papua New Guinea with cannibals waiting for the next big fat American climber to arrive? Of course, I would have to be truthful, but I struggled for ways to verbalize how my mission in life coincided with that point in our relationship. Michelle was pregnant. The expedition was scheduled for April of 1994, when she would be seven months along. Our relationship had been kindled when I spotted her in the crowd at a Seven

Summits program I was presenting for the Spokane Mountaineers. She was aware of my obsession with climbing. But now I struggled to find the right words and the right context for putting my climbing ambitions on the same playing field with my love for Michelle. Overwhelmed with that objective, I just blurted it out to her one day with the grace of a cowboy trying to sort out his feelings for his girlfriend and his horse.

"Michelle, I really want to travel to New Guinea someday to try and climb Carstensz Pyramid. My good friend Glen Porzak has been working years to secure all the required permits to try the climb, and he called me. He finally got the permit from the government."

"Just what is a Car Stand Pyramid?"

Obviously, I hadn't communicated very well, and I tried my best to downplay the danger. "It's pronounced 'kahr-stuhnz,' and it's a little mountain in the middle of a jungle in New Guinea."

"God, another mountain?" she said as her eyes looked into my soul. "Haven't you climbed enough mountains?" At first she was aghast, but slowly edged toward being supportive. "What will that take for time? A week or two?"

Again, telling the truth was painful: "Well, no, actually, it could be a month."

"So when are you planning this expedition?" she finally queried after a long pause. "After the baby I hope!"

Telling the truth at that moment felt like trying to pass a massive, jagged kidney stone out my mouth. "Well, not exactly. The permit and prime climbing season is in May." The silence made me squirm, but this time it was wrenching as Michelle looked straight ahead and came to grips with the situation. She convinced me she would be all right, and then I convinced myself she was being honest.

"I'm going down to rewrite my last will with my attorney tomorrow morning," I said. Having totally exhausted my courage just to come clean to Michelle, I didn't dare tell my parents, as they had already suffered years of anxiety over my addiction to danger. They would find out soon enough.

On April 22, 1994, the stellar team of climbers Glen Porzak had chosen was set to meet in Los Angeles International Airport. Michelle was seven months pregnant with Kelly, and as the minutes drew closer to board the plane,

I felt a welling up of guilt, selfishness, fear, anxiety, depression, and failure as a father. Just what the hell was wrong with me? The question pounded in my cranium until I felt everyone in LAX was staring at me. Adventure had taken my commonsense hostage. I was begging the Almighty for answers and help and getting no response. But as I wrestled with my demons, Michelle was the one who had to be stronger. Unbeknownst to me as I flew off, she went into false labor. I wasn't there to assist. Her mother helped her through the crisis.

JUNGLE JOURNEY

The 14-hour flight from LA was consumed in conversation about Watergate and the life of Richard Milhous Nixon, whose death was announced over the aircraft radio just after takeoff. The flight landed in the small town of Biak, which was a World War II landing strip in the Schouten Islands, and then we changed aircraft to fly to the thatched roof houses of Nabire on the north coast of Irian Jaya. After overnighting in a windowless motel, we flew 100 miles over dense jungle in a Twin Otter to the village of Illaga at 8,700 feet in the central highlands of the island. Looking out the window at the density of the jungle, the rugged mountains, and the deep gorges, everyone figured that if the pilots didn't come back for us, we would never be seen or heard of again.

When we approached the highland village, the pilots made several passes before attempting to land the twin-prop plane on what appeared to be a 20-degree angled airstrip fouled with stumps that protruded through lush grass. I had brought a camcorder for filming the expedition, and with no flight crew to make me keep my seat belt on, I went up the aisle directly behind the pilots and started recording what they were seeing out the front window during the approach. When the wheels "touched" ground all I remember is seeing the roof of the plane as I backflipped down the aisle all the way to the rear seats. I stood and grabbed the backrest of two empty seats as tightly as I could with my hands, but the plane bounced a second time and I flipped again. The wheels were tough enough to withstand this "crash" landing and eventually we stopped, but my camera was broken. That was the bitter end of my expedition movie making.

When our small tribe of white male climbers crawled off the 19-passenger plane, we appeared almost as strange to the natives as the native warriors seemed to us. Reading and seeing pictures about the Dani tribe was a galaxy away from reality. Not a word was uttered by our team. Before our eyes were a dozen naked men with skin as black as coal, wearing only penis gourds strapped to their bodies by small cords around their waists. The bare-breasted women were only slightly more covered in knee-length raffia grass skirts. Young boys wore junior penis gourds and the little girls were nude. The natives were staring at us like deer dazed by headlights and we suddenly were uneasy to be so porcelain white and so completely clothed as our winged time machine dropped us off in the Stone Age. These people had no other access to written history or the invention of the wheel. A couple of the men were holding hand-made wood-handled axes fitted with stone adzes for cutting trees and digging yams and potatoes.

"When in Rome, do as the Romans do: is that how we fit in here?" I whispered to Gerry Roach. He turned and laughed, but I saw the fear in his eyes. I felt like shouting, "I'm very sorry for our appearance people," but managed to keep my mouth shut. The pilots remained in the cockpit as we climbed down the ladder from the plane. We found out later that they'd heard a report over their radio of a possible uprising. We unloaded our baggage and the plane was quick to leave.

We pitched our tents on a relatively flat spot on the airstrip, and the next morning we prepared the porters and food for the expedition. I asked Porzak for a "leave of absence" to take a one-hour trek into the jungle to visit the mummified remains of an esteemed Dani leader. I had read and heard that this revered man was the tribe's version of our George Washington, and I wanted to see the site and snap a photo. After a sweaty trek up the mountainside on a marginal trail, I followed my Dani guide to a small thatched hut. He unlocked a large security chain on the entrance and opened the door to reveal the eerie repose of a 400-year-old skeleton with dried skin seemingly shrink-wrapped to the bones. The skull, which had hollow eye sockets, was topped off with a bird of paradise feather cap. The corpse of the smallish man was sitting upright on a wicker chair with his penis gourd intact. I was told the Dani bring this mummy out as the center of attention for special ceremonies and celebrations.

Standing with the Dani guide who took me to
their mummified leader. I am on the right.

The first third of the 75-mile trek to the base of Carstensz was through the world's thickest jungle called "the heart of darkness," and we got off to a dim start. Apparently there had been miscommunication with Ripta, our government-assigned Indonesian liaison officer from Manila. He had overseen the purchase of local vegetables—yams, sweet potatoes, berries, and bananas—to be loaded into bilums (string bags) for the porters to carry. We were well up the trail before we realized our expedition had launched with only half the amount of locally procured food needed for the trip as scheduled. Walking out of Illaga was pleasant at first, going down a winding trail for several miles

341

between grass huts and fields of snorting pigs. The porters were strung out, most of them carrying potatoes to sustain themselves over the next two weeks. The jungle portion of the journey began after passing the idyllic village of Pinapa.

The first day on the route up and into the heart of darkness reduced our pace to slow, silent pain and desperation. The seven Americans on this team had been on a combined total of 32 Himalayan expeditions, and none of us had ever seen or experienced trekking anywhere in the world that remotely compared with the so-called trail through this jungle of Irian Jaya. The route was unmarked; only the native Dani guide knew the path over the sharp limestone roughly carpeted with moss. Thin trees had toppled into every step of the path, with tree roots wrapped over exposed rocks and blowdowns. For the first couple of miles there was no solid ground to walk on. We sometimes resorted to crawling and grabbing roots with our ungloved hands. When we could actually walk, our boots often would disappear ankle deep or even knee deep into thick boggy mud. We traveled uphill thorough this wet slime, then slightly down into a creek bed, and then back up on a side hill through roots and under ferns, creepers, and spiky palms for a thousand feet.

After a full day of this madness, we were horrified to look down from a small clearing to see that we had traveled only a ridiculously short distance from Illaga. With the same expenditure of time and effort on a typical "trail" we would have covered 20 or 30 miles. In the jungle, we'd gained only about five miles at best. The tree canopy was impenetrable in some areas, rendering day into night. Mammoth plants prospered under any openings that allowed sunshine to filter through to the jungle floor. When they could catch some solar rays some of these spiky native plants rivaled trees for size.

The flora was well watered as this jungle is one of the rainiest places on earth. May is the driest month. Our mornings were always clear, but the clouds would build and, starting around noon, dump about an inch of rain in four to six hours each day. Ages ago the Dani figured out what to wear in this warm, moist environment: nothing! My typical trekking attire—knickers or pants, wool socks, gaiters, and boots—became soaked and heavy in the afternoon, so I did as the locals do, or at least as much as my modesty allowed. I stripped down to just nylon shorts. The Dani grew up barefoot and their feet were calloused and tough enough to hike the toughest terrain without shoes. Of course, my feet were much too tender to go barefoot, but I had packed a pair of tennis shoes, an extra item my teammates did not bring, and they were soon jealous.

A large rock provided temporary shelter from the pouring rain as we reached our first campsite, and the Dani quickly cut wood and built a fire. Being on the equator, darkness dropped like a curtain just minutes after the sun set. The rain soon stopped, the fog dissipated and in the clear atmosphere of 11,000 feet the stars lit up the sky. As our climbing team ate crackers, peanut butter, a little cheese, lemonade, rice, potatoes, and soup, I was enthralled by the efficient Dani as they cooked their dinner of sweet potatoes and pork over the open fire. After eating they huddled closely around the flames and began to chant songs that would make Mozart weep. The porters swayed arm-in-arm and sang music that seemed to come from the heart of space. Their vocal cords were like instruments making harmony with deep guttural bass and baritone vibrations. The chants seemed like a mix of the Australian Aboriginal didgeridoo and Zulu melodies. The collective sound was a resonating triumph of their souls. Tears crept down my cheeks as I listened. During the evening, two or three of the Dani would take turns sleeping while the others huddled and continued to chant as one with the universe above them.

The sky was crystal clear on the third morning and from a small clearing on our "trail" we could see to the distant horizon. The skyline resembled an old man lying on his back with his mouth open exposing grey buckteeth. Some of these limestone peaks were covered in white banners of the small remaining glaciers. We could see our destination, the summit of Carstensz, or Puncak Jaya as it is called in Indonesia. Between us and Carstensz Pyramid was a 40-mile traverse through karst limestone formations similar to Bryce Canyon National Park, and glacial moraines left just 4 degrees from the equator during the last ice age. Formed from water-soluble limestone, the plateau had countless caves. Streams often plunged straight down into dark holes and out of sight into the bowels of the earth. This highland was created in the late Miocene Melanesian orogeny, or mountain building process, as the whole island was pushed upward to an extreme height by the oblique collision between the Australian and Pacific plates. The limestone I occasionally chipped at was several hundred million years younger than the limestone formations on the summit of Everest. I relished breaks in the traveling to search the rocks for skeletal fragments of marine organisms like coral and foraminifera. Just the thought of all the time and forces of nature on display in this landscape kept a smile on my face.

Our party celebrated liberation from the heart of darkness on the evening of April 30. We were still a two-day trek from the base of Carstensz, but our campsite in the middle of the plateau with views in all directions brightened everyone's mood. The Dani built a huge campfire. That afternoon, one of them had killed a small bird and ate it for lunch, causing a lot of excitement among the porters. Another sort of excitement bounced through camp after the fire and festivities faded. "Just what the hell is wrong with you, Ripta?" I blurted after he'd jumped in and out of our tent and other tents several times, making sleep impossible.

"Well, for you sir it is no problem, but for me, I could be taken hostage by the neighbors," he said in a clearly nervous voice. He was concerned about the potential of encountering another tribe, one of the many tribes that had never seen foreigners. The Danis feel that the Indonesians have taken their land, and, justifiably, they want it back. Conflicts are not uncommon, Ripta told me. "In 1989, four Indonesian students were killed at this very spot by the Dani guerillas," he said. "It's not a problem for you sir, but these war people might grab me and use me for dinner."

"Ripta, it's the middle of the night. How could the Fore or Asmat tribe tell the difference between you and me?"

"Well sir, all I can tell you is they would know. Last year they took four Indonesian trekkers hostage and they were killed. They hate us Indonesians only. The students were probably eaten as they were butchered beyond recognition and only parts of their bodies were found. They do not like the white visitors either, but they left them alone."

"The Asmat left the white people alone because whites eat bad food," I explained as though I knew what I was talking about. "Our food is loaded with preservatives that make all Americans reek. Today I saw you eating a half a can of Pringles potato chips. Now you smell terrible just like me!" I continued, waving my arms wildly. "It's like a repellant to cannibals."

Ripta stared back, nodded, and, if he understood what I said, he seemed to believe it. He turned and went into the night to his tent, enabling me at least to get some sleep—for better or worse. I had a nightmare as I slept that added to the drama. I dreamed that Michelle had left me while I was on this expedition. I searched for her when I got home and found out that she had moved in with another man.

The trip was full of notable but less earth-shaking dramas. The next morning, for example, I unwittingly sat on an ant nest and spent the rest of the day picking little pismires off my body and pack. More enjoyable was the ringside seat we had for the impressive athletic performance of a porter who chased, outran, and captured a huge rat the size of a baby kangaroo. The Dani would have it for dinner, as no food item was wasted.

As our journey continued, the spectacular mountain peaks stood out like teeth along a saw blade. On the seventh day of trekking, we settled into a five-hour uphill grind to New Zealand Pass at 14,750 feet, where fleeting glimpses of Carstensz through rain and mist revealed our proposed route to the summit. The view was a quick reminder that the climbing challenge ahead would be technically much harder than Everest, but in the meantime we were numb struck with the severity of simply getting there. The trek was physically and mentally intense. Down the other side of the pass we came upon the remains of a dead man whose skull had been removed and stuck on the top of his spear. Ripta said the Dani had died of exposure trying to climb over the pass from the north side.

Down and down we hiked into the huge valley beneath the great North face of Carstensz before finally making Base Camp on May 2 at 13,430 feet. Our climbing team arrived at this milestone with cuts, bruises, sore muscles, and aching feet but thankful to still be alive. Two ducks swam in a small lake next to our campsite. They were the first ducks we had seen on the journey, a curiosity I might have pondered longer had I not been exhausted. In all the reading and research my teammates and I had done, the rigors of the trek to the base of Carstensz were never detailed. The climb had been chronicled and previous mountaineers had described their observations and fascination with the Dani, but none of the accounts we found prepared us for the grunt work just to reach the mountain.

Perhaps our predecessors had conspired in a morbid little game of suppressing the surprise of a week-long walk and climb through a bog muddled with hills, tangled tree roots and moss-covered spiny branches that confound your movements from below, from the sides, and from above. The uninitiated don't think of the jungle in terms of vertical gain. The initiated do. In Nepal, climbers ascend a total of 22,500 feet from their start at Lukla to the top of Mount Everest, racking up 11,000 feet during the seven-day, 43-mile hike to Base Camp. The cumulative elevation gain from Illaga to the summit of Carstensz is a whopping 36,000 feet, which includes about 33,000 feet of cumulative gain in the seven-day, 70-mile trek to the base of the mountain.

CLIMBING CARSTENSZ

"Ripta, I notice you've been eating all of our Pringles!" I joked trying to make light of the Indonesian's sudden appetite for "stinky" American snacks.

"Yes sir, I think the American food has worked for me."

"Now your body odor is as bad as ours. When we get down from climbing the mountain you can make the trek out without worrying about the guerrillas."

At the camp below one of the world's great mountains, our American team including Porzak, Roach, Dave Graber, Chris Pizzo, Wayne Hutchens, and Mike Browning couldn't wait to get our hands on the vertical rock face that posed 2,594 feet of rock climbing to the summit. We knew by the pioneers, including Heinrich Harrer of Eiger fame, that the ascent was a grade four, and the rock climbing was severe. The hardest pitch was listed as a tough 5.8, but everyone was up for the task.

We started at 5:15 a.m. on May 3. The first 1,000 feet of climbing was unroped class three and four with some low fifth class exposed leads up water-filled gullies. Higher up, the angle steepened on solid limestone ribs that were sharp and spiny. Leather gloves would have been helpful in protecting our hands, but we didn't have any. The prickly ridges, I surmised, were made of coquina or pieces of coral and seashells, while others seemed to be made of calcite, dolomite, or quartz crystals that made the surface as abrasive as diamond grit sandpaper. (I was frustrated to have so many unanswered questions about the fascinating mineralogy. I wish we'd have had a geologist on the team.) No one wanted to chance a slip or fall for fear of being shredded into mincemeat.

After a couple of hours scaling the original route that Harrer had taken on the main north face, we reached an exposed ridge at 15,000 feet just as a cloak of fog and morning mist engulfed our mountain. I had read stories of the incredible views from this spot where climbers could look over remnants of the glaciers that Jan Carstensz had seen in 1623 from the ocean 80 miles to the south. We donned our raingear and continued climbing through fog and drizzle on faith that the peak was still up there beyond our couple hundred feet of visibility. Working up an alpine ridge with slick footholds and exposure to the north and south faces of the mountain, we came to a gap that required some navigating to get around. With that problem solved, we continued up the ridge for several hundred feet to a prominent point to another gap, this one large and exposed. Using slings we draped around a limestone horn, we anchored a rope and rappelled into the gap for 150 feet of vertical drop that would have been too treacherous to down climb over the wet rock. From the gap we traversed onto an exposed ledge system on the south face. None of the reported magnificent views were visible down the face as Ripta and I gathered hardware from our sacks and took the lead.

Ripta went first up an awkward vertical crack system carefully placing pitons and wedges in the rock for protection. This was the crux of the climb, and with the water cascading over the rock, the next 300 feet of climbing turned desperate. Slick slabs with small holds stretched between three small overhangs that had to be surmounted. The rain transitioned to snow as we ascended, and I struggled to follow Ripta while making sure the anchors were sound at the belay stances for our teammates to follow. The relief of gaining the ridge again on a lower angle slope was temporary. The summit ridge was riddled with dangerously loose boulders, so we moved even slower to avoid dislodging anything that might tumble toward our partners below. After negotiating two more wide gaps that required careful belaying to crest, we could finally see the summit just 200 feet above.

Reaching the misty top of Carstensz was the culmination of a lifetime's work for Roach, Porzak, and me. We climbed the last several feet arm in arm to bag the "eighth" of the Seven Summits. Teammates gave us a standing ovation as we slapped each other on the back. We hoped in vain that the clouds would part if only for a second so we could view the mighty jungle below us on both sides of the mountain. To make sure the euphoria didn't float us too far from reality, Ripta pointed to a snow slope a few feet below the summit and said, "This is where my friend fell off."

Climbing the final ridge to the summit of Carstensz.

I wasn't sure I heard him correctly and asked, "You mean he fell off the top?"

"Yes sir, Mr. Chris, my great climbing partner fell off the top and went all the way to the bottom," he said pointing down the south face into the fog and snowflakes. Then he pointed to a small steel plaque that memorialized the climber. Ripta succeeded in focusing our attention on the next task. We started down with utmost caution, well aware that 90 percent of climbing accidents occur on the climb down, not the climb up. After descending about 500 feet, the snow turned to rain. At the rappel point off the hard cliff, Ripta and I prepared to go first to set up the ropes. Just as he began to lean back on the rope I noticed an oversight and instinctively yelled, "RIPTA! RIPTA! STOP!" His carabineer was not hooked from the rappel rope to his safety belt. He was just one move away from joining his friend 2,000 feet down the south face. After hours of safely negotiating difficult climbing, this one lapse nearly became another classic case of tragedy on the descent.

I fended off mental and physical fatigue by dwelling on the importance of getting back home to Michelle and the baby. We reached Base Camp at 6 p.m., and I fell asleep exhausted but pleased with our achievement. The next day was devoted to catching up on sleep mixed with wandering around the small lake as more rain drenched the landscape.

On May 5 we climbed the Sudirman Range's third highest peak, an unnamed mountain at the time, and on May 6 we bagged East Carstensz Peak and enjoyed wonderful southward views of Carstensz. I found fossils of seashells and sea crustaceans clearly visible in the bedded rock layers. A 1936 aerial photo of the mountain icecap I'd seen showed glaciers, but they were almost entirely melted away a half century later. Ripta pointed out a steel pole placed by geologists showing the glacier had retreated another 15 feet from the previous year.

The mornings usually dawned clear, but the fog, rain, and snow started to come earlier each day. Our gear was saturated as we broke camp at 8:30 a.m. on May 7, but our team made time to pick up all our garbage. We had been doing this routinely before leaving each camp. Litter from previous trekkers fouled every campsite we passed, so we also cleaned up after them. We were determined to leave a good example for our liaison and porters to proudly model for future groups. Ripta and the Dani would watch us with intense curiosity as we gathered the smallest bits of paper, cans, empty freeze-dried food wrappers, worn-out socks... and stuff them into a large duffle bag to carry out to Illaga. Burnable material was piled into the bonfire each night. Every other scrap of trash was hauled out on our backs. We explained to Ripta and the Dani many times why we were determined to keep their wilderness landscape clean, but the concept was foreign to them. They deemed it a waste of energy. The look on their faces indicated their bewilderment with the mysterious ways of the white man.

On most mountaineering expeditions, the trek out from base camp is easier and much faster than the trek in. This wasn't the case here. Climbing Carstensz and its neighbors was the easiest part. The six-day hike back to Illaga was no picnic. The rainfall was increasing each day, making the path, if you dare to call it that, softer and more dangerous than we'd experienced the previous week. About 1,000 feet from the crest of New Zealand Pass we descended 1,200 feet into a wide gully thick with foot-high grasses that grew up from a foot or so of sodden sponge-like moss. With each step my foot would sink ankle deep or deeper into muddy goo that sometimes concealed sharp spines. All the way down this gully we slipped and fell on our asses as we flailed and reached for spiny branches in vain attempts to remain erect. Swearing at the top of our lungs didn't help our plight. I was battle-scarred with bloody cuts and bruises and the sorest feet I have ever experienced when we finally made it to the lake below the pass and a better-defined trail. But the misery wasn't over as we slogged forward in the mud through tree roots, tangles of moss-covered branches and ponds of oozing crud in between jagged limestone outcrops. Mud wrestling would be considered a prettier and more refined sport.

MOTHER OF ALL SINKHOLES

On the trek over the limestone plateau into Base Camp, we had walked by some huge depressions. Large streams flowed toward them before disappearing mysteriously. Agreeing that none of us would ever walk this path again, we made a group decision to seize the opportunity to explore everything on the plateau that looked interesting. The next day, we veered off from our approach path, figuring a new route couldn't possibly be worse than where we had been, and bushwhacked through small forests and more of the same bog and slippery moss as we followed a large creek. Normally a stream would flow out some sort of valley, but this one was headed for a depression that seemed to be about a mile across with no obvious exit. The suspense grew with the roar of rushing water ahead. Soon our curiosity was rewarded as we peered in awe over a cliff where a waterfall was cascading for a thousand feet into a mammoth hole and cave. A quarter mile across this huge sinkhole were two more streams of the same size also pouring down into the black hole, which conjured up notions that this might be the anus of our earth.

Ripta said many more sinkholes and caves are scattered through the highlands. "A couple years ago I took some geologists up here and they put some colored die in the water," he said in his soft voice. "It came out 80 miles to the south near the coastline in some artesian waterfalls."

Porzak and I climbed down into the abyss and got as close as we dared to watch this confluence of water gush into the cave and drain into the blackness. Most of the world's notable caves are in limestone. The water-soluble rock on this plateau at elevations over 11,000 feet was exposed to tremendous amounts of annual rainfall and other factors that gathered water through cracks and weaknesses to form underground rivers. Judging by the volume of water flooding into this chasm, the caves hidden in the bowels of the earth had to be huge. I was thankful that the spelunker bug had never bit me. Descending into one of these caves would be tempting, but that likely would be far more dangerous than climbing expeditions above ground.

After reaching the crest of the plateau at 12,000 feet, we hiked four more days to reach Illaga. The daily rain and high humidity kept us clean from the waist up, but we were caked with mud from the waist down. Wildlife sightings were few beyond bugs like moths and beetles, as well as small birds. We had frequent encounters with field rats, which the Dani would catch and eat whenever they could. The climbers welcomed any diversion from the trek's high misery index. We were all nursing cuts that were bleeding through our socks and boots. Roach and I felt as though we may have fractured bones in our feet. The pains would persist for days, but I felt a surge of relief when I finally could lie on the ground and relish the feeling one can experience only in the complete exhaustion of successfully completing a grueling expedition.

The day we were supposed to leave was the first sunny day of the expedition. We took advantage of the weather, hiking around the village, trading a pocketknife or leather belt for locally made beads, bows, arrows, and penis gourds. I had heard about the local Dani carpenter who made stone axes, so Roach and I set out to find him. Arriving at his hut, the man brought out two of the finest hand-crafted stone axes. The only other tools of this type I had seen were in the American Museum of Natural History in New York. The Dani do not use numbers. They clench a fist for "five," and hold up two fists for "10." He held up two fists. Neither Roach nor I could tell if this meant a hundred, a thousand, or what. We went to get Ripta, who said, "The Dani man wants 10 US dollars, not five!" It was a lesson in local economics. The man had devoted three months each to hone the curved rock to razor sharpness as well as fitting and carving the hardwood handles. I held up $10 and a huge smile came over his face. I handed the man my bill, and he gave me the axes. Both of us were very satisfied.

Our team had extra time to absorb the local culture as our chartered plane did not arrive on the day it was scheduled. We were told there had been an "incident" a couple days earlier. "The local schoolteacher is leading a guerilla movement against the Indonesians whom they feel intruded on their land and people," Ripta explained in his best English. "When the plane landed a few days previous to our return, the tribe stormed the plane, and the local police shot a pig that belonged to a native to show force. The scene got out of hand and scared the pilots badly enough so they would not fly back in."

This incident had the Indonesian government scrambling to find two more pilots who would risk flying into Illaga to pick us up. Being aware that natives often took visitors hostage so they could demand money or guns, the tensions ran high among our American group. Usually the anxiety of whether you'll see your family again occurs at a scary moment high on a mountain, not at the airstrip.

Our spirits brightened the next morning, May 12, when our eager ears heard our chartered flight buzzing in with two new pilots in the cockpit. We soon departed from the edge of civilization and the next moment that matters was arriving in Spokane, walking down the airport causeway and seeing Michelle, who was blooming in her eighth month of pregnancy.

"Chris, you were missed, really missed!" said Julie, Michelle's sister-in-law.

I'd been looking forward to a long kiss with Michelle, and nearly melted in her arms as I hugged her and our child at the same time.

"Well, how did the expedition go?" Michelle asked.

"It was a journey," I said, a bit surprised at my inability to immediately verbalize the experience. "I can't explain it really. It was a journey."

The women were satisfied with those words at that moment. It was good to be home.

A month later, I found myself in the mix of another ordeal, laboring through labor with Michelle, surprised at how much effort goes into being on the sideline, and finally watching the birth of my daughter Kelly. She greeted the world surrounded by nurses, doctors, clean hospital walls, shiny stainless-steel equipment, bright lights, and the compiled knowledge of centuries of medical science all in one delivery room. Before leaving the Illaga airstrip, I had noticed a pregnant Dani woman. I couldn't help but wonder about her baby. Kelly and the Dani child would grow up with separate struggles in a world of constant change. One of my dreams for Kelly is that she will one day share a bit of that child's heritage and savor the most beautiful singing I have ever heard in the highlands of the wildest place on earth.

NEW BEGINNING

I met Michelle in December of 1985 at a Spokane Mountaineers wedding party for Bob Christianson. I liked her instantly. I was still married but separated from Sharon at the time and taking care of my son Jon and daughter Jae. I persuaded Michelle to go on a couple of dates. Understandably, she did not want to go further with a relationship while I was still married. My divorce from Sharon took a tumultuous four more years to finalize.

In March of 1993, I presented a slide program for the Mountaineers. Michelle was in the audience and we met again. This time I wasn't going to let her go. We ventured to the Canadian Rockies to climb Mount Athabaska together, went to Stehekin in the North Cascades to bushwhack into Trapper Lake, and backpacked into the Gospel Hump Wilderness of Idaho. In October of 1993 Michelle was pregnant with Kelly. I had been determined to NEVER EVER get married again, but we both wanted kids. When I grabbed her from the Spokane Mountaineers program audience, Michelle also grabbed me, even though she was fully aware of my obsession for climbing mountains. I took off for the Carstensz expedition in April of 1994. Kelly was born two months later, helping me slowly change my mind about marriage. I proposed in August of 1994 and Michelle accepted.

With our baby daughter on my back, we hiked, and dragged a less-than-mountain-hardened preacher up from Priest Lake, Idaho, to the summit of Mount Roothaan. With Chimney Rock and the Selkirk Mountains in the background, we were married on a warm, beautiful windless September 24th.

Words from the Wild

- When asked, "What surprises you most?" the Dalai Lama said, "Man, because he sacrifices his health in order to make money. Then he sacrifices money to recuperate his health. And then he is so anxious about the future that he does not enjoy the present. The result being that he does not live in the present or future; he lives as if he is never going to die, and then he dies having never really lived."
- "Two roads diverged in a wood and I, I took the one less traveled by, and that has made all the difference." —Robert Frost

Twenty-Six

Into Thin Hair

THE GRAY MATTER INSIDE THE CRANIUM is the control room for some 30 trillion cells in the adult human. This center of body functions is designed to handle routine operations automatically, but the portion of the user manual regarding emotions gets very thick and technical.

I believe that my brain was hardwired to climb in a way that often overrides feelings. Climbing to me is linear and intense. It's similar to surfing, where you fix your eyes on the horizon while feeling the ocean. While climbing, I envision the top as I feel the mountain with my hands and feet—and the feeling is pure joy. Therefore, I climb. The harder and higher the mountain, the deeper my desire. Passion for reaching summits feeds my mind, body, and soul like gasoline to an engine.

I recognize that "joy" is not the first word most people would choose to describe their feelings while climbing an exposed cliff. I've questioned my longings. What was the purpose of all this mountain climbing? Was it to find joy and happiness? Is happiness the pursuit of life? If mental toughness is the main ingredient for success, where does the mental toughness come from?

I once told my sister, "You either got it or you don't. Success in life is predetermined by your nature, and a man's nature will determine his fate."

"Well, just what do you mean by that?" she snapped. "What about hard work? Dad taught us that with hard work you could attain any goal!"

I responded to that challenge by stepping onto my soap box and lecturing my little sister with the know-it-all confidence of a big brother. "Look Sue, people are born with certain genetic gifts, and no matter how hard you work at something, if your goal is unrealistic it won't work."

"I think people are born for certain tasks," I continued preaching to Sue. "Finding out what you're good at allows you to maximize the results of hard work to improve your lot in life. I could never play the piano like Van Cliburn or hit a baseball like Babe Ruth, no matter how hard I worked at either of those activities. Cliburn's hands spanned 12 keys. Ruth had 20/15 vision and could see the threads on a baseball coming in at 90 miles per hour. Ruth was a big man with a natural swing! I have none of those physical gifts or the hand-eye coordination. Hard work would never get me to that level."

Shakespeare seemed to be on a similar soap box when he wrote, "All the world is a stage, and all the men and women merely players. They have their exits and their entrances; and one man in his time plays many parts, his act being seven ages." Infant, schoolboy, lover, soldier, justice, pantaloons, second childhood, and finally sans everything.

For 50 years of my life, taking one step at a time, I was able to climb up and back down through about 4.7 billion years of geologic history to see and feel this astounding earth more intimately than most people could imagine. As a youngster I thought going into space would be the ultimate adventure. However, I've lived my dream discovering planet Earth, and what a beautiful dream it has been.

Words from the Wild

- As a teenager, I felt that I could find the answer to life's mysteries by climbing into The Death Zone. Some of my friends are still there. I was lucky to climb into thin hair.

About the Author

After a long career as a General Contractor, Chris now serves as president of the Dishman Hills Conservancy board in Eastern Washington and spends his time working to conserve the area that helped spark his love of climbing. He lives in Spokane, Washington with his wife, Michelle, and dog, Ueli, and despite his thin hair, he still loves getting outside and enjoying nature any way he can. He wears a hat to keep his head warm.

CPSIA information can be obtained
at www.ICGtesting.com
Printed in the USA
BVHW070354110122
625723BV00002B/3